Many Russian novels of the nineteenth and twentieth centuries have made a huge impact, not only inside the boundaries of their own country but across the Western world. *The Cambridge Companion to the Classic Russian Novel* offers a thematic account of these novels, in fourteen newly commissioned essays by prominent European and North-American scholars. There are chapters on the city, the countryside, politics, satire, religion, psychology, philosophy; the Romantic, Realist, and Modernist traditions; and technique, gender, and theory. In this context the work of Pushkin, Dostoevskii, Tolstoi, Turgenev, Bulgakov, Nabokov, Pasternak and Solzhenitsyn, among others, is described and discussed. There is a chronology and guide to further reading; all quotations are in English. This volume will be invaluable not only for students and scholars but for anyone interested in the Russian novel.

THE CAMBRIDGE
COMPANION TO THE
CLASSIC RUSSIAN
NOVEL

CAMBRIDGE COMPANIONS TO LITERATURE

THE CAMBRIDGE
COMPANION TO THE
CLASSIC RUSSIAN
NOVEL

EDITED BY
MALCOLM V. JONES
University of Nottingham

AND
ROBIN FEUER MILLER
Brandeis University

CAMBRIDGE
UNIVERSITY PRESS

PUBLISHED BY THE PRESS SYNDICATE OF THE UNIVERSITY OF CAMBRIDGE
The Pitt Building, Trumpington Street, Cambridge CB2 1RP, United Kingdom

CAMBRIDGE UNIVERSITY PRESS
The Edinburgh Building, Cambridge CB2 2RU, United Kingdom
40 West 20th Street, New York, NY 10011–4211, USA
10 Stamford Road, Oakleigh, Melbourne 3166, Australia

© Cambridge University Press 1998

First published 1998

Printed in the United Kingdom at the University Press, Cambridge

Typeset in Sabon 10/13 pt. [CE]

A catalogue record for this book is available from the British Library

Library of Congress cataloging in publication data
The Cambridge companion to the classic Russian novel / edited by Malcolm V. Jones and Robin Feuer Miller.
p. cm. – (Cambridge companions to literature)
Includes index.
ISBN 0 521 47346 2 (hardback). ISBN 0 521 47909 6 (paperback)
1. Russian fiction – 19th century – History and criticism.
2. Russian fiction – 20th century – History and criticism.
I Jones, Malcolm V. II. Miller, Robin Feuer, 1947–   . III. Series.
PG3098.3.C33   1998
891.73'009 – dc21   98–33220
CIP

ISBN 0 521 47346 2 hardback
ISBN 0 521 47909 6 paperback

CONTENTS

Part 3: The literary tradition

Part 4: Structures and readings

    ROBERT BELKNAP

13 Gender   251
    BARBARA HELDT

14 Theory   271
    CARYL EMERSON

    Guide to further reading   294
    Index   298

NOTES ON CONTRIBUTORS

ROBERT BELKNAP is Professor of Slavic Languages at Columbia University. He is the author of numerous articles on Russian literature; his books include *The Structure of "The Brothers Karamazov"* and *The Genesis of "The Brothers Karamazov."*

JOSTEIN BØRTNES is Professor of Russian Literature at the University of Bergen. His books include *Visions of Glory: Studies in Early Russian Hagiography*.

CARYL EMERSON is A. Watson Armour III University Professor of Slavic Languages and Literatures at Princeton University. She is translator and author of several books on Mikhail Bakhtin, on Russian music, and of articles on Russian nineteenth-century prose, philosophical thought, and readings of Dostoevskii, Tolstoi and Pushkin. She is also General Editor of *Studies in Russian Literature and Theory* for Northwestern University Press.

SUSANNE FUSSO, Associate Professor of Russian Language and Literature at Wesleyan University, is the author of *Designing "Dead Souls": An Anatomy of Disorder in Gogol*, and co-editor with Priscilla Meyer of *Essays on Gogol: Logos and the Russian Word*. She is now writing a study of Dostoevskii's *Adolescent*.

BARBARA HELDT is Professor Emerita of Russian, University of British Columbia. She is author of *Terrible Perfection: Women and Russian Literature*, translator of Karolina Pavlova, *A Double Life*, *Kozma Prutkov: The Art of Parody*, and author of numerous articles and contributions to symposia on Russian literature.

MALCOLM V. JONES is Emeritus Professor in Residence at the University of Nottingham. The author of books and articles on Tolstoi, Dostoevskii and other aspects of Russian literature and intellectual history, he is also President of the International Dostoevsky Society and has recently retired as General Editor of *Cambridge Studies in Russian Literature*.

W. GARETH JONES is Professor of Russian at the University of Wales, Bangor. His publications include books and articles on aspects of the Russian eighteenth-century enlightenment, Tolstoi, Chekhov, and other topics from Russian nineteenth- and twentieth-century literature.

ROBERT A. MAGUIRE is Bakhmeteff Professor of Russian Studies at Columbia University. His books include *Red Virgin Soil: Soviet Literature in the 1920s*, *Gogol from the Twentieth Century: Eleven Essays*, and *Exploring Gogol*. He has also translated widely from Russian and Polish.

HUGH McLEAN is Professor Emeritus at the University of California, Berkeley. He is author of *Nikolai Leskov: the Man and his Work* and articles on Pushkin, Gogol, Tolstoi, Kushchevskii, Chekhov, Maiakovskii and Zoshchenko.

ROBIN FEUER MILLER is the author of *Dostoevsky and "The Idiot": Author, Narrator, and Reader* and of *"The Brothers Karamazov": Worlds of the Novel*, as well as of essays on Russian and comparative literature. She edited *Critical Essays on Dostoevsky* and co-edited Kathryn Feuer's *Tolstoy and the Genesis of "War and Peace."* She is Dean of Arts and Sciences and Professor of Russian and Comparative Literature at Brandeis University.

LESLEY MILNE is Reader in Modern Russian Literature at the University of Nottingham. She is the author of books and articles on twentieth-century Russian satire. Her most recent books are *Mikhail Bulgakov: A Critical Biography* and an edited volume, *Bulgakov: The Novelist-Playwright*.

GARY SAUL MORSON is Frances Hooper Professor of the Arts and Humanities at Northwestern University and has written studies of Dostoevskii, Tolstoi and Bakhtin. Best known for his theories of "prosaics" and "sideshadowing," his most recent book, *Narrative and Freedom: The Shadows of Time*, won the René Wellek award.

ROBERT RUSSELL is Professor of Russian at the University of Sheffield. He is the author of books and articles on Valentin Kataev, Russian drama of the 1920s, and other aspects of twentieth-century Russian literature.

VICTOR TERRAS is Henry Ledyard Goddard University Professor Emeritus, Brown University, Providence, R.I. A native of Estonia, he immigrated to the United States in 1952, where he resumed his academic career, interrupted by the war, in 1959. He has taught Russian and Comparative literature at several American universities. He is the author of many books and articles on Russian literature including *A History of Russian Literature*.

ANDREW WACHTEL is Professor of Slavic Languages and Literature at Northwestern University. He is author of books and articles on the representation of childhood in Russian culture, on the writing of history by Russian novelists, on the ballet *Petrushka*, and on Russian art and music.

The Cambridge Companion to the Classic Russian Novel is not a history of the Russian novel. It is a collection of essays chiefly about those Russian novels and novelists – émigrés excepted – that have made a significant impact on world literature and about the tradition that they represent. It is in this sense that the word "classic" is used, not to confer status, but to acknowledge effect. Forty years ago, Harold Orel, remarking that the importance of the Russian novel in English literary history could hardly be overemphasized, wrote:

> Henry James referred to Turgenev as "le premier romancier de son temps"; George Moore, who admired Tolstoy's "solidity of specification," referred to *Anna Karenina* as the world's greatest novel; Robert Louis Stevenson interpreted Dostoyevsky's *Crime and Punishment* as a room, "a house of life," into which a reader could enter, and be "tortured and purified"; Galsworthy sought "spiritual truth" in the writings of Turgenev and Tolstoy; and Arnold Bennett compiled a list of the twelve greatest novels in the world, a list on which every item came from the pen of a Russian author.[1]

Lists varied, but the cult of the Russian novel reached its apogee in England in the years following the First World War. In 1931, by which time he had established himself as one of the most promising young English novelists of his generation, William Gerhardie sketched the stylistic features which, in his view, young writers of his time most admired and strove to cultivate. He included among his exemplars Pushkin, Lermontov, Chekhov, Tolstoi, Dostoevskii, and Turgenev. Gerhardie was showing off, his judgments more witty than profound. Yet on an impressionistic level the notes that he strikes are instantly recognizable: Pushkin's lyrical power and paganism; Lermontov's elegiac quality combined with his Byronism;

---

[1] Harold Orel, "Victorians and the Russian Novel: A Bibliography," *Bulletin of Bibliography* (January–April 1954), 61; quoted in George Zytaruk, *D. H. Lawrence's Response to Russian Literature* (The Hague and Paris: Mouton, 1971), p. 36.

Chekhov's miraculous naturalness and consumptive cough; Tolstoi's life-imparting breath conjoined, alas, to his foolishness; Dostoevskii's pathological insight but extravagant suspiciousness; Turgenev's purity in reproducing nature marred by his sentimentalism.[2] These are the familiar burdens of the Russian soul, mediated through the great prose works of the nineteenth century, as familiar to us as the strains of Shakespeare, Austen, Dickens, Trollope, James, Twain, Hemingway, Conrad, an inalienable part of the modern literary sensibility and, in the view of many, its crowning achievement. Born in St. Petersburg in 1895, Gerhardie himself has some slight claim to being regarded as a "Russian novelist" and might be suspected of favoritism. Yet, with his polyglot background, he was able to draw inspiration from a wide range of European literature. The significant thing is that, once again, the Russians occupy a dominant place.

By adoption, or perhaps by absent-mindedness, we recognize the great Russian realist novels as our classics, an integral part of that interactive web of the modern imagination which found one of its most notable expressions in the novel and which prompted D. H. Lawrence to declare (and the world-famous Russian theorist of the novel Mikhail Bakhtin to imply by his choice of subject) that the novel is among the greatest intellectual achievements of the modern mind.[3] We think of them, as we do of the works of Tchaikovsky or Kandinskii, as part of our common heritage, yet extending it in ways which eluded our native-born writers. For they are also in some ways strangely alien to us – strangely Russian – and it is perhaps unsurprising that the Russians themselves have made concepts such as "defamiliarization," and the distinction between "one's own word" and "the alien word," central features of their theories of the novel. Russia, and its literature, has always been conscious of being torn between East and West, where "East" has ranged from Constantinople to the Tatar hordes, and "West" has incorporated the whole of Europe and its cultural progeny.

Before exploring that thought further, it is worth pausing to raise a further question prompted by Gerhardie's list: what Russian names would an anglophone novelist of the 1990s wish to add to it and what would be his or her comments on them? This is a quite difficult question. In 1834, the Russian critic Vissarion Belinskii concluded that there was no such thing as Russian literature, only a few isolated peaks of achievement by outstanding individuals. That might seem to be the common judgment on the Soviet

---

[2] William Gerhardie, *Memoirs of a Polyglot* (London: Robin Clark, 1990; first published 1931), pp. 164–65.

[3] Zytaruk, *D. H. Lawrence's Response*, p. 74.

novel some 160 years later. In *Cancer Ward* Solzhenitsyn's narrator says of one of his characters that he was rather frightened at the thought of how many writers there were. In the last century there had only been about ten, all of them great. In this century there were thousands; you only had to change a letter in one of their names and you had a new writer. There was Safronov and there was Safonov, and more than one Safonov apparently. And was there only one Safronov? No one could possibly have time to read all their books, and when you did read one, you might just as well not have done. Completely unknown writers floated to the surface, won Stalin prizes, then sank without trace.[4] Solzhenitsyn's character is, of course, caricaturing the achievements of the Soviet novel, which are greater than he would allow. But, searching his or her mind for familiar names, our contemporary writer would probably begin by reciting the same ones as Orel or Gerhardie, the "ten" great novelists of the last century. Then, depending on his or her knowledge of the twentieth-century Russian literary scene, a number of others would tumble out: Solzhenitsyn for certain, and then perhaps Belyi, Sholokhov, Pasternak, Bulgakov . . . The *cognoscenti* might add Zamiatin or Pilniak, Olesha or Platonov. And those with an even more intimate knowledge of the tradition would no doubt wonder whether they should include Karolina Pavlova, Goncharov, Aksakov, Saltykov-Shchedrin, Leskov, Gorky, Sologub, Bunin, Fedin, Leonov, Aleksei Tolstoi, and more recent writers such as Vasilii Grossman, Tendriakov, Trifonov, Bitov, Voinovich, Petrushevskaia, Tatiana Tolstaia, Rasputin, Erofeev, Aksenov or Zinoviev, who have been quite extensively published and written about in the West. But there is an important difference. The Russian writers in Gerhardie's list repaid their debt to Western literature a hundredfold. They inspired both admiration and imitation across the globe. Those in our supplementary list, while having undoubted claims to the attention of the well-read reader of our time, and in the cases of Bunin (1933), Pasternak (1958), Sholokhov (1965), and Solzhenitsyn (1970) even attracting Nobel Prizes, have not significantly fed back into the Western literary tradition and seem unlikely ever to do so. The two exceptions are perhaps Belyi, whose novel *Petersburg* has been much admired as a modernist classic, and Bulgakov, whose influence Salman Rushdie has openly and gladly acknowledged.[5] The great mass of Soviet novelists, even the good ones, seem unlikely ever to achieve ongoing international acclaim, let alone classic status.

[4] A. Solzhenitsyn, *Rakovyi korpus* (Paris: YMCA Press, 1968), p. 110.
[5] See Arnold McMillin, "The Devil of a Similarity: *The Satanic Verses* and *Master i Margarita*," in Lesley Milne (ed.), *Bulgakov, the Novelist-Playwright* (Luxembourg: Harwood Academic Publishers, 1995), p. 232.

In Belinskii's time, the problem was to escape the thrall of Western European literature and establish an "organic" tradition on a comparable or superior level, which Russia could call its own. This it did, it is commonly claimed, through the dual heritage of Pushkin and Gogol, establishing, as Robert Belknap shows in his essay, a new conception of narrative technique, resulting in what Henry James called "baggy monsters" and "fluid puddings," but which later readers came to regard as a key discovery of the Russian novel,[6] which has spiralled back into Western literature in the modernist period. Caryl Emerson, in her essay, shows how the Russians themselves have theorized this achievement.

In the twentieth century, at least from the late 1920s to the post-war period with its succession of thaws and freezes, Russian literature, prolific though it was, would seem to have lain under a curse, from which only a few outstanding individuals contrived a heroic escape, and often enough by a reverse trajectory, through achieving recognition, though not imitation, in the West. This book does not radically challenge this thesis, though it does demonstrate that the soil in which these outstanding writers grew continued to be fertilized by the on-going Russian literary tradition, a tradition which is now in the 1990s showing signs of a new flowering, enriched perhaps by a period of enforced dormancy.

Contributors to this book were asked to write on their particular subjects with an eye to a list of writers whose claim to the status of "classics" is widely agreed, but with the freedom to vary names in the list in deference to the demands of their topic. They were also advised that the essays were not to be conceived as extended encyclopedia articles but would, we hoped, offer new, even idiosyncratic, insights into the subject, informed, where relevant, by recent political and cultural developments. The extent to which we have succeeded is for others to judge. Of course, the strategy, the topics and the list (the very idea of which echoes the unfashionable idea of a literary canon) are all open to debate. But this is a risk which we have chosen to take. We hope that the resulting essays will be of interest to undergraduate, graduate and general readers wishing to discover the common ground between the Russian and the Western novel as well as the characteristic features which Russia has brought into the tradition. They will have to look elsewhere for encyclopedic coverage and for strict consistency of approach. The volume opens with essays by Robert Maguire and Hugh McLean on the twin themes of the city and the countryside, thereby setting out the unique landscape of the Russian novel. The second

---

[6] See Caryl Emerson's essay in this book and Donald Fanger, "On the Russianness of the Russian nineteenth-century novel," in Theofanis George Stavrou (ed.), *Art and Culture in Nineteenth-Century Russia* (Bloomington: Indiana University Press, 1983), pp. 40–56.

section addresses specific cultural themes with which the Russian novel is widely associated: the often baleful influence of politics (W. Gareth Jones), the tradition of satire which was in many respects a response to it (Lesley Milne), the religious tradition of Russian Orthodoxy (Jostein Børtnes), the relationship of the Russian novel's famed psychological depths to the social setting (Andrew Wachtel), and the philosophical dimension established by the three nineteenth-century giants (Gary Saul Morson). In the third section, Susanne Fusso explores the contribution of the Romantic tradition to the development of the Russian novel while Victor Terras seeks to define the sources and nature of Russian Realism. Robert Russell examines the emergence in the early part of the twentieth century of the Modernist tradition. Finally, in part four, Robert Belknap discusses the peculiar features which characterize the Russian plot and Barbara Heldt asks about the effects on women's writing of a novelistic tradition which was the exclusive preserve of powerful male writers. The last essay, by Caryl Emerson, both gives an overview and critique of Russian theories of the novel and, by implication, furnishes a variety of possible solutions to the problems raised in this introduction and in the essays which follow.

Malcolm V. Jones
Robin Feuer Miller

ACKNOWLEDGMENTS

The editors would like to express their appreciation to all the contributors, not least for their patience and cooperation in the face of an editorial policy which continued to evolve in matters of detail as the essays came in, and also to Drs. Kate Brett and Linda Bree at the Cambridge University Press for their unflagging support as the agreed deadline repeatedly gave way to external pressures. Finally the editors wish to express their gratitude to Melanie Cumpston, formerly of the Department of Slavonic Studies at the University of Nottingham, for her help in preparing the typescript for submission to the Press, and to Hazel Brooks of Cambridge University Press for her unfailingly sympathetic and efficient copy-editing.

NOTE ON TRANSLITERATION AND TRANSLATION

The Library of Congress system of transliteration from Cyrillic has been used. This includes proper names, though hard and soft signs (which are included in the notes) have been omitted in names in the text of the book. The only exceptions to this rule are names which have become so familiar in English in another form that they would be unrecognizable if this policy were strictly adhered to (e.g. Tchaikovsky, Herzen) and the names of tsars (Alexander I). Like any other policy attempting a compromise between user-friendliness and faithfulness to a particular system, this inevitably leads to some inconsistencies (for example Herzen appears also as Gertsen where works by him in Russian are referred to in the notes) but the editors thought that this would not mislead anyone who is able to read Russian and would not interest anyone who is not.

All translations of quoted extracts are by the appropriate chapter author unless otherwise specified.

CHRONOLOGY

1802	Death of A. N. Radishchev (1749–1802)
1807	Treaty of Tilsit (with Napoleon)
1812	Napoleon invades Russia and enters Moscow
1814	Alexander I enters Paris with his troops after defeat of Napoleon V. T. Narezhnyi's *A Russian Gil Blas*
1818–26	N. M. Karamzin's *History of the Russian State* (12 vols.)
1822	A. S. Pushkin's poem "The Prisoner of the Caucasus"
1823–31	A. S. Pushkin's *Evgenyi Onegin*; published in full, 1833
1824	A. S. Pushkin's poem "The Gypsies"
1825–55	Reign of Nicholas I
1825	Death of V. T. Narezhnyi (1780–1825) Decembrist Revolt (led by Guards officers seeking to establish a constitution)
1826	Death of N.M. Karamzin (1766–1826)
1829	F. V. Bulgarin's *Ivan Vyzhigin*
1830	A. S. Pushkin's *Tales of Belkin*
1832–34	M. Iu. Lermontov's *Vadim*
1832	N. V. Gogol's "A Bewitched Place"
1833	A. S. Pushkin's *The Queen of Spades* A. S. Pushkin's poem "The Bronze Horseman"
1834–36	A. S. Pushkin's *The Captain's Daughter*
1834	V. G. Belinskii's ground-breaking critical articles *Literary Reveries*, arguing that Russia has no national literary tradition
1835	N. V. Gogol's *Taras Bulba*, "Nevskii Prospekt" and "Notes of a Madman"
1836	P. Ia. Chaadaev's *First Philosophical Letter* arguing that Russia has made no contribution to universal history N. V. Gogol's "The Nose"
1837	Death of A. S. Pushkin (1799–1837)
1840–41	M. Iu. Lermontov's *A Hero of Our Time*

1841	Death of M. Iu. Lermontov
1842	N. V. Gogol's *Dead Souls* and *The Overcoat*
1843–59	K. K. Pavlova's *Quadrille*
1846	D. V. Grigorovich's *The Village* F. M. Dostoevskii's *Poor Folk* and *The Double*
1847	D. V. Grigorovich's *Anton Goremyka* N. V. Gogol's *Selected Passages from Correspondence with Friends* V. G. Belinskii's *Letter to Gogol* circulated I. A. Goncharov's *A Common Story*
1848	K. K. Pavlova's *A Double Life* Death of V. G. Belinskii (1811–48) F. M. Dostoevskii's "White Nights"
1849	I. A. Goncharov's "Oblomov's Dream"
1852	Death of N. V. Gogol (1809–52) L. N. Tolstoi's *Childhood* I. S. Turgenev's *A Sportsman's Sketches*
1853–56	Crimean War (between Russia and the combined forces of Britain, France, and Piedmont)
1854	L. N. Tolstoi's *Adolescence*
1855–81	Reign of Alexander II
1855–57	I. A. Goncharov's *The Frigate Pallada*
1855	N. G. Chernyshevskii's treatise on *The Aesthetic Relations of Art to Reality*
1856	S. T. Aksakov's *A Family Chronicle* and *Recollections* I. S. Turgenev's *Rudin*
1857	L. N. Tolstoi's *Youth*
1858	S. T. Aksakov's *Childhood Years of Grandson Bagrov* A. F. Pisemskii's *A Thousand Souls*
1859	I. A. Goncharov's *Oblomov* I. S. Turgenev's *A Nest of Gentlefolk* Death of S. T. Aksakov (1791–1859) Death of F. V. Bulgarin (1789–1859) L. N. Tolstoi's *Family Happiness* N. A. Dobroliubov's essay "What is Oblomovitis?"

1860	I. S. Turgenev's *First Love* I. S. Turgenev's *On the Eve*
1861	The Emancipation of the Serfs, followed by a series of reforms in the early 1860s Death of N. A. Dobroliubov (1836–61) F. M. Dostoevskii's *The Insulted and Injured* A. F. Pisemskii's *An Old Man's Sin*
1862	I. S. Turgenev's *Fathers and Children*
1863	N. G. Chernyshevskii's *What is to be Done?* L. N. Tolstoi's *The Cossacks* F. M. Dostoevskii's *Winter Notes on Summer Impressions* A. F. Pisemskii's *The Troubled Sea*
1864	V. P. Kliushnikov's *Mirage* F. M. Dostoevskii's *Notes from Underground* N. S. Leskov's *No Way Out*
1865–69	L. N. Tolstoi's *War and Peace*
1866	F. M. Dostoevskii's *Crime and Punishment*
1867	I. S. Turgenev's *Smoke*
1868	F. M. Dostoevskii's *The Idiot*
1869–79	M. E. Saltykov-Shchedrin's *The History of a Town*
1869	I. A. Goncharov's *The Ravine*
1871–72	F. M. Dostoevskii's *The Devils*
1872	N. S. Leskov's *Cathedral Folk*
1873	N. S. Leskov's "The Sealed Angel" and "The Enchanted Wanderer"
1875–80	M. E. Saltykov-Shchedrin's *The Golovlev Family*
1875	F. M. Dostoevskii's *A Raw Youth* N. S. Leskov's "At the End of the World"
1877	L. N. Tolstoi's *Anna Karenina* I. S. Turgenev's *Virgin Soil*
1880	F. M. Dostoevskii's *The Brothers Karamazov*
1881–94	Reign of Alexander III
1881	Assassination of Alexander II

1910	I. A. Bunin's *The Village* Death of L. N. Tolstoi (1828–1910)
1911	I. A. Bunin's *Sukhodol*
1912	A. A. Bogdanov's *Engineer Menni*
1913	Maksim Gorkii's *Childhood*
1914–18	First World War
1915	V. V. Maiakovskii's poem "A Cloud in Trousers"
1916	Andrei Belyi's *Petersburg* (in book form)
1917	Nicholas II abdicates in February; he is succeeded by a Provisional Government; in October the Bolsheviks seize power E. I. Zamiatin's "Islanders"
1918–21	Civil War and period of War Communism
1920–21	E. I. Zamiatin's *We* (published for the first time in Russian in 1952 and in the USSR in 1988)
1920	E. I. Zamiatin's "Mamai"
1921–22	Boris Pilniak's *The Naked Year*
1921–40	A. N. Tolstoi's *A Tour of Hell*
1922–23	A. N. Tolstoi's *Aelita*
1922	Andrei Belyi's *Petersburg* (revised, shortened edition)
1923	Union of Soviet Socialist Republics (USSR) formally established D. A. Furmanov's *Chapaev*
1924	Death of V. I. Lenin K. A. Fedin's *City and Years* A. S. Serafimovich's *The Iron Flood*
1925	Beginning of Maksim Gorkii's uncompleted novel *The Life of Klim Samgin* M. A. Bulgakov's *The White Guard* F. V. Gladkov's *Cement*
1926	Isaac Babel's *Red Cavalry* Death of I. A. Furmanov (1891–1926)
1927	Death of F. K. Sologub (1863–1927)

1947–54	"Cold War" between the Soviet bloc and the West
1949	Death of A. S. Serafimovich (1863–1949)
1953	Death of I. V. Stalin Krushchev elected First Secretary Death of I. A. Bunin (1870–1953) L. M. Leonov's *Russian Forest*
1956	I. G. Erenburg's *The Thaw* Death of A. A. Fadeev (1901–56)
1957	Boris Pasternak's *Doctor Zhivago* Death of A. M. Remizov (1877–1957) Launching of Sputnik I
1958	Death of F. V. Gladkov (1883–1958)
1960	Death of Iu. K. Olesha (1899–1960) Death of Boris Pasternak (1890–1960)
1961	Iurii Gagarin is the first to travel in space
1962	Cuban missile crisis A. I. Solzhenitsyn's *One Day in the Life of Ivan Denisovich*
1963	M. M. Bakhtin's *Problems of Dostoevskii's Poetics* (revised edition of 1929 book on Dostoevskii) A. I. Solzhenitsyn's "Matrena's Home"
1964	Fall of Khrushchev; he is succeeded by Brezhnev and Kosygin
1966–67	M. A. Bulgakov's *The Master and Margarita*
1966	F. A. Iskander's *The Goatibex Constellation*
1967	Death of I. G. Erenburg (1891–1967)
1968	A. I. Solzhenitsyn's *Cancer Ward* A. I. Solzhenitsyn's *The First Circle*
1973–75	A. I. Solzhenitsyn's *The Gulag Archipelago*
1973	F. A. Iskander's *Sandro from Chegem* V. Erofeev's *Moscow Circles* M. A. Bulgakov's *The Master and Margarita* (full, Moscow edition)
1974	Aleksandr Solzhenitsyn is expelled from the USSR

1975	Death of M. M. Bakhtin (1895–1975) V. N. Voinovich's *The Life and Extraordinary Adventures of Private Ivan Chonkin* (published in the USSR in 1988–89)
1976	V. G. Rasputin's *Farewell to Matera* A. Zinoviev's *Yawning Heights* (published in USSR in 1990) Iu. V. Trifonov's *House on the Embankment*
1977	Death of K. A. Fedin (1892–1977) Death of V. V. Nabokov (1899–1977)
1978	A. G. Bitov's (1937–) *Pushkin House*
1979	V. N. Voinovich's *Pretender to the Throne* (published in the USSR in 1990)
1982	F. A. Iskander's *Rabbits and Boa-Constrictors* (published in the USSR in 1987) Death of Brezhnev; Iurii Andropov elected as General Secretary
1984	Death of Andropov; Konstantin Chernenko elected as General Secretary Death of M. A. Sholokhov (1905–84) Death of Chernenko; Gorbachev elected General Secretary
1985	Gorbachev and Reagan meet at Geneva
1986	Death of V. P. Kataev (1897–1986) V. N. Voinovich's *Moscow 2042* (published in the USSR in 1990) Explosion at Chernobyl nuclear reactor Academician Sakharov released from detention in Gorkii Policy of *glasnost'* and *perestroika* announced at XXVII Party Congress
1988	Celebration of millennium of Russian Orthodox Church
1990	Yeltsin resigns from Communist Party
1991	Yeltsin elected President of Russia August coup against Gorbachev Abolition of USSR (December)

1

MALCOLM V. JONES

Introduction

What does give the classic Russian novel its power over the imagination? There have been many attempts to define its unique features and to account for its rise to pre-eminence in such unpromising soil. Underlying most analyses is the perception that Russian literature achieved its stature in a dialectic (or dialogue) with Western European literary traditions. Bakhtin has provided a theoretical model for this process in a shift from regarding the Western tradition as "authoritative discourse" to regarding it as "inwardly persuasive discourse"; in other words from a mental attitude which saw Western traditions as providing unsurpassable achievements which could only be imitated or rejected, to one which assimilated them to native Russian experience as part of a process of growth-in-dialogue: a complex dance in which the partners now lightly touch, now embrace and now draw apart, at times melting into a common movement and at times loudly asserting their difference.

The double helix comes unbidden to the modern mind as a model of this process. And that is no doubt one of the major reasons for the extraordinary fascination which the Russian novel has exercised over the Western reader. It is not simply that Russian writers have always had the Western tradition at the back of their minds, and woven it into their own tradition, trying to overcome what Harold Bloom has famously called the anxiety of influence. It is that for the first time Russian literature is reflecting back to Western readers a profounder, broader, more complex and, it often seems, more authentic, view of themselves, a view which puts in question not only Western achievements, but also the Western literary heritage as embedded in the novel itself. To put it more simply, Russian novels force us to ask questions about ourselves, about novels, and more broadly about human discourse, as well as about the physical world they purport to convey.

A key role in this process – characterized by a profound inferiority complex and a countervailing impulse to discover and assert an authentic national voice – was played in the last century by the Russian intelligentsia, for whom the novel was the primary medium of debate. The intelligentsia was both a channel for the assimilation of Western culture and a vehicle for the affirmation of Russia's own unique experience and values and (potential or presumed) contribution to world civilization. Educated Russians of all social classes were heirs both to Western cultural traditions, which they shared with their European and North American counterparts, and their own cultural and historical roots, which were uniquely theirs and which retained a strong sense of otherness. The novel appeared and achieved respectability in Western Europe just at the right moment to act as a vehicle for this ambitious programme. By the 1830s it had come of age in Russia too. Moreover, a more capacious and appropriate vehicle could hardly have been designed for the purpose. The novel was capable, as Bakhtin has famously argued, of absorbing all other genres. As Russians discovered, no field of contemporary human discourse – except perhaps the strictly technical or scientific – was debarred. Imaginative fiction could be manipulated in all sorts of ways unavailable to more direct forms of discourse and, above all, it was capable of relating, as no other medium could, broad social, political, philosophical and religious questions to the existential experience of the individual through the medium of narrative, thus facilitating entry to these questions at a variety of different levels. Through the evolution of its narrative techniques, the novel had proved capable of engaging the interest of the reader simultaneously at the level of story and, as modern theory has it, at the level of "ideal author".

The great novels of the nineteenth century could be, and often were of course, read simply for entertainment. The majority of readers, unlike the writers, were women and the novels often read aloud *en famille*. Richard Ware draws our attention to a contemporary account of the reception of *Anna Karenina*, according to which most readers regarded the novel simply as entertaining and absorbing reading, an opinion held not only by short-sighted aristocrats but even by some contemporary critics.[1]

Another account recalls that there was neither singing nor laughter on the days when a new issue of *Russkii vestnik* appeared with a fresh installment of Dostoevskii's *The Brothers Karamazov*. When all were gathered, the family took their places round the table with a green shaded lamp in the middle, and the reading aloud began. Everyone took turns to read and there was no pause until they reached the final page. Faces alternately turned pale and burned with excitement; the voice of the reader shook. The reading was then followed by detailed discussion of every movement in the souls of the characters and by attempts to guess what would happen next.[2] In a delightful essay on *War and Peace*, Nikolai

Bakhtin (Mikhail Bakhtin's brother) recalls how, like many Russian readers, he had, by dint of reading and rereading, come to know the characters in the novel like real-life friends and acquaintances. Then he confesses that actually he had never read the whole of Tolstoi's great novel from cover to cover. He had just dipped into it again and again.[3]

But, whatever its primary appeal to the reading public, the significance of the nineteenth-century novel will not be fully grasped unless it is understood that each new volume to appear was part of the ongoing debates in the literary journals, the salons and the private apartments of the intelligentsia. Neither Tolstoi's *Anna Karenina* (1875–78) nor Dostoevskii's *The Brothers Karamazov* (1879–80) can be appreciated as phenomena of their time apart from the discussions on marriage and the family inspired by Chernyshevskii's novel *What is to be Done?* (1863). No more, in a later period, can Bulgakov's *The Master and Margarita* be wholly appreciated apart from its satire on the Soviet literary scene and, on a broader scale, on the Soviet system itself. The aim of literature was not merely to entertain, to instruct or even to reflect reality. It was to seek "the measure of life" in all its dimensions, together with an understanding (and this was a particular feature of its Russianness) of the limitations of the human mind in attempting to grasp its meaning. At the beginning of the nineteenth century, Russian culture experienced two irresistible imperatives (both exemplified in Pushkin's and Gogol's work): to grasp and represent in imaginative literature the full range of contemporary reality, exemplified in such concepts as the *narod* (the Russian people), *the rodina* "motherland"), the vast, primitive, anarchic Russian countryside, the history and the symbolism of her capital; and to understand their place in history. This latter quest sometimes embraced the idea of national historical mission, which at times, for example in Dostoevskii's hands, became messianic. Though most of the nineteenth-century intelligentsia lived and worked in the city, the two capitals of St. Petersburg and Moscow, and experienced all the strains of urban life, they were fully aware of the countryside, populated by the oppressed peasant classes, their lives lived out among the beasts they tended. Yet, some thought these same peasants were possessed of superior spiritual insights, often associated with ancient peasant beliefs and folk traditions, such as those celebrated in the novels of Leskov in the nineteenth century and the works of the "village prose" writers (Belov, Rasputin and others) in the twentieth. The liberal intelligentsia (Turgenev, Aksakov, Tolstoi) were themselves often landowners and experienced the tension between the landowner's love of the rural idyll and guilt at the price others had to pay to preserve its semblance. Increasingly, as the nineteenth century wore on, the countryside was seen not just as the repository of Russia's spiritual heritage, but also as the setting for a social and moral degeneration in which all classes were caught up. Although overlaid by more recent historical events, two world wars, the Revolution and Civil War, the collectivization programme, the purges and the collapse of the Soviet Union, these dimensions have continued to dominate the Russian experience and its representation in fiction to the present day.

That the idyll of the Russian countryside was deeply flawed struck some (Saltykov-Shchedrin, Bunin) so painfully that it seemed to plunge them into a grotesque, nightmarish gloom. Others (Goncharov, Aksakov) presented it more ambiguously. Turgenev and Tolstoy, perhaps, preserved their love of the Russian countryside best. What all the nineteenth-century novelists seem to be acutely aware of is the ultimate futility and hubris of Russia's repeated attempts to subject the vastness and majesty of nature to the human will, together with the inadequacy of human reason fully to comprehend life's meaning. The theme has its first memorable expression in Pushkin's great poem "The Bronze Horseman"; it is central to Tolstoi's philosophy of history in *War and Peace*; it underlies Dostoevskii and the long anti-rationalist tradition in Russian thought, the fate of Bazarov in Turgenev's *Fathers and Children*, the failure of the Bolshevik experiment in Pasternak's *Doctor Zhivago*, the collapse of Platonov's anarchic *Chevengur*, and the tragic–comic depiction of a Moscow thrown into confusion by a visit from the devil in Bulgakov's *The Master and Margarita*.

And its source is to be found, like those of many of the other leitmotifs of Russian intellectual and spiritual life, in the uncompromisingly anti-rationalist traditions of the Orthodox Faith, traditions thrown into relief by its anti-Catholic and anti-Protestant stance. In his essay Jostein Børtnes shows the impact of Russian Orthodoxy on those major novels which most strikingly exemplify its influence, but its pervasive effect is very widely evident in Russian culture, in the structuring function of religious myths (for example the Easter myth or the Apocalypse), in the presence of folk religious types (for example the Holy Fool) and artefacts (the icon), as well as in a pervasive Anti-Rationalism and preference for apophatic (negative) theology. Elsewhere, John Garrard[4] has reminded us that, for better or for worse, Russia was not a part of the Roman Empire, nor did it experience directly the fruits of the Renaissance; nor was it a part of the Roman Catholic tradition which the Roman Empire adopted and which embraced the Renaissance. This made the grafting on of European culture in the modern period all the more problematic and the attempt all the more fascinating. Even where Anti-Rationalism was not explicitly made a virtue, as with the progressive Westerners, its influence ran very deep, until in the twentieth century, in one of those periodic attempts by Russia's rulers to seize history and nature by the scruff of the neck, the power of science and technology to overcome all natural obstacles temporarily became Holy Writ and gave rise to a completely new dominant in Russian culture.

It seems momentarily to have escaped Gerhardie's attention that one prominent feature of the Russian novel is its deep moral seriousness, its uncompromising wrestling with seemingly intractable social and political problems no less than with the "accursed questions" of philosophy and religion, questions which, as Tolstoi was aware, professional philosophers often consider to be unanswerable because misconceived and which the great novels of Western Europe address only obliquely, if at all. It is a signal characteristic of the Russian novel that it takes *seriously* (i.e. as indicative of what is essential in life) aspects of human experience frequently banished to the fringes of the secular European novel, to the extent that they may actually become organizing principles of the narrative, and hence, by implication, of that everyday experience which the narrative seeks to express. Not only does religion sometimes play this organizing role, but so do folklore, the dream, the supernatural, metaphysics, and that peculiarly Russian state of mind which critics call *poshlost'* ("self-satisfied mediocrity") and which, in Gogol's work, facilitates that strange slippage between the material and the surreal (and/or supernatural) which is his hallmark.

This deep seriousness is in part a consequence of the vastness of Russia and of its searing historical experiences, some self-inflicted, some inflicted by external enemies. It is in part a consequence, according to some, of the passion, the complexity, the broadness of the "Russian soul," combining the spirit of Europe with the spirit of Asia, with a tendency to seek extreme, maximalist solutions to the problems of keeping both individual soul and political body under some sort of control. Undoubtedly it is also in part the consequence of working within the context of an oppressive political order, as Gareth Jones explains. As Alexander Herzen wrote, in his "Open letter to Michelet" (1851), the ghastly consequences that attended the written word in Russia inevitably increased its effectiveness:

> The free word is listened to with love and veneration, because in our country, it is uttered only by those who have something to say. The decision to publish one's thoughts is not lightly made when at the foot of every page there looms a gendarme, a *troika*, a *kibitka*, and the prospect of Tobolsk or Irkutsk.[5]

It is as if throughout the history of the Russian novel there was always a third, silent participant in the dialogue, alongside the writer and the reader, the oppressive presence of the Russian state and its apparatus of censorship and repression. Just as in Soviet Russia free conversation on politically sensitive issues was inhibited by fear of being overheard by an agent of the

KGB, so throughout the history of Russian literature the spectre of imprisonment, exile, execution or psychiatric supervision played its role in fashioning what was thought, felt, written and said, and how it was expressed. The frequency with which Russian literature actually deals explicitly with these themes, or some metaphorical equivalent, is therefore hardly surprising. Such a predicament gave rise to ingenious, Aesopian techniques for fooling the authorities, to saying what had to be said metaphorically rather than directly, for cultivating what Bakhtin called "the word with a sideways glance." Most notably it gave rise to the tradition of the satirical novel, to which Lesley Milne's essay is devoted. Of course there were sunny interludes, periods when the censorship was relaxed. But they could never be relied upon to last.

Partly in spite of and partly because of this situation, the imaginative world of the Russian novel seems to stretch out endlessly in space and time and at the same time is capable of focusing on the subtlest movements of the inner world of the individual psyche, from the historical vastness of Tolstoi's *War and Peace* and Sholokhov's *The Quiet Don,* to the tense psychological and physical enclosure of a Dostoevskian novel, from the daylight naturalism of Turgenev's *Fathers and Children*, to the apocalyptic fantasy of Bulgakov's *The Master and Margarita*, from the unremitting satirical gloom of Shchedrin's *The Golovlev Family* to the tragic lyricism of Pasternak's *Doctor Zhivago.*

Each Russian writer mapped out the territory in his own way and although their works certainly echo each other and develop each other's achievements, rarely could the work of one be mistaken for that of any other. There has been much discussion of various categories of "realism" in Russian literature (Critical Realism, Romantic Realism, Fantastic Realism, Revolutionary Realism, Socialist Realism). One could equally well discuss categories of "Russianness" and indeed, though scorn is nowadays often poured on the idea of the "Russian soul," such terms may still focus discussion of similarities and differences.[6] The point is that, in spite of their pervasive adherence to the principle of "realism," none of the great Russian novelists was a naive Realist, or even a Naturalist in the French sense. Each of them, as we have noted and as several of the essays demonstrate, sought and discovered organizing principles for their perception of experience in realms beyond the material and the immediate. They all understood the limitations of language in expressing human experience. Some, like Gogol, exploited these for satirical and comic purposes. Others, like Dostoevskii, turned them into a structural principle of their fictional world. As Victor Terras argues, Realism was in some measure a negative conception, a move away from Romanticism.

But it was also a sustained attempt by a series of highly gifted writers of fiction to redraw the parameters of human experience, to capture, through their own personal sensibilities, the essence of Russian humanity. This essential Russianness would be recognized by readers in all its splendor and misery and would subsequently stand in for Russia in the minds of generations of foreign admirers and color their perceptions of it. Each novelist absorbed those narrative techniques which the European novel had developed and which suited him best and went on to push those techniques in new directions, sometimes stretching them to their limits and sometimes, as with Gogol or Leskov, importing features of the Russian (or Ukrainian) folk tradition which gave their works new and surprising twists. The traditions of European Romanticism were grist to their mill. The pervasive influence of Rousseau on the widely read Tolstoi is generally conceded. Turgenev drew inspiration from his contacts, literary and personal, with the great French writers of his day, Flaubert, Maupassant, Sand, the Goncourts, Mérimée. Among Dostoevskii's favorite novelists were George Sand, Victor Hugo, Balzac and Dickens (the "Romantic Realists"). He even learnt from the French Gothic novelist Eugène Sue, and from Rousseau.

One aspect of their "realism" is the attention Russian novelists pay to the experience of the everyday (*byt* as it is called in Russian), the social reality round about. The popularity of the "physiology" ("*fiziologiia*") and the feuilleton (*fel'ton*) among the writers of the Natural School, fostered by Belinskii in the 1840s, was an important formative influence, as were the novels of Dickens, Sue and Balzac. This surfaces in Bakhtin's theory of the novel in what Morson and Emerson call his conception of the "prosaic,"[7] a theme which Gary Saul Morson takes up in a different context in his contribution to this volume. The feel for the physicality of the experienced world is to be found in all the great Russian prose writers, from Pushkin to Platonov, from Pasternak to Petrushevskaia. It is not, as I have hinted, a naturalistic accumulation of minutiae, but a sense of the telling detail. It is true even of Dostoevskii, whom Merezhkovskii contrasted to Tolstoi as the "seer of the spirit" to the "seer of the flesh". Many of the images we take away from Russian novels are in fact physical details: Akakii Akakievich's overcoat, the smell and the sounds of the Haymarket in Raskolnikov's St. Petersburg, Anna Karenina's unruly little curls, Rusanov's cancer, Zhivago's rowan tree and flickering candles, Pilate's attar of roses. Such examples find parallels in Western realist novels. But in Platonov, whose *Chevengur* is belatedly becoming recognized as one of the most significant Russian novels of the Soviet period, material reality even takes on metaphysical significance. Thomas Seifrid has written that if Platonov portrays man's existence as a tragic subordination to corporeality, then the ultimate fear troubling this vision is that nothing but matter truly exists.[8]

If the material, whether of the town or the countryside, plays a notable part in Russian realism, so too does a characteristic which Marshall Berman has ascribed to "the modernism of underdevelopment," a tendency in one powerful tradition of the Russian novel, represented in both the Gogolian and the Pushkinian lines, to question the reliability of our perceptions and to stand nervously on the threshold of an abyss which opens up as soon as confidence in the solidity of the prosaic world is eroded. Beyond the abyss is a world which seems to be structured by the arbitrariness of the dream rather than the solidity of common sense and reason. It is as if "all that is solid melts into air," Berman tells us, quoting, of all people, Karl Marx. It is the ability of the Russian novel to render the sensation of life in the no man's land between the prosaic, everyday, common-sense world and the world of fantasy, dream, folklore, madness, that is one of its hallmarks. Of course the focus on minute physical detail is as much a feature of the dream life as it is of waking experience, perhaps more so. Those critics who tell us that the Jerusalem sections of Bulgakov's *The Master and Margarita* are more realistic than the Moscow chapters sometimes forget that. This sensation is enhanced for Western readers by the fact that, aside from the deployment of narrative techniques, the subject matter itself hovers on the brink of the familiar and the unfamiliar, "one's own world" and "an alien world."

The Modernism of underdevelopment is closely allied to the tendency in Russian literature which is often called – somewhat misleadingly perhaps – "Fantastic Realism." Ranging from the grotesquerie of Gogol's "The Nose," through the frankly supernatural of a small number of Turgenev's and Chekhov's tales and the diablerie of Bulgakov's novel, but also including Dostoevskii's masterpieces, Fantastic Realism in the Russian tradition places a huge question mark against the reliability of common sense, the healthy, the self-evident, the reasonable, and the rational in human experience, and the ability of logic and science to contain it and plumb its depths. It also raises profound questions about our ability ever to discern the boundaries between a world apparently governed by these principles and the realms of dream, fantasy, the supernatural, poetry, the spirit. It is of course in these respects heir to the Romantic and precursor of the modern and post-modern, of Freud, Kafka and the Existentialists. But it is positivistic realism – all that is solid – that it explicitly takes as its point of departure, and our confidence in it which it seeks subtly, by one means or another, to subvert. There is a degree of play in this. There is also an intense seriousness. How could it be otherwise in a country which was required for seventy-five years to subscribe to systematic, state-sponsored fantasy; in which science itself was put at the service of ideology, where statistics almost always meant lies, and where the outcome, far from being playful and escapist, was the kind of experience expressed by Solzhenitsyn in his *First Circle* or Zinoviev in *Yawning Heights*? Solzhenitsyn's works internalize the principle of institutionalized fantasy and it becomes the structural principle which dominates and distorts the everyday experience of millions of people in his world. The twentieth century, no less than earlier epochs, can furnish many horrific examples of societies being fashioned to accord with systematic fantasies. Perhaps the Russians foresaw this and sensed the danger more clearly than most. If so, it did not prevent them from experiencing it as cruelly as any.

Fantastic Realism, then, which both celebrates the non-rational and warns against the terrifying abyss to which it may be the gateway, turns out to be an obsessive fascination of the Russian imagination. It takes many forms, from the appeal of extreme ideological positions – an appeal experienced no less by Tolstoi than by Fedorov, Dostoevskii, Bakunin or Lenin – to fascination with the folkloric, the demonic and the grotesque – Gogol or Bulgakov – an awareness of being part of powerful, impersonal, irresistible historical processes – Tolstoi again, Sholokhov, Bulgakov – or a sense that the patterns of history and personal experience find their meaning in religious categories, for instance, the motifs of death and resurrection (the Easter myth), of crisis, judgment and vindication (the myth of the Apocalypse).

It is perhaps significant that it was a Russian, Mikhail Bakhtin, who introduced into literary theory the term "chronotope," a term which constantly reminds us of the fourth (temporal) dimension of what traditional criticism was wont to call "setting." In theory, all narrative has its own chronotope, just as it has its own setting. But in practice Bakhtin is particularly interested in a relatively small number of particularly striking or recurrent chronotopes for which he found convenient labels, for example, the chronotopes of the carnival, the provincial town, the salon, biographical time, the road, the threshold, each with its own characteristic space-time coordinates and modes of narrative.

One chronotope which does not figure in Bakhtin, and not at all prominently in writing about him – this may incidentally be a key to the dissatisfaction many have felt with his treatment of Dostoevskii – is the apocalyptic. But given the nature of the Russian historical experience it is not surprising that the apocalyptic tradition should have exercised such a hold on the Russian imagination. David Bethea recently published a book on this subject[9] in which he analyzed the way in which the apocalyptic tradition is handled in Dostoevskii's *The Idiot*, Belyi's *Petersburg*, Platonov's *Chevengur*, Bulgakov's *The Master and Margarita*, and Pasternak's *Doctor Zhivago*. The book is remarkable as much for the idea as for the realization, for it throws into relief a facet of the Russian novelistic tradition, the importance of which, though now obvious, had somehow eluded literary criticism, except when dealing with individual writers.[10] In passing, Bethea draws attention to a number of features of this tradition which demonstrate that far from being a minor feature of the Russian imagination, it turns out to be a major organizing principle. For example, he links it with both the revolutionary and the utopian traditions. The real-life visions of such revolutionary activists as Mikhail Bakunin were imbued with apocalyptic motifs, in which a secular Revolution replaces the Second Coming and an earthly utopia replaces the "new heaven on earth" to come. As Tolstoi's narrator says in "The Kreutzer Sonata," "According to the doctrine of the Church the world will come to an end, and every scientific doctrine tells us the same thing" (chapter 11). The Second Coming and the coming of the Revolution merge in the writings of the Symbolists, most memorably in Blok's poem, *The Twelve*, where the figure of Jesus appears in the snowstorm to lead the revolutionary band. They merge again in expectations of a glorious life built on completely new lines in which humanity will be free from oppression and conflict, in which the righteous (the proletariat) will be vindicated and the sinners (the bourgeoisie) eternally damned. In Pasternak's novel, all, Marxists and non-Marxists alike, experience a sort of elemental upsurge of energy, interpreted by some in a poetic, Schellingian sense, by others according to the Bolshevik creed. The sense of history moving at breakneck speed towards a final and catastrophic dénouement was foreshadowed in Gogol's image of the troika. With hindsight it is possible to see that Russian history actually was rushing towards such a catastrophe, that those Russian writers who sensed it were right in their intuitions, though in most cases wrong in the way they characterized it. The apocalyptic mode of interpreting history had a long pedigree in Russian culture, linked to the notion that Moscow was the Third Rome and that there would be no fourth, and surfacing even in the thought of such disparate thinkers as Nikolai Berdiaev and Iurii Lotman. The tendency for Russia to define itself by radical breaks and maximalist strategies is all part of the apocalyptic package. What some Western critics have seen as a lack (the failure of Russia to garner the fruits of the Graeco-Roman classical tradition) is seen in this perspective as an irresistible organizing principle of historical experience, by no means unique to Russia, but unusual in its pervasive influence on the shape of narrative fiction.

The phenomenon does not cease with the Revolution. The three post-revolutionary novels selected by Bethea are very different from each other in other ways, but share this apocalyptic structure. Apocalypticism, with its play on symbols, merges into Modernism and it comes as no surprise that it arrives there courtesy of Gogol, Dostoevskii and the Symbolists.

The Symbolist–modernist novel, exemplified by Belyi's *Petersburg*, and discussed in Robert Russell's essay, foregrounds through its style as well as through its subject-matter the disintegration of the subject. Dostoevskii's narrators had sometimes raised questions about the status of their own narrative and jumped unpredictably between incompatible narrative points of view. The narrator of *Petersburg* goes further. He cannot resist the temptation to suggest that his narrative is nothing but cerebral play. John Elsworth has argued that the entire system of relationships in the novel may be governed by occult forces.[11] No less important is the sense that the normal conventions of fiction are about to explode in our faces, and this subversion of realist or representational narrative conventions in favor of techniques of defamiliarization extends to all branches of culture in the extremely rich period of innovation and experimentation of the late tsarist and early Soviet periods. In art, it should be remembered, this was the period not only of Symbolism but also of Neoprimitivism, Cubofuturism, Rayonism, Suprematism and Constructivism.[12] Where the printed word was concerned a radical fragmentation often extended to typographical devices (for example in the work of Belyi, Kruchenykh, Kamenskii, Zdanevich, Maiakovskii), and not only in poetry. *Petersburg* itself contains some thirty cases of typographical devices (major indentations) used to suggest a shift in consciousness through visual effect.[13]

What actually occurred after 1917 was neither a Second Coming nor a Utopia, though it was often represented in millennial terms. It was, perhaps, more in the nature of a Purgatory (always a questionable concept in Orthodox theology), a period of waiting in which a purifying suffering would be rewarded (or not rewarded in the case of the sinner/bourgeois/kulak) with a future paradise. Marxist-Leninists called this period "the dictatorship of the proletariat." But whatever it was called, Russian literature felt the need to reflect a paradise deferred, placing it in a situation not unlike that of the Christian Church in the first century AD. The failure of the millennium fully to materialize gave rise, among other, less notable literary phenomena, to the genre of dystopia (Zamiatin's *We*) and the dynamic of Platonov's unique novel, *Chevengur,* neither of which appeared in full in Russia until the period of *glasnost'*.[14] Both these novels end in the apparent victory of state bureaucracy over the forces of individual spontaneity and idealism. In *We*, this conclusion seals the triumph of a scientifically organized totalitarian state over the individualism of its citizens. In *Chevengur*, the depressing ending concludes the Quixotic quest of the hero for the home of true socialism but seems to imply that this is the inevitable consequence of the sort of anarchistic political idealism celebrated in such novels of the Civil War period of Revolutionary Romanticism as Pilniak's *Naked Year*. The utopian programme of the inhabitants of Chevengur is presented as entirely futile. Gorkii was right in seeing in the novel a profound ambiguity: it is both utopian and anti-utopian. Its centre of gravity is located beyond and above both. But, most important of all, this centre of gravity is not spiritual: the myth has been secularized; the spiritual has become material.

Translated into practical, political terms, the predicament faced by Platonov was also the predicament faced by the new Soviet State and those who supported it. The issue was how, if at all, the Revolution could be secured by a judicious balance of spontaneity and political force. The State was supposed to be withering away, yet spontaneous, anarchist, naive Communism was demonstrably not capable of creating the brave new world envisaged by the Bolsheviks. The idea of revolution as a spontaneous, elemental, natural force is reflected in many a novel of the early Soviet period as well as in its better-known reflection in Pasternak's *Doctor Zhivago*.[15] Katerina Clark has argued convincingly that the spontaneity/ consciousness dialectic is the structuring force that shapes the master plot of the Socialist Realist novel and not, as might be thought, the class struggle itself. The characters in Platonov's novel never graduate to political consciousness. Socialist Realists were supposed to put this right by providing models for the Soviet citizen, more or less bewildered by the failure of the Soviet State to "wither away" as Marx and Lenin said it should. Although the term "Socialist Realism" was coined only in 1932, the official Soviet view was that it had been evolving for the last quarter of a century. Precursors such as Gorkii's *Mother* (1906), Furmanov's *Chapaev* (1923), Serafimovich's *The Iron Flood* (1924), Fadeev's *The Rout* (1927), Gladkov's *Cement* (1925) and the first two parts of A. Tolstoi's *Tour of Hell* (1923–41) were all written and published before the key date.[16] What was now needed, in Zhdanov's phrase, was "a combination of the most matter-of-fact everyday reality with the most heroic prospects,"[17] resulting in what Clark calls its "proclivity for making sudden, unmotivated transitions from realistic discourse to the mythic or utopian" and "the absence in it of those features that can be seen as exploration or celebration of the objective/subjective split: parody, irony, literary self-consciousness, and creative or complex use of point of view."[18] In a sense Soviet society was making the same implausible claim as the Catholic Church in the early

Middle Ages, and trying to fend off heretics with the pretense that the millennium had already arrived.[19] The heroes of the Socialist Realist novel often displayed characteristics familiar from medieval Russian religious and secular narratives and the trajectory of their plots often followed the familiar Christian pattern of death, transfiguration and resurrection. While these novels may be, and were, called classics of Socialist Realism, they have never been recognized as classics of world literature and the thousands of novels which followed the models of Socialist Realism generally failed to transcend their level of achievement. On the other hand, their cultural significance is of great interest. The novels of the high Stalinist period attempt to celebrate that triumph of heroism, science, technology and reason over the forces of anarchy and nature which the mainstream of Russian culture had always problematized. Regrettably, therefore, they find no place in this volume.

However, there are notable novels among the exemplars of Socialist Realism, outstanding examples being Leonov's *Russian Forest*, A. Tolstoi's *A Tour of Hell*, and Sholokhov's *The Quiet Don*. Of these, *The Quiet Don* is the most widely celebrated in the West. Like no other novel, *War and Peace* included, it conveys a sense of the vastness, primitiveness and violence of Russia, the Cossack lands, and the instinctual forces and values which impel ordinary, unprivileged men and women in their struggle for survival and supremacy against forces over which the individual has no control. Although it is hailed as one of the great *Soviet* novels, the irony is that the heroes and heroines belong to the wrong side (the Whites) in the Civil War, as do the Turbins in Bulgakov's novel of 1925, *The White Guard*. The hero, Grigorii Melekhov, experiences and himself lives the physical violence and mental anguish of his time and place. Sholokhov's masterpiece conveys the life of the Don Cossacks in a period of upheaval through brilliant physical descriptions, but also through his rendering of the timeless values and traditions of the Cossacks themselves.

Not all Russian novels are inspired by a sense of the apocalyptic, even where they display a strong sense of history. Counterbalancing this tendency is another which reminds the reader that beyond the turmoil, the world of nature, of which humanity is a part, continues on its course, ever renewing itself as season follows season and generation succeeds generation. The Turgenevan tradition, as represented by his best-known novels, *Rudin*, *On the Eve* and *Fathers and Children*, in many ways foreshadows the revolutionary novel, but lacks its conviction of the saving power of the Revolution. Nor is it inspired by a vision of impending national doom. In Turgenev's fictional world heroism consists in the constant reaffirmation of humane values by the individual in the face of an unresponsive universe.

Tolstoi was not free of the Russian penchant for philosophizing, prophesying and following through principles to the bitter end. Yet his greatest works of imaginative fiction are structured by quite different principles, in which the physical, the mentally balanced, natural continuity and renewal are underlying structuring principles. Ironically, Bakhtin's principle of dialogue (which he wishes to deny Tolstoi) is actually particularly strong in him. So is his sense of the immediacy of the present moment and of the process of becoming as it is observed, on which Tolstoi is actually stronger than he is on historical processes. Time is cyclical, death and disaster are followed by renewal. This is not apocalyptic time, but it does once again echo a basic Christian structure. It is again the Easter motif, the cycle of death, transfiguration and resurrection, but grafted onto a perception of the world structured by the pagan rhythms and seasons of the natural world rather than, as with Dostoevskii, an apocalyptic framework. Consciously or not he built these motifs into the title of his best-known novel, *War and Peace*.[20] Where the apocalyptic occurs in Tolstoi, for example in Pierre's masonic speculations, it appears as a deviation from the norm as it would in an English realist novel. The motif of death and resurrection embraces both the nineteenth century and the revolutionary novel. Only the dark gloom of Saltykovian or Buninesque satire seems to exclude the possibility of rebirth and renewal.

Bakhtin saw Tolstoi's novels as built round such chronotopes as "biographical time" and "the salon." There are, of course, others, particularly in the vast historical panorama of *War and Peace*, but there is no denying that Tolstoi's salons and his biographies both partake of that sense of breadth in physical time and space which Dostoevskii had sought and found in the inner reaches of the human spirit.

Words and expressions like "measure," "classical mean," or "understatement" do not immediately spring to mind when writing of the major Russian novelists. Yet one only has to mention the names of Pushkin, Turgenev and Chekhov, all, it is true, the writers of shorter fiction, and the enormous influence of the first of these, to be reminded that there is more to the Russian novel than the traditions we have been discussing. The novels of Pushkin and Turgenev have never had the impact on the imagination of the Western reader of the other classics we have discussed (save perhaps those of Turgenev in France), and Chekhov did not write novels at all. Yet they represent vital, lasting strains in the Russian tradition, strains often appreciated better by native Russians than by foreign admirers. Above all they are models of verbal economy, of aesthetic form, a measure and constant reminder of the ideals which Russian literature is capable of achieving and from which their more unruly successors depart in full knowledge of their parentage.

Pushkin was not simply the first great figure in the tradition, revered continually from his day to this. His spirit has lived in the novels of others, through quotation, allusion, contrast, and more complex forms of inter-textuality, from his immediate contemporaries and successors Lermontov and Gogol, to such contemporaries of ours as Andrei Bitov. The way in which this strain has lived on as an ideal in the world of loose, baggy monsters as well as in the more restrained prose of some of his more direct literary descendants is well shown in Susanne Fusso's essay.

All the novelists mentioned in this introduction are men (which is why some of our contributors use the masculine pronoun when referring to Russian novelists). There have been no outstanding women prose writers in Russia until very recently. It is not entirely clear why this should be. In our own century some of the finest of Russia's poets have been women. A list of the classics of English literature of the late eighteenth, nineteenth, and twentieth centuries would contain a substantial list of outstanding women novelists, many of whom have long been acknowledged as such and have never been in need of rediscovery. It does not appear to be the case that Russian women were more disadvantaged than English women during either the nineteenth or the twentieth centuries. As Catriona Kelly tells us, the number of women writers grew steadily in the early nineteenth century and writing by women continued to develop its own diverse traditions over the next 170 years, but she nevertheless concludes that "between its origins in the late eighteenth century and the present day . . . Russian women's writing [exists] in the interstices of patriarchal culture."[21] The study of Russian writing from feminist perspectives has, however, been developing apace in recent years and as a consequence one of our essays reminds us that the Russian novel is based on an essentially male viewpoint. That this fact does not carry with it the necessary implication that the Russian novel is either inaccessible or an affront to women readers is evident. But it does underline its gender-bias, a fact which Barbara Heldt's essay does something to redress.

The constant balance and counterbalance between the various traditions of the Russian novel – the Pushkinian and the Gogolian, the Dostoevskian and the Tolstoian, the Modernist and the Socialist Realist, the utopian and the dystopian, above all the tendency towards the fantastic, with the disintegration of the subject and the text, set against the affirmation of the primacy of the physical and the material – have resulted in a literary tradition which, for all its subversive questioning of novelistic discourse, has never entirely lost its grip on common-sense reality. This is no doubt why its most influential theorist, Mikhail Bakhtin, still continued unblushingly to use such concepts as "author," "realism" and "subject" in an age when structuralism and post-structuralism was radically problematizing such notions in the West. In one of the final turns of the double helix, it is this twentieth-century theory of the novel, rather than a tradition of Soviet novels, which has come back to invigorate Western literary theory in our own day and once again brought us to recognize the power of the Russian mind to interrogate our own traditions.

NOTES

1. Richard Ware, "Some Aspects of the Russian Reading Public in the 1880s," *Renaissance and Modern Studies*, 24 (1980), 27; quoted from S. F. Librovich, *Na knizhnom postu* (Petrograd–Moscow, 1916), p. 99.
2. Ware, "Some Aspects," p. 28; quoted from E. N. Lebedeva, "Kak prezhde chitali knigi – stranichki vospominanii," *Vsemirnyi vestnik*, 10 (1908), 7.
3. Nicholas Bachtin, *Lectures and Essays* (Birmingham: University of Birmingham, 1963), p. 28.
4. John Garrard (ed.), *The Russian Novel from Pushkin to Pasternak* (New Haven: Yale University Press, 1983), p. 3.
5. A. I. Gertsen, *Sobranie sochinenii v tridtsati tomakh* (Moscow: AN SSSR, 1954–60), vol. VII, pp. 329–30.
6. See Robert Belknap (ed.), *Russianness: Studies of a Nation's Identity* (Ann Arbor: Ardis, 1990).
7. Gary Saul Morson and Caryl Emerson, *Mikhail Bakhtin, Creation of a Prosaics* (Stanford University Press, 1990).
8. Thomas Seifrid, *Andrei Platonov* (Cambridge University Press, 1992), p. 110.
9. David Bethea, *The Shape of Apocalypse in Modern Russian Fiction* (Princeton University Press, 1989).
10. See Rufus Mathewson, *The Positive Hero in Russian Literature*, 2nd edn (Stanford University Press, 1975) on the impact of French Socialism on the apocalyptic trend in Russian thought.
11. J. D. Elsworth, *Andrey Bely: A Critical Study of the Novels* (Cambridge University Press, 1983), pp. 88–116.
12. John E. Bowlt (ed.), *Russian Art of the Avant Garde, Theory and Criticism*, rev. edn (London: Thames and Hudson, 1988).
13. Gerald Janecek, *The Look of Russian Literature, Avant-garde Visual Experiments 1900–1930* (Princeton University Press, 1984). On Belyi's novels, see pp. 25–44.
14. *Chevengur* appeared for the first time in full in Russian in 1988; *We* appeared for the first time in Russia in 1988.
15. See Richard Freeborn, *The Russian Revolutionary Novel: Turgenev to Pasternak* (Cambridge University Press, 1982), pp. 77–122, "Revolution and instinct."
16. English translations of substantial extracts of Furmanov's *Chapaev*, Serafimovich's *The Iron Flood*, Gladkov's *Cement*, Fadeev's *The Rout*, Ostrovsky's

How the Steel was Tempered and Sholokhov's *The Fate of a Man*, all classics of the Socialist Realist novel, can conveniently be found in Nicholas Luker (trans. and ed.), *From Furmanov to Sholokhov, an Anthology of the Classics of Socialist Realism* (Ann Arbor: Ardis, 1988).

17. Katerina Clark, *The Soviet Novel: History as Ritual* (Chicago and London: University of Chicago Press, 1981), p. 34; quoted from "Rech' sekretaria CK VKP(b) A. A. Zhdanova," *Pervyi s"ezd pisatelei. stenograficheskii otchet* (Moscow: Ogiz, 1934), p. 4.

18. Clark, *The Soviet Novel*, pp. 37, 39.

19. Comparisons might also be made with the Victorian Evangelical novel, on which see, for example, Robert Lee Wolff, *Gains and Losses, Novels of Faith and Doubt in Victorian England* (New York: John Murray, 1977).

20. It may be noted that the only chapter with a title in *Anna Karenina* (part v, chapter 20) is called "Death" and his third and last novel is entitled *Resurrection*.

21. Catriona Kelly, *A History of Russian Women's Writing 1820–1992* (Oxford University Press, 1994), p. 443.

I

THE SETTING

2

ROBERT A. MAGUIRE

The city

Russia is unique among European states for having had two capitals during much of its modern life: St. Petersburg and Moscow. The first was founded in 1703 by Peter the Great, and became the administrative, political, and cultural capital. In these respects, it displaced Moscow, whose history went back at least four hundred years. But Russians continued to regard the older city as the spiritual center of the country; even the tsars, who presided in Petersburg, went to Moscow to be crowned; and the Bolsheviks reconfirmed its traditional importance by moving the government back there in 1924. Each city has come to represent very different and often conflicting values, as we shall see, and each has functioned as a pole around which the vexed question of Russia's character and destiny has revolved.

Since the early nineteenth century, St. Petersburg and Moscow have figured prominently in the Russian novel. But many of the issues that attach to them are far older. In Kievan Rus, the first East Slavic state, cities were not only centers of culture, but enclosures against domestic and foreign enemies. It is instructive, and perhaps psychologically significant, that in Slavic languages, the word for "city," as in Russian *gorod* and Church Slavonic *grad,* has no etymological connection with the Latin *civis* and its derivations in English and the Romance languages, but instead goes back to the Indo-European root designating an enclosed place. Counterparts are found in such words as English "garden," Latin *hortus,* and Irish *gort* ("cultivated field"). Russians were hardly unique in feeling that the world at large was hostile and must be shut out. What is unusual is the persistence of this feeling throughout the nation's history. The sources of potential danger were early identified in ways which have also persisted. Under the year 862 (AD) in the *Primary Chronicle* (twelfth century), we read that the Eastern Slavs, unable to govern themselves, turned west to the Varangians, or Vikings, with the following request: "Our land is great and bounteous, but there is no order in it. Come to reign and rule over us."[1] The result was Kievan Rus. A century later, according to the same source,

Great Prince Vladimir wished to import a major religion to replace the native paganism, and for various reasons settled on Eastern Christianity, then centered in Byzantium. Even if the *Chronicle's* accounts are legendary, they register the early presence in the national mind of two foreign elements, traditionally called "West" and "East," terms which the Russians have used for centuries in pondering their national identity. To be sure, both elements are viewed favorably in the *Chronicle*. But never having quite melded, they have often been seen as threats to the integrity of native enclosures – political, cultural, psychological – and have inspired ambiguous feelings. "West" may stand for good order and high civilization, but also for tyranny and soullessness. "East" may betoken beauty and a truth rooted in the senses, but also mindless cruelty and destructiveness. Enclosure, East, and West form a cluster of motifs that, with many variations, have helped shape a literary version of the city which is peculiar to Russians.

In the first great work of Russian literature, *The Song of Igor's Campaign* (1186), "East" is a negative concept, embodied in the vast steppes that are inhabited by the Kumans, a people of Turko-Mongolian origin with no settled way of life. Without consulting the senior prince, Igor sets forth from his town to join battle with them far to the east, is defeated and captured, but eventually escapes and makes his way back. For the author of the poem, the town is a secure, nurturing bastion, and Igor acts unwisely and rashly in leaving it to seek personal glory. A century later, the threat from the East became catastrophic reality when the Mongols, or Tatars, swept westward and destroyed the old Russian state. Towns remained intact; many developed a lively local literature. But it was not until the fourteenth century that one of them, Moscow, began to expand until it achieved predominance.

A considerable body of writing celebrated medieval Moscow as the corporealization of the national idea. Despite its enormous vitality, however, this city-state felt frequently beleaguered from both East and West. Only gradually did it open itself to the world outside. The most spectacular of these openings came with the founding of St. Petersburg in 1703. Military, commercial, and cultural considerations figured in Peter's decision, but the city soon acquired deeper meanings, which writers were quick to exploit. A notable instance is Vasilii Trediakovskii's poem "Praise to the Izhorsk Land, and to the Reigning City of St. Petersburg" (1752). Here the city is treated, in typical eighteenth-century fashion, as a monument to enlightened reason. This was the view that prevailed for nearly half a century thereafter. Gradually, however, darker sides began to emerge, particularly in response to the poetics of Sentimentalism, another international literary movement that reached Russia late in the 1700s. Nature came to be identified as the locus of vitality and authenticity; the city, of artificiality, insincerity, and deception. Nikolai Karamzin's short story "Poor Liza" (1792) has been exemplary for generations. And it was Karamzin, in his *Memoir on Ancient and Modern Russia* (1810–11), who was one of the first to deconstruct the eighteenth-century view of St. Petersburg in these terms. He chided Peter for setting the city "amidst rippling swamps, in places condemned by nature to be unpopulated and barren. . . . How many people perished, how many millions and how much labor were expended to realize this objective? One might say that Petersburg is founded *on tears and corpses . . .*" The lesson for this Sentimentalist was that "man shall not overcome nature!" Less familiar in this context, but destined for an equally long life, was the exemplum of a genuinely Russian city, which he set forth many pages earlier and obviously expected his reader (primarily Tsar Alexander I) to prefer to Petersburg: "A small town that was barely known before the fourteenth century . . . raised its head and saved the fatherland (by defeating the Mongols). Honor and glory to Moscow! . . . The Moscow princes accomplished this great work not by personal heroism . . . but solely by virtue of a wise political system that was consonant with the circumstances of the time."[2]

When Pushkin employed these same contrasts, he could count on practiced responses in his readers. *Evgenii Onegin*, a "novel in verse" (1823–31), opens in St. Petersburg. There are just enough mentions of landmarks, climate, and real-life personalities to make it instantly recognizable to any Russian: the Summer Garden, the Nevskii Prospect, the white nights, Talon's French restaurant, a cluster of turn-of-the-century playwrights. It is largely an upper-class and therefore Europeanized city that Onegin and the narrator frequent, with its tireless round of parties, balls, and evenings at the theater. Like the city itself, Onegin is a composite of foreign fashions, ideas, and styles. Now and then Pushkin introduces the lower orders – coachmen, merchants, peddlers, bakers, cabbies – mainly by way of ironic contrast with the idle aristocracy. Presently, however, a more familiar contrast is introduced, as Onegin, bored with Petersburg, goes off to his country estate: "For two days," we are told, "he found novelty" in a landscape imported in effect from the eighteenth-century idyll, "lonely fields,/ The coolness of a densely shaded grove,/ The babble of a quiet brook" (1, 54). But soon he is no more satisfied there than any of his numerous literary progeny would be, and, in his relationship with the neighboring Larin family, he turns destructive, breaking Tatiana's heart and killing Lenskii, her sister's fiancé, in a duel.

Outlined this way, the plot draws on conventions that would evoke an immediate response in any reader of "Poor Liza." But Tatiana is no simple peasant girl, and no ordinary victim of urban lust: her view of life derives not so much from good instincts as from the perusal of foreign novels, and is therefore suspect. Pushkin also plays with the Moscow/Petersburg contrast. Tatiana's family, worried about her spinsterhood, takes her to Moscow to meet eligible men. If Petersburg is Onegin's city, and Onegin has proven unworthy of Tatiana, then Moscow, we suppose, is bound to yield an authentically Russian man who will help Tatiana discover the authentically Russian woman beneath the foreign veneer. Pushkin bolsters our expectations with a brief portrait of "white-stoned Moscow" that is far more appealing and more "Russian" than his Petersburg. He cites the "golden crosses" of the "ancient cupolas" that "blaze like fire," the nostalgia that this view inspires in the poet when he is in exile, and even the name itself, "Ah, Moscow! . . . How much the Russian heart finds blended in this sound!" (VII, 36). The poet does not fail to remind us of the city's refusal to submit to Napoleon during the invasion of 1812 – a rejection, in effect, of foreign ways – and he provides a rapid tour of the main thoroughfare, where bustle and disorder prevail, in contrast to the austere grandeur of Petersburg. The social scene that engulfs Tatiana looks like a warm, extended family, mostly female, unlike the chilly, male-dominated *haut-monde* of Petersburg. But instead of feeling at home, Tatiana "looks and does not see,/ She loathes the stir of this society;/ She feels stifled here" (VII, 53); and she yearns to be back in the country. She might as well be in Petersburg, where everyone seems to be unhappy; and that in fact is where we find her as the poem ends, married to a prince, ornamenting society, and painfully aware that her existence is empty. In his ironic way, Pushkin undoes the traditional contrast by pronouncing the two cities essentially the same, and even making us wonder whether the old urban/rural contrast really holds, if Onegin and Tatiana cannot find fulfilment in either place.[3]

Pushkin's *The Bronze Horseman* (1833) is far shorter than *Onegin*, but it left a far deeper mark on the developing theme of Petersburg in Russian literature. The Introduction begins with Peter the Great standing in a mist-shrouded, barren landscape, and, "filled with great thoughts," vowing to establish a city that will "strike terror in the Swede" and "cut a window through on Europe." This rehearses the eighteenth-century idea that intention is father to the deed. Suddenly "a century has passed," perhaps in response to the question Trediakovskii had posed in his poem, "What will it be like after a hundred years have passed?" There follows an elaboration of wonders also remarked by the earlier poet: the magnificent symmetries of "palaces and towers," the steady flow of visitors "from all corners of the earth," and the displacement of Moscow. Had Pushkin left matters at that, the poem would be merely a superior imitation of an eighteenth-century model. But with part I, the imagery and tonality undergo an abrupt change, as a flood falls "like a frenzied beast" upon the city. Evgenii, a humble civil servant, is introduced, the first of the "little men" that were to populate Russian literature for the next century. He escapes the devastation, but goes mad when he discovers that his fiancée has perished. Thereupon he roams the city, "A stranger to the world . . . Neither beast nor man/ Neither this nor that, neither a denizen of the world/ Nor a dead spectre," hereby becoming the progenitor of hundreds of literary spectres in Petersburg settings. Finally he encounters the equestrian statue of Peter the Great in the Senate Square, and threatens it: "Just you wait!" Thereupon the statue leaps off its pedestal, and pursues him through the city until he dies. Legions of Russian writers and critics have puzzled over the meaning of this encounter: the individual sacrificed to the stern, impersonal purposes of the state, retribution visited on the subjects of those power-mad rulers who presume to challenge the forces of nature? In any event, Pushkin once again opens the conventions to serious question.[4]

Gogol was the first of the great writers after Pushkin to accord Petersburg a central place in his work, in terms that owe much to his predecessors and profoundly influenced his successors. His earliest recorded impressions of the city date from a letter he wrote his mother in April 1829, in which he describes a cheerless, eerily silent metropolis, where "everything is crushed, everything is mired in idle, trivial pursuits." This is the city which, with further indebtedness to Pushkin, later figures in his short stories. Appearances to the contrary, the eighteenth-century conventions are present, only with a peculiarly Gogolian twist. A colorful, bustling city of the kind beloved by Trediakovskii turns up in "Nevskii Prospect" (1835), but it is the product of a mind unhinged by lust, "all [Piskarev's] feelings were ablaze and everything before him was veiled in a kind of mist. The sidewalk swept off beneath his feet, carriages and their trotting horses seemed to stand still, the bridge stretched and broke in mid-arch, a house stood roof downward, a sentry box hurtled toward him, and the sentry's halberd seemed to flash upon his very eyelash, along with the gilt letters of a signboard and the scissors painted on it." This prepares us for the theme of the unreal city that is introduced at the very end, in one of the most fertile passages in Russian literature: "It tells lies at any hour, this Nevskii Prospect does, but most of all when night falls in a dense mass upon it . . . and when the devil himself lights the street lamps for the sole purpose of showing everything as it really is not." Here "light" serves to parody the eighteenth-century idea of Petersburg as an emblem of the Enlightenment.

"The Overcoat" (1842) is Gogol's most famous work, and its treatment of St. Petersburg has shaped much of Russian urban literature. The main character, Akakii Akakevich, is a "little man" in the mold of Pushkin's Evgenii, but undergoes considerable development. As a copy-clerk, he at first simply accepts what he has been handed, and performs his mindless routines contentedly. Once he leaves his office, however, he is at the mercy of the city, which is bleak and hostile. Still, there are hints that he is capable of a kind of creativity that makes the city unchallenging, even congenial. "But if Akakii Akakevich did look at anything [outside his office], on it he saw his neat, evenly copied lines." The comment has greater point when we remember that much of Petersburg is laid out rectilinearly, and that across the river, on Vasilevskii Island, the streets are called "lines." Akakii's gift, if not necessarily a parody of the "great thoughts" that enabled Peter to make of the real world anything he wanted, establishes him as a character who presumes that he can deal with his surroundings, even change them for the better. But this apparently harmless fantasy proves to be the kernel of larger ambitions, which end by destroying him. Their instrument is the new overcoat, which comes to represent for Akakii something more than a protection against the icy winter wind: full acceptance by his fellow-clerks, perhaps an opportunity for sexual fulfilment, in short, qualities that most human beings take as their due. In Gogol's world, however, aspirations to social and psychological mobility always involve enormous risks; *hubris*, or overstepping, is as unwise there as in ancient Greece. Punishment soon follows. The coat is stolen off Akakii's back as he walks through late-night streets and enters "an endless square, its houses barely visible on the far side, looking like a fearful desert." In spiritual literature, the desert is often a place of illumination and self-discovery. In Gogol's story, Akakii discovers a self that is stripped of illusion; but the sudden illumination (ironically, nocturnal, as in "Nevskii Prospect") of his true state is too overwhelming for him to survive. Just as Petersburg itself (following Pushkin) no longer functions as an enclosure against hostile nature, so the overcoat can no longer conceal Akakii's ordained position in life, which, Gogol seems to say, is that of mere copy-clerk.[5]

Gogol's Petersburg is phenomenologically unreal. Perhaps that is why there are so few topographical markers in his urban landscapes, and few references to such traditional motifs as enclosure. Ultimately, he regards this city as deeply un-Russian, even as non-place. We might expect him to hew to convention and advance Moscow as a vital native alternative. He does so only once, in an article of 1837, where, in a detailed comparison of the two cities, Moscow comes off as unmistakably Russian in its open-hearted, slovenly, "feminine" ways. But even here, Gogol has reservations. Perhaps borrowing from *Evgenii Onegin*, he philistinizes "femininity" to mean a profusion of marriageable girls and a craze for fashions. And even while deeming Moscow's intellectual life more vigorous than Petersburg's, he reminds us that it too is largely imported from abroad.[6] For truly Russian settings, Gogol turns to small provincial towns, but he finds them even less vital. When he did eventually focus, in *Dead Souls*, on the question of the national identity, his reference point was not Petersburg or Moscow, but all of Russia – and a phantasmal Russia of the future at that.

By this time, it was clear that many different kinds of verbal discourse – histories, guidebooks, newspapers, even popular anecdotes – had begun to contribute to the developing myth of St. Petersburg. But belles-lettres were by far the most important, not only because they now occupied a central position in the national culture, but because they tended, especially in the form of the novel, to exploit and absorb other genres. The work of Fedor Dostoevskii is crucial in these respects. He was born in Moscow, but received his higher education in St. Petersburg, spent most of his life there, and made it the setting of many of his works. Moscow does not really figure in his fiction; other cities and towns are either provincial or foreign; his urban geography therefore resembles Gogol's. Several Petersburgs are evident in his early writings: fantastic and menacing, as in *The Double* (1846); enchanting and magical, as in "White Nights" (1848); sordid and harsh, as in *The Insulted and Injured* (1861). In *Notes from Underground* (1864), the narrator aphorizes a conventional theme when he calls Petersburg "the most abstract and premeditated city on the surface of the earth. (There are premeditated and unpremeditated cities.)"[7] He finds evidence at hand in the form of trendy contemporary issues like socialism, science, and utilitarianism. Against them he deploys caprice, anger, and even compassion, which are Dostoevskii's versions of the "irrational" sides of the city that Pushkin had found in vengeful nature, and Gogol in drives for power, sex, and self-aggrandizement.

Of Dostoevskii's four great novels, it is *Crime and Punishment* (1866) that most creatively draws on tradition to create a haunting picture of nineteenth-century Petersburg. Among the major ingredients are Western influences, the impoverished orders of society, and enclosure. But in every case, Dostoevskii takes these elements to an extreme, and gives them a new slant. For example, Raskolnikov is chock-full of the social, political and anthropological ideas of the day, despises them as the products of "other people's intelligence" – thereby raising the borrowing motif long associated with Petersburg – yet uses them to justify his murder of the old pawnbroker, only to discover that his motives for the crime involve far more than ideas, whatever their source. Urban poverty had been registered by Pushkin and Gogol, but in Dostoevskii's novel, it establishes an overwhelming presence, with a relentless series of shabby rooms and stinking streets. Like Dickens, with whom he is often compared, Dostoevskii is well aware that poverty has no history. That is perhaps why he offers few glimpses of the famous sights and monuments, which would of course open into the past. He keeps us focused on the present; and by compressing this present into a mere two weeks, he creates a suffocating psychological enclosure from which escape seems impossible. While taking full advantage of the enormous variety of human types present in any large modern city, he contrives to have all the characters touched in one way or another by Raskolnikov's thoughts and actions. Yet by adopting a third-person narration, he makes the point that Raskolnikov himself is subject to larger forces, and is not simply projecting his own mind onto the city. In this hermetically sealed literary world, objects, events, and people are intertwined; any action, however trivial, can generate enormous consequences, like the conversation Raskolnikov over-hears in the eating-house between two people he does not know (part I, chapter 6), which he takes as permission to commit the murder. Ironically, Raskolnikov, once convicted of the crime, exchanges the prison of Peters-burg for the "freedom" of exile in Siberia. But as his dreams in the Epilogue show, the city, and all it has come to stand for, cannot be readily forgotten. Indeed, Dostoevskii, in a major revision of the tradition, does not regard Petersburg as an aberration. He offers no mitigating or contrasting order, be it the countryside, nature, or Moscow; the city focuses and intensifies what is happening in Russia at large. As Luzhin puts it: "All these innovations, reforms and ideas of ours – all these have touched us in the provinces too; but in order to see everything and see it more clearly, one must be in Petersburg."[8] Many later writers would take note.

Dostoevskii's achievement as an urban novelist is all the more striking when we consider the far more conventional Petersburg set forth in the writings of three of his illustrious contemporaries, Ivan Goncharov, Ivan Turgenev, and Lev Tolstoi. In Goncharov's first novel, *A Common Story* (1847), Aduev, a naively idealistic young man, moves to the capital from his country estate in hopes of becoming a famous writer. But he cannot cope with the pitiless demands of the city and with the cynicism of his wealthy uncle, and settles for an undistinguished existence. *Oblomov* (1859), Goncharov's masterpiece, restates many of the same situations in a far more mature and compelling way. Ilia Ilich Oblomov comes to St. Petersburg from Oblomovka, his estate, to take up a job in the civil service, and to find a wife. He abandons the first after two years, and fails totally with the second. When the novel opens, a decade later, he occupies a spacious, centrally-located apartment, but remains uninvolved in the life of the city, which casts only a shadowy presence throughout. Instead, he lies on a couch in one room, attended by his elderly servant Zakhar, and reminisces about Oblomovka, a paradise that owes much to literary idylls of the eighteenth century. In fact, his estate has fallen on hard times, and, as the sole heir, he has plenty of work awaiting him there. Though intelligent and well-meaning, he cannot bestir himself to return, any more than he can seek a purposeful life in the city. He is the most celebrated instance of the kind of displaced, or "superfluous" character initiated by Onegin, which throughout the nineteenth century was often regarded as regrettably typical of the Russian character. Turgenev, for one, usually killed such characters off. Goncharov's solution is more ingenious. He decides to bestow happiness on his hero by moving him to a location that combines city and country: the suburb. (*Oblomov* may in fact be the first piece of suburban literature in Russia.) There he settles down in the well-run house of the widow Pshenitsyna, who becomes a mother–wife figure and makes his life a "living idyll," like the Oblomovka of old. Eventually he dies of inactivity and gluttony. Although he has achieved personal fulfillment, it is devoid of the kind of social concerns that Russian readers had come to expect in literary characters.

Turgenev writes mostly about provincial Russia. But the city, particularly Petersburg, is a constant if nearly silent presence in his six novels. The best is *Fathers and Children* (1862). It is set in 1859; but in a long flashback, we are told that the young Kirsanov brothers left their estate in the 1840s and went to Petersburg for formation, Pavel as a Guards officer, and Nikolai as a civil servant. Pavel is ruined by the experience, and becomes one of those deracinated characters that literary tradition had already taught readers to associate with the capital. It is probably not coincidental that his patronymic is Petrovich, or "son of Peter," meaning perhaps Peter the Great, and if so, reminding us of the perennial question of the national identity. That question is more palpably raised by Pavel's Western habits, like his Anglophilia and his fondness for European spas, and, contrastively, by certain "Eastern" features of his dress and rooms, such as a fez, Chinese slippers, and Turkish carpets. Nikolai is in danger of displacement, also being a Petrovich, and, like Oblomov, having resigned his government job in disillusionment. What saves him is his decision to return to and manage the family estate, where he forms a liaison with his housekeeper's young daughter, who exemplifies deeply Russian values. As the novel opens, he is being visited by his son, Arkadii, who has brought with him Bazarov, a friend and mentor. Both are recent graduates of St. Petersburg University. There Bazarov has become infected with Western ideas, and is now an exponent of "nihilism" (*nigilizm*), a foreign word for a foreign concept, around which the intellectual and moral conflicts of the book cluster.

Structurally, Turgenev honors a pattern that goes back to Pushkin and Gogol, whereby alien, usually urban values are suddenly introduced into a vital, self-contained world, often a country estate. In Gogol it is the entity that disintegrates (as in "Old-World Landowners" or *The Inspector General*). In Turgenev the opposite occurs. Bazarov dies; Pavel ends his visit to resume a life of aimless wandering in Europe. Arkadii, however, comes to see that the "soil" is where he belongs, with a wife and children in his future. As the son of a country doctor, Bazarov really belongs there too; and Turgenev, an accomplished ironist, makes the point by having him buried in his parish churchyard. We are meant to conclude that Petersburg at best serves as an arena where young men may test themselves, but that it cannot provide an authentic way of life for a Russian.

Much the same idea shapes Tolstoi's novella *Family Happiness* (1859). Here Masha has to leave her idyllic family estate, plunge into the empty social round in Petersburg, and jeopardize her marriage in order to learn that true values reside in the country, with husband and children. An antipathy to Petersburg is apparent from the opening pages of *War and Peace* (1865–69). For Tolstoi it is a foreign, upper-class city, whose inhabitants lead lives that are "insignificant, trivial, and artificial . . . concerned only with phantoms and reflections of life." Pierre Bezukhov, the hero, feels out of place there, and his marriage to the socially accomplished but stupid Hélène is a disaster. Still, the experience shows him what he is not, and points him toward discovering an authentic self. The most important stopping-place on that long route is Moscow, which is treated as the antithesis of Petersburg in virtually every respect. Tolstoi does not dwell on topographical *realia*, but he brings in all levels of society to show that this city is a vital, organic entity, and stands for Russia as a whole. Even though Moscow's upper classes have been somewhat tainted by foreign ways, as the celebrated scene of Natasha's evening at the opera reminds us, the solid Russian core remains, waiting to be uncovered. That happens in 1812. Tolstoi's graphic account of Napoleon's occupation of the city re-enacts the old Russian pattern of borrowing from abroad, and shows a way out that Petersburg never took, as the inhabitants burn and then desert the city. Burning of course is a traditional symbol of purification, and it enables Tolstoi to make the important point that Moscow – and by extension, Russia – is less a place than a state of mind: "Everything had been destroyed, except something intangible, yet powerful and indestructible." It is here that Pierre, as a prisoner of the French, "attained the serenity and contentment which he had formerly striven in vain to reach," an "inner harmony" which creates in him a feeling of oneness with all humans, nature, and the universe.[9] Eventually he settles in the countryside; but the two urban experiences, however different, have been essential prerequisites to this discovery of true place.

Yet Tolstoi never allows us to forget that it is character which shapes place, and that place, so regarded, is relatively unimportant. An early version can be seen in *The Cossacks* (1863), where Olenin tires of the empty life of his fellow-aristocrats in Moscow (which is identical in this respect to Petersburg) and seeks authenticity among the "simple" folk of the Caucasus. But his preconceptions are too powerful; the quest is fruitless; and he ends up with no proper place at all. This is what happens to the heroine of *Anna Karenina* (1875–77). Both Petersburg and Moscow are treated contemptuously in this novel; the countryside is extolled as the spiritual and moral center of Russian life; but it is ultimately Anna's flaws of character that prevent her from making healthy choices, and doom her to disaster.

Around the turn of the century, fiction writers began to explore new themes, like industrialization, the rising middle class, business entrepreneurship, and class warfare. Cities and towns were the preferred settings, and blacks and grays the preferred coloration, in the spirit of Dostoevskii and Gogol, but with an admixture of French Naturalists like Zola. These trends are generously represented in the works of Maksim Gorkii, especially in *Mother* (1906), his most famous and influential novel, which offers an adulatory account of the rising revolutionary movement in ways that left an indelible mark on all Soviet literature: it has rightly been called "the archetype of the socialist realist novel."[10] Revolution also drives the plot of Andrei Belyi's *Petersburg* (first version in book form, 1916; revised, 1922), but that is all the two novels have in common. Gorkii's is propaganda; Belyi's is an ambitiously conceived and intricately woven work of art, which most readers of Russian literature have come to regard as the greatest urban novel of the twentieth century.

The story is set in 1905, when Petersburg, at nearly two million the largest city in the Russian Empire, stood at its height culturally, but was being racked by social unrest that would culminate in revolution. Belyi creates a tissue of detail that makes the city vividly present, indeed almost a character in its own right. In addition to climate, topography, architecture, and the famous streets and monuments, he brings in the great intellectual and cultural issues that engaged educated people, and the political discontents that knew no class boundaries. So particular are the events he describes that we can date the action of the novel, although he does not do so, as unfolding between 30 September and 9 October. It is on them that he builds his fictional plot. It moves linearly. But the lines intersect several great circles, which dip back into time past, ahead into an apocalyptic time future, and even into an astral "fourth dimension." One consequence is the appearance in fictional present time of characters and events from Russian history. Peter the Great – man and equestrian statue – is the most important. Belyi also draws heavily from earlier Russian fiction, thereby reminding us how much of the identity of Petersburg has been created by writers. "Was that the shadow of a woman darting onto the little bridge to throw herself off?" the narrator asks at one point. "Was it Liza?" in an allusion to the heroine of Tchaikovsky's operatic version of Pushkin's story "The Queen of Spades" (1833). "No, just the shadow of a woman of Petersburg." But it could have been Liza too, in the world as Belyi arranges it. He not only makes no attempt to conceal his borrowings, but ensures that we see them too. This is very much in keeping with the Russian tradition of "literariness" (*literaturnost'*), which does not prize "originality" in the sense that most non-Russian Western cultures do. The character of the old senator, Apollon Apollonovich, is the richest beneficiary of this tradition, embodying as he does certain attributes of the god Apollo, after whom he is named, the greenish ears of Anna Karenina's husband, the devotion to bureaucratic drudgery of Gogol's Akakii Akakevich, and the reactionary politics of Konstantin Pobedonostsev, the real-life Procurator of the Holy Synod. Belyi also avails himself of much of the complex mythology that had grown up around the city by his time, with heavy doses of the Bible, Rudolf Steiner, and German philosophy. It finds forceful expression in the images of enclosure, East, and West, all of which are intertwined. Most particularly they are associated with Apollon Apollonovich. He regards Russia as a vast, threatening expanse, an "icy plain" that is "roamed by wolves," and is frightened by the rising tide of violence in the country, which he identifies not only with revolutionaries, but with "Eastern" elements variously defined as Mongolians and Turanians. These fears prompt him to seek refuge behind apparently secure enclosures, like Petersburg itself, the thick walls of his magnificent house, Comtean positivism, and the undeviating routines of domestic and official life. But everything he tries to exclude is either already present within any given enclosure, himself included, or gains easy access to it; and at any moment he can find himself whisked out of his rooms, his city, and his body into the fourth dimension.

What is true of Apollon holds for Belyi's novel at large. Nothing is clearly delineated; everything blends and blurs, so that conventional markers like "fact" and "fiction," "past" and "present" are ultimately meaningless. Even Belyi's system of language relies on polyvalence and ambiguity, as we might expect in a Symbolist writer. In these ways too, *Petersburg* reveals the presence of the same impulse that drove all the

Russian arts of the early twentieth century toward a conflation and synthesis of genres, styles, and materials. As a result, we are offered no reliable phenomenological world, no narrator who explains or even hints at the way things "really" are. By the end of the novel, characters, narrator, and readers find themselves in a state of confusion and puzzlement, much like readers of Gogol, Belyi's favorite writer. Nothing is left of those "great thoughts" which had originally created the city. Paradoxically, the most thoroughgoing novel ever written about Russia's capital city ends by writing Petersburg, and perhaps even Russia itself, out of existence. Belyi began work on a sequel to this novel, which was to be entitled *The Invisible City*. There, he said, he would no longer "rummage around in vileness," but would "depict wholesome and ennobling elements of 'Life and the Spirit.' "[11] But it was never written, perhaps because wholesomeness and nobility are qualities conspicuously absent in earlier fictional treatments of St. Petersburg.

Much of the imagery of Petersburg, however, moved to other venues. One was utopian societies, often highly technological, as in Aleksandr Bogdanov's *Red Star* (1908) and *Engineer Menni* (1912). In early Soviet times, Aleksei Tolstoi's *Aelita* (1922–23) enjoyed wide popularity. It begins in a Petersburg ravaged by revolution and civil war, an "insane city" of empty, wind-swept streets, boarded-up buildings, and freezing interiors, like all of Russia at the time. No alternative being available, two committed urbanites, the scientists Los and Gusev, build a rocket ship and set out for Mars, where, amidst a desolate landscape, they come upon the magical, sparkling capital city of Soatsera. Unfortunately, it is controlled by an evil tyrant, Tuskub, who wants it annihilated, arguing – in what looks like a throwback to Sentimentalist anti-urbanism – that "the force that is destroying universal order – anarchy – emanates from the city. A laboratory for the preparation of drunkards, thieves, murderers, savage voluptuaries, ravaged souls – such is the city." It turns out, however, that Tuskub is interested merely in hanging on to power, and Gusev, intent on preserving this marvelous city, leads a band of rebels. He fails, and, with Los, escapes back to Petersburg. Four years have passed, and with them, a transformation has occurred: Petersburg has become "one of the really chic cities of Europe," no longer bleak and empty, but bustling and purposeful, with the Nevskii Prospect (in a look back perhaps at the landscape of Belyi's novel) "filled with people, flooded with light from a thousand windows, fiery letters, arrows, and revolving wheels above the roofs." What has made the difference is purposeful labor and a new technology. Los himself is now employed in a factory, where he is "building a multi-purpose engine of the Martian type. It was assumed that his engine would revolutionize the very foundations of mechanics, and eliminate all the imperfections of the world's economic system."

Aleksei Tolstoi was not alone among writers of the 1920s in abhorring raw nature, seeing cities as models for an ideal society, and assuming that they could be created on this earth. The trick was to find the right people to run them. Nor was he alone in celebrating technology, and identifying it as an urban phenomenon: that was to be a Soviet habit of mind right up to the end of the system in 1991. In Russia, as elsewhere in the industrialized world, there had been considerable discussion, since the late nineteenth century, of the impact of technology on human beings, for better or worse. The best-known exponents of a kind of technological Romanticism were the so-called "Smithy" poets of the 1920s, like Gastev, Kirillov, Kazin and Gerasimov, and the novelist Fedor Gladkov in *Cement* (1925). At first glance, Tolstoi should be numbered among them. Yet he tells us, in an odd turn of phrase, that Los "did not really believe that any conceivable combination of machines was capable of solving the tragedy of universal happiness."[12] This puts Tolstoi in the camp of the skeptics, who were numerous in the 1920s. Most prominent among them was Boris Pilniak, who explored the man/machine relationship in a number of novels. And in Evgenii Zamiatin's *We* (1921), skepticism spilled into sheer hostility to create the most celebrated dystopia in Russian literature.

The time is the remote future; the place, the Single State, a technologically advanced, rigidly regulated city, which has been surrounded by a green glass wall to keep out the untamed world beyond. It looks like the kind of society that Apollon Apollonovich had dreamed of creating. In fact, Zamiatin draws heavily, though silently, on Belyi's novel for particulars of setting, characterization, imagery, and themes.[13] However, he reduces these particulars to the absurd, especially in his treatment of science and technology, which in any event are virtually absent in *Petersburg*. Technology has built the Single State, and has also devised a rocket ship (described in the imagery of industrial Romanticism) to export "happiness" to other worlds. One catch is that technology has become oppressive, as graphically demonstrated in the Machine, the State's instrument of execution, which punishes the crime of individuality by disintegrating the perpetrators.

We was deemed subversive by a Bolshevik political culture that glorified cities and technology, and it was not published in the Soviet Union for many years. With the removal of the capital to Moscow in 1924, however, writers found a less dangerous and more productive setting for many of these same themes. We might have expected them to devise a new literary code. Instead, they simply borrowed parts, large or small, of the Petersburg

one, their task made easier by the fact that literary Moscow had traditionally functioned mainly as an antithesis to Petersburg, had never developed a
particularly specific code of its own, and, in any event, was probably too
ancient and potent a symbol of Russian nationalism for accommodation to
the needs of a supposedly internationalist age.

An early case in point was Boris Pilniak's *The Naked Year* (1921). To be
sure, it is set in a provincial town, not a metropolis. But this town has a
kremlin, or fortress, as did many others; and Pilniak uses it to evoke
Moscow, which in turn displays several of the conventional features of
Petersburg. The most striking is "Chinatown," whose name derives from an
early confusion of the word for "China" (*Kitai*) with *kita*, the sixteenth-
century term for the wooden fence (later a stone wall) that delimited the
central part of Moscow. At one stroke, Pilniak combines the motifs of
Easternism and enclosure, insists that they coexist with "Western" phenomena typified as bowler hats and briefcases filled with stocks and bonds,
and suggests that the Revolution, for all its vaunted novelty, merely enacts
these familiar images and juxtapositions.[14] If Andrei Belyi read this novel,
he must have given a smile of recognition.

Enclosure and Easternism, however, proved unproductive in other
Moscow novels, perhaps because of the new emphasis on internationalism.
The themes of urban crime and squalor did pass over, with Leonid Leonov's
novel *The Thief* (1927) among the most notable instances. So did the
themes of bureaucracy and technology, along with many familiar character-
types. Mikhail Bulgakov's *The Master and Margarita* (1928–40) makes
more extensive use of these materials than any Soviet novel set in the
capital.

Here we see a mostly middle- and lower-class city of the late 1920s,
where lawlessness and chaos prevail. To judge by newspaper accounts of
the time, this Moscow had a basis in actuality. But in Bulgakov's hands,
such actuality soon proves elusive and evanescent, spun as it is out of
rumor and gossip, projected onto ever-shifting temporal and spatial planes
(even a "fifth dimension"), constantly invaded by supernatural powers, and
narrated in a variety of styles and dictions, including an interpolated
historical novel about Christ and Pilate. Most striking is its "literariness,"
as evinced in massive and obvious importations from fictions of centuries
past, both Russian and foreign, such as *Alice in Wonderland* and *The
Golden Ass*. As in Belyi's *Petersburg* (always a powerful presence), all are
as "real" as anything else in this nightmarish city. Especially important as a
theme and an engine of the plot is demonism, which also imbibes
generously from literary sources. Readers will easily recognize Dostoevskii's *Double* (1846), Gogol's "Overcoat", and some of his *Dikan'ka*

Tales as well, especially "A Bewitched Place" (1832), which could serve as an unofficial subtitle for the whole novel. But it is the figure of Woland, a refugee from Goethe's *Faust*, who neatly conflates the old Petersburg themes of foreignness, literariness, and demonism. He is the most "positive" of all the weird and unsavory characters in that he at least provides a way of escaping the oppressive enclosure that is everyday Moscow. The chief beneficiary is the heroine, Margarita, who becomes a witch, with decidedly Gogolian characteristics. Presumably she is dead, but there is no telling for sure.

By the time Bulgakov began his novel, the political climate had become decidedly inhospitable to latter-day Petersburgs. No doubt that is one reason why it was not published until the late 1960s. Far more cautious, and ultimately, far more representative, was the picture of Moscow in one of the greatest works of the 1920s, Iurii Olesha's *Envy* (1927). Like many Soviet writers of the time, Olesha exploits the conflict between the "old" values of tsarist Russia and the "new" values that inspirited the Revolution and the developing Soviet system. He embodies them in six characters and sets them in a Moscow of his own time. The "old" have obvious antecedents in the literature of Petersburg: Ivan Kavalerov, as an impractical dreamer, resembles Oblomov; Kavalerov, the ne'er-do-well and failure, looks back to many a Dostoevskian character; and Annechka is a devouring female of a type frequently found in Gogol. The "new" people embody the "correct" attitudes of the Soviet 1920s: a dedication to urbanism, a transformation of the world through technology and purposeful labor, and the elimination of negative thoughts and feelings. Yet here too Olesha looks to prototypes in the literary Petersburg of old: Andrei, the commissar, is a jumped-up Akakii Akakevich; and Volodia and Valia, the ideal Soviet youths of the future, resemble the antiseptically purposeful people, often revolutionaries, that populate such nineteenth-century novels as Nikolai Chernyshevskii's *What Is to Be Done?* (1863). Olesha's version of the "new" Moscow is also highly ambiguous. He makes scarcely a mention of the *realia* that mark the city for even a casual reader; except for a few place-names, we could be in any large modern urban center. Possibly he may be reminding us, no doubt ironically, of yet another politically correct idea of the 1920s: that Moscow, as the headquarters of the world Communist movement, should have no purely Russian coloration. This may be why only the "old" characters are so intent on relishing palpable, local objects, whether charming (Kavalerov's trodden blossom or almond sliver), menacing (Ivan's humanized machine Ophelia), or wondrous (Annechka's bed). But such details are not particular to Moscow, or for that matter, to Russia; the city loses its specific identity, and begins to stand for the country as a whole. In these senses, *Envy* prepared the way for at least three decades of Socialist Realist novels, which would revive the centuries-old theme that Moscow is more an idea than a place.

Actually, Pilniak had been among the first, in *Naked Year*, to foresee this development when he depicted provincial towns as mini-Moscows. By the early 1930s, the official aesthetic of Socialist Realism obliged all writers to do the same. Thus, in Mikhail Sholokhov's *Virgin Soil Upturned* (1932–60), Davydov, a metal worker by trade and a Communist by conviction, is sent from the city to bring order to a collective farm. Although he has a lot to learn about rural life, the Party takes for granted that his political attitudes, urban to the core, are adequate to any situation, regardless of locale. Ultimately the lines between city and country were to be erased altogether, at least in theory. But it did not follow that a politically enlightened farmer could function just as effectively in the city: the chronic Bolshevik distrust of rural Russia prevailed. (Significantly, Davydov is killed by enraged peasants.) The country was becoming progressively urbanized, with Moscow setting the political, social, intellectual and technological norms. Eventually this tendency found expression in the notion of "agro-cities," which was proposed by Nikita Khrushchev in the 1950s, but never went very far.

Urban settings continued to predominate in Soviet literature during the so-called "Thaw," that period of comparative political relaxation which got under way around 1956. The better writers, however, began to find more interesting ways of handling them, now that they were freer to disregard the dictates of Socialist Realism, with its penchant for generalization and typology. Many showed an interest in recording the trivia of life, which would not have been possible under Stalinism. Iurii Trifonov, for one, specialized in representing the ordinary, frequently banal routines of domestic life as lived out in Moscow. Aleksandr Solzhenitsyn has also been a meticulous recorder of quotidian details. Far more than Trifonov or most of his contemporaries, however, he is interested in myth-making, often in terms that are familiar to readers of earlier urban literature. One of them is enclosure. *One Day in the Life of Ivan Denisovich* (1962) is set in a forced labor camp, as are the three volumes of *The Gulag Archipelago* (1973–75); *Cancer Ward* (1968) takes place mainly in a hospital located in a large city. *The First Circle* (1968) unfolds in Moscow and environs, with many different enclosures: the city itself, the Kremlin, the Liubianka prison, the *sharashka*, or special labor camp, the tight world of the Party privileged. All overlap, and together comprise the gigantic enclosure that is the Soviet Union. This Moscow bears no resemblance to the nurturing, authentically Russian city of old. It is more like literary Petersburg from Pushkin through

Belyi, a conglomeration of isolated individuals whose identity is largely shaped by a bureaucracy obsessed with dehumanizing trivia.

Many other writers of this period – and Solzhenitsyn himself to some extent – began to rediscover the countryside as a contrasting realm of salubrious moral values. In Boris Pasternak's *Doctor Zhivago* (1957), the countryside is where the title character goes to escape the privations and dangers of a Moscow torn by Revolution and Civil War. There he learns that all life, large or small, past or present, human or vegetable, is interconnected and sacred, that essentials lie in homely daily details, and that authentic humanity and true art depend on one's ability to achieve a "tranquil and broad outlook which elevate(s) the particular instance to a universality that is familiar to all." But Pasternak enriches this "country" theme by introducing an "Eastern" motif, which had been virtually absent from Soviet urban fiction since the 1920s. Not only does Zhivago settle far to the East, in the Urals region, but just before he leaves Moscow, he sees a mysterious boy "with narrow Kirghiz eyes, in an unbuttoned reindeer coat with fur on both sides, the kind people wear in Siberia or the Urals." He understands that this boy is his "death," meaning, perhaps, the death of an old way of life, and rebirth into a new one. If so, then what Pasternak draws on here is the tradition of the vital, life-affirming, and essentially Christian East that goes back to the *Primary Chronicle*. The literary conventions of the nineteenth century might lead us to suppose that once Zhivago abandons Moscow and embraces the rural east, he achieves personal fulfillment. Pasternak refuses such an easy and obvious solution. Zhivago's life in Moscow is shown to be a necessary preparation for his spiritual and artistic discoveries. It is there that he begins to see that the whole edifice of pre-revolutionary culture has been false, that the Revolution has been beneficial in knocking it down and revealing essentials, as expressed in the "joy of living" an "ordinary" existence, and that he is powerless to interfere in the processes of history or the natural rhythms of life. And it is to Moscow that he ultimately returns, like most of the surviving characters in the novel. He understands that despite its shabbiness and poverty, Moscow is "still a big, modern city," and that such cities are "the only inspiration for a truly new, modern art," speaking as they do the "living language of our time . . . the language of urbanism," which is "incessantly stirring and rumbling outside our doors and windows." Zhivago himself does not live long enough to turn these insights into art. Perhaps it is just as well: he retains something of the aesthete in his make-up, and Pasternak would not have us think that the city is simply material for a good poem. Perhaps that is why his death is followed by an epilogue in which the narrator states that Moscow is not merely "the locale of these events," but is itself "the real heroine of a long story," the most Russian of subjects, indeed a "holy city," the embodiment, we might say, of an authentically Russian life that knows no polarities, but is organic, unitary, and vital. The similarity to medieval views of Moscow, and, more recently, to Tolstoi's view in *War and Peace,* though unremarked, is obvious.[15]

There is no place for Petersburg in Zhivago's world, or, for that matter, in much of the Soviet literature written since the 1920s. But the theme is not dead. In 1978 Andrei Bitov's *Pushkin House* appeared. The edifice that inspires the title is the famous institute for literary research of the Academy of Sciences, located on Vasilevskii Island in St. Petersburg. We are therefore not surprised to find that, in the spirit of Belyi, the novel cites or alludes to many well-known works of Russian literature, draws characters, situations and themes from them, and treats them all as part of the ongoing life of the city in the 1960s. Bitov need not even be very specific about the sights and landmarks: mere hints and echoes serve to situate any reasonably literate reader. Yet the novel seems luxuriant, mainly because Bitov relishes the particulars of ordinary life. For the most part, he treats them with warmth and affection. That in itself represents a sharp departure from the Petersburg literary conventions, and probably explains why he has no need for a contrasting Moscow or countryside.

Pushkin House was one of the last big novels with a city theme to be published in Russia. Indeed, novels of any kind are rarer now; literature itself has fallen on hard times; creative energies are being directed elsewhere. But given the traditional importance of fiction for reflecting and shaping the national mind, it is likely that Russia will again need its writers, and likely too that the novel, and with it the theme of the city, will revive and continue to resonate.

NOTES

1. In *Pamiatniki literatury drevnei Rusi. Nachalo russkoi literatury XI – nachalo XII vekov* (Moscow: Khudozhestvennaia literatura, 1978), p. 37.
2. Karamzin's memoir was published as a supplement (*prilozhenie*) to A. N. Pypin, *Obshchestvennoe dvizhenie v Rossii pri Aleksandre I*, 4th edn (St. Petersburg: Tipografiia M. M. Stasiulevicha, 1908), pp. 491–92, 481, 483. The italics are Karamzin's.
3. A. S. Pushkin, *Polnoe sobranie sochinenii v desiati tomakh* (Moscow: Nauka, 1962–66), vol. V, pp. 32, 155–56, 163.
4. Ibid., vol. IV, pp. 379–97.
5. In Gogol, *Polnoe sobranie sochinenii*, 14 vols. (Moscow–Leningrad: AN SSSR, 1937–52), vol. III. The quotes from "Nevskii Prospekt" are on pp. 19, 46; from "Shinel," on pp. 145, 161.

6. Gogol, "Peterburgskie zapiski 1836 goda," in *Polnoe sobranie sochinenii*, vol. VIII, pp. 177–79.

7. In Dostoevskii, *Polnoe sobranie sochinenii v tridtsati tomakh* (Leningrad: Nauka, 1972–90), vol. V, p. 101.

8. Ibid., vol. VI, p. 115.

9. In Tolstoi, *Polnoe sobranie sochinenii* (Moscow: Khudozhestvennaia literatura, 1929–64), vol. IX, p. 258; vol. XII, pp. 3, 211; vol. XI, pp. 96–97.

10. Victor Terras, "Gorky," in Victor Terras (ed.), *Handbook of Russian Literature* (New Haven: Yale University Press, 1985), p. 181.

11. Belyi, Letter to Aleksandr Blok, December 28, 1912 (January 10, 1913), in V. Orlov (ed.), *Aleksandr Blok i Andrei Belyi. Perepiska* (Moscow: Izd. Gosudarstvennogo Literaturnogo Muzeia, 1940), pp. 301, 309. For the quotations from Belyi's *Petersburg*, see the 1928 edition as published in Moscow (Khudozhestvennaia literatura, 1978), pp. 58, 78.

12. The quotations are taken from the first edition, as published in *Krasnaia nov'*, 1 (1923), 74; 2 (1923), 55, 57. Most of the passages cited were removed from subsequent editions of the novel, and "Petersburg" was changed to "Petrograd" – all understandable "improvements" in light of the new political climate. "Universal happiness" in the last quotation sounds peculiar – perhaps it is a misprint for "unhappiness" – but it does not alter Tolstoi's idea that technology has its limitations.

13. For a detailed discussion of Zamiatin's indebtedness to *Petersburg*, see Robert A. Maguire and John E. Malmstad, "The Legacy of *Petersburg*. Zamiatin's *We*," in John Elsworth (ed.), *The Silver Age in Russian Literature* (New York: St. Martin's Press, 1992), pp. 182–95.

14. In Pilniak, *Izbrannye proizvedeniia* (Moscow: Khudozhestvennaia literatura), pp. 46–47.

15. Pasternak, *Doktor Zhivago* (Ann Arbor: University of Michigan Press, 1959), pp. 465, 211, 500, 501, 530–31.

3

HUGH McLEAN

The countryside

Certainly since the time of Theocritus, and doubtless long before that, weary city dwellers have sought – or at least thought about seeking – escape from their noisy, bustling, confining urban world into the tranquillity, spaciousness, and presumed leisure of the countryside. In such moods nature generally appears to them in her most benign aspects: warm but not hot, green, fertile, vivifying, motherly. The country resident, on the other hand, may feel an equally powerful impulse to escape: from the isolation, boredom, discomforts, and dangers of rural life to the security, social connectedness, and relative cultural richness of the town, where people can collectively defend themselves against a nature often not at all benign, as well as against less than benign fellow creatures.

The anti-urban urge has been a theme of literature almost since literature has existed at all. The Western tradition offers a long procession of passionate pastoralists, from Theocritus and Vergil down to Rousseau and beyond. Despite the fact that only a tiny minority of them actually lived in cities, the Russians absorbed the pastoral tradition enthusiastically if belatedly, themselves producing such elegant poetic celebrations of the bucolic life as Gavrila Derzhavin's delightful idyll "To Evgenii; Life at Zvanka" (1807).

In the novel, celebration of the countryside makes a splendid beginning in *Evgenii Onegin*, Pushkin's great novel-in-verse, the progenitor in theme if not in form of so many distinguished descendants. *Evgenii Onegin* embodies that triangle of vividly contrasted settings later powerfully exploited by Tolstoi: majestic, imperial, "European" St. Petersburg; comfortable, historic, ultra-Russian Moscow; and a lyric countryside filled with idyllic nests where the gentry played at realizing the Theocritan ideal. "Flowers, love, countryside, idleness, / Fields! I am devoted to you with all my heart"[1] proclaims the narrator-poet, marking this as a distinction that separates him from his hero, who soon tires of live-in "eclogues." It is an attachment the narrator shares with his nature-loving heroine, Tatiana, who even in her last incarnation as a Petersburg *grande dame* still longs to return to her bucolic birthplace. Despite the boredom, however, Onegin does settle down easily enough to the life of a country squire, in a prototypical setting the narrator describes as a "charming little place,"[2] complete with a manor house perched on a hill, a brook, meadows, fields of grain, and a garden serving as "the refuge of meditative Dryads."[3] There Onegin lives the life of an "anchorite," amusing himself with reading, horseback riding, wine, "fairly inventive" dinners, and on occasion the "young and fresh kiss"[4] of one of his dark-eyed serf girls.

Onegin has, however, brought with him, both in his luggage and within himself, some of the trappings of urban culture; these set him apart from the local gentry, whose conversation inescapably turns around such prosaic rural concerns as haymaking and hunting dogs. Their greater cultural sophistication draws together Onegin and Lenskii, the latter fresh from his studies at Göttingen, although Lenskii, unlike Onegin, is willing to let the charms of love draw him into rustic social life. Eventually even the anchorite Onegin is caught in the toils of love, as Tatiana follows up her letter with direct confrontation in the garden. The manor garden as a locus of love declarations, later an almost automatic reflex in the nineteenth-century Russian novel, especially Turgenev's, thus makes an early appearance in *Evgenii Onegin*, although in an image reversed from the conventional one, with the female offering love and the male rejecting it.

Pushkin takes us through the whole sequence of seasons in the country, showing not just the spring and summer idylls, but also chilly, rainy autumn, and best of all, the crisp, clear Russian winter, felt as exhilarating both by the "triumphant" peasant who opens the first sleigh-road and the frolicsome lad who harnesses himself to the sled on which his dog gets a ride. The winter, the time of nature's death, is the appropriate time for the fatal duel that ends Lenskii's brief life and propels Onegin onto his "journey." A year later Tatiana is taken over the same sleigh-roads to Moscow, to be auctioned off at the "bridal fair."

The majority of inhabitants of the Russian countryside, the actual peasant farmers on whom the country's life depends, make only the briefest cameo appearances. Onegin's perhaps urban-generated liberalism induces him to shift his serfs from *barshchina* ("corvée," i.e. work for the landlord) to *obrok* ("quitrent," i.e., payment to the landlord in money or in kind),[5] much to the consternation of his conservative neighbors; but it never seems to occur to him to question his right to live as a complete parasite and in comparative luxury off the labor of these slaves.

It will be almost two decades before Russian literature will bring these slaves into literary focus. In the meantime, Onegin's journey, retracing the poet's own exilic wandering, takes him into the more exotic regions of the expanding Russian empire, the picturesque Crimea, with its memories of ancient Greek settlements and Tatar seraglios, and most of all the Caucasus, which served beautifully as Russia's answer to Byron's Near East: towering, majestic peaks, dramatic waterfalls and colorful natives, admirable in the reckless dash of their brave warriors, the exotic charm of their women, the alluring otherness of their (mostly) Muslim customs.

These scenes, already etched into the Russian consciousness from Pushkin's *Prisoner of the Caucasus* (1822), were given their classic novelistic incarnation in Lermontov's *A Hero of Our Time* (1840), where the Caucasus provides an ideal backdrop for another tragic romance between a callous, "burned-out" Russian officer and a vulnerable Circassian maiden, and also for a classic, purely Russian "society tale" of sexual rivalry, set in one of the region's fashionable watering places.

Back home in Russia proper, the idyllic setting of the gentry estate was given a much less benevolent exposure by Gogol. In his story "Old-world Landowners" (1835) Gogol had already, under the guise of what masquerades as an idyll, in fact vividly epitomized what Marx and Engels later called the "idiocy of rural life."[6] If looked at too closely, Gogol's lovable Baucis and Philemon are actually walking exemplars of the grossest gluttony and empty-headed futility. Now the same theme was writ large in his great novel *Dead Souls* (1842). Even the plot of this satirical masterpiece was indicative of the fatal weakness that before the end of the century would bring ruin to so many Russian gentlefolk: their addiction to living on borrowed money. The attempt of Gogol's anti-hero, Chichikov, to swindle the state by mortgaging dead instead of live serfs is only an *outré*, criminal instance of the egregious fiscal irresponsibility characteristic of most gentlemen.

Chichikov's acquisitive excursions outward into the countryside from the town of NN confront him and the reader with a series of stupefying specimens of degenerate gentry whose environs are perfect metonymies of their lifeless souls. In the garden of bland, sentimental, pretentious Manilov, for example, there is a gazebo ludicrously labeled "Temple of Solitary Meditation." The bully, windbag, and liar Nozdrev lives among kindred spirits – a huge pack of dogs to which he was "like a father," while his human children interest him little. Solid, stolid Sobakevich is at least a good manager of his domain, viewing his peasants as an extension of himself. Their no-nonsense homes have no carved ornaments or other frills, but are built to last. In contrast, the huts of miser Pliushkin's serfs have deteriorated to the point of disintegration, their occupants having absconded to the tavern or the open road. In Pliushkin's neglected garden, however, nature has created a wonderful, tangled wilderness, described by Gogol in wonderful, tangled sentences. In that garden the remnants of human plans and efforts to impose order on nature have long since been submerged to the point of obliteration in luxuriant verdure.

The second volume of *Dead Souls* was supposed to embody a less negative image of the Russian countryside, a world peopled by landowners some of whom, at least, were trying to realize the practical program of beneficent agricultural and serf management that Gogol later outlined in his *Selected Passages from Correspondence with Friends* (1847). The ideal is presumably realized on the estate of Konstantin Kostanzhoglo, where everything is orderly and in good repair, the peasants have "some sort of intelligent expression on their faces," and the manor house is crowned by a huge (pre-electric) spotlight that lights up his lands for fifteen versts (ten miles) around. The spotlight aptly symbolizes the "enlightening" aspect of Kostanzhoglo's benign concentration camp, which bears a startling resemblance to the regime of peasant control and agricultural management actually instituted a century later on Soviet *kolkhozy* and *sovkhozy*. Russian peasants, Gogol clearly believed, were by nature lazy dolts who required the strictest supervision from their God-appointed masters. If all landowners were like Kostanzhoglo, he thought, then serfdom could be the basis for a society not merely tolerable, but actually ideal.

The winds of history, however, were blowing in a different direction. By the late 1840s it was becoming increasingly clear, even in the upper reaches of Nicholas's hidebound government, that serfdom would eventually have to go. It was wasteful and inefficient; as agricultural managers the gentry were negligent, ill-qualified, and ineffective; the peasants had neither incentive nor adequate opportunity to improve their lot by hard work, thrift, and investment. And of course serfdom was flagrantly inhumane. Peasants were helplessly subject to the whims of their owners or the latter's deputies, who not only managed the peasants' labor and disposed of its fruits, but had almost unlimited power over their lives and bodies. In the 1840s Russian literature at last assumed the task of opening the country's eyes to the cruel realities of the peasant's lot.[7]

To be sure, peasants were something of an international fashion at the time, as witness famous novels by George Sand, Berthold Auerbach, and Harriet Beecher Stowe; but no doubt harsh economic conditions in the Russian countryside and a growing recognition of the inhumanity of the serf system independently impressed on Russian writers the timeliness for them of the peasant theme. At any rate, the Russian reading public was jolted in the mid-1840s by two powerful, pioneering novellas produced by a writer long respected in Russia, but little known abroad, Dmitrii

Grigorovich. Grigorovich's *The Village* (1846) and *Anton Goremyka* (1847) for the first time offered Russian readers a close look at the realities of everyday peasant life, and a look not "downward" but as if from within. In *The Village* this view-from-within is rendered still more poignant by the doubly vulnerable status of the central character. Akulia is an orphan girl taken in, very reluctantly, by a neighbor's household when her mother dies. Akulia's life is one of unmitigated oppression not so much by her owners (who for the most part are scarcely aware of her existence, though they do, by blindness and caprice rather than malice, later force her into an unsuitable marriage) as by other peasants – first her step-parents and then her husband and in-laws. And even that oppression, it increasingly transpires, is mostly a by-product of the overwhelming social fact about the Russian countryside: poverty.

For most Russian peasants in the nineteenth century were *poor*. Their wretched houses were smelly, dark, drafty, and crowded. The peasant diet was extremely limited: cabbage soup, kasha (porridge), potatoes, and rye bread were the staples, and in years of bad harvests there was real hunger and even starvation. Few could afford real shoes or boots, instead making do in winter with bast wrappings, made from the inner bark of lime trees. Defenses against disease were those of folk medicine: herbs and magic incantations. Until the *zemstvo* reforms of the 1860s schools for peasant children were almost non-existent. Serfs were subject to the capricious authority of their owners and could be sold with or without land. Corporal punishment was widely used. Life was bleak and without much prospect of improvement, at least until industrialization late in the century made possible a mass migration of peasants into the cities to become industrial workers. In the meantime the chief escape and entertainment, at least for men, was consumption of alcohol, a practice which unproductively siphoned off the small amount of disposable income the peasants had.

Most of these woes are exhibited in *Anton Goremyka*, whose hero, an exceptionally kind, responsible peasant, is driven by both malice and circumstances to the last limits of despair. We have the testimony of Lev Tolstoi, then a university student, of the "great impression" made on him by this tale.[8] Its colors, however, must have seemed unbearably dark to most of the reading public. Surely not all peasants were "poor wretches"; surely the sun sometimes shone on the Russian village. Perhaps in quest of this more balanced view Ivan Turgenev shouldered his gun and undertook to explore the countryside of Orel Province. The ultimate result was his splendid *The Sportsman's Sketches* (1852), perhaps his greatest book.

Turgenev's work, like Grigorovich's, is an extension to the countryside of the so-called "physiologies," already applied to urban environments in

Nekrasov's *Petersburg Miscellanies* (1845–46). As a literary form, the physiology was an early manifestation of the developing school of Realism: a basically descriptive rather than narrative genre, in which high value is placed on "truth." In his rural physiologies Turgenev dealt not only with peasants, but with gentry as well, and even with some of the intermediate classes, though he avoids the clergy. In general, he finds an inverse relationship of virtue and attractiveness to social standing. Turgenev's peasants, for the most part, are agreeable, responsive, complex, articulate human beings, whereas landowners are eccentric, self-indulgent, twisted, and incomplete in their humanity, with no special qualifications at all for the function they are supposed to fulfill in rural life, that of agricultural managers.

The very first of the sketches, "Khor and Kalinych" (1847), offers a contrast of two very different human types, showing that male peasants, far from being an undifferentiated mass of bearded look-alikes, offer a wide range of varieties. Khor is as far removed as could be imagined from Anton Goremyka. No doubt highly exceptional in his achieved independence and prosperity, he is an intelligent, enterprising peasant businessman, a markedly successful manager of his domain, allowed a large degree of freedom by his owner as long as his substantial quitrent payments are kept up. His friend Kalinych, on the other hand, is by nature a romantic, a true child of nature, more at home in the woods than under a roof, utterly uninterested in "getting ahead."

Turgenev's roving camera reveals numerous examples of the cruelty and pain engendered by the serf system itself, quite apart from the nearly universal poverty. Particularly injurious is the capricious interference by owners in their serfs' private lives, such as refusal to allow love-marriages, as is the case in "Ermolai and the Miller's Wife." More egregious cruelty is not unknown. In "The Bailiff" the landowner Arkadii Penochkin, a refined, French-speaking aesthete, has a servant flogged because the wine has not been warmed to his satisfaction; and when a family of peasants in a distant village appeals to him against a bailiff whose extortions have reduced them to despair, Penochkin angrily dismisses their complaint, leaving the infamous bailiff free to exact his revenge.

Turgenev is also at pains to show that Russian peasants are by no means lacking in what the educated classes call "culture." Though different and unwritten, their oral culture is no less real and meaningful than the literate one taught to the gentry in schools. In "The Singers" Turgenev's persona, along with an intensely involved audience of peasant enthusiasts, witnesses a musical contest between two expert vocal acrobats, either of whom, had their circumstances been different, might well have graced the operatic stage.

Some of the finest pages in *A Sportsman's Sketches* are devoted to nature herself, seen apart from the human fauna that exploit and often despoil her. The hunter's last sketch, "Forest and Steppe," is an early instance of those virtuoso nature descriptions that became a much admired feature of all Turgenev's art, displaying his acute perceptions, his detailed, almost scientific knowledge of plant and animal life, his painterly eye for nuances of shading and color, and his unsurpassed power over the rich resources of the Russian language, by means of which he transforms literature into a graphic art.

Country scenes play an important part in most of Turgenev's novels more narrowly defined, such as *Rudin* (1856), *A Nest of Gentlefolk* (1859), *On the Eve* (1860), and *Virgin Soil* (1877), though he never again invoked the peasant theme as centrally as he had done in *A Sportsman's Sketches*. In Turgenev's greatest novel, *Fathers and Children* (1862), the action is again exclusively concentrated on the life of the gentlefolk in their several nests. They are, however, themselves differentiated by class: the plebeian "nihilist" student Bazarov, son of a country doctor, introduces a disruptive force into the tranquil world of the more aristocratic Kirsanov family, giving them the implied message that they are both parasitic and outmoded. Though he may partly agree with this assessment, Turgenev seems to take malicious satisfaction in showing that the plebeian Bazarov is no more successful than the aristocrats at communicating with real peasants.

Moreover, Bazarov is no more immune than the Kirsanov brothers to the charms of the lovely Fenechka, the softly deferential plebeian beauty Nikolai Kirsanov has taken as mistress and later makes his wife. Bazarov's flirtation with Fenechka provokes an absurd duel with Pavel Kirsanov, who is himself guilty of lusting after Fenechka. These scenes take place in a series of idyllic settings evoked in Turgenev's typical lyric prose, mostly on the Kirsanov estate, but with contrastive excursions both to the neighboring town and to the modest property of Bazarov's parents. All the landscapes are summer ones, incidentally; Turgenev tends to avoid winter scenes.

Hunting itself is seldom at the center of attention in *A Sportsman's Sketches*, but hunting for its own sake did have a major part to play in Russian literature. Hunting is, after all, an archetypal human activity. Originally part of man's eternal quest for food, it was then extended to encompass the protection of agriculture and domesticated animals from predators. By the nineteenth century, however, it had become primarily a "sport," an entertainment engaged in by country people, mostly gentry, but with peasant participation. Only toward the end of the century was much notice taken of its cruelty and destructiveness.

Both hunting and fishing play an essential part in the great trilogy of Sergei Aksakov, *A Family Chronicle* and *Recollections* (1856) and *Childhood Years of Grandson Bagrov* (1858). (Earlier, Aksakov had written the Russians' classic practical manuals on both hunting and fishing.) In the trilogy all the main themes associated with the Russian countryside are present: country life vs. town life; a child's discovery of nature; man's conquest of nature through agriculture; serfdom; Russian conquest of new lands, involving subjection of non-Russian native peoples; and ecological problems, including deforestation and destruction of wildlife habitats.

As in *Evgenii Onegin* and many other Russian novels, the contrast between life in the town and life on a gentry estate is a central device in Aksakov's novels, woven into the very fabric of the plot, where it acquires a genetic dimension associated with two basic strains in the lineage of grandson Bagrov. On the paternal side, Bagrov's father and heroic grandfather are quintessential country squires, presiding in due succession over a substantial domain in the Ufa region, some 300 miles east of Kazan, wrested by the grandfather both from wild nature and from the nomadic Bashkir tribesmen who had been its owners. Bagrov's mother, on the other hand, is very much a townswoman. At first the family lived in Ufa, while the father pursued an official career, but on the death of *his* father they moved for good to the Bagrov estate. The narrator, whose Bagrov blood responded powerfully to all the country stimuli – fishing, hunting, farming, and simply nature herself – was thus confronted with a difficult emotional conflict, one that extends through the whole novel: a much adored mother who not only did not share his enthusiasm for these country attractions, but actually tried to bar him from them, as either dangerous or somehow degrading.

Despite his mother's resistance, the country experiences that bring about the boy Bagrov's awakening to nature are among the most strongly felt and formative of his life, described by Aksakov both with the detailed precision of careful observation, and with an emotional exuberance that still avoids all sentimentality or prettifying. As in *Evgenii Onegin*, all the seasons are covered: the rigors of a winter journey by sleigh during a blizzard (one is made acutely aware of the eternal Russian struggle with cold – man the "naked ape" who has chosen to live in a frigid climate for which nature has provided him with no bodily defenses); the exultation as spring at last breaks winter's hold, ice and snow begin to melt, the birds come back, and the boy can escape the long imprisonment indoors; the lushness of summer, with its freedom and manifold activities of peasants and gentry alike; and finally, the sense of completeness in autumn, with its harvest festivities and rest from summer toil.

Bagrov's grandfather and his father, unlike many Russian landowners, were attentive agricultural managers, and the boy Bagrov observes their activities with fascination. Once, while watching the peasants prepare the land for sowing, the boy asks and is allowed, though reluctantly, to try peasant work himself. But the experience is quite unlike that of Konstantin Levin in *Anna Karenina.* Trying to harrow the ground, Bagrov lacks peasant know-how, cannot walk easily on the ploughed land, cannot make the horse obey him. The peasant boy guiding him laughs at his difficulties, Bagrov feels humiliated, and the experiment is not repeated. Class barriers are not so easily crossed.

Unlike *A Sportsman's Sketches,* Aksakov's trilogy makes no effort to bring the question of serfdom into primary focus; indeed, the atmosphere of nostalgia for a gentleman's beautiful childhood on an estate farmed by serfs would seem to exclude much expression of protest. Yet some revulsion against cruelty and injustice does penetrate the nostalgia. The tempestuous rages in which old grandfather Bagrov indulges from time to time, committing physical mayhem against his serfs and family alike, are a repellent manifestation of a social system that endows a male master with unbridled power over all the human beings in his domain. The boy Bagrov is also revolted when he sees his grandmother, herself a victim of her husband's violence, take out a whip and flog a serf girl who had done her spinning work badly.

The theme of ecological deterioration, so prominent in our times, is anticipated by Aksakov, as it was later by Chekhov. The domestication of wild lands, a process actively represented by grandfather Bagrov, inevitably brings with it destruction of wildlife habitats and thus less abundant fish and game. Bagrov as fisherman and hunter is thus at odds with Bagrov as farmer, and he finds no way to resolve the contradiction. He celebrates his grandfather's pioneering enterprise, but at the same time laments the destruction of the wilderness which this enterprise causes.

In 1859, a year after *Childhood Years of the Bagrov Grandson,* there appeared another major text in the Russian pastoral tradition, Ivan Goncharov's *Oblomov* (actually the most pastoral part of the novel, "Oblomov's Dream," had appeared separately as early as 1849). Again as in Aksakov, the pastoral theme is invoked in the form of nostalgia for a lost, idyllic world of childhood. The present of the hero, Ilia Oblomov, is irrevocably fixated in the urban world of St. Petersburg. Duty, however, demands that he return to the rural scenes of his childhood and assume full responsibility for the now neglected lands he has inherited. Hopelessly indolent, he can never summon the energy actually to fulfill his duty. How much more pleasant to do it all in fantasy, to return via "dream" to the Oblomovka of the past!

The nostalgia of the return is, however, less pure than Aksakov–Bagrov's. First of all, the purpose of the imaginary recovery of childhood is classically psychoanalytic (at least in the modern reader's eyes): to seek an explanation for the hero's crippling psychological disabilities, a quest Aksakov in no way shares. The answer clearly emerges: the pathologically overprotective upbringing of an adored gentry child with no siblings, doted on and cosseted by parents and an extended family, sheltered from every possible danger, real or imaginary, with every wish instantly fulfilled by obsequious servants. The indolence of Oblomov's mature years is already instilled in him in childhood, both by the example of the extraordinarily inactive adults with whom he lives, and by their fear-ridden effort to stifle in him any spark of independence, vigor, or adventure.

A contrast later central to the novel has its roots already at the time of "Oblomov's Dream": the "Russian" indolence of the Oblomovs vs. the "German" efficiency and enterprise of the Stolz family, whose father manages a nearby estate and also runs a boarding school. These "German" virtues, however, are never actually exhibited as manifested in agriculture, and indeed throughout the novel the Stolz side of the contrast remains largely a theoretical abstraction. But Ilia Oblomov's "Russian" indolence is all too palpable. His parents' life closely resembles that of Gogol's old-world landowners: utter idleness, the days punctuated only by the biological rhythms of eating and sleeping. No one really does anything else. The inevitable changes brought about by the passage of time are simply lamented; the ideal world would be for every day to be exactly like the one before. The Oblomov motto of total inertia is succinctly formulated by the mistress: "One should pray more to God and not think about anything."[9]

Standing behind his inert hero, Goncharov is aware that not all is well at Oblomovka, idyllic as it may seem. The indolence has gone so far that even basic house repairs are not made. A balcony long decrepit and ruled out of bounds to the family (but not to their serfs) at last collapses and falls, fortunately crushing only a family of chickens. Farming seems to be left entirely to the peasants themselves, the master's supervision consisting only of sitting by the window and asking passing peasants what they are doing and why. Serfdom seems almost benign in this lazy atmosphere, but some ugly signs nevertheless appear. For instance, the fourteen-year-old Ilia lies on his back so that his servant, Zakhar, can put on his stockings and shoes. If something displeases him in the procedure, "he will let Zakharka have it on the nose with his foot."[10] If Zakhar should complain, he will receive a "light blow with the fist"[11] from Oblomov senior. Ilia Oblomov escapes from Oblomovka to an abortive official career in St. Petersburg, but he cannot escape its spirit of inertia and dependence, which cripples him for life. Oblomov illustrates vividly a fundamental paradox about a serf society: the nominal masters or "parents" are often in effect children, and spoiled children at that, nurtured and cared for by their "parent" slaves.

The pastoral theme plays a prominent part in both of Lev Tolstoi's great novels. The action of *War and Peace* (1865–69) is of course projected back to a much earlier era, the age of Alexander I, when Russian society (at least in retrospect) had seemed much more stable, confident, and, as it were, morally valid, despite the presence of serfdom, its merits demonstrated by the great victory over Napoleon. All three major families in the novel own country estates, which, as in Gogol, metonymically reflect their owners' characters. Ilia Rostov epitomizes the irresponsibility of the archetypal Russian gentleman: mortgage your lands to the hilt, live lavishly, and hope your children can marry money (in this case they succeed). Pierre Bezukhov inherits vast holdings on which he intends to introduce far-reaching reforms. Few reforms, however, are actually accomplished, for Pierre lacks the perseverance and practical capacity to see to it that his orders are carried out. Old Nikolai Bolkonskii, a former general, has imposed on Bald Hills (*Lysye gory*) an eighteenth-century rationalist, quasi-military regime. His son Andrei, assuming ownership of an estate at Bogucharovo, exhibits some of the same rationalist traits, but with an admixture of new, liberal ideas. There he is able successfully to implement most of the reforms Pierre dreamed of in vain, including a scheme for peasant emancipation. Nevertheless, it is the Bogucharovo peasants who, seduced by strange superstitions, threaten to revolt when the French armies are at the gates and Princess Maria is alone in charge. Serendipitously, Nikolai Rostov arrives just in time to teach them who is boss, partly by strategic use of his fists.

Hunting is also a gauge of character in Tolstoi, as well as an opportunity for vivid narrative. Maintaining a lavish hunting establishment, Ilia Rostov still enjoys the excitement of the chase, though old age has diminished his physical powers and his judgment. His son, Nikolai, however, has all the dash and passion of the born hunter. And even Natasha, showing that her native Russianness is unspoiled by her aristocratic upbringing, enters fully into the spirit of the hunt and emits a squeal of exultation when she sees that the dogs have run down a hare.

In *Anna Karenina* we see Russian society at a much later period, the 1870s. Town and country are again vividly contrasted, always in favor of the latter, and with penetrating subtleties. True country people, epitomized by Konstantin Levin, have real roots in the soil. The country is their natural home; they belong there and live fully only there. But others, like Levin's half-brother Koznyshev, Stiva Oblonskii, Vronskii, and Anna Karenina herself, are only visitors in the country; their real life is in the city. Stiva, in typical gentry fashion, is selling off the timber on his wife's lands for less than it is worth to merchants who know its value very well. Vronskii spends vast sums of money to recreate in the country all the luxuries of urban life and adds some supposed benefactions for the peasants. But his charities are felt as alien and out of proportion, like the cows he imports from Switzerland. He is simply playing "squire." And on Vronksii's estate Anna is only a guest, not the mistress, an alien body in an alien world.

The antipode to these unassimilated urban transplants is Konstantin Levin, Tolstoi's ideal country gentleman, a thoroughly engaged and committed full-time farmer. And Levin's apotheosis is the great mowing scene, when his physical strength enables him to wield a scythe with the best of the peasant mowers, thus obliterating the social distance between himself and the "people" and becoming one of them, at least for a day. In this sublime saturnalia of sweat he experiences real ecstasy, a total obliteration of self.

Later in his life Tolstoi advocated more drastic means for reconciliation of the classes: voluntary renunciation of their property by landowners. Though few gentlemen – not even Tolstoi – adopted this utopian programme of their own accord, a great many in effect did so involuntarily, losing their lands through forced sale or foreclosure. The decline of the gentry in the nineteenth century remains a crucial sociological fact, most powerfully epitomized in literature in Saltykov-Shchedrin's *The Golovlev Family* (1880), surely one of the gloomiest books ever written.

Here the degeneration of the gentry is far more than economic; indeed, in the novel's early parts it is not economic at all, as if to demonstrate that there are worse forms of degradation than bankruptcy. The first-generation matriarch, Arina Petrovna Golovleva, is – atypically – a good, industrious manager and succeeds in adding to the family's assets. But it is all for naught. The family for whose sake she has toiled is in a state of catastrophic moral and psychological disintegration, incapable even of enjoying, let alone conserving their wealth. Her husband is a shiftless drunkard who mostly lies in bed writing obscene poetry. Their eldest son, Stepka, after squandering property devolved on him by his mother, returns to live like an animal in an outbuilding in the Golovlev estate, killing himself with vodka. Another son, Pavel, also drinks himself to death. A daughter, Anna, marries against her mother's will, is deserted by her husband and dies, leaving two orphaned daughters, the chief representatives of the third generation. But the ultimate specimen of moral decay – and the crowning glory of the novel – is the third son, Porfirii or "Iudushka" (little Judas), one of the most unforgettably repulsive characters in literature: pointlessly, pettily acquisitive, impenetrably hypocritical and self-righteous, endlessly mouthing self-justifying moral aphorisms, untouched by any feeling of human connectedness. One of his sons commits suicide when his father disinherits him; the other embezzles government money and is sent to Siberia, where he dies, his father refusing to help him. The two orphan girls complete the process of degeneration. First running away to become provincial actresses, they sink into a mire of vulgarity, becoming virtual prostitutes. One ends by committing suicide, the other destroys herself in the good Golovlev way, with alcohol.

For all of these people the greatest and most beneficial event in their lives is death, and an all-encompassing spirit of emptiness and death pervades the book. Even the landscape is redolent of death: bare, endless fields stretching into the distance, sodden villages like black dots contrasting with the white churches of the village cemeteries. It is hard to imagine any redemption or hope reaching the utter bleakness of the Golovlevs' grim world.

In the early twentieth century Ivan Bunin's novel *Sukhodol* (1911) seems a direct echo of *The Golovlev Family*. It shows a gentry family in an even more extreme state of hopelessness and decay, if that can be imagined. At the end of *Sukhodol* a once imposing manor house, now in ruins and unheated, is inhabited by three shivering elderly women. One of them is totally insane. She and another are the only survivors of the noble Khrushchev dynasty; the third is a former serf who still feels bound to the family, though it has treated her cruelly. For such a family there can be no future but death and extinction.

Bunin's social pessimism, however, goes further than Salytkov's, encompassing the peasantry as well. His novel *The Village* (1910) shows a brutalized, deracinated, alcohol-poisoned peasant class, scarcely capable even of the farming tasks they supposedly know by instinct. They have lost any vestiges of the vibrant folk culture celebrated by Turgenev. An equally somber picture of peasant life had been presented earlier in Chekhov's famous story "Peasants" (1898), which had shocked the Russian public, used to the much more benevolent view of the peasantry found in the work of populist writers like Nikolai Zlatovratskii.

Bunin's *Village* contrasts the lives of two brothers of peasant origin. One of them, Tikhon, has made money in the town by ruthless acquisitiveness. He eventually is able to buy the estate of Durnovka, where his great-grandfather, in the days of serfdom, had been exposed to be devoured by hunting dogs for the crime of stealing his master's lover. But the acquisition brings Tikhon little satisfaction, economic or emotional. The life led there by its peasant inhabitants has become one of unrelieved, squalid barbarism, grimly observed from the decrepit manor house by Tikhon's agent, his brother Kuzma, himself a sort of failed village philosopher. Farming at Durnovka is carried on sloppily and lazily; there is constant strife and bickering, both among families and within them, frequently erupting into ugly scenes of violence. After a year in Durnovka, Kuzma and Tikhon both only long to get away: "to the town, as far as possible from these cutthroats."[12] Bunin's village is a world devoid of any social cohesion or morality, where irrational, often self-destructive people act out their basest instincts. Although in general Bunin seems to believe that the instinctual life is all that matters, that neither social forms, ideologies, nor culture have much real influence on human behavior, he nevertheless also appears to think that conditions in the Russian countryside actually deteriorated after the emancipation of 1861. Gentry and peasantry decayed together, and the ruin that descended on the country after 1917 was not unexpected.

The countryside was certainly not a primary concern of the urban-centered modernists who dominated the Russian literary scene in the decades before the Revolution. Nevertheless, at least one major novel must be mentioned as an exception to this rule, Andrei Belyi's *The Silver Dove* (1910). In this characteristically symbolizing novel most of the action takes place in three locales, each supposedly characteristic of the Russian countryside, but at the same time functioning at a high level of symbolic abstraction. The village of Tselebeevo lies between the gentry estate of Gugolevo to the West and the town of Likhov to the East. Gugolevo represents the heritage of Western civilization and culture, the bearers of which were the upper classes, including the gentry and intelligentsia. Likhov, the home of the dissenting religious sect of the "Doves," symbolizes the East, perceived by Belyi as chaotic, irrational, primitive. The hero, Petr Darialskii, is torn between the two: an intellectual rooted in Western culture, engaged to a gentlewoman, he is powerfully drawn, partly by sexual attraction, to a coarse peasant woman, Matrena, and hopes through her to lose himself in the peasant mass. The "doves" want Darialskii to sire a "savior" on Matrena; when he becomes disillusioned and seeks to escape the entanglement, they murder him. This plot was, of course, a symbolic representation of one of the most troublesome problems that had afflicted Russian society since the eighteenth century, the enormous cultural gulf separating the educated classes from the "people," and Belyi's novel was a prophetic illustration of the virulent class hatreds that were to be unleashed and acted out in the Civil War of 1918–20.

The topic of the Civil War was to dominate much of the literature of the first post-revolutionary decade, and its leading new novelist, Boris Pilniak, took up this theme, using ideas and techniques derived directly from Andrei Belyi and to some extent from Bunin. Pilniak's most characteristic novel, *The Naked Year* (1921), utilizes typical Belyi-esque devices – "musical" prose, fragmented structure – to represent the chaos of Russian provincial life during the "naked" year, 1919. In that fateful time nature herself participates in the country's destructive orgy of violence and death. As in Blok's "The Twelve," cruel, symbolic snowstorms sweep across the land, in Pilniak singing nonsense, neo-Soviet words: *gviuu, gaauuu, gla-vboommm*.

A neo-Slavophile, Pilniak enthusiastically endorses the "Eastern," elemental, instinctive, ultra-Russian side of the dichotomy symbolized in *The Silver Dove*, indeed carrying the confrontation much further than Belyi had done. Pilniak sees the Revolution as the upheaval of "Scythian," atavistic, peasant Russia, gleefully and violently casting off the encrustations of Western civilization imposed on her since the reforms of Peter the Great, and he exults in the destruction. The two most "Western" classes in old Russia, the landed gentry and the merchants, are shown as hopelessly degenerate, ripe for the slaughter. The noble Ordynin family, like Bunin's Khrushchevs, had long ago squandered their landed property. Though they had temporarily recouped their position by a marital alliance with a rich merchant family, all of their wealth has now been swept away by the Revolution save a cellar full of decaying keepsakes. Also like the Khrushchevs', their decline, more than economic, is biological, genetic. The father is mad, the mother in an advanced state of degeneracy, and most of the children variously defective.

Pilniak's "Scythian" view of the Revolution was of course not at all to the liking of the new Bolshevik rulers. In their official view, Soviet Russia was, to be sure, a workers' and peasants' state, but the far more numerous peasants were very much the junior partners in this coalition. They had to be reshaped and pulled along the path of progress by the workers, who in turn had to be properly indoctrinated and led by a Party dominated by intellectuals. During the 1920s, and even more so in the 1930s, formidable pressure was brought to bear on writers to embrace and propagate this "correct" understanding of the historical process.

Even the most well-intentioned writers, however, found it difficult to embody the official formula in actual works about the peasant experience. When foregrounded in fiction, genuine peasant emotions, thoughts, and attitudes tended to overrun the dogma. Something like this seems to have happened with Mikhail Sholokhov's epic novel *The Quiet Don* (1928–40). Focusing on a highly specific social milieu, the Don Cossacks, one he knew well from personal experience, Sholokhov's artistic integrity overpowered his – no doubt sincere – Communist convictions. Instead of rehearsing an acceptable Party parable, much to the consternation of official critics Sholokov produced a many-sided, comprehensive picture of a peasant society in turmoil, thoroughly ambiguous in its political implications. The central hero, Grigorii Melekhov, perfectly exemplifies the difficult choices faced by the Cossacks, whose age-old military allegiance to the tsarist state and gut-level attachment to their lands and possessions conflicted with a yearning for social justice, especially among the poor. The Cossacks are forced to choose among political movements and armies that represent alien objectives coming from the larger outside world, Reds vs. Whites, neither of whom stood for what the Cossacks wanted. Grigorii vacillates back and forth between them, for a time identifying with a hopelessly quixotic third force, a movement for Cossack independence. At last totally isolated, he comes to a tragic end – not the buoyantly optimistic finale expected of the exemplary Communist morality.

As in *War and Peace*, the often horrifying narrative of war and violence in *The Quiet Don* is relieved by vividly realized scenes of "peace": Cossack life described with ethnographic thoroughness, and within it, Grigorii's intense personal relationships – his parents, his brother and sister, his wife and children, his passionate adulterous love affair. Also following Tolstoi, Sholokhov projects the human violence against the background of a lyrically perceived but "indifferent" Nature, rendered with detail and precision of vocabulary worthy of Turgenev.

Before he had brought his epic novel to a conclusion, Sholokhov was pressured into undertaking a new project, a novel dealing with the "hot" subject of collectivization. Entitled *Virgin Soil Upturned*, this work proved even more difficult for Sholokhov to complete. The first volume was duly published in 1932, while collectivization was still going on, but the second one did not appear until 1960! In this novel Sholokhov's adherence to Party doctrine was much clearer, freer of ambiguities, than had been the case in *The Quiet Don*. Collectivization was to be represented "correctly," as a class struggle within the village. The better-off *kulaks* were to be displaced and dispossessed, "liquidated as a class," their property seized and incorporated into collective farms. Although the impetus was supposed to come from the righteously vengeful zeal of the village poor, the real organizer of this social revolution was the Party, represented in the novel by a sterling ex-worker named Semen Davydov. In between the kulaks and the poor were the "middle" peasants, the majority, pulled in both directions – envious of the kulaks, but reluctant to pool their lands and animals into the collective. And to make the class line-up – and the message – even clearer, Sholokhov has the kulaks ally themselves with dark conspirators from the old regime, who lure them with the undying dream of Cossack independence, to be achieved with (illusory) armed aid expected from the West.

This officially certified series of confrontations might have produced a lifeless and stereotyped piece of Party propaganda. In Sholokhov's hands, however, *Virgin Soil Upturned* almost succeeds in becoming genuine literature. The social turmoil of that tumultuous time is on the whole convincingly represented, grounded in Sholokhov's intimate knowledge of the Cossack world he depicts. The sufferings of the kulaks are not glossed over, nor is the fact that for many of them their only crime was that they had been good, thrifty farmers. (To be sure, at least one presumably representative kulak, Iakov Ostrovnov, shows his intrinsically evil kulak nature by starving his old mother to death.) Many characters come believably to life, and even the true-blue Communist Davydov is granted a less than exemplary love life, finding it difficult to choose between a sexy adulteress and a pure, dedicated teenager. But the anti-Soviet conspiracy, led by two ex-tsarist officers, one of them a Pole, is thoroughly preposterous, and it comes near to destroying all credence in this otherwise talented novel.

The title of *Virgin Soil Upturned*, if not its actual content, anticipates and symbolically represents over-ambitious and, in too many cases, ultimately disastrous Soviet projects for transforming nature: literally, Khrushchev's ill-advised effort to solve the perennial grain shortages by bringing under cultivation steppe lands where the water supply was only marginally adequate; and figuratively, countless other projects – damming rivers, changing their courses, placing factories so that their wastes could be discharged into rivers and lakes. The end result of all this has been to turn the former Soviet Union into an ecological disaster area from which it may take decades to recover. Hymnic celebrations of these hubristic assaults on nature were characteristic literary products of "socialist realism."

The peasant theme, though certainly not the countryside, is almost completely absent from one of the most celebrated Russian novels of the Soviet period, Boris Pasternak's *Doctor Zhivago* (1957), though the author does take the opportunity, through one of his characters, to pronounce his judgment that collectivization had been a dismal failure, necessitating a huge, terror-based cover-up, aimed at "teaching people not to judge and think."[13] This wholesale repudiation of collectivization, impossibly heretical in 1957, became the stock-in-trade of the "village prosaists" of a later era, especially after the advent of *glasnost'*. All the novel's characters come from the intelligentsia, shown struggling through the chaotic events of War and Revolution, mostly in the cities but with periodic shifts of scene to rural areas, particularly to a region in the Urals similar to the one where

Pasternak himself had lived in 1915–16. There Iurii Zhivago experiences the joy of union with nature through physical labor. "What happiness it is to work from dawn to dusk for yourself and your family, to build a shelter, to cultivate the earth in the quest for food, to create your own world, like Robinson Crusoe, imitating the Creator creating the universe."[14]

In general, Zhivago displays an acute sensitivity to Nature, best expressed in his poems, which form an integral part of the novel. Yet prose descriptions are often equally poetic, conveying not simply rapture at Nature's beauty, but a sense of wonder and reverence before her infinite variety, her changeability, her power. Pasternak's Nature, unlike Pushkin's, is not at all indifferent to human affairs, but actively participates in them like the rowan tree that holds out two snowy arms to welcome Zhivago.

As Zhivago's name suggests (deriving from the Russian adjective for "living" or "alive"), the whole novel is a hymn to Life, perceived as a deep, self-renewing force of nature, far more fundamental than the deluded, blood-stained efforts of those who claimed to be reshaping it. And at the core of this Life is Love. Nature herself wills the love of Iurii Zhivago and Lara Antipova: the earth, the sky, the clouds, and the trees insist on it. In the intensity of their love the lovers feel at one with the universe, part of its beauty, alienated from those who were foolishly seeking to exalt man over the rest of nature.

During the Stalin period and its immediate aftermath Russian writers continued to turn out a constant stream of officially approved novels dealing with peasant themes and the countryside. Most of these have been gratefully submerged in the "memory hole" that has swallowed up much of the written-to-order propaganda of that era, but a few may merit a more lasting place in Russian literature. One such is Leonid Leonov's *Russian Forest* (1953), one of the first Soviet novels to revive the "ecology" themes dating back to Aksakov and Chekhov: the problem of conservation, wise management of the vast timberlands of northern Russia and Siberia, many of which were being wantonly devastated in the fever of "socialist construction." This theme was to be invoked more boldly in the work of many of the *derevenshchiki* ("village prosaists") prominent in the 1960–1980 period.

The novel was also not the primary genre of the *derevenshchiki*, who mostly gravitated from the largely descriptive and factual *ocherk* or "sketch" dominant in the 1950s to the short story and novella. Some longer novels were nevertheless written by members of this group, which includes Valentin Rasputin, Viktor Astafev, Vasilii Belov, Boris Mozhaev, Fedor Abramov and several others. Limitations of space regrettably preclude extended discussion here of these interesting writers.[15]

The village prosaists obviously owe a considerable debt to Aleksandr Solzhhenitsyn, whose story "Matrena's Home" (1963) adumbrated many of their central themes: celebration of rural Russia and its old-time denizens as a repository of traditional culture, morality, and values, doubly threatened by encroachments from urban industrial society and contamination from Communist dogma.

Valentin Rasputin's powerful novella *Farewell to Matera* (1976) must serve here as a characteristic, if superior, specimen of this extensive literature. The huge Bratsk hydroelectric project in Siberia involved damming the Angara River, in the process inundating forever a fertile island where generations of peasants had led good, traditional Russian lives. Seen in their last season before the man-made flood, the inhabitants divide by generations, the young generally accepting the change in the name of progress and opportunity. But the story focuses on the old, especially a group of old women, who lament the destruction of their familiar world. These women, a living link to the peasant culture of the past, as human beings are deeper, more thoughtful, and wiser than their descendants.

The novella thus poses the most fundamental of "countryside" questions, many of which had been anticipated by writers of earlier times. These questions, of course, are also relevant outside Russia. Is "progress" worth its costs? How much land, and what land, should be allocated to agriculture, how much to urbanization, and how much left wild? Aksakov and Chekhov had asked these questions in the nineteenth century, and they are very much on the agenda today. Could we not manage our factories without massive pollution and environmental destruction? In general, could we human beings not learn to live in better harmony with nature, making measured use of her bounty to fill our needs, but without destroying either her beauty or her capacity for self-renewal?

NOTES

1. A. S. Pushkin, *Evgenii Onegin*, I, 56, in Pushkin, *Polnoe sobranie sochinenii v desiati tomakh* (Moscow: Nauka, 1962–66), vol. V, p. 33.
2. Ibid., II, 1 (p. 36).
3. Ibid.
4. Ibid., IV, 38–39 (p. 92).
5. Ibid., II, 4 (pp. 37–38).
6. Karl Marx and Friedrich Engels, *The Communist Manifesto,* ed. Samuel H. Beer (Arlington Heights, Ill.: 1955), 14.
7. Or reassumed: Aleksandr Radishchev's *Journey from St. Petersburg to Moscow* had made a noble effort in this direction as early as 1790, but his book was of course suppressed.

8. N. N. Gusev, *Lev Nikolaevich Tolstoi: Materialy k biografii s 1828 po 1855 god* (Moscow: Izdatel'stvo AN SSSR 1954), see illustration facing p. 241.

9. I. A. Goncharov, *Polnoe sobranie sochinenii v vos'mi tomakh* (Moscow: Goslitizdat, 1952–55), vol. IV, p. 134.

10. Ibid., p. 145.

11. Ibid.

12. I. A. Bunin, *Sobranie sochinenii v deviati tomakh* (Moscow: Izdatel'stvo khudozhestvennoi literatury, 1965–67), vol. III, p. 118.

13. Boris Pasternak, *Doktor Zhivago* (Ann Arbor: University of Michigan Press, 1959), p. 519.

14. Ibid., p. 286.

15. The reader is referred to the excellent study by Kathleen F. Parthé, *Russian Village Prose: The Radiant Past* (Princeton University Press, 1992).

2

THE CULTURE

4

W. GARETH JONES

Politics

From the very beginnings of modern Russian literature, Russia's writers have consciously dealt with politics. Following Peter the Great's death in 1725, there was a danger that his modernizing reforms would be frustrated by conservative forces. Consequently in 1729 Feofan Prokopovich who had been a fervent panegyrist for Peter, proposed to his younger protégé Antioch Kantemir, a writer of satires against the anti-Petrine reactionaries, that they should consider themselves members of a "Learned Watch" dedicated to the defense of the westernizing reforms. Assuming a distinct ideological position, these Russian writers were not content with being mere reflectors of the political scene, but chose to play an active part in the political process. In future, this had serious consequences. By placing themselves close to the seat of autocratic power, writers inevitably encouraged the Russian autocrats to seek to control their production and their lives. At the close of the century, the minor writer I. F. Bogdanovich could even propose that writers be dressed in uniform and given ranks commensurate with the distinction of their service to the state.[1] The strict discipline implied by that "uniform" has been present throughout most of the history of modern Russian literature; its links with politics have made its writers subject to the control of censorship and to the sanctions of exile, imprisonment or even execution.

Russian literature's long political engagement was recognized in the title *The Government and Literature in Russia* that Plekhanov, the father of Russian Marxism, suggested to the revolutionary writer Stepniak in 1888 for a work to be written in English. But the repression suffered by Russian writers as a result of their close involvement with politics was highlighted in the book's prospectus: it would be a "martyrology of Russian literature," beginning in the eighteenth century with Novikov and Radishchev and continuing with Pushkin, Lermontov, Turgenev, Griboedov, Polezhaev, Kostomarov, Shevchenko, Dostoevskii, Mikhailov, and Chernyshevskii, and would lead up to Plekhanov's contemporary Russia where "almost all the talented writers of the present day have been or still remain in exile."[2] Plekhanov, Russia's leading Marxist at the time, could not have foreseen that the martyrdom of Russia's writers would continue into the twentieth century, long after the establishment of an avowedly Marxist regime in 1917.

Russian writers not only courted their martyrdom by volunteering to embrace politics, but indeed were often obliged, in the absence of other channels of expression, to be the sole focus of political discourse. It was a role they fully recognized. When encouraging the young Tolstoi's first steps as a writer in 1856, Nekrasov underlined the commitment required by the particular nature of Russian society: "You will do still more when you understand that in our country the role of a writer is above all the role of a teacher and, as far as possible, an intercessor for the mute and oppressed."[3] Despite the young Tolstoi's wish at that time not to be trammeled by politics, by the close of the century he too had assumed the role of the radical oppositionist. And the authority of the novelist challenged that of the autocrat. Suvorin, the editor of *New Age* (*Novoe Vremia*), the leading conservative journal, realized that "we have two tsars, Nicholas II and Lev Tolstoi. Nicholas II can do nothing with Tolstoi, cannot shake his throne, whereas Tolstoi without any doubt is shaking the throne of Nicholas and his dynasty."[4]

The writer's calling, described by Nekrasov and embraced by Tolstoi, has been, of course, the traditional role of poets and writers who more often than not in the history of world literature have been conscious spokesmen for a particular society or for a whole people. The modern novel, a genre that seeks to set its characters against a broad social canvas, might be expected to have provided an excellent vehicle for the writer as prophet of the nation. Developing as it did during the age of Romanticism, the European novel seemed well poised to express the collective nationalism that sprang from the Romantic spirit with its quest for national origins and delight in historical local color. Paradoxically, however, the Romantic age also insisted on the overriding importance of the immediate personal experience of the individual. Since politics with its concern for public actions and events did not accord well with this individualistic Romantic outlook, the notion was formed that politics should have no part in imaginative literature. "Politics in a work of literature," remarked Stendhal in a famous quip, "is like a pistol-shot in the middle of a concert, something loud and vulgar": but he went on to say, "and yet something which it is impossible to ignore."[5] Stendhal's own novels are indeed packed with politics as proof of this. However, to some extent he resolves the paradox of placing a Romantic with his individual outlook against the broad social and political background of a novel by endowing his heroes with a special perspective. Their standpoint is that of a small, beleaguered group of intellectuals facing a sluggish and corrupting society, celebrated in his phrase "the happy few." The Russian novelists who appeared after Stendhal in the early nineteenth century also found it impossible to turn their attention away from politics. And they shared his standpoint of an élite intelligentsia, although, burdened as they were by the Russian noble intelligentsia's collective guilt for serfdom and deep sense of alienation, they might be better described as "the unhappy few." They also shared the relationship that Stendhal's novels had to a revolutionary historical event. The consequences of the French Revolution of 1789 were the source of the Frenchman's novels. Similarly, a series of cataclysmic turning points was to direct the concerns of Russia's novelists: 1825 and the Decembrist Revolt, 1861 and the Emancipation of the Serfs, 1905 and the First Russian Revolution, 1917 and the Bolshevik Revolution, 1956 and De-Stalinization. 1991 and the dissolution of the Soviet Union may prove another such defining moment.

It was the conspiracy against the autocracy by young noblemen, many of them his own friends, ending with their tragic defeat of 14 December 1825 that was central to much of Pushkin's writing. He was obsessed by the causes of the debacle and the necessity of an action which seemed doomed to failure. To make sense of the rebellion and its aftermath, he was to turn to the past and the popular upheavals of Russian history. But even in his "novel in verse," *Evgenii Onegin*, the first great Russian novel, although it might appear that Pushkin is concerned only with the private worlds of his characters, Onegin is presented as a representative figure of the generation of young Russian noblemen who became Decembrists. This is made explicit only in the unpublished tenth chapter where Onegin is described as moving in Decembrist circles. Although in the end the abiding interest of Onegin is Pushkin's portrayal of a man crippled by lack of commitment in love, the same flaw of non-commitment in the Russian character might have been one of the reasons why the Decembrist Revolt had failed. In setting aside the notion of his tenth chapter, Pushkin may have understood that the novel would become unbalanced if great political events intruded too forcibly on the intimate world of his hero, but, in any case, he would have been obliged to yield to the rigors of the draconian censorship established by Nicholas I in response to the Decembrist Revolt.

The impediments to publishing any work in the 1830s which could treat more overtly Pushkin's concern with rebellion was shown by the case of his unfinished novella *Dubrovskii* which had difficulty passing through the censorship when it was published posthumously. In *Dubrovskii* Pushkin quotes verbatim the transcript of a lawsuit which took place in Tambov between 1826 and 1832 resulting in the unjust expulsion of a poor landowner by a rich one, Troiekurov. The law officers who come to take possession for Troiekurov are burned alive in Dubrovskii's manor house. Dubrovskii, the fireraiser, is admired by his people for his revolt against oppression. Again the portrayal of the individual rebelling against the consequences of overweening power, the theme given dramatic intensity in Pushkin's narrative poem, *The Bronze Horseman*, was at the heart of *Dubrovskii*. However, as is apparent in *The Bronze Horseman*, Pushkin's attitude to political power was ambivalent. He was as impressed by its exercise as he was appalled by its consequences.

This ambivalence was present in Pushkin's response to the Pugachev rebellion of 1773–75. Not only did he write an official history of the rebellion, with the support of Nicholas I who gave him privileged access to the archives, but also *The Captain's Daughter*, a novel set in the time of the rebellion. Both history and novel were written side by side and completed together in 1836. Comparing them highlights the particular strengths of the novel as a literary form, and the way in which it could deal with politics despite the censorship. In the *History* it is the narrative of significant events and campaigns that predominates; the episode recorded in the *History* on which *The Captain's Daughter* is based is a mere illustration of the atrocities of the Pugachev rebellion. Pugachev storms a government fort, hangs its commander before the eyes of his young wife who is then raped by Pugachev. Forced to become his mistress, she is eventually murdered by his followers who fear her influence over him. The politics of rebellion in the novel work on the individual lives of characters but it is their personal experiences that occupy the foreground. Pushkin had demonstrated in *The Captain's Daughter* how the Russian novelist could achieve that delicate balance between the portrayal of political power and the rebellion against it by creating fictional characters who, although insignificant to a historian's eyes, appeared to be more vibrantly alive than the historical personages among whom they move. If *Evgenii Onegin*, as a novel of contemporary society, could not explicitly portray its hero as a potential political rebel, the historical novel could allow Pushkin more latitude.

The example of Walter Scott, whose novels enjoyed great vogue at the time, enabled Pushkin to present *The Captain's Daughter* as a historical romance safely located in the past. It was no accident that its plot follows a pattern similar to that of Scott's novel *Waverley*, but the rebel campaigns described by Scott are for him long ago and far off. His novels have no bearing on any contemporary political upheaval in Britain. The Decembrist Revolt would have cast a different light on *The Captain's Daughter*. Read in the aftermath of the Decembrist Revolt, Grinev's words at the close of chapter 13 rang out with particular poignancy: "May God preserve us from witnessing a Russian rebellion, meaningless and merciless!"

The use of fictionalized history to convey the interplay of power and rebellion was also made by Pushkin's contemporary, Nikolai Gogol. The anarchic atrocity at the heart of the rebellion against autocratic power in *The Captain's Daughter* recurs in the barbarous cruelty depicted in Gogol's *Taras Bulba*. Read on its own, *Taras Bulba*, weaving together events of the fifteenth, sixteenth and seventeenth centuries, may appear to be more like the comfortably distanced romances of Scott and works by the faithful Russian followers of his conventions, like Narezhnyi and Zagoskin. Gogol's tale, however, belongs to a cycle of stories that made up the novel *Mirgorod*. And the lightning flashes of the historical romance of *Taras Bulba* were finally grounded in the present day of *Mirgorod*'s last story, "The Tale of how Ivan Ivanovich quarrelled with Ivan Nikiforovich." Again a political rebellion was illuminated, and one not unconnected with the Decembrists, for the time of the two Ivans' quarrel was given as 1831, the year of a major Polish rebellion against the tsar. *Taras Bulba* on its own would have been a work to rally anti-Polish sentiment. But Gogol shows how by 1831, the time of his two Ivans, the heroic idealism of *Taras Bulba*, the valorous comradeship in defense of the Orthodox faith, had degenerated into mean spite.

"The Tale of how Ivan Ivanovich quarrelled with Ivan Nikiforovich" was a jaundiced portrayal of how aristocratic virtues had withered away to be supplanted by the seediness of the local bureaucracy and military, which maintained Nicholas I's repressive regime after 1825. The tale anticipates the social satire of *The Government Inspector* and *Dead Souls*. Its political bite did not escape the censor who excised certain passages, while reviewers in the Petersburg press, supportive of the regime, castigated the tale for being "dirty" and "vulgar." The denunciatory tone was conveyed by the literary journal *The Northern Bee* (*Severnaia pchela*) when it wrote "Why show us these rags, these dirty scraps however skilfully they are presented? Why portray the ugly picture of the backyard of life and humanity without any apparent aim?"[6] Supporters of the regime easily recognized the subversive edge of Gogol's comedy despite his vehement denials that he had any political axe to grind. Critics of the autocracy were certainly even quicker in realizing how Gogol was an example of how literature could be used to express their protest.

It is Vissarion Belinskii (1811–48), the leading spirit behind the radical, revolutionary movement, who ensured that the political resonances of the early Russian novels would not go unnoticed. Belinskii was aware that the repressive intellectual climate of his day channeled political thought into forms of imaginative expression. The writer, therefore, was obliged to be an agent in any political reform. As a consequence *Evgenii Onegin* and *Dead Souls* could both be read as indictments of the social system, with Pushkin and Gogol, however much it went against their political grain, being enlisted as liberating agents of progress.

A key article by Belinskii appeared in the September 1835 issue of the literary journal, *Telescope (Teleskop)*. His "On the Russian tale and the tales of Mr Gogol" extolled the novel as the only worthwhile modern genre, differentiated "ideal" from "real" literature, and gave preference to the realistic novel which reproduced life "in all its nakedness and truth." Belinskii stressed the analytical role of literature operating on life as a "scalpel" to reveal "all its wickedness, and all its frightening ugliness."[7] This was the advantage of the new tendency in literature headed by Gogol which uncovered the warped social relations of serf Russia. Belinskii championed Gogol as the leader of the *Natural School* whose uncovering of Russia's social vices implied the need for political reform.

Later in his "Letter to N. V. Gogol," written from the safety of Western Europe in 1847, as a riposte to Gogol's claim that his work had no political import, he revealed his understanding of the Russia that he believed Gogol had shown in nakedness and truth:

> [Russia] presents the frightful picture of a country where human beings trade in human beings without even having the justification so cunningly used by the American plantation owners in their claim that a negro is not a human being: a country where people call each other not by proper names but by nicknames like Vanka, Steshka, Vaska, Palashka; a country, finally, where not only are there no guarantees for the individual personality, honor or property, but there is not even a proper police system, but only vast corporations of various bureaucratic thieves and plunderers![8]

This might well have been Belinskii's reading of *Dead Souls*, and it led him to spell out the political program needed to replace a world deadened by the inhuman system of serfdom with civilization, enlightenment and humanity. "The most vital national problems in Russia today are the abolition of serfdom, the repeal of corporal punishment, and the strictest possible implementation of at least those laws that do exist." *Dead Souls* had been read by Belinskii, as he had read *Evgenii Onegin*, primarily as an indictment of Russian society. The first task was to overthrow the old order, before proceeding to promote the new progressive world. For the moment the Russian novel's political role would have to be one of criticism and destruction: the surgeon's scalpel rather than the sculptor's chisel.

In his "Letter to N. V. Gogol," Belinskii made manifest the political role of the novelist as he saw it and as it would be accepted by the Russian radical intelligentsia:

> Literature alone, despite a barbarous censorship, still has vitality and forward movement. That is why the calling of the writer is so honored among us, why literary success comes so easily even with a little talent; that is why the title of poet or writer has eclipsed the glitter of epaulettes and multicolored uniforms; that is why a so-called liberal tendency, even one unsupported by real talent, is rewarded with general attention, and why there is such a sudden drop in the popularity of great writers who, sincerely or not, offer themselves in the service of the Orthodox Church, autocracy and nationality.[9]

Belinskii regretfully had to cite Pushkin with his political ambivalence as an example of the latter, but he went on to reiterate that "The public is right. It sees Russian writers as its only leaders, defenders, and saviors from the darkness of autocracy, orthodoxy and nationality." It must be remembered, of course, that the official policy of the Russia of Nicholas I was "Autocracy, Orthodoxy and Nationality."

Not only did Belinskii highlight the political import of writers such as Pushkin and Gogol, but he suggested, when identifying and promoting new talent, that the treatment of political themes was a requirement for aspiring novelists. It was Belinskii who proclaimed to Dostoevskii, when he was a young and obscure writer, that his *Poor Folk* had revealed the misery of the life led by the downtrodden minor officials at the bottom of the bureaucratic pile. In return, committed young writers acknowledged Belinskii as their mentor. One of the charges brought against Dostoevskii when he was arrested for subversive activities in 1849 and condemned to death was that he had circulated Belinskii's banned "Letter to N. V. Gogol" which was not approved for publication until 1872.

While in such works as Dostoevskii's *Poor Folk* and Herzen's *Who is to Blame?* the stifling, inhuman effect of a pernicious urban society was castigated, the radical response read between the lines was that any amelioration could be sought only in the Utopia of a socialist, collectivist future. The position of Russia's serfs was different: to effect a radical change in their state, no utopian vision was needed but the actual abolition of serfdom.

Again it was Belinskii who underlined the message inherent in Turgenev's sketch "Khor and Kalinych" – the first in the series that was to become *A Sportsman's Sketches* – where the independent Russian peasant Khor flourished despite "very unfavorable circumstances" which was Belinskii's code for serfdom. Nurtured by Belinskii's criticism, Turgenev was fully aware of his political role. *A Sportsman's Sketches* was the first work of fiction that could be said to have had direct political consequences; it played its part in the agitation that led to the Emancipation of the Serfs in 1861. Turgenev wrote of *A Sportsman's Sketches* later that "under this title I collected and concentrated everything against which I had taken a decision to struggle to the end – with which I had sworn never to compromise. It was my Hannibal's oath; and it was not I alone who took that oath then."[10] Turgenev entered into the ideological debates of his time, making a political point against the Slavophiles, by presenting his flourishing peasant as a supporter of the arch-Westernizer Peter the Great who was for the peasant the truest of Russians. Only the spectre of the censorship prevented Turgenev from adding to the series of stories the projected "Russian German and Reformist" whose main character would embody the repressive essence of the Nicholaevan regime.

When the collected stories of *A Sportsman's Sketches* were published in a single volume in 1852 the political force of the work was well summed up in a censor's denunciation of its harmful consequences in a report to the Minister of Popular Education. The censor who had passed *A Sportsman's Sketches* for publication was dismissed and Turgenev himself was exiled by decree of Nicholas I to his estate.

Although Belinskii had died in 1848, his influence lived on and not only through the pages of the young writers he had championed – Turgenev, Herzen, Annenkov, Dostoevskii and Nekrasov. The aura of Belinskii spread throughout Russia. In 1856 Ivan Aksakov, a Slavophile distrustful of Western ideas, discovered to his grief that

> The name of Belinskii is known to every thinking man . . . There is not a country schoolmaster who does not know – and know by heart – Belinskii's letter to Gogol. If you want to find honest people, people who care about the poor and the oppressed, an honest doctor, an honest lawyer not afraid of a fight you will find them among Belinskii's followers.[11]

There were many followers who steadfastly maintained the link between the novel and politics. The most brilliant and compelling example was N. A. Dobroliubov whose death from consumption at the age of 25 in 1861 ensured that he would be remembered for the optimistic ardor of the totally committed youthful radical, not cooled by the experience of age. He had the added advantage of writing at a time when change at last seemed possible. Political reform, which had seemed so impossible when Belinskii died in 1848 in the year of Europe's abortive revolutions, became a distinct possibility in the euphoria following the death of Nicholas I in 1855, the end of the Crimean War in 1856 and the accession of the reforming tsar, Alexander II. After 1858 the government allowed open discussion of reforms in the press and the new liberalism came to a head with the Emancipation of the Serfs in 1861. Using literary commentary as a means for raising political issues, Dobroliubov led the assault on Russia's social system from the pages of the radical journal, *The Contemporary (Sovremennik)*. More impatient and dogmatic than Belinskii, Dobroliubov distilled the prescriptive essence of his forerunner's thinking. Literature's function was to be a means of propaganda for radical ideas. So dominant was Dobroliubov's strident personality that it was thought by contemporaries that he had been the model of the "new man" for a number of novelists including Turgenev's Bazarov in his *Fathers and Children*. It is a curious example of how life and art combined. The force of Dobroliubov's polemics seemed to be acknowledged by novelists who felt obliged to include within their fictional world the image of the man who insisted that their fiction was only valid if it furthered the political agenda proposed by him in the real world.

It was with the milestone of the 1861 Act of Emancipation that the Russian novel acquired its revolutionary status, despite the qualms of its mainly liberal and noble authors. From now on it would not limit itself to reflecting society and being a forum for opinion but would also present images of radical change. Not only did the Emancipation of the Serfs promise to overthrow the last vestiges of the feudal order but men would be freed from grinding labor by the new technological discoveries of natural science and women would be liberated from their position of social inferiority.

That 1861 was perceived as a transforming moment was indicated by the very titles of Russian novels and critical articles. Such was Dobroliubov's "When Will the Real Day Come?": the title of his review of Turgenev's *On the Eve* (1860). To hasten that real day, it was necessary to dispense with the superfluous men and replace them with "men of action and not of abstract, always somewhat Epicurean, reasoning."[12] The task prescribed by Dobroliubov for writers as their political responsibility was to search out this "new man" and present him to the Russian public.

Another key essay by Dobroliubov clearly shows how his reviews of contemporary novels were camouflage for political statements. "What is Oblomovitis?" (1859) took as its starting point Goncharov's novel *Oblomov* which had presented a smiling picture of a country squire sunk in sloth. For Dobroliubov, however, Oblomov's idleness was no laughing matter but a social disease that revealed the dysfunction of Russian society. He went further, discovering that most Russian novels hitherto had projected weak, ineffectual characters deformed by their egoism. With a sweep of his net, Dobroliubov put the heroes of Pushkin's *Evgenii Onegin*,

Lermontov's *A Hero of Our Time*, and Turgenev's *Rudin* into the same category. All had been corrupted by the rottenness of serfdom and the stagnation of the repressive regime needed to sustain it. Past literature had correctly identified the main symptom of Russia's political decay. Literature's task was now to promote the image of the new man whose hour was about to strike.

Russian novelists, responding to the tremendous pressure of the conflicting political currents of the day instinctively as artists, might not have needed the goad of radical critics. Yet the effectiveness of Dobroliubov's criticism is seen in Turgenev's response to the charge in his "What is Oblomovitis?" that all the main characters were ineffectual. In 1860 Turgenev made a crucial change to his novel *Rudin* which had first appeared in 1856. At the end of the original version Rudin becomes a homeless wanderer: in the revised 1860 edition he perishes on the Paris barricades waving a red banner, a hero alongside his brother revolutionaries. The redeeming of Rudin as a *révolté* coincided with Turgenev's conception of Bazarov, the new man who was to be the hero of his *Fathers and Children*. In its reference to a generational change, the very title of *Fathers and Children* again pointed to the historical watershed of 1861. Bazarov embodies many of the traits of the "new man": he has no noble pedigree, he scorns any attempt to idealize the peasantry and rejects art, liberal reformism, divine revelation, all institutions based on custom. His total negation of civilizing values explains his title of "nihilist." He declares himself committed only to the objective lessons of natural science. He is subject to nobody and is his own man, totally independent. He is clearly projected into the future as a "man of the sixties," a representative of the "children" in revolt against the principles and faith of their "fathers," the "men of the forties." Making the characters representative of precise historical decades is as significant as the exact placing of the novel in 1859. It is a feature of all Turgenev's novels that chronicle and evaluate the "body and pressure" of time that they describe eternal human concerns in the particular political crux of an exact time.

The political impact of *Fathers and Children* was immediate when it was published in the spring of 1862 following the Act of Emancipation. That Turgenev had succeeded in bringing to life the "new man" in his hero Bazarov was proved by the swift reaction of all shades of the political spectrum. There was considerable disagreement as to Turgenev's intention. His friend Annenkov wanted to know whether Bazarov was to be taken "as a fruitful force for the future or as a disgusting boil on the body of a hollow civilization to be lanced as soon as possible."[13] Most critics were convinced that Turgenev had taken sides and remonstrated with him.

Among the radicals Dmitri Pisarev was almost alone in approving the picture of Bazarov as someone with whom the honest and fearless youth could identify.[14] The most vitriolic assault on Turgenev's supposed sympathies came from *The Contemporary*, the journal previously edited by Chernyshevskii and Dobroliubov, which argued that he had indeed painted a disgusting boil, a repellent caricature of the young radicals.[15] Consequently, to his dismay, Turgenev was relegated to the camp of the reactionaries. The stormy political wrangle on Turgenev's true intentions continued to rumble on through the century, and indeed echoes of the great debate still reverberated a century later.

Fathers and Children was a novel with political consequences in that it helped the various political persuasions to demarcate themselves more clearly. It brought into focus the main issues that separated the "children," the impatient radicals of the sixties, from the "fathers", the long-suffering liberals of the forties. It gave a name, Nihilism, and with it substance to the amorphous yearnings of a new generation. And it politicized the Russian novel in a new way for *Fathers and Children* was answered, not only by reviews and polemical articles in the thick journals, but by another novel: Chernyshevskii's *What is to be Done?*.

Chernyshevskii was a political prisoner in the Peter and Paul Fortress in St. Petersburg for his activities as a radical publicist when he wrote *What is to be Done?* between December 1862 and April 1863. Although a lax censorship originally allowed it to be published in *The Contemporary* in 1863, as soon as the intent of the novel was revealed it was banned until the 1905 revolution. Its proscription and the treatment of its author gave it a remarkable prestige among the radicals. In his treatise of 1855, *The Aesthetic Relations of Art to Reality*, Chernyshevskii had argued that art could only be an auxiliary to real life and that its function must be to act as a "textbook for life." *What is to be done?* was an example of such a textbook. Without any of the ambiguities of *Fathers and Children*, it presents lucid models of the new men and women, bent on bettering humanity through the continual purification and strengthening of its essentially good nature through guild socialism, women's liberation and enlightened self-interest. At the centre of the novel stands the paragon figure of Rakhmetov, chaste, monastic yet enigmatic – a man who has become a superman of "a new breed" by submitting himself to a socialist doctrine. The prophetic tone of the novel was enhanced by the four dreams – it would be more apt to call them visions – which come to the central figure of Vera Pavlovna, culminating in the fourth vision when she sees her promised land with its eternal summer guaranteed in the electrically-lit, aluminum Crystal Palace where all social problems have been resolved. The

visionary enthusiasm of the novel and the sense of the compelling personality of its martyred author ensure that *What is to be Done?* retains its
appeal. What is certain is that as a political "textbook for life" it satisfied
the yearnings of thousands of eager disciples. They included the young
Lenin and his elder brother who was executed for revolutionary activities.[16]

That the years of debate leading to the Emancipation of 1861 and the
immediate aftermath should have led to a politicized literature is hardly
surprising. Nor is it surprising that the radical extremism of Chernyshevskii
should have elicited a vehement reaction against it. Anti-nihilist novels
with their telling titles streamed from the press in the wake of Pisemskii's
The Troubled Sea (1863), a diatribe against the younger generation;
Leskov's *No Way Out* (1864), Aksharumov's *A Complex Affair* (1864),
Kliushnikov's *Mirage* (1864), Avenarius's *The Plague* (1867), Goncharov's
The Ravine (1869).[17] The political divide between the generations of the
1840s and 1860s, made manifest by Turgenev's *Fathers and Children*,
continued to fascinate Russians. Particularly poignant was the situation of
Dostoevskii who had been banished as a child of the "forties" and had now
returned into the altered world of the sixties. His response was *Notes from
Underground* (1864) which signalled a turning point in his career and
prepared the groundwork for his major novels. Dostoevskii's intention
seems to have been to throw overboard the idealists of the forties who
included his own youthful self, the writer of *Poor Folk*. Not only the men
of the forties are attacked in *Notes from Underground*, however, but also
the new men who had recently appeared, for the work is aimed against
Chernyshevskii, the acknowledged leader of the new generation and in
particular his "textbook for life," *What is to be Done?* Chernyshevskii had
chosen the Crystal Palace in London as his symbol of the triumph of
rational technology and social organization; Dostoevskii deliberately
shattered this symbol with his hero of *Notes from Underground* who rebels
against the notions of utilitarian self-interest and perfection. Chernyshevskii would be content with a perfecting of political institutions;
Dostoevskii highlighted the permanent rebellious state of his own man
from the underground who would never be satisfied with any political
structure. His hero outradicalizes the radicals, as later the heroes of his
major novels will do.

Crime and Punishment which followed *Notes from Underground* is
remarkable for combining within the main character, Raskolnikov, both
the rationalist whose life is based on self-interest and the subversive "underground man" with his irrational Napoleonic aspirations. By splitting the
"new man" from within in *Crime and Punishment*, Dostoevskii sunders the
idea of the monistic nature of man for whom a lucid "textbook for life"

could be written. While the murder committed by Raskolnikov can only be indirectly linked with the growing number of political assassinations by "nihilists" in the late 1860s,[18] Dostoevskii's novel *The Devils* had its source in real political unrest in the summer of 1867. His young brother-in-law, a student liable to be embroiled in the troubles, was persuaded by the Dostoevskiis to leave Moscow for the haven of Dresden where they were living at the time. Dostoevskii discussed the life and ideas of the student world with his brother-in-law and, according to his wife,[19] it was from these conversations that Dostoevskii conceived the idea of depicting the political movement of the time in one of his novels, and of modeling one of the main characters, Shatov, on the student Ivanov who was later to be killed in 1869 on the orders of the revolutionary terrorist Nechaev. Initially the novel was to be a "pamphlet novel," aimed against the revolutionaries. In the end the pamphleteer in Dostoevskii was to be shouldered aside by the artist with his urge to grapple with universal philosophical and religious questions in his portrayal of Stavrogin. No longer was the novel solely concerned with political polemics, but the original pamphleteering kernel remained an integral part of it. *The Devils* features the Verkhovenskiis, father and son; like *Fathers and Children*, it is an examination of warring generations. Dostoevskii, however, deepens Turgenev's sense of the interdependence between the two generations. The older Verkhovenskii, Stepan Trofimovich, has spawned a son, Petr, who has exploited but distorted the ideals of his father's generation, transmuting the idealistic liberal humanism of the 1840s Westernizers into a shallow nihilistic opportunism, to become a dim reflection of the sinister, amoral Nechaev whose revolutionary ambition had culminated in murder. Other characters also caricature representatives of political trends criticized by Dostoevskii. Shatov is an extreme Slavophile who transforms the nation into his God. Kirillov is an extreme Westernizer who follows the thesis that mankind is God. The representation of Nechaev's activities in *The Devils* led to an impassioned political debate on the forms of revolutionary action in the early 1870s.

Dostoevskii is polemicizing as well with Turgenev who is caricatured in the novel as Karmazinov, a writer attacked for his increasingly tendentious novels. Dostoevskii was particularly incensed by Turgenev's latest novel *Smoke* (1867). Turgenev, moving in Russian émigré circles abroad, had been implicated in a political affair which had obliged him to beg for clemency and accept exoneration from the Russian authorities. Consequently he was shunned not only by the young radicals but also by the older progressives. His sense of rejection was distilled into the bitterness of *Smoke*. Slight of plot, *Smoke*, set in Baden-Baden during a few August days in 1862, is a vehicle for a series of satirical vignettes depicting the radical left-wing of the Russian intelligentsia as well as members of the right-wing establishment. The element of political pamphleteering in *Smoke* sets it apart from Turgenev's other novels, as does the mediating of Turgenev's personal views through the mouth of Potugin, the narrator. Although its preoccupation with issues long since dead may make it appear dated, some aspects are more enduring, particularly the two problems posed by Potugin: firstly, the Russian need to find a leader and secondly, Russia's ambivalent attitude to the West. Potugin's policy is that only the best essence of European civilization should be emulated by Russians, since Russian culture is impoverished. Again the Crystal Palace is used to underline Potugin's argument. Imagine, he said, the Great Exhibition with the discoveries of each nation in turn withdrawn from the exhibits; the withdrawal of Russia's contributions would leave the exhibition unchanged "because even the samovar, bast shoes, the shaft-bow, the knout – these famous products of ours – were not invented by us."[20] The novel as a political pamphlet restates Turgenev's moderate Westernist viewpoint: his belief in reason against the vaunted Russian intuition, his belief in Western intellect rather than the Russian soul.

Turgenev's last novel *Virgin Soil* was even more of a pamphlet novel contrasting the conservative landed squirearchy with the young populists. It has been suggested that the only way of understanding *Virgin Soil* is in terms of the doctrine of Soviet Socialist Realism.[21] Characters are divided into black and white according to their political credentials. The pure populists include a positive hero Solomin, a factory manager, anticipated in a preparatory sketch as a necessary contrast to the Russian utopian prophet: "one must place a real practical man American-style who gets on quietly with his job like a peasant ploughing and sowing."[22] It provides an uplifting message for the future. It can be seen as a prototype of the political novel of the twentieth century with Solomin extolled in the novel's last chapter as one of the "strong, grey, monochrome men from the people" to whom the future belongs.

Although there seems to be a great divide between this figure and the early Rudin romantically brandishing his red banner on the 1848 Paris barricades, Turgenev was adamant at the end of his life that they were the product of the same impulse. "The author of Rudin written in 1855," he wrote, "and the author of *Virgin Soil* written in 1876 is the same man. I endeavored during all that time as far as my strength and ability permitted with conscientious objectivity to portray and embody in fitting types what Shakespeare calls 'the body and pressure of time'; and the swiftly changing faces of Russian people from cultured society which was the main object of my observations."[23]

While the "body and pressure of time" pushed Turgenev into writing novels which were more and more structured on broad political divisions, his great contemporaries Dostoevskii and Tolstoi seemed to mount a determined critical resistance to the dominant spirit of their age that demanded political engagement. Dostoevskii in particular challenged all the modish assumptions and currents of his own time, revealing the irrational in human behavior which must undermine any rational political program. Likewise in his *War and Peace*, Tolstoi directed his readers away from the "body and pressure" of their own time to consider the instinctive behavior of the masses and the folly of seeing war, that ultimate expression of power politics, as a process that could be explained by historical analysis. The rejection in *War and Peace* of all historical explanations of human behavior in terms of social developments implied a rejection of the sense conveyed by *Fathers and Children* that one generation, that of the sixties, must be related, even if antipathetically, to the preceding one. Yet both Dostoevskii and Tolstoi incorporate into their novels topical political issues of the day which had resulted from the great reforms of the sixties that followed the revolutionary Emancipation of the Serfs in 1861. Even such a minor reform as the vain attempt to control alcoholism in 1863 by changing the licensing laws supplied Dostoevskii with the crucial sub-plot of the Marmeladov family in *Crime and Punishment*; and the consequences of the transformation of Russia's legal system was explored in the portrayal of the new kind of professional enlightened prosecutor in the character of Porfirii. Later in *The Brothers Karamazov* the new jury system imported from Western Europe would be examined critically and shown to be unworkable in Russian society. Even factual newspaper reports could be incorporated within the fiction as Dostoevskii did in *The Devils* by using reports of the long trial of the Nechaevists who had murdered the student leader Ivanov.

In his *Anna Karenina* Tolstoi likewise drew heavily on the burning political issues of the day, particularly those concerned with the reforms. The establishment of a system of local government councils, the *zemstva*, by Alexander II was a key part of the reconstruction of the Russian state and Konstantin Levin, initially an enthusiastic *zemstvo* member, is shown to have lost his ardor for the institution as it had been undermined by the self-interest of its participants. The same self-seeking infects the laudable endeavors of Karenin, a high ranking state official, to deal with injustices suffered by national minorities in the Russian Empire. Tolstoi is exceptional among the novelists of his time in dealing with the human mechanics of the political processes at local and state level. Even today's reader can comprehend the disappointment of men of Levin's temperament in the souring of idealistic reform. The reader of the 1870s responded more keenly to the novel's response to the flux of contemporary political events such as the populists' "going to the people" movement with which Levin flirted.

The measure of the force of the novel's political impact was that Katkov, the Slavophile editor of the *Russian Herald* (*Russkii Vestnik*), in which *Anna Karenina* was appearing, refused in 1877 to publish the concluding part, in which the motives of Russian volunteers for the Balkan war in support of Serbian independence were put into question.

It must be remembered that the political ambit of all those novels of the sixties and seventies was emphasized because they were serialized in the thick journals, such as Chernyshevskii's and Dobroliubov's *The Contemporary* and Katkov's *Russian Herald*, where the serialized fiction was accompanied by critical, philosophical, and political articles. The symbiosis between fiction and real social criticism was also emphasized by the habit of characters within the fiction of writing such articles. Both Raskolnikov in *Crime and Punishment* and Ivan Karamazov in *The Brothers Karamazov* write articles which are pivotal to the novel. In *Anna Karenina* both Konstantin Levin's brothers are writers, Nikolai, the socialist crank, and Sergei Koznyshev, his half-brother, whose political treatise, *An Essay Reviewing the Foundations and Forms of Government in Europe and Russia*, to which he had devoted six years of his life, is met by total silence.

The dispiriting indifference to Koznyshev's work seems to foretell the stagnation in Russian political thought in the 1880s and 1890s. With the accession of Alexander III after the assassination of Alexander II in 1881, a repressive regime was brought into being that attempted to suppress all oppositionist political activity and the intellectual debate that nurtured it. With the dousing of political debate, the great age of the Russian novel seemed to have ended. The closing years of the nineteenth century were a period referred to as one of "small deeds" and chronicled mainly by the minor forms of the novella, short story and sketch rather than the novel. Only Tolstoi remained of the great novelists and he had demonstratively turned his back on art to become a moral teacher. The moralist speaks out loudly in Tolstoi's *Resurrection* (1899) which was read as such an assault on the Russian Imperial regime and Russian Orthodoxy that it resulted in Tolstoi's formal excommunication by the Church. *Resurrection*, however, was a rare reminder of the past glories of the Russian novel's ability to shake political faiths. Chekhov, the greatest writer of the period, despite his genius in capturing the anguish of the age in such stories as "Ward 6", set his face against any overt political statement. "It is no good for an artist," he wrote to Suvorin, his publisher who had chided him for avoiding the burning questions of the day, "to concern himself with what he does not understand. For specialist problems we have our specialists; it is their business to pass judgment on the peasant commune, on the fate of capital, on the harmfulness of drunkenness, on boots, on women's complaints."[24]

It was not until Russia experienced another cataclysmic political event, the First Russian Revolution of 1905, that politics re-emerged as a dominant force in a Russian novel. Gorkii's novel *Mother* (1906) stood out as a work planned to serve the cause of Revolution. The novel is a semi-documentary, based on the real-life story of an exiled political activist Petr Zalomov and his mother Anna Zalomova who was known to Gorkii as a boy. Gorkii's personal involvement in the 1905 Revolution when he was imprisoned and then exiled also lay behind the novel. As in Turgenev's later novels, many of the characters are mouthpieces for political trends – international socialism, anarchism and revolutionary socialism – and the central political message is spelled out by the son at his trial. The stark political theories, however, are humanized since their exponents are seen through the compassionate, caring eyes of the central character of the mother. It is the suffering of the "children," and particularly that of her only son, that transforms the proletarian mother into a Madonna-like character. Appreciating the oppressed revolutionary workmen as tormented Christian martyrs, she comes to understand the sacrifice inherent in the revolutionary vocation and transfers her devotion from the Orthodox Church to political activism. A future paradise on earth bought with revolutionary blood replaces her previous faith of personal immortality in heaven.

The two themes of a quasi-religious transformation of society and the projection of a positive hero apparent in Chernyshevskii's *What is to be Done?* are certainly evident in Gorkii's *Mother*. Although the effect of Gorkii's novel was captured by a friend who told him, "Now everyone's talking not about Turgenev's *Fathers and Children* but about Gorkii's *Mothers and Children*,"[25] one striking difference between *Mother* and its predecessors, Turgenev's *Fathers and Children* and Chernyshevskii's *What is to be Done?*, is that it did not inspire other novelists to grapple with the implications of its characters' standpoints as happened in the 1860s and 1870s. It acquired a singular reputation but little resonance in other novels. The best selling novels of its day such as Artsybashev's *Sanin* and Sologub's *The Petty Demon* were deliberately apolitical. If novelists responded to the revolutionary pressure of their age, then the response was reflected in avant-garde techniques rather than ideological themes. Advances in the novel's technical boundaries, revolutions in its form, were achieved above all by Belyi's *Petersburg*, which, despite its treatment of events with potential political significance, may be seen as political only in its deliberate assumption of an anti-political stance.

Even the triumph of the Bolshevik Revolution in 1917 did not immediately resurrect the committed political novel. Indeed, the most trenchant criticism of prescriptive, exemplary literature came from the Bolshevik writer Evgenii Zamiatin shortly after the triumph of Bolshevism in 1917. His anti-utopian novel *We*, written in 1920–21, questioned the model Crystal Palace of Chernyshevskii's *What is to be Done?* in its portrayal of a totalitarian Single State enclosed in a city of glass. The hero of *We*, D-503, totally absorbed in the collective state, discovers his individuality through falling in love with a female number I-330 who turns out to be the leader of a revolutionary cult bent on shattering the entropy of the Single State symbolized by the city of glass. Zamiatin was also countering the populist extremists who had elevated the "people" into their God, and so challenged a heresy to which Gorkii had succumbed and promoted in *Mother*. Gorkii's *Confession* of 1908 ended with a prayer to "the almighty, immortal people!," "and there shall be no other gods in the world but thee, for thou art the one God that creates miracles!" It was the same divine "people" to whom Nilovna in Gorkii's *Mother* had transferred her religious faith. Zamiatin might well be referring to this aspect of *Mother* when he makes D-503 in his "Entry No. 22" sardonically record the parallel between the Single State which gives him passive contentment and the fellowship of Christians, "our only (though very imperfect) forerunners: for them passivity was a virtue, pride was a vice, and they understood that *We* belonged to God, *I* to the devil."

Although Zamiatin's *We* was banned, he played a leading part in the Serapion Brotherhood, a focus of the diffuse trend known as the *poputchiki* or "fellow-travelers." Although Bolshevism had imposed a totalitarian political regime on Russia, literary politics remained surprisingly pluralistic in the 1920s. While the fellow-travelers gave general support to the regime, they were in agreement with Chekhov's view that writers in addressing human experience should be content with producing evidence and not attempt to be judges. The outstanding novels of the early Soviet period are content to chronicle the cataclysmic events of the Civil War without providing a focused political viewpoint.

Such apolitical objectivity was not allowed to go unchallenged. An opposing faction of writers, the On Guardists, demanded detailed Party regulation of all literature by the Bolsheviks. In the Communist Party discussions on its policy towards literature in 1924 and 1925, although the On Guard view was rejected, the right of the Party to guide literature was asserted with the setting up of the centralized All-Union Association of

Proletarian Writers (VAPP). Even when this became the more rigid RAPP (Russian Association of Proletarian Writers), there were still attempts, ultimately in vain, to maintain some equilibrium between the conflicting Russian traditional understandings of the novel's purpose. In the balance was the view of literature as presenting a true representation of reality, and the opposing view that literature should be prescriptive, set forth models of behavior and be an auxiliary to the policy of "changing the world" at the heart of Stalin's first Five-Year Plan (1928–1933).

By 1934 Russian novelists had become subject not only to one publishing system, one Writers' Union, but to the one official doctrine of Socialist Realism. The doctrine's three tenets – *partiinost'* ("party-mindedness"), *ideinost'* ("ideological content") and *narodnost'* ("nationality") – emphasized the spirit of collectivism which permeated Socialist Realism. The triad bore a striking resemblance to the official motto of Nicholas I, "Autocracy, Orthodoxy, Nationality," against which Belinskii had inveighed in his "Letter to N. V. Gogol."

Political dogmatism now dictated the content of Russian novels. The criteria for assessing them were primarily political rather than purely literary. Those novels of the 1930s, however, that were hailed as the most effective in promoting the new ideology did not fit into the prescription of Socialist Realism. Mikhail Sholokhov's *The Quiet Don* (1928–40) was the Soviet novel *par excellence* but as Mathewson suggested,[26] it challenged every tenet of Socialist Realism in the tragic fate of the hero, Grigorii Melekhov. The novel, chronicling the counter-revolution of the Don Cossacks, focuses on the contradictory and confused Melekhov who strives to grasp and make sense of the shifting kaleidoscopic politics of his own age. It is that riven, shifting Melekhov that puts *The Quiet Don* outside the prescribed pattern of extolling single-minded proletarian or Party heroes.

Yet, novels, such as *The Quiet Don,* that escaped the narrow confines of the new dogma, were paradoxically cited as exemplars of Socialist Realism. Novels as disparate as Gorkii's *Mother* and *Klim Samgin* (1936), Furmanov's *Chapaev* (1923), Aleksei Tolstoi's *A Tour of Hell* (1921–40), Nikolai Ostrovskii's *How the Steel Was Tempered* (1932–34), and Fadeev's *The Young Guard* (1945/1951), were to be the models for the new politicized literature after 1932. Socialist Realism may be viewed not so much as the imposition of Stalin's totalitarian will on Russia's novelists, but as the distillation of attitudes assumed in the Soviet novel of the 1920s which were in turn derived from nineteenth-century experience.

The Russian Revolution of 1917 had not led to a new world for Russian literature. With the establishment of Stalinism in the early 1930s, it seemed to the contrary that the traditions of the nineteenth century had reasserted themselves with a new vigor. As far as literature was concerned, it has been argued that Stalinism appeared as a reprise of the militant materialism of the 1860s.[27] The propagandistic novels which were required seemed to be a new version of the novels represented by Chernyshevskii's *What is to be Done?* It has also been argued that the positive heroes prescribed by Soviet doctrine had their source, not in Marxist theory, but in the fictional heroes of Chernyshevskii and Gorkii.[28]

With Stalin's death in March 1953 the policies associated with him began to decompose. The period became known as the "Thaw" (*Ottepel'*), and the title of Ilia Ehrenburg's novel *The Thaw* in 1956 was proof of the novelists' enduring role in channelling political attitudes. It was 1956 that proved to be the pivotal year when in February Khrushchev's speech at the Twentieth Party Congress denounced Stalin for his repression. *The Thaw* clearly celebrated de-Stalinization in its portrayal of a society frozen in deep inertia being thawed by the warm sincerity of its main characters. But *The Thaw* essentially retained the model, exemplary hero of the Socialist Realist novel: it was only the purpose of the hero that was adjusted. The other landmark political novel that appeared in the same year as *The Thaw* was Dudintsev's *Not by Bread Alone* which again preserved the essence of the Socialist Realist pattern while adjusting the conflict: a lowly, powerless representative of the common people overcomes the resistance of a Stalinist party apparatus.

Novelists, like the politicians of the Thaw period, were too rooted in Stalinism and the Stalinist doctrine of Socialist Realism to free themselves totally. The metaphor of the "Thaw" was well suited to the real situation: despite the experience of fresh warmth, the solid ground of Stalinist politics remained unchanged. The excavation and moving of that ground would be a political imperative of the post-Thaw years.

In literature it was carried out mainly by the growing publications of memoirs, reminiscences and diaries in such literary journals as *New World* (*Novyi mir*). Not only did the memoirs restore the suppressed memory of Russia but they also challenged, perhaps at first unconsciously, two fundamental tenets of Socialist Realism. The memoir literature emphasized the objective, cognitive role of literature which had been relegated in favor of a purposeful, agitational depiction of life. It also replaced the positive hero's political exhortation with the private voice of ordinary people, buffeted by revolution, purges and warfare, yet obliged to stay silent. In his editorial to the fortieth anniversary number of *New World* in 1965 Tvardovskii showed how conscious the journal was of the effect of its deliberate policy of memoir publishing. That editorial was linked with Solzhenitsyn's work. It placed Solzhenitsyn's *One Day in the Life of Ivan Denisovich* (1962) within the memoir genre as it may well have placed Pasternak's *Doctor Zhivago* (1957), ironically rejected by *New World* in 1956, for *Doctor Zhivago* corrected Russia's amnesia by restoring lost memories of the revolutionary years. In her own memoir *Hope against Hope* Nadezhda Mandelstam recognized that Pasternak's novel was a remembrance of things past, an attempt to determine his own place in the swift-flowing movement of days, and to seek understanding of this movement.[29] *Doctor Zhivago* shared with the memoir literature generally a concern with apparent trivialities of day-to-day existence rather than a concern with great events and personalities. In this way it made the same political statement as *A Captain's Daughter* with its regard for the individual and the rebel against the state. Alongside these memoirs, yet linked with them, was the open publication of works, which had long been repressed, by authors who in some cases were long dead. Even the public acknowledgment of authors such as Babel, Bulgakov, Pilniak, Zamiatin and Zoshchenko was a political act in the post-Thaw period. The most significant example of an exhumed work was undoubtedly Bulgakov's *The Master and Margarita*, finished just before the author's death in 1940 but not published until 1966–67. Set in Moscow in the late twenties or early thirties, it too, when it appeared in the mid-sixties, was part of the memoir literature.

If Stalinism was guided by the experience and the models of the nineteenth-century novelists in prescribing its politicized literature, then the process of de-Stalinization after 1956 also drew on the same traditions to dismantle those prescriptions. In the courageous challenge made to political censorship by such works as *Doctor Zhivago*, *The Master and Margarita* and Solzhenitsyn's novels, in their banning and eventual publication, Russians recognized a reprise of their nineteenth-century political history. The authority of liberal "thick journals" such as *New World* was itself reminiscent of their influential predecessors such as *The Contemporary* of the 1850s and 1860s which gave a platform to Belinskii, Dobroliubov, Nekrasov and Chernyshevskii and promoted new, politically engaged novels. Pasternak's *Doctor Zhivago* followed Pushkin's example in *The Captain's Daughter* in seeking to make sense of Russian history and Russian rebelliousness by illuminating the life of individuals. Bulgakov in *The Master and Margarita* derived inspiration from Gogol's treatment of social reality through fantasy. Bulgakov, Pasternak and Solzhenitsyn, all of whom suffered political repression, were candidates for inclusion in a "martyrology of Russian literature" such as Plekhanov had envisioned in 1888. Yet, paradoxically, all three, like Pushkin in his time, had been close to the seat of central power: Bulgakov and Pasternak were given special acknowledgment by Stalin, while Solzhenitsyn was favored by Khrushchev's direct intervention authorizing publication of his *One Day in the Life of Ivan Denisovich*. Proof of the continuing close relationship between the novel and political power was the choice of a novelist, Chingiz Aitmatov, to propose Gorbachev formally as first President of the Soviet Union. Will the dissolution of that Union in 1991 herald a new development in the political novel as Russia's novelists take their bearings on a new revolutionary milestone? The immediate reaction of Russia's prose writers seems to be an attempt to evade the burden of their traditional role as spokesmen and prophets by deliberately avoiding political engagement, or even by constructing texts that do not fit into the traditional novel genre. In time, of course, that attitude, adopted in defiance of a long tradition of political engagement, may well be seen as a challenging political stance.

NOTES

1. Iu. M. Lotman, *Sotvorenie Karamzina* (Moscow: Kniga, 1987), p. 22.
2. G. V. Plekhanov, *Literatura i estetika*, 2 vols. (Moscow: Khudozhestvennaia literatura, 1958), vol. II, pp. 7–8.
3. N. A. Nekrasov, *Sobranie sochinenii*, 8 vols. (Moscow: Khudozhstvennaia literatura, 1965–67), vol. VIII, p. 189.
4. Quoted by E. Lampert in Malcolm Jones (ed.), *New Essays on Tolstoy* (Cambridge University Press, 1978), p. 145.
5. Stendhal, *Racine et Shakespeare*, chapter 5.
6. N. V. Gogol, *Sobranie sochinenii*, 6 vols. (Moscow: Khudozhestvennaia literatura, 1952–53), vol. II, p. 325.
7. V. G. Belinskii, *Polnoe sobranie sochinenii*, 13 vols. (Moscow: Akademiia Nauk, 1953–59), vol. I, p. 267.
8. Ibid., p. 213.
9. Ibid.
10. I. S. Turgenev, *Polnoe sobranie sochinenii i pisem*, 28 vols. (Moscow–Leningrad: Akademiia Nauk, 1960–68), vols. I–XV, *Sochineniia*, vol. IV, p. 408.
11. Quoted in Isaiah Berlin, *Russian Thinkers* (London: Hogarth Press, 1978), p. 150.
12. N. A. Dobroliubov, *Sobranie sochinenii*, 9 vols. (Moscow–Leningrad: Khudozhestvennaia Literatura, 1961–64), p. 103.
13. V. A. Arkhipov, "K tvorcheskoi istorii romana I. S. Turgeneva *Ottsy i deti*," *Russkaia literatura*, 1 (1958), 148.
14. Berlin, *Russian Thinkers*, pp. 282–83, 286.
15. M. A. Antonovich, "Asmodei nashego vremeni," *Sovremennik* (March 1862), pp. 65–114.
16. Lenin is quoted in Rufus W. Mathewson Jr., *The Positive Hero in Russian Literature*, 2nd edn. (Stanford University Press, 1975), p. 82 and Richard Freeborn, *The Russian Revolutionary Novel: Turgenev to Pasternak* (Cambridge University Press, 1982), p. 24.
17. For an account of these novels and their background, see Charles A. Moser, *Antinihilism in the Russian Novel of the 1860s* (The Hague: Mouton, 1964).

18. See Richard Peace, *Dostoyevsky: An Examination of the Major Novels* (Cambridge University Press, 1971), p. 28.
19. A. G. Dostoevskaia, "Vospominaniia," in A. Dolinin (ed.), *F. M. Dostoevskii v vospominaniiakh sovremennikov*, 2 vols. (Moscow: Khudozhestvennaia literatura, 1964), vol. II, p. 74.
20. Turgenev, *Sochineniia*, vol. IX, p. 233.
21. Richard Freeborn, *Turgenev: The Novelist's Novelist* (London: Oxford University Press, 1960), p. 169.
22. Turgenev, *Sochineniia*, vol. XII, p. 314.
23. Ibid., p. 303.
24. A. P. Chekhov, *Polnoe sobranie sochinenii i pisem*, 30 vols. (Moscow: Nauka, 1974–82), *Pis'ma* vol. III, p. 45.
25. L'vov-Rogachevskii quoted in Freeborn, *The Russian Revolutionary Novel*, p. 51.
26. Mathewson, *The Positive Hero*, p. 232.
27. James H. Billington, *The Icon and the Axe: An Interpretive History of Russian Culture* (London: Weidenfeld and Nicolson, 1966), p. 534.
28. Mathewson, *The Positive Hero*.
29. See Max Hayward, *Writers in Russia: 1917–1978* (London: Harvill, 1983), pp. 209–10.

5

LESLEY MILNE

Satire

The first two great satirical novelists in Russian literature are Nikolai Gogol (1809–52) and Mikhail Saltykov (1826–89), who wrote under the pen-name of Shchedrin. Many major Russian writers, from Aleksandr Pushkin through Lev Tolstoi and Fedor Dostoevskii to Aleksandr Solzhenitsyn, have used satirical depiction in their novels, but it could never be said that satire is characteristic of their work as a whole. It is Gogol and Shchedrin who between them set the points of reference for the Russian satirical novel.

Of course satire existed in Russian literature before Gogol, but not in the form of a novel of European stature.[1] An important element in the development of the Russian satirical novel was the picaresque tradition. In its classic form, which originated in Spain in the mid sixteenth century and in the following centuries spread throughout Europe, the picaresque novel is the retrospective autobiography of a rogue, the *picaro*.[2] In Russia, as elsewhere, the picaresque was disseminated chiefly through its French model, Alain Lesage's *Gil Blas* (1715–35). Its popularity is demonstrated by two Russian imitations, *A Russian Gil Blas*, by Vasilii Narezhnyi (1814) and *Ivan Vyzhigin* by Faddei Bulgarin (1829), which was subtitled *A Russian Gil Blas* on its first appearance. Where Bulgarin's novel defends the existing social order, Narezhnyi uses the same literary model to opposite political effect, and the last three parts of his six-part novel were in fact banned by the censor. Narezhnyi constructs a classic picaresque tale, in that the hero tells the story of his own past life, spent traveling around the country in the service of various masters; he becomes corrupted by the debauchery of the world, until the moment of his repentance when his integrity is restored, thus providing the moral basis for his retrospective account. The story-line is packed with adventures, but also with robustly satirical episodes exposing abuse of power in high places. Narezhnyi's *Russian Gil Blas* shows how the picaresque novel, plotted around the travels of an anti-heroic or unheroic central character, develops into a satirical panorama. The first Russian novel of this type to achieve a universal reputation was Gogol's *Dead Souls*.

Dead Souls, part 1 of which was published in 1842, is not classically picaresque in that it is not the first-person narrative of the rogue himself. It is, however, picaresque in that it recounts the travels of its scoundrelly central hero, Pavel Ivanovich Chichikov. The idea of *Dead Souls* started off with an anecdote which Gogol said was provided by Pushkin. In Russia of the 1830s there was a census once every ten years and landlords were required to pay poll taxes for any male serfs, even if they died between censuses. The serfs, or "souls" (as they were termed in both official and customary parlance) were dead, but on lists they were still alive; a swindler could therefore buy them cheaply. Given that financial status was determined by the number of "souls" owned, he could thus become a man of property; he could use his "souls" to obtain a piece of land on which to settle them, acquire a mortgage on them and thus begin to build a real fortune on a non-existent commodity. It has been argued that Chichikov's enterprise is implausible, because serfs could only be sold with their families.[3] Be that as it may, there is something definitely shady about the whole business.

Chichikov's reason for wanting to purchase dead souls is not explained in the novel until the end of part 1, and it is never understood by the inhabitants of the provincial town of NN, into which Chichikov rides in his britzka in the novel's opening paragraph. The town is a collective image of mediocrity, venality, triviality, affectation and complacency, all portrayed with festive comic exuberance. Round Chichikov's activities the towns-people generate absurd spirals of rumor, and then when they seek to know the truth, whom do they ask? They turn, of course, to Nozdrev, who is a frivolous and reckless liar.

The town of NN, concerned only with externals, took Chichikov to its heart and, externally, Chichikov offers nothing to which anyone could take exception. He is neither handsome nor ugly, neither too fat nor too thin, not old but not too young either. His chameleon ability to flatter and please is constantly on display. Externally, he is very fastidious, with smoothly-shaven cheeks and a chubby body that is very well cared for: it is rubbed with a special soap that adds whiteness to the skin, then sponged and eau-de-cologned. We too would have been taken in by Chichikov, as the author tells us towards the end of chapter 11 in an admonitory address to the reader.

In his travels round the town of NN trying to purchase dead souls, Chichikov encounters various local landowners. All are characterized according to a set formula. One feature is isolated and exaggerated to the exclusion of all others and it is expressed in every aspect of that landowner: name, physique, clothes, house, furniture, food and drink, serfs, wife and children (if any), reaction to the proposed sale of the dead souls. Where the cloyingly sentimental Manilov gives Chichikov the souls for nothing, the bear-like Sobakevich drives a hard bargain and Nozdrev makes them the wager in a game of draughts; Pliushkin, the hyperbolized embodiment of miserliness, sells Chichikov his runaway serfs as well, and Korobochka, the manic housekeeper, becomes obsessed with the market price for "dead souls." As for Chichikov, in chapter 11, the final, summarizing chapter of part 1, we at last discover the character trait which he embodies: it is the vice of "acquisitiveness," which turns all his positive qualities, such as intelligence and fortitude, to naught. The denseness of detail in these characterizations produces an illusion of life while at the same time evoking a spiritual darkness. All the characters are dead souls in a moral sense.

Despite the fact that Chichikov in part 1 travels only about thirty miles round the town of NN, the text of *Dead Souls* conjures up a sense of vastness. This is evoked by the lyrical digressions of the third-person narrator, which from chapter 7 onwards articulate the author's vision. The soaring rhetoric of these digressions is counterbalanced by the constant need to return to Chichikov, and this alternation between the lofty and the comic was to create a productive model for Russian satirists in the future. One of the most famous passages in all of Russian literature, often cited and even more frequently parodied, is the finale to part 1 of *Dead Souls*, where Chichikov's britzka spawns an image of the troika that then becomes a "bird-troika," which in turn symbolizes Russia in headlong, divinely-inspired flight while other nations step aside to make way for her. This last chapter of part 1 reveals to the reader the pathos behind the author's comic inspiration: Chichikov's adventures have in fact been about Russia, ramshackle, drowsy and straggling, but also full of great potential when viewed "from the beautiful distance" of Rome, where Gogol wrote most of part 1. There is mention of "the laughter visible to the world and the tears which it neither knows nor sees," tears of sublime anticipation which hint at a prodigious apotheosis in part 11, for Gogol cherished an artistic plan whereby Chichikov would undergo a moral regeneration. When the conversion of Chichikov refused to happen as the writing of part 11 progressed, Gogol interpreted this as meaning that he himself was unredeemable. All great satirists hope by their writings to change the world for the better. In Gogol this sense of vocation was so strong that he hounded himself to death by his perceived failure to live up to it.

The writer's moral obligation to society was an idea shared and propagated by Russian literary criticism in the nineteenth century. In the tradition set by Gogol's great contemporary, Vissarion Belinskii (1811–48), the critic was also bound by this same duty to guide and instruct society. When Gogol depicted stagnation and corruption, radicals like Belinskii assumed that this was a protest against Russia's political structures. Gogol's *Selected Passages from Correspondence with Friends*, published in 1847, came as a shock: in this collection of writings (very few of which were passages from actual "letters to friends") Gogol affirmed the entire social, legal, ecclesiastical and political *status quo*. Belinskii responded as to an act of personal betrayal, writing Gogol a famous letter which, although not published until 1872, circulated in manuscript and became one of the great radical texts of the Russian nineteenth century.[4]

For Saltykov-Shchedrin, as for Belinskii, it was an article of faith that the writer should lead society on the road of reason, self-awareness, development and progress. It was not from the "beautiful distance" that Shchedrin viewed his contemporary Russia. He served as a government official from 1844 to 1862, when his contentious views forced him to take early retirement, and again from 1865 to 1868, when the government retired him once and for all. He was vice-governor of Riazan and later of Tver, and by 1868 he had reached a civilian rank equivalent to that of general in the army. In government service he tried honourably to practice liberalism in what he saw as a very temple to anti-liberalism. As a satirist he vented his civic rage in the open contempt of his mockery. His two major satirical novels are *The History of a Town* (1869–79) and *The Golovlev Family* (1875–80).

Mikhail Bakhtin identified two different types of laughter in his book *Rabelais and His World*, published in Moscow in 1965: the festive, life-affirming laughter of the carnival and a mocking, negating, rationalist "laughter that does not laugh."[5] Shchedrin's laughter is of the latter type. In *The Golovlev Family* the comic element is almost entirely absent. The Golovlevs represent the decline and decay of the Russian landowning gentry, with all the author's revulsion against this way of life (which he saw in his childhood on the family estate) concentrated on these characters. A particular distillation of loathing is reserved for the portrayal of the last member of the family, Porfirii. *The Golovlev Family* describes a life of limited horizons and monumental idleness. These features are evoked by Goncharov in *Oblomov* through the mock-idyll of "Oblomov's dream" (1849), but on the Golovlev estate they have turned viciously destructive. One by one the members of the family die from drink or despair, choked to death by the suffocating atmosphere that is embodied in Porfirii Golovlev. His character can be encapsulated in two words: hypocritical bloodsucker.

Having thus defined him once and for all, the author then adds layer upon layer of confirmation. The only comic touch in the novel is Porfirii's mode of speech, whiningly unctuous, larded with diminutives, a greasy little escape route from all moral responsibility; but constant repetition of examples eventually provokes in the reader that reaction of nauseated horror experienced in the novel by Porfirii's victims. The world of *The Golovlev Family* is a complete anti-idyll. It is the most unmitigatedly cheerless work in all of Russian literature, but, paradoxically, the vigorous contempt with which Shchedrin pursues these characters of his own mocking and grotesque creation produces an exhilarating effect.

The History of a Town is an allegory, presented in the form of a parody of Russian history of the eighteenth and early nineteenth centuries. Actual historical events and characters are parodied, for example the tour of southern Russia on which Potemkin conducted Catherine the Great in 1787, and the reactionary policies of Count Aleksei Arakcheev in the last years of Alexander I's reign. The "history," full of deliberate anachronisms, is written in a pastiche of both the twelfth-century historical chronicles and the officialese of the eighteenth- and nineteenth-century Russian empire. Beneath this level of parody, however, the satire is didactically savage. The town represents Russia and its name, Glupov, is derived from the adjective *glupyi*, meaning "stupid." This is not "wisdom in reverse," nor a comically endearing Sillytown, but just plain downright Stupidsville. The myths of Rus, Russia and autocracy are demolished by a rationalist laughter that denies them any legitimacy. The governors of Stupidsville are at best frivolous incompetents and at worst lunatic tyrants. Shchedrin's satirical devices here include grotesque fantasy, for example in the chapter "The music box" where the town governor instead of a head has a music box that can play only two tunes: "I'll ruin you" and "I won't stand for it." This fantastic element is one means by which the satire in *The History of a Town* transcends the parody of a particular historical empire to achieve a more universal reference to despotism in general. The view of "the people" is likewise refracted through grotesque exaggeration. Here Shchedrin creates a darkly comic effect through the contrast between the matter-of-fact tone of the narrative and the brutal events described. In the "Tale of the six town governesses" the townspeople turn into a lynch mob whose violence escalates to the point where the only sound in the town is the "splat-splat-splat" of bodies hitting the ground after being thrown from the belfry. The positive ideal of the people as embodiment of the idea of democracy is revealed through its opposite: these inhabitants of Stupidsville, who continue to welcome each new governor with ever the same delight and awe. The novel ends on an ambiguous note, which used sometimes to be interpreted as heralding a revolution but in view of the clues embedded in the text must be seen as announcing a reign of political reaction so extreme that the chronicler falls silent. A tradition of satire is its use of "Aesopian" language, the expression of a fundamental truth in the form of a fable. In *The History of a Town* the historical parody is an Aesopian language in which to discuss Russia's historical legacy and political mentality.

Satire continued to flourish in the sketch, the drama, and short prose forms through to the first decades of the twentieth century and in the 1920s Mikhail Zoshchenko created a new point of reference for Russian satirists with his use of the first-person narrator in his very short stories, typically two to three pages in length. But satire itself presented a problem for the Soviet regime. There was a line of argument which held that satire – whether the author wishes it or not – automatically attacks the state system (Belinskii's misunderstanding of Gogol's political intent in *Dead Souls* providing a potent historical example). The arguments against satire gained ground from the late 1920s onwards, and to employ satire as a mode of discourse became increasingly dangerous.[6] Gogol and Saltykov-Shchedrin had been able to reach their readers through the normal processes of publication. Among the major satirical novelists of the 1920s and 1930s only the partnership of Ilia Ilf and Evgenii Petrov reached a contemporary Soviet readership. The novels of Ilf and Petrov, *The Twelve Chairs* (1928) and *The Golden Calf* (1931) were published in the Soviet Union as soon as they had been written. The two other major satirical novels of the period, Evgenii Zamiatin's *We* and Mikhail Bulgakov's *The Master and Margarita*, have a different publishing history. Bulgakov's novel, written 1928–1940, was not published until 1966–67. Zamiatin's *We* was written 1920–21 but was not published in the Soviet Union until 1988.

Ilia Ilf (1897–1937) and Evgenii Petrov (1903–1942) occupy a special place in Russian literature. They both died young (Ilf of tuberculosis, Petrov in a plane crash during the war) but during their short literary life they wrote two of the funniest novels in the Russian language and created a character of mythic proportions: Ostap Bender, whose turns of phrase are part of the national stock of quotations. The authors killed him off at the end of *The Twelve Chairs*, but, like Sherlock Holmes, he proved resurrectable and they were able to continue his career in *The Golden Calf*. In the new collective society Ostap is an arch-individualist. Uninterested in building socialism, he is in search of a fortune: the diamonds hidden in one of a set of twelve chairs in the first novel; the money of a secret millionaire in the second. Like Chichikov, Ostap Bender is a traveling rogue, but there the resemblance ends. Where Chichikov is unsavory, Ostap is splendid:

when we meet him again at the beginning of *The Golden Calf* he is described as young, athletically-built and handsome, with chiselled features like those of the head on a coin. Ostap Bender has a well-developed sense of irony and the authors gave him their own wit and style. His stature is matched by his area of operation: he roams over the vast geographical spaces of Soviet Russia, deploying ingenious ways of relieving people of money. Some of these are masterpieces of comic inspiration, as in chapter 36 of *The Twelve Chairs* when Ostap notices that there is only one place in the tourist resort of Piatigorsk that does not charge an entrance fee: the cliff path with a view of the spot where Mikhail Lermontov fought his fatal duel, now marked by an evil-smelling puddle. Ostap promptly remedies this omission, taking money for the view of the puddle. All the tourists pay the charge – including a party of policemen on a guided tour. *The Twelve Chairs* reflects the period in which it is set: the New Economic Policy (NEP), with its scope for a measure of private enterprise. But by 1928 when the book was published NEP was in its last throes. The Soviet Union was entering the period of the "Great Leap Forward" which precipitated the country into industrialization, collectivization and, as eventually became apparent, the lethal grip of Stalinism. *The Golden Calf* reflects the onset of this new era. Ostap in his pursuit of the Soviet "underground millionaire" (who has to keep his riches a secret because they are illegal in this new society) in chapter 15 sets up a fictitious bureau to which he gives the name Horns and Hoofs, for the office ostensibly handles the distribution of these items. The implied whiff of diablerie here is one of Ostap's ironic jokes, but when he returns to the town in chapter 35 he finds that the office has taken on a real existence and has been incorporated, name and all, into the local bureaucratic structures.

The Twelve Chairs and *The Golden Calf*, in the tradition of the picaresque, use the rogue and his travels in order to focus the satirical exposure of society. But in the context of the debates at the time, the satire had to have an ideologically sound target. The finale of both novels established a firmly "Soviet" moral and thus provided a measure of protection; the target of the mockery could be readily labelled as "relics of the past." Emigré critics, sympathetic to Ostap Bender's anarchic individualism, were equally confident that the novels were in fact mocking the absurdities of the Soviet regime. Both interpretations are correct. Ilf and Petrov believed in socialism but saw no reason to suppress their youthful merriment. Fortunately for the authors – and for the Russian reading public over the subsequent decades – the Soviet literary establishment proved able to accommodate them as licensed jesters. There was a period at the end of the 1940s when the novels came under attack and were not reprinted. One of the manifestations of the post-Stalinist "Thaw" in literature, however, was the republication in 1956 of *The Twelve Chairs* and *The Golden Calf*.

For the generation that came of age in the Thaw, the irrepressible, irreverent comic spirit of these two novels was part of the new freedom of that period. Ilf and Petrov parodied everything. The plots themselves are parodies: of the quest novel in *The Twelve Chairs* and the detective novel in *The Golden Calf*. Parody can also, of course, be a potent weapon for mocking and challenging authority. Clichés of post-revolutionary literature, theatre and cinema are joyously sent up by Ilf and Petrov, along with the Soviet habit of making interminable speeches about the international situation. The authors showed no more respect for the giants of Russian literature: the Tolstoian rejection of earthly values was travestied in *The Twelve Chairs* in the tale of the hussar-monk Aleksei Bulanov, and Dostoevskii's letters to his wife were wickedly parodied in the novel's subplot, in the letters that Father Fedor sends home. The parody extends even into the socialist holy of holies, the works of Marx and Lenin. Marx, echoed by Lenin, had said that the liberation of the proletariat must be achieved by the proletariat itself.[7] On the walls of a provincial club in chapter 34 of *The Twelve Chairs* this has been creatively deformed: a poster left over from a lecture on life-saving proclaims "Assistance to the drowning lies in the hands of the drowning themselves." In the late 1920s and 1930s most readers would have encountered the original before they met the parody. It is safe to say that since the 1950s most readers of *The Twelve Chairs* have met the parody first, which has the effect of comically alienating the original and undermining its authority. The laughter of Ilf and Petrov, tolerated by the establishment, was a force for intellectual liberation.

The laughter of Mikhail Bulgakov (1891–1940) proved less easy for Soviet literature to assimilate. In a letter of 28 March 1930 to the Soviet government he declared his deep skepticism with regard to the revolutionary process taking place in Russia.[8] This is reflected in his satirical story *Heart of a Dog*, which describes a surgical experiment that goes wrong and can be read as a parody of the great socio-political "experiment" of the Russian Revolution. *Heart of a Dog* was written in early 1925 but was not published in the Soviet Union until 1987. *The Master and Margarita*, after lying unpublished since its author's death, had reached the Soviet reader two decades earlier. The impact of *The Master and Margarita* upon literary Russia was liberating to the point of revelation.

The novel's list of characters was unusual for a start: the devil, in the guise of Professor Woland, paying a visit to Moscow; Pontius Pilate, governor of Judea in the time of Jesus Christ; and the figure of Jesus himself, here named Ieshua. One of the most haunting narratives in Western culture, the tale of the Passion of Christ, was retold in this novel. For half a century militant atheism had been part of official Soviet ideology and for most Soviet readers this was their first encounter with the cultural heritage of the Bible. Small wonder, then, that *The Master and Margarita* created a literary sensation, which was further enhanced by its use of the fantastic. Here were the familiar streets of Moscow, and here was the devil, walking down them, accompanied by a retinue which included a cat that paid for itself on trams and was a crack shot with a revolver. In the 1960s Bakhtin's literary theories, suppressed during the years of Stalinism, were re-entering Russian intellectual life. Bulgakov's novel was an exciting example of Bakhtin's theory of carnival laughter which, by breaking away from everything that is humdrum and generally accepted, allows the possibility of a completely new order of things.[9]

The activities of Woland and his suite generate the novel's satirical energy. Woland as a character can be compared to Ostap Bender, with the latter's sardonic magnificence here raised to a higher power. As an agent through which to organize a satirical exposure of society, the devil has the advantage of being both omnipotent and fantastic, traveling freely through space and time. Bulgakov's Woland cannot be equated with evil, for to do so makes nonsense of the novel, where he works for good. It is because of him that the Master and Margarita are reunited and the Master's novel, which is the Pilate chapters of *The Master and Margarita* itself, is preserved from destruction. In this sense Bulgakov's novel is a story about itself: the story of how a text, written against the spirit of the time in which it is composed, survives against all the odds in a fantastic realm that exists in parallel to the "real" world. One of the reasons why the novel could be published in the Soviet Union in 1966–67 in a censored form, and why the full text could be published in Moscow in 1973, is that the activities of Woland and the antics of his retinue create a screen – a dust cloud of diablerie, a noisy, carnival diversion – while the "novel about Pontius Pilate" is being smuggled through.

Analysis of the novel's satirical "hit-list" reveals that many of the targets are members of the literary and theatrical world. Of the two, it is the theatre people who escape most lightly: their sins are in the main venial ones of drunkenness, inefficiency and telling lies on the telephone. The irresponsibility of selling stale fish sandwiches in the theatre buffet is, however, serious enough to warrant a refined psychological punishment: prediction of the buffet manager's death from cancer. (Bulgakov trained and practiced as a doctor before turning to literature as a career.) Bulgakov was a dramatist as well as being a prose writer, and satirized his relationship with the Moscow Art Theatre in the unfinished novel *Teatral'nyi roman* (1936–37), translated under the title *Black Snow*. In *The Master and Margarita* the theatrical satire is in a slapstick mode, with the occasional sinister undertone. The literary satire is altogether more vengeful, as shown by a comparison of the two severed heads in the novel. When the theatre compère Bengalskii has his head torn off by Woland's cat during the performance at the Variety Theatre in chapter 12, this is reversible: Bengalskii's head is restored to its proper place on his shoulders. When the literary critic and journal editor Mikhail Berlioz is decapitated (by a tram) in chapter 3, he dies a gruesome death and his head is turned into a skull-goblet from which Woland in chapter 23 can drink a toast. Berlioz is being punished for an intellectual crime. He misused his considerable erudition to lead the young poet Bezdomnyi astray. He thus represents those members of the pre-revolutionary intelligentsia who turned into timeserving beneficiaries of the Soviet literary establishment. This new establishment buys ideological loyalty through the distribution of privileges. By the time that Woland and his henchmen leave Moscow, such centers of privilege as the Writers' Club and the special currency shop are charred and smoking ruins.

The Master and Margarita satirizes a society that has abandoned individual responsibility and conscience. This same theme is treated in nonsatirical mode in the five chapters of the novel (chapters 2, 16, 25, 26 and 32) which tell the story of that encounter in ancient Jerusalem between the Roman governor, Pontius Pilate, and the young Jewish philosopher, Ieshua. Pilate, under the historical and ideological pressures of the moment, commits an act of moral cowardice, for which he atones throughout the millennia until, at the end of the novel, he is granted release. Pilate's sin was to condemn to death a perfectly innocent man. This was one of the "mass sins" of the epoch in which the novel was written, an age of ideological extremes, in which Stalin's Russia and Hitler's Germany acted as mirror images of one another. The Pilate story in *The Master and Margarita* dramatizes the conflict between individual conscience and political expediency and, in its conclusion, demonstrates the possibility of forgiveness. *The Master and Margarita* is a great comic novel in which the satirical element is only one part of a larger whole.

The name of Mikhail Bulgakov re-entered the mainstream of Soviet culture from the Thaw onwards. The name of Evgenii Zamiatin (1884–1937) took longer to return. Zamiatin emigrated from the Soviet Union in 1931 and died in Paris. *We* was first published in English, French and Czech translations between 1924 and 1929; the first complete Russian text appeared in New York in 1952. The centenary of Zamiatin's birth provided a wonderful opportunity for comparison of *We* with George Orwell's *1984*, but both novels were unmentionable in print in a Soviet book or journal except in glancing references to them as "malicious pamphlets on the Soviet regime."

We is an anti-Utopia which uses science-fiction as a vehicle for social and political satire. Zamiatin was inspired by H. G. Wells, whose science-fiction he saw as providing an example of "mathematics and myths, physics and fantasy, blueprints and miracles, parody and prophecy."[10] This description is a statement of his own artistic method in *We*. Zamiatin was at home in the world of physics and mathematics for he was a marine architect who lectured on marine engineering at the St. Petersburg Polytechnic and spent 1916–17 in Britain supervising the construction of Russian icebreakers in shipyards on the Clyde and the Tyne. When in *We* he evokes both the religious zeal for compulsory salvation and the human desire for comfortable conformity, Zamiatin is parodying what he saw in Britain as well as prophesying on the basis of experience in post-revolutionary Russia. The plot outlines structures of control which correspond to a particular type of human mind-set. This is intellectual satire in the Shchedrinian mode, but where Shchedrin wields the Russian knout of sarcasm Zamiatin prefers a weapon that in an essay on "The New Russian Prose" he described as altogether more "European": the sword of irony.[11]

We is a novel of ideas which takes up the Dostoevskian debate on the nature of freedom, happiness and humanity. Its style is deliberately "modern," with recurring images that bring the ideas into swift and sharp focus, and it is full of ironic devices stemming from its use of the first-person narrator. A Utopia describes an ideal state or commonwealth; a dystopia depicts an ugly state system. The first irony is that our narrator thinks he is writing a Utopia, while we readers fast realize that this is a dystopia. On the very first page the narrator waxes lyrical about "ideal unfreedom"; he clearly enjoys obeying the rules of collectivity which the state imposes. Even his diary, that most personal of records, is written with the intention that it should be used as state propaganda. But he finds himself drawn into a rebellion against the state and here another level of irony enters: a discrepancy between what our narrator believes to be true and what is really the case. He offers us his own perspective on his circumstances, but we can deduce that the situation is very different from what he thinks. Other characters are concealing from him their true selves and purposes and he, meanwhile, is struggling with a new ironic twist to the meaning of "we": not the harmonious collective acting in unison but the two halves of a divided self, one of which now longs for the delirium of love and freedom, while the other wants to return to the original comfortable certainties in which there were no questions, just exclamations of praise for the system.

The satirical thrust of *We* is anti-Utopian, in that it is against the very idea of Utopia. Utopia leaves no room for questions: how can it, if it is ideal? Utopia is static, unchanging. But that is counter to the whole spirit of intellectual enquiry which should characterize the human race. This central idea of the novel is expressed in Entry 30 of the narrator's diary, where he is challenged to name the final number. When he protests that the number of numbers is infinite and it is therefore impossible to name the last one, he is told that the same is true of revolutions. The state ideology in which he had been educated had a myth of the "last revolution," but there is no "last revolution" just as there is no "last number." Zamiatin's novel expresses a warning that the Russian Revolution with its utopian dreams could, by regarding itself as the "last revolution," ossify into a static system intolerant of enquiry, incapable of self-renewal and sustainable only through oppression.

The major satirists of the 1920s and 1930s were born before the Revolution and, with the exception of Petrov, had all their schooling in the pre-revolutionary period. The next generation of satirists was entirely "home-grown." Fazil Iskander (born 1929) and Vladimir Voinovich (born 1932) started their literary careers in the Khrushchev era, that time of optimism in which it seemed that the Stalinist legacy could be overcome.

Iskander, an Abkhaz who lives in Moscow and writes in Russian, is both a poet and a prose writer. His prose, which on the surface appears very casual, in fact reveals the close affinity between poetic cadence and comic timing, an effect achieved by the author's presence in the text either as first-person narrator or as raconteur. He moves the plot along through a series of digressions, mostly comic but sometimes lyrical and, on occasions, openly moralistic. All these features are evident in the short novel *The Goatibex Constellation* (*Sozvezdie kozlotury*), a favorite with Russian readers ever since its first publication in 1966. The creature of the title, a cross between goat (*kozel*) and ibex (*tur*), becomes a symbol of Khrushchev's agricultural policies, which combined reform with a tendency to push particular initiatives too far. In popular wit these became identifed with the one word *kukuruza* ("maize or Indian corn"), widely sown as a result of a propaganda campaign but often in defiance of local climatic conditions. Of course by the time Iskander's novel was published Khrushchev had been ousted and his schemes officially derided as hair-brained, but the phrase *kozloturizatsiia zhivotnovodstva* ("the goatibexation of animal-breeding") goes beyond Khrushchev's corn and sounds suspiciously like a parody of *kollektivizatsiia sel'skogo khoziaistva* ("the collectivization of agriculture"), that cornerstone of Soviet ideology since the end of the 1920s. The preposterous word *kozloturizatsiia* casts a shimmer of doubt on the wisdom of *kollektivizatsiia*. Iskander's mockery is, however, always genial. *The Goatibex Constellation* belongs to a rare category: books that are both written and read with a smile.

Iskander managed to balance on an ideological tightrope, as shown by his novel *Sandro from Chegem*. The novel is composed of a series of self-contained stories and was published in the Soviet Union in 1973, but in abridged form; the complete edition appeared first in the West in 1979. In the introduction to the novel the author states that it was conceived as a parody of the picaresque. Sandro, the hero, is clearly a rogue; but his cunning is part of the cultural tradition he represents, the patriarchal society of Iskander's native Abkhazia. This, depicted with humor and admiration, stands as a kind of touchstone against which the Soviet era is measured. The novel is a mock epic, with Sandro maneuvring his way through the historical events of his time and adjusting to various types of regime. One of the story-chapters which was not published in the Soviet Union until 1988 is "Belshazzar's Feast," describing a banquet at which Sandro encounters Stalin. Sandro, though initially caught up in the universal awe of Stalin, retains his faculties of sharp-eyed observer. He thus offers a focus through which Iskander can depict this banquet as an anti-carnival, a travesty of the traditional Caucasian rites of hospitality. The form chosen by Iskander for *Sandro from Chegem*, individual stories linked by character and setting, enabled him to publish some in the West and some in Russia according to the possibilities of the moment. It also enabled him to continue adding new stories to the Sandro epos, although events in Abkhazia since the break-up of the Soviet Union have cast a retrospective shadow. After the former Soviet republic of Georgia was recognized as an independent state in 1992, Abkhazia fought a war of independence from Georgia, declaring itself a nation state in 1993. Today's war-ravaged zone presents a bleak contrast to the well-tended landscape of Iskander's fictional Abkhazia in *Sandro from Chegem*.

Iskander's short novel *Rabbits and Boa-Constrictors* was published in the West in 1982 and in the Soviet Union in 1987. It is Shchedrinian in its concern with the relationship between "the authorities" and "the people" in the two separate kingdoms of the title. The kingdom of the boa-constrictors represents the Soviet regime, with parodic speeches, slogans and songs. The boa-constrictors keep the rabbit population in a state of terror by the device of "hypnosis." One of the rabbits (a figure whose distant human prototype is Solzhenitsyn) proves that the "hypnosis" does not in fact exist and is simply a product of the rabbits' own fear. This discovery should bring liberation to the rabbits, but it does not. It has by now become clear that the rabbit kingdom is also a parody of the Soviet regime, with the populace kept in a state of subjugation by the constant promise of Cauliflower, a comically inspired metaphor for Communism. Because no one has ever seen cauliflower, it is depicted on the state banners in wonderful rainbow hues. Meanwhile in the kingdom of the boa-constrictors another discovery has been made: hypnosis is not needed; the snake simply has to wrap its body around the rabbit and suffocate it. At this point the jungle turns into a parody gymnasium as the snakes go into training to develop the stomach muscles they now need in order to kill their prey. Thus new methods of control evolve and the law of the power-jungle prevails. *Rabbits and Boa-Constrictors* is a sombre fable embroidered with brilliant comic detail.

Vladimir Voinovich is the creator of Ivan Chonkin, a character to rank in European literature with Jaroslav Hašek's good soldier Šveik. The first two parts of *The Life and Extraordinary Adventures of Private Ivan Chonkin* were written 1963–70 and published in the West in 1975. Volume II (parts 3 and 4), entitled *Pretender to the Throne*, was published in Paris in 1979. In 1980 Voinovich emigrated to Germany and was deprived of his Soviet citizenship. It was only in 1988–89 that Chonkin reached the Soviet reader in a Soviet publication. Volume II followed in 1990.

Chonkin has two lines of literary genealogy. He is a refutation of the "positive hero" of Socialist Realism and a reincarnation of one of the best-loved characters of Russian folklore, Ivan the Fool. Where the "positive hero" is a very paragon of ideological soundness, Chonkin is a simpleton who never understands the language of ideology. This device of the character's "not understanding" is a means by which the satirist can expose the gap between official rhetoric and plain reality. In the traditional tales, Ivan the Fool starts off life in the most underprivileged of situations: ugly, dirty and of low birth, he is the character whom everyone else pushes around. This is exactly the position of Chonkin at the beginning of the novel. But in the course of the tale Ivan the Fool accomplishes heroic feats and emerges at the end, handsome and triumphant, to win the hand of the princess in marriage. He is an anti-hero who is in fact a cleverly masked ideal hero. The same is true of Chonkin, who in a series of hilarious plot-twists, comes to display not only a native Russian ingenuity but also the ideal Soviet virtues of loyalty, labor and valor, exposing the absence of these qualities in the society around him.

The satirical panorama in *Chonkin* is achieved not by making the hero mobile but, on the contrary, by fixing him to the spot. In volume I Chonkin is sent to guard a plane with instructions (which he fulfils almost to the letter) not to stray a step from it; throughout volume II Chonkin is in prison. He is, however, the hub around which the whole plot wheels, gathering sweep and momentum and generating multiple misunderstandings. By the end of volume I a Soviet general and a regiment have been diverted from the war to deal with Chonkin, but by the end of volume II he has invaded the dreams of both Stalin and Hitler and, unbeknown to all historians of the Second World War apart from the narrator, Chonkin has saved Moscow.

Voinovich in an interview with *The Literary Gazette* (*Literaturnaia gazeta*) of 20 June 1990 (p. 8) revealed his plans for the last part of the novel, in which Chonkin at the end of the war is to find himself in the West, where he stays, becoming owner of a large American farm (the modern equivalent of marrying the princess), and even flying his own plane. He returns to Russia with a trade delegation in the Gorbachev era and seeks out Niura, who in volume II was pregnant with his baby. Their meeting is a sad one. He has a smile of porcelain-crowned teeth while she has no teeth at all. Thus Voinovich confronts his comic hero of Russian folklore with Russia's historical tragedy, embodied by Niura. It is possible that Voinovich will complete his Chonkin story not in a separate volume but as part of his autobiographical testament, *The Grand Design*, the first installment of which was published in 1994. This reflects the fact that the writing of Chonkin changed the course of its author's life by causing him to be ejected from his native land.

In 1982 in Germany, looking back at Russia from the painful distance of exile, Voinovich started his novel *Moscow 2042*. It was published in the West in 1986 and in Russia in 1990. *Moscow 2042* is in the Zamiatin line of satirical science-fiction, while the title acknowledges the debt to Orwell's *1984*. Moscow in 2042 is a parody of the Moscow that Voinovich left in 1980, with its characteristics exaggerated to grotesque absurdity. The humor is provided by the first-person narrator, an exiled writer who time-travels sixty years ahead from 1982 and finds his native land celebrating the centenary of his birth (Voinovich here making his alter-ego a decade younger than himself). In the novel there is another writer-figure who participates in both centuries and whose prototype is Solzhenitsyn. Voinovich subjects this contemporary giant to the same methods of parodic portrayal as he employs in his depiction of Moscow: grotesque extrapolation. The resulting caricature of course gave great offense but it raises a fundamental point about the Russian tradition in which a writer has moral authority greater than that of the State. Voinovich's satire of Solzhenitsyn subjects this idea to critical examination: just because a major writer is in opposition to the State does not necessarily mean that his ideas should be uncritically embraced. The narrator leaves a Moscow of 2042 which has overnight changed all its ideological signs and emblems while remaining fundamentally the same in its mentality of worshipful acquiescence. To this extent, although with a different emphasis, Voinovich's novel concurs with the gloomy model proposed in Iskander's *Rabbits and Boa-Constrictors*. But Voinovich has the eternal optimism of the satirist who hopes that his fiction will operate as a kind of "prophecy in reverse" and, by predicting things, prevent them.

Intellectual life in the Soviet Union in the 1970s and the first half of the 1980s was characterized by a mood that can with hindsight be identified as *fin-de-régime*. A work that expresses this most clearly is *Yawning Heights* (*Ziiaiushchie vysoty*) by Aleksandr Zinovev (born 1922). Written in 1974–75 and published in the West in 1976, it is a novel that recalls the original meaning of the word satire: a mixture or mish-mash. Six hundred separate fragments of text each with its own title and composed in different styles are linked by recurring topics of conversation between and about the characters, generically labelled as "Writer," "Artist," "Dauber," "Bawler." The prototypes of some can be identified, "Truth-Teller," for example, being Solzhenitsyn (whose importance in Russian culture of this period is demonstrated by the appearance yet again of a "Solzhenitsyn-character"). Zinovev was a distinguished academic philosopher before he turned fiction-writer, and the satire is Shchedrinian in its intellectual ferocity. Stupidsville here is the town of Ibansk, a name which is a pun on the most common Russian forename combined with the Russian verb *ebat'* ("to fuck"). The title too is a pun, achieved by altering the first letter in the word "shining" (*siiaiushchii*) to transform it into "yawning" (*ziiaiushchii*). *Yawning Heights* evokes a towering fraud and an abyss of boredom. The fragments of text with their mercilessly aphoristic formulations reflect the circularity, frustration, and despair of the arguments conducted during this period by the Russian intelligentsia, cramped and isolated for want of an open forum for public debate. In 1978 Zinovev was forced into emigration, where he has continued to write, using the same fragmentary form. Sheer volume has weakened the effect, but the impact made in its time by *Yawning Heights* has to be recognized.

The circularity of despair is enacted in another mode by Venedikt Erofeev (1938–1990) in *Moskva–Petushki*, variously translated as *Moscow Circles*, *Moscow Stations* and *Moscow to the End of the Line*. This short novel was written in 1969 and first published abroad in 1973. Intensely funny and full of literary allusions, it is composed in a style which achieves lyrical pathos while simultaneously imitating the inebriated state of its first-person narrator named, like the author, Venedikt Erofeev. It is his mono-logue during a journey from Moscow to Petushki, which he never reaches because he is too drunk to get off the train, and it carries him back to his starting point. He is both traveling rogue and drunken innocent. With all the refinement of a connoisseur he introduces us to cocktail recipes that have poetic names like "The tear of a young Communist girl" but contain throat-searing ingredients like varnish and anti-perspirant for the feet. This is Russian intellectual jokery stripped to its living soul and laughing through all too visibly drunken tears. The drunkenness is both real and metaphorical, representing a refusal to participate in any of the require-ments of official society. The book's poignancy lies in the way that this deliberate self-destruction is transformed through the work of art into an act of self-creation.

Erofeev's book was first published in the Soviet Union in 1988–89; *Yawning Heights* appeared in a Soviet publication in 1990. With the partial exception of Bulgakov, the Soviet publication dates of previously banned satirical works thus all fall within the period 1987–90, when novels written sixty years apart were being published virtually simultaneously. The satirical novel here simply exemplifies the "catching up" that occurred in every area of culture during the first period of *glasnost'*. Of course copies of banned literature had been in secret circulation long before then, but this was patchy and risky, particularly for youngsters or those without position or patronage. Now these books could be not only read but also discussed openly and in print. Intellectual Russia plunged into an orgy of reading from which it emerged, giddy and blinking, into the new post-Soviet era.

The first question now must be whether Soviet satire can retain its relevance in post-Soviet conditions. That begs the further question of how different the conditions are going to be. *Dead Souls* has, after all, outlived serfdom. In terms of the satirists themselves, they fall into two categories: those like Shchedrin, Zamiatin and Zinovev, who deal with structures and whose work will appeal primarily to intellectual circles; and those writers whose books can reach a mass readership. It is easier for the novel with a strong central hero to capture the popular imagination, and certainly the initial post-Soviet period offers plenty of scope for roguery, with numerous enterprises that resemble Chichikov's "dead souls" or Bender's "Horns and Hoofs." The present situation in Russia can in turn be expected to produce a crop of satirical works, for times of sudden transition with their attendant incongruities have generally been fruitful for the writing of satire. How the post-Soviet Russian state will tolerate its satire remains to be seen, which leads back into the question of how different the new society will be, and in what ways.

NOTES

1. Charles A. Moser (ed.), *The Cambridge History of Russian Literature*, rev. edn (Cambridge University Press, 1992), see index for: Kantemir; Sumarokov; Krylov; Novikov; Griboedov; *The Tale of Frol Skobeev* (p. 36); and Mikhail Chulkov's *The Comely Cook*, or *The Adventures of a Debauched Woman* (pp. 69–70).
2. Christine J. Whitbourn (ed.), *Knaves and Swindlers: Essays on the Picaresque Novel in Europe* (London, New York, and Toronto: Oxford University Press, 1974).
3. T. E. Little, "Dead Souls," in Whitbourn (ed.), *Knaves and Swindlers*, p. 115.
4. Vissarion Belinsky, "Letter to N. V. Gogol," in W. J. Leatherbarrow and D. C. Offord (trans. and ed.), *A Documentary History of Russian Thought* (Ann Arbor: Ardis, 1987), pp. 130–35.
5. Mikhail Bakhtin, *Rabelais and his World*, trans. Hélène Iswolsky (Cambridge, Mass.: The MIT Press, 1968), p. 45.
6. Robert Russell, "Satire and socialism: the Russian debates," *Forum for Modern Language Studies*, 30, 4 (1994), 341–52.
7. Karl Marx, Inaugural address to the International Workingmen's Association (1864): "the emancipation of the working class must be won by the working class itself." V. I. Lenin, Speech at the Fourth Conference of Trade Unions and Factory Committees, Moscow (27 June–2 July 1918): "the emancipation of the workers must be done by the workers themselves."
8. J. A. E. Curtis, *Manuscripts Don't Burn. A Life in Diaries and Letters: Mikhail Bulgakov* (London: Bloomsbury, 1991), p. 107.
9. Bakhtin, *Rabelais and his World*, p. 34.
10. E. Zamiatin, "H. G. Wells," in Zamiatin, *A Soviet Heretic: Essays by Yevgeny Zamyatin*, trans. and ed. Mirra Ginsburg (Chicago and London: University of Chicago Press, 1970), p. 270.
11. Zamiatin, "The New Russian Prose," in Zamiatin, *A Soviet Heretic*, p. 103.

6

JOSTEIN BØRTNES

Religion

Speaking of the "Russian novel," we often refer to the classical canon of highly individual works by the great nineteenth-century Russian authors. It is, however, also possible to define the "Russian novel" somewhat differently, as an open adaptive system in which the individual works are parts of a continuous development. In this system, characters and events are represented according to a set of patterns, or schemata, that are subject to constant variation when applied to the social world around us and to the processes that take place in people's minds. These are the two basic aspects of narrative – the "landscape of action" and the "landscape of consciousness" – the two landscapes that according to Jerome Bruner characterize this mode of thought as opposed to the logico-scientific, or "paradigmatic" mode.[1]

The outer landscape of action unfolds according to an action pattern, or plot. But in this landscape of action changes occur because of changes taking place in the inner landscapes of the characters involved. To understand a narrative is therefore to have an understanding of the changes both in the characters' inner landscape of thought and in the outer landscape of events. The two are aspects of the same, since, as Michael Carrithers puts it, "the metamorphosis of thought entails the metamorphosis of social relations and vice versa."[2] In the following, our attention will be centered on the function of art and religion in the "dual landscape" of the Russian novel, understood as an open adaptive system.

The idea of a "dual landscape" – the interaction between characters and plots – is particularly appropriate in the study of the Russian novel. The characters, the plight into which they have fallen, and their consciousness, are here so closely interwoven that we understand the characters only as they are revealed to us in the sequence of events, in constant interaction with their surroundings and with one another. In this sense, it is the imaginative application of the narrative mode to novel-writing that enables us as readers to move so easily from literature to the extra-literary spheres of self-knowledge, social theory, religion and politics. Each novel is a *possible world*, its protagonists *potential characters* that come to life through the reader's imaginative understanding.

By the middle of the last century, the problem of selfhood had become acute in Russia. The ideal of self in Orthodox anthropology, based on the story of man being created in God's image and likeness, was no longer universally accepted. In Orthodox anthropology, to be created in the image of God is to have the possibility of restoring the divine likeness that was lost through the Fall. This task assigned to every Christian was made possible by the Incarnation. In the human figure of Christ, divine likeness is realized to a perfect degree, and all Christians may consciously, by an act of their own free will and to the extent of their possibilities, enter upon the task of creating in themselves the likeness of God in imitation of Christ's archetype.

The idea of Christian self-realization in imitation of Christ is deeply embedded in the divine service of the Orthodox Church, and its visual expression is found in the art of the icon. It is part of a religious heritage of all Russians brought up in the Orthodox faith. Towards the end of the eighteenth and at the beginning of the nineteenth century, however, the validity of Orthodox anthropology was increasingly questioned as Russian intellectuals came under the spell of the Enlightenment and were deeply stirred by Rousseau's idea of the inborn goodness of "natural man," his idea of an uncorrupted natural self hidden by layers of repression caused by socialization and acculturation.

Rousseau's ideas are at the center of Russian debate about society and the nature of man during the 1780s and 1790s, when people like Fonvizin and Radishchev often developed their views of human nature and society in polemical opposition to the Genevan philosopher. According to the Tartu semiotician Yurii Lotman, Fonvizin, in particular, attacked Rousseau's idea of the natural goodness of man, arguing that man is born with the rudiments of vice and inclined towards evil from childhood on. To Fonvizin, therefore, the child acquires a self not by being set free from social constraints, but by integration into the ethical and religious whole of a just society, not to be confounded with the selfish and fragmented Russian society of the day.[3]

A different reaction to Rousseau is found in the writings of the Russian freemasons. In their rejection of Rousseau's anthropology, they come closer to Montesquieu's thesis of an inborn evil from which a person can free himself only through moral rebirth as a precondition of a just organization of society. Yurii Lotman locates the beginning of the "great argument with Rousseau" in late eighteenth-century Russian freemasonry, "the essence of which was formulated by Dostoevskii in his drafts for *A Raw Youth*, when he says about his hero: 'He hates the Geneva ideas (i.e. philanthropy, i.e. virtue without Christ) and does not recognize anything natural in virtue'." (Lotman, "Russo i russkaia kul'tura," p. 87).

The dichotomy of "man is evil by nature" and "man is good by nature" became a constant feature in nineteenth-century Russian thought. It is symptomatic of the fate of Rousseau's natural man in Russia that Pushkin in his poem *The Gypsies* (1824) represents the whole idea of innocent nature as a myth and in his hero demonstrates the impossibility of becoming "natural" by casting aside the vestments of civilization.

The dilemma was deepened with the arrival of the Romantic cult of the genius. In Russia, as in the rest of Europe, this cult found striking expression in the adoration of Napoleon, in whose genius Hegel saw an incarnation of the "spirit of history." In his philosophy, history is moved forward through the actions of "world-historical individuals," whose mission sets them apart from the rest of humanity and exempts them from the ethical laws of ordinary people.

There is an early allusion to the Russian cult of Napoleon in *Evgenii Onegin*, in stanza XIV of the second chapter:

> To us all others are just zeros
> And we ourselves the chosen few.
> We all aim at becoming Napoleons;
> The many millions of two-legged creatures
> Are only tools for us[.]

To Pushkin, in contrast to Hegel, Napoleon more and more stood out as the supreme symbol of individual egoism in post-Enlightenment European philosophy. Yurii Lotman has argued that the "We" of these lines, from whom the poet distances himself through his irony, refers to a whole generation of Russian Romantic egoists, including many of the Decembrists, whose ideas Pushkin did not share and of which he became increasingly critical. To Pushkin, Napoleon's achievements were a manifestation of political amoralism and readiness to sacrifice everything in order to satisfy his own personal ambitions, qualities that in Pushkin's view were the ethical equivalents of political despotism.[4]

Ten years later, Pushkin embodied this Napoleonic mentality in the figure of Hermann in *The Queen of Spades*, a hero with "at least three crimes" upon his conscience, whose comrades are repeatedly struck by his resemblance to Napoleon.

But Hermann's individual egoism manifests itself in the private, not in the public sphere. His amoralism is much more akin to Julien Sorel's in Stendhal's novel, *The Red and the Black* (*Le rouge et le noir*, 1830), another of Napoleon's emulators in the nineteenth-century novel, and to Raskolnikov in *Crime and Punishment* (1866) whose admiration for Napoleon has taken complete possession of the "inner landscape" of his mind. Like Raskolnikov, Hermann seeks to rob an old woman of her treasure in order to satisfy his personal ambitions, bringing suffering upon himself by killing her, just as Raskolnikov must suffer when he murders the old pawnbroker and her sister.

It is more difficult to see a Napoleonic hero in Chichikov, the adventurous rogue who dominates the scene in the first part of Gogol's unfinished novel, *Dead Souls*, published in 1842. But when the provincial authorities try to identify this unknown buyer of "dead souls," "among a number of shrewd suggestions there was, strange to say, one to the effect that Chichikov might be Napoleon in disguise":

> thinking it over each for himself, they found that Chichikov's face, when he turned round and stood sideways, was very much like a portrait of Napoleon.
> (*Dead Souls*, chapter 9)

As Lotman has pointed out, however, there is a functional resemblance between the three. All three are tempters, incarnations of evil; Hermann and Raskolnikov as manifestations of Romantic egoism, Chichikov as their comic counterpart.[5]

In Gogol, as well as in Pushkin, the optimistic and revolutionary ideologies underlying the philosophical anthropology of the Enlightenment and Romanticism were reinterpreted in the light of their own tragic vision of the moral universe. Gogol's *Dead Souls* was intended as Christian epic in the form of a novel. In its unfinished part II, Chichikov should have continued to buy dead souls, but also should have gotten involved in other illegal activities, been caught, thrown into prison, and deported to Siberia. Here, he should have undergone a spiritual resurrection and begun a new life. The same fate awaited Tentetnikov, the ne'er-do-well hero of part II. Deported to Siberia for his participation in subversive political activity, he should have "woken up" and begun a new life together with Ulenka, the general's daughter. But to Gogol and his contemporaries Ulenka's heroic behavior would have been associated with the wives of the Decembrists who had chosen a life in Siberian exile together with their husbands.[6]

In the unfinished part II of *Dead Souls*, Gogol's narrative imagination has outlined a pattern of events which in the outer "landscape of action" may be divided into the three phases of a transitional rite as summarized by Victor and Edith Turner in their article "Religious Celebrations": first a phase of transgression, culminating in the separation of the hero as a criminal from the rest of society and his spiritual "death." This phase of *separation* is followed by the *liminal* phase (from *limen* meaning "threshold" in Latin), a kind of social limbo. The liminal phase may be broken down into three major events: (1) the communication of *sacra*, i.e. of symbolic things and actions representing society's religious mysteries, (2) *ludic recombination* (from Latin *ludus*, "play," "jest," etc.) – the free and playful rearrangement of traditional cultural factors in new and unexpected configurations, however bizarre and outrageous, and (3) the fostering of *communitas*, defined as "a bond uniting people over and above any formal social bonds." The Turners compare *communitas* to Martin Buber's "flowing from I to Thou": it "does not merge identities; instead it liberates them from conformity to general norms, so that they experience one another concretely and not in terms of social structural . . . abstractions." The third phase, the phase of *reaggregation*, or *reincorporation*, marks the triumph over death, and resurrection to a new life.[7] In the Russian novel, the patterns of archaic *rites de passage* are "individualized" in the sense that the authors not only experience the traditional liminoid phenomena of Russian culture, but *create* their own variations on the cultural heritage.[8]

What is missing from the action pattern of Gogol's novel when seen in the light of this scheme, is the factor by which the reversal of events and the hero's spiritual metamorphosis are brought about. To judge from Aleksandr Bukharev's conversations with Gogol, however, it looks as if he had intended Chichikov's "resurrection" to come as a result of the tsar's direct intervention. But the idea was never realized, and it is easy to see why. Bringing the tsar into the phase of liminality would have resulted in a carnivalization of his figure and everything he symbolized. It is only when we come to the classical novels of the 1860s and 1870s that this problem is solved. And it is solved by bringing art and religion into play in the process of transforming the hero's self.

The first of the great novelists to apply this method is Turgenev in *Fathers and Children* (1862). Bazarov, the hero of the novel, has been alienated from the world of his parents and the traditional values of Russian society. They have been replaced by a set of ideas acquired through the study of modern Western materialism. The journey back from university to spend the summer holiday with his parents takes him through the ambiguous chronotope which from our present point of view we recognize as liminal. It is a time-space in which the *sacra* of the "fathers" are ridiculed and distorted in the most absurd ways when seen with the eyes of the "children." But the reversal of traditional values is only one aspect of the action pattern. Bazarov's savage criticism of contemporary Russian society and the idealism of the older generation demonstrates their inability to live up to their own high standards. At the same time, however, Bazarov in the course of the novel embraces every position he has denounced: he defends his honor by fighting a ridiculous duel, falls in love, and when rejected realizes that love is much more than the purely physiological phenomenon of his theories. When, eventually, he returns to his parents and begins to share his father's practice as a country doctor, he is finally reintegrated into the fabric of daily life and responds to its prosaic needs.

Bazarov's journey is a process of reintegration. But it is also a communication of the sacred, represented in the words, images, and actions from the Christian sphere that Turgenev has mounted into Bazarov's story, often in an ironic way that conceals the deeper meaning of the novel's religious symbolism.

The image of the sacred appears in the fresco of the Resurrection of Christ that Bazarov drives past on his way to Anna Sergeevna, the woman with whom he falls in love. But it is typical of liminality that the sacred image has been distorted and all attention is drawn to the marginal figure of a dark-complexioned warrior "lying outstretched in the foreground" (chapter XVI), whereas the central motif of the angel of the Lord who, according to St. Matthew 28:2–4, "descended from heaven," is passed over in silence. The motif of the angel has been detached from the Resurrection image and appears in "ludic recombination" with Anna Sergeevna, the "angel from heaven" whose arrival at Bazarov's deathbed inspires his father with new hope that this son will be saved (chapter XXVII).

Through an ironic recombination of the sacred and the profane, Anna Sergeevna is transformed into a symbol of love as the cosmic force by which Bazarov is reborn to a new life beyond death. During their last encounter, when he knows that he is already dying, Bazarov points at his powerless body, lying "outstretched" before him, just like the body described in the fresco painting. The repetition is all the more remarkable since the word is not a common one, and it occurs only twice in the whole novel, establishing a correspondence between Bazarov and the warrior in St. Matthew, who, for fear of the angel, "became as dead."

At this point of the story, Bazarov has reached the stage of reaggregation, when he will be reunited with the sacred power of the holy rituals:

> Father Alexis performed the last rites of religion over him. When he was anointed, when the holy oil touched his breast, one of his eyes opened, and it seemed that at the sight of the priest in his robes, the smoke from the censers, the candles before the icon, something like a shudder of horror was reflected in his lifeless face.
>
> (chapter XXVII)

The story of Bazarov's new life begins in the epilogue, where he is resurrected in the loving memory of his parents, and the flowers on his grave "tell us not only of eternal peace alone, of that great peace of 'indifferent' nature; they tell us, too, of eternal reconciliation, and of life without end." (chapter XXVIII).

Modern readers do not immediately recognize these last lines of *Fathers and Children* as quotations – the phrase "indifferent nature" is taken from Pushkin's poem, "When I wander along noisy streets," the other "life without end" from the Orthodox funeral hymn "With the holy, O Lord, give Thy servant peace." To contemporary readers, however, the allusions hidden in the final paragraph were quite clear. Herzen even found it necessary to warn Turgenev in a letter that his "requiem at the end with its distant approach to the immortality of the soul is fine, but dangerous."[9] Today, we have to rediscover this "distant approach to the immortality of the soul" in order to understand the meaning of Bazarov's death as part of his life story.

In Russian literary criticism of the time, Bazarov was seen as the first literary depiction of the "new man" of the 1860s. Dostoevskii's Rodion Raskolnikov, the hero of *Crime and Punishment* (1866), is another. And the close affinity between them was immediately recognized. Bazarov and Raskolnikov were both regarded as serious attempts to understand the "nihilist" mentality of the new young people, not as a wild and pre-posterous aberration, but as a tragic distortion of the mind, leading to severe suffering. From a literary point of view, both are descendants of the Napoleonic hero of Russian Romanticism. In Bazarov, this is implicit in his role as an outsider, his scorn for humanity, and his idea of himself as a giant. In Raskolnikov, on the other hand, the idea of becoming like Napoleon has become an obsession.

Crime and Punishment begins by representing the hero in the phase of separation. He withdraws from the rest of the world in order to plan the murder of the old pawnbroker, the acid test by which he is going to prove to himself that he is one of the "extraordinary" men, the movers of history, who, like Napoleon, are all natural criminals who never hesitate to shed blood, provided that the blood is shed to their own advantage.

It is not difficult to recognize in Raskolnikov's theory the same dis-tinction as in *Evgenii Onegin* between the "chosen few" and the "millions of two-legged creatures." What is new in Raskolnikov's version is his extension of exceptional people to comprise all *"new people"*, including himself. By internalizing the theory of Romantic egoism, Raskolnikov becomes a "foreign translation" (part II, chapter 6), an expression used about him and his likes by his friend Razumikhin. From the moment he conceives his crime to the moment of his confession, Raskolnikov lives in a kind of social limbo, representing the first stage in the second, central phase in his story, the phase of liminality. In this liminal phase, Raskolnikov enters a chronotope that no longer coincides with the time–space perception of normal experience. When he falls ill and suffers a mental breakdown, time closes in on him in a way that corresponds to the way his disease confines him to his lodgings, which to his mother give the impression of a "tomb" (III, 3). From this liminal state he is to emerge only gradually, in a process that will eventually lead to his reintegration, his return as a resurrected person to the prosaic world of everyday life that opens up as a potential future towards the end of his story.

This process begins when Raskolnikov meets Sonia Marmeladova, the prostitute with whom he, the murderer, develops a relationship based on their common status as social outcasts. Initially he sees in her a possible ally against society. But her love, sprung from her Christian faith, gives her a sacred power, the power of the weak and powerless, which in their encounters penetrates his consciousness, enabling Raskolnikov to see his plight in the light of the symbolic message of the New Testament. When Sonia, at his "strange request" (IV, 4), reads out to him the story from St. John about the Raising of Lazarus, the possibility of a resurrection and new life begins to take form in his mind.

The whole atmosphere of this scene is one of *ludic recombination*: the sacred message of the Gospel is quoted verbatim in Sonia's words and communicated to the murderer by her, the prostitute. At the same time, the Christian *sacra*, the cross and the New Testament, are displayed in the very room where she receives her clients. And in this room Raskolnikov realizes that by killing the old woman he killed his own self: "There and then I did myself in, at one blow, forever! . . . But it was the devil who killed the old woman, not I . . ." (v, 4). But it is in this room, too, that Raskolnikov accepts the cypress-wood cross from Sonia, clearly recognizing the significance of his act: "This, then, is the symbol of my taking up the cross" (VI, 8).

From this point onwards, the Gospel accounts of Lazarus' resurrection, and of Christ's death and Resurrection, form a pattern underlying the representation of Raskolnikov's descent into the hell of the Siberian prison, where in his dream about the plague Raskolnikov finally conquers the forces of evil that have transformed his mind into an inferno.

Siberia is above all the landscape of liminality in the Russian novel. From his confinement Raskolnikov views the land of freedom across the river that divides the world of the convicts from the free world outside. And here, on the bank of the river, Raskolnikov's regeneration begins one early morning in the second week after Easter – the feast celebrating Christ's descent into hell, his victory over death, and Resurrection – it begins at the moment when for the first time in their life together Sonia understands that he loves her, and when he knows "with what infinite love he will now expiate all her sufferings" (Epilogue, 2). This is the moment of pure *communitas*, when "love has resurrected them, and the heart of each held endless springs of life for the heart of the other" (Epilogue, 2).

By juxtaposing his own story with the New-Testament narrative about the resurrection of Lazarus and the Easter celebration of Christ's Resurrection, Dostoevskii has brought together two different registers, one sacred, the other profane, establishing a complex relationship of equivalence and difference between Christ's archetype and Raskolnikov's process of restoring his own self in the image of the archetype. The fundamental pattern underlying this juxtaposition is that of thematic variation, a movement from the theme to the discovery of a new variation, a "slippage," to use Douglas Hofstadter's term.[10]

In *Crime and Punishment*, the slippage from archetype to variation represents Dostoevskii's radical understanding of the Gospel. Every human being, even a murderer, is a potential image of Christ.

The slippability of archetypal patterns depends on their *underdetermining character*, allowing for both approximate predictability and innovation, for repetition with constant variation. They are not like fixed schemes that can only be reproduced over and over again, but flexible and adaptable to constant contextual change and reinterpretation.

In Dostoevskii's œuvre, the adaptivity of the regeneration pattern is most evident in his last novel, *The Brothers Karamazov* (1880). The theme of death and resurrection is anticipated already in the epigraph to the novel, the words from John 12:24 about the corn of wheat that "if it die, it bringeth forth much fruit." After the murder of their father, the central characters of the novel – the brothers Ivan, Alesha, their elder half-brother Dmitrii and the bastard Smerdiakov – go through a crisis that in the lives of each of them can be described as a variation of the same theme as that underlying Raskolnikov's story.

The pattern is most easily recognizable in the novice Alesha's return to the world after the death of his spiritual father, the elder Zosima. The account of Alesha's transition reaches a climax when in a state of drowsiness at the elder's coffin he hears Father Paisii read about the wedding in Cana and the words of the Gospel merge with his own in a vision of the dead Zosima among the wedding guests, inviting him to come into the presence of Christ in the image of "our Sun": "And you see our Sun, do you see Him? . . . Do not fear Him. He is terrible in His Majesty before us, awful in His sublimity, but infinitely merciful. He has made Himself like unto us from love and rejoices with us" (book VII, chapter 4). With a last glance at his spiritual father, lying in the coffin "with the icon on his breast and the peaked hood with the octangular cross, on his head" (book VII, chapter 4), Alesha leaves the cell and walks out into the night. "The silence of the earth seemed to melt into the silence of the heavens. The mystery of the earth was one with the mystery of the stars . . ." Overcome, he falls onto the earth, embraces it and kisses it; "with every instant he felt clearly and, as it were, tangibly, that something firm and unshakeable as that vault of heaven had entered into his soul. It was as though some idea had seized the sovereignty of his mind. He had fallen on the earth a weak youth, but he stood up a resolute champion, and he knew and felt it suddenly at the very moment of his ecstasy. 'Someone visited my soul at that moment,' he used to say afterwards" (book VII, chapter 4).

Alesha has passed from one stage to another through the internalization of Zosima, his spiritual father figure, and his ideas. Now he is ready to follow the elder's last command: "Within three days he left the monastery in accordance with the words of the elder, who had bidden him to 'sojourn in the world'" (book VII, chapter 4). And when at the very end of the novel, after Iliushechka's funeral, he gathers around him a group of boys – about twelve of them – at the stone where Iliushechka's father had wanted to bury his son, the whole scene suggests the archetypal image of Christ surrounded by his apostles. With his farewell speech in remembrance of the dead boy, Alesha establishes a new community, or *communitas*, in which the dead boy is transfigured into a living presence in each of them. This experience of eternal memory – the *Vechnaia pamiat'* of the funeral hymn – creates an awareness of immortality that culminates in an enraptured confession of faith in the Resurrection. Alesha has become the founder of a new, alternative Christian community outside the monastery and outside the official Russian Church. From this point of view, Alesha's return to the world is no less radical than Raskolnikov's.

As variations of the same pattern, the process of liminality in the lives of Alesha's brothers is less complete. And the degree of completeness depends on each brother's involvement in the murder of their father. Dmitrii comes next to Alesha in degree of innocence. As the innocent suspect he faces deportation to Siberia if found guilty. In his prison cell, he undergoes a metamorphosis not unlike Alesha's:

A new man has risen up in me. He was hidden in me, but would not have come to surface, if it hadn't been for this blow from heaven . . . And what do I care if I spend twenty years in the mines . . . It is something else that terrifies me now: that the resurrected man may leave me! . . . we shall be in chains

and there will be no freedom, but then, in our great sorrow, we shall rise
again to joy, without which man cannot live nor God exist . . .

(book XI, chapter 4)

Ivan, Alesha's full brother, is the last manifestation of the Romantic rebel in
Dostoevskii's world. Ivan rejects the idea of a natural goodness in man,
maintaining that there is no virtue if there is no belief in God and
immortality, and that without this belief everything is permitted. But he
finds himself in a dilemma, unable to decide whether or not he himself
believes in the immortality of his own soul.

Like his brothers, Ivan is on the road to rebirth. In his case, the process
of liminality takes the form of a personality split and mental derangement.
His mind is turned into an intellectual limbo where the universal questions
of God's existence and immortality are "turned inside out" (book V, chapter
3). "Ivan is a tomb" says Dmitrii. To Alesha, "Ivan is an enigma" (book V,
chapter 3), until, finally, he begins to understand what his brother is going
through: "God, in whom he did not believe, and God's truth were
conquering a heart which did not want to submit" (book XI, chapter 10).

Ivan's personality split leads to an internalized dialogue in which
different voices strive to gain control over his mind in a struggle objectified
in his dystopian prose poem, "The Grand Inquisitor," and in his interview
with the devil, in whose words he recognizes "everything that is stupid in
his own nature, outgrown, thrashed out in my mind long ago" (book XI,
chapter 9).

Ivan's dialogue with the devil makes it clear, as Victor Terras has
observed, that "behind his Grand Inquisitor's professed compassion for
suffering humanity, there is hidden a deep hatred of human freedom and of
the image of God in man."[11] From a generic point of view, Ivan's poem is a
travesty of the temptation of Jesus in the desert, or, in anthropological
terms, a *ludic recombination* of Christian elements into a grotesque and
melodramatic encounter between Christ, returned to earth, and his satan-
ized vicar. But not only the Grand Inquisitor is a projection of Ivan's mind.
The silent figure of Christ listening to the Inquisitor's nocturnal diatribes is
another, or, more precisely, the figure symbolizes another Ivan, formed in
the image of Christ's divine archetype.

In Ivan's abstractions, as well as in the reasoning of his Grand Inquisitor,
logic has replaced the dynamic indeterminacy of life that we find in
Dmitrii and Alesha. In Ivan's "Legend of the Grand Inquisitor," the moral
and political totalitarianism of the Roman Church is seen as a product of
Western European civilization and its identification of truth with right
reasoning and positive concepts. In contrast, Alesha's account of the Life of

Father Zosima – Dostoevskii's answer to the Legend – represents truth as part of the common experience of life, inexhaustible as life itself. In Orthodox theology, this refusal to exhaust knowledge of the truth in rational terms and definitions is called the "apophaticism" of knowledge. "This apophatic attitude leads Christian theology to use the language of poetry and images for the interpretation of dogmas much more than the language of conventional logic and schematic concepts," according to the Greek philosopher Christos Yannaras, to whom apophaticism is the great contribution of Greek Orthodoxy to modern Christian thought.[12]

In nineteenth-century Russia, the revival of the theology of the Greek Church Fathers led to a revival of Orthodox apophaticism. To lay theologians like Dostoevskii, the apophatic, or negative way of knowing God through "dissimilar similarities" became an important means of breaking away from the petrified dogmas and eternal truths of the official Russian Church. In the lives of his characters truth is never something given, but something to be found and verified in common experience and in communion with others.

Ivan's road to ethical rebirth begins when he accepts responsibility for the murder of his father. Realizing that Smerdiakov has acted as his "double," deciding to take his guilt upon himself and confess to the crime, Ivan is overcome by a feeling of joyful happiness that his mental anguish has come to an end. He has reached a new stage in the process of liminality, symbolized by his rescue of the half-frozen peasant. By this act of compassion Ivan is following the hagiographic pattern of his namesake, St. John the Merciful, whose rescue of a frozen beggar he was unable to understand in his dialogue with Alesha earlier in the novel.

The confession is not the end of Ivan's liminality, however. It only marks his transition to a new stage, not to the nether world of the Siberian mines – which is Dmitrii's lot – but to an eclipse of his self in the darkness of the unconscious, an internal hell in the landscape of his mind and the beginning of a rebirth.

Smerdiakov, the perpetrator of the crime, hangs himself. But before this act of self-condemnation, he, too, has gone through a kind of transition rite, symbolized by the long white stocking that so terrifies Ivan at their last meeting. As Richard Peace has pointed out, white had a particular significance for the Russian religious sect of the Castrates. They referred to themselves as "The White Doves," dressed in white, and referred to the actual act of castration as "whitening." His Castrate-like features have been underlined earlier in the novel, but now a number of details seem to indicate that he has gone through the final rite of initiation to the sect.[13]

The relationship between Ivan and Smerdiakov, his double, is a variation of the pattern underlying the relationships between Stavrogin and his satellites in *The Devils* (1872). In a process we might call "demonic kenosis," Stavrogin empties his own ideas and ideologies into the minds of his followers, who, in their turn, project his teachings back onto Stavrogin in an attempt to transform him into a living symbol of the ideas they have made their own, only to discover that Stavrogin is but an empty impostor, symbolizing nothing but nothingness.

In Russian literature the problem of idolization, of men creating gods in their own image, may be traced back to Gogol. To *Dead Souls*, where the officials project their ideas of Napoleon and even of Antichrist onto Chichikov, but above all to his comedy *The Inspector General* (1836), where the provincial civil servants project their collective fears onto the figure of Khlestakov, transforming him into a living image of their own ideas of what a government inspector must be like.

In Dostoevskii's *The Idiot* (1868), the idolization theme is combined with the impostor theme in a way that not only anticipates *The Devils*, but in a way that turns the impostor comedy into a religious tragedy.

Prince Myshkin, the central character, arrives back after several years in Switzerland, an enigmatic figure, whom his new acquaintances try to define by projecting onto him their own ideals. The debauchee and non-believer Rogozhin regards him as a *iurodivyi*, or "holy fool," simply because of his sexual inadequacy. To the young girl Aglaia he is an incarnation of her literary hero, the Poor Knight of Pushkin's ballad, whereas to Nastasia Filippovna, the "fallen woman," he comes as a potential redeemer. All these different interpretations are made possible by Dostoevskii's narrative technique in the first part of the novel. As Robin Feuer Miller has observed, the Prince is here characterized through his parables and stories after a model provided by the portrayal of Christ in the Gospels, thereby making his figure even more enigmatic and sphinxlike.[14]

But Myshkin is not the redeemer Nastasia Filippovna and the readers are led to believe. His initial role as a savior changes in the course of events, until he becomes an agent of perdition, incapable of preventing Rogozhin's murder of Nastasia Filippovna and the terrible blood wedding at the end of his sojourn in Russia.

To understand this development, we have to study the symbolism underlying the novel's action and represented in a series of execution stories told by Myshkin and his interlocutors throughout the four books of the novel: Legros's death by guillotine in Lyons and the firing squad execution; Dubarry's beheading; Ippolit's potential execution, were he to commit murder; the impalement of Stepan Glebov under Peter the Great; and the beheading of Sir Thomas More. These executions are all variations on the archetypal execution of Christ, symbolized in the novel by Hans Holbein's Basel painting of Jesus in the tomb – *Der Leichnam Christi im Grabe* – that so fascinated Dostoevskii when he saw it in 1867.

Holbein's painting is referred to in passing by the Prince in one of the opening chapters, and later, when Rogozhin shows him a reproduction of it in his father's house, Myshkin comments that "some people may lose their faith by looking at that picture" (II, 4).

The symbolic meaning of the painting, however, is only explained towards the end, when the dying Ippolit gives an extended description, or ekphrasis of the picture. According to Ippolit, there is in Holbein's picture no trace of the extraordinary beauty that painters usually try to preserve even in representations of the crucified Christ. What we see is the dead body of a man who has undergone unbearable suffering, a naturalistic rendering of how any man's corpse would look after such suffering. Looking at the picture:

> you are involuntarily struck by the idea that if death is so horrible and the laws of nature are so powerful, then how can they be overcome? How can they be overcome when even He has not conquered them now? . . . The picture seems to give expression exactly to the idea of a dark, insolent, and senselessly eternal power, to which everything is subordinated, and this idea comes to you involuntarily. (III, 6)

In Ippolit's interpretation, the Holbein painting becomes a representation of the "demythologized," unresurrected Christ of nineteenth-century radical theology, epitomized in David Friedrich Strauss's *Das Leben Jesu* (*The Life of Jesus*, 1835) and Ernest Renan's *La Vie de Jésus* (1863). Jesus is represented by Renan as a person "in whom was condensed all that is good and elevated in our nature." But with his historian's eye Renan sees Jesus as a human being whose life "finishes with the last sigh." As for the legends about the Resurrection, their main source is supposed to be the "strong imagination" of Mary Magdalene.[15]

The story of Prince Myshkin demonstrates the impossibility of an *imitatio Christi* based on the particular image of Christ posited by nineteenth-century liberal theology. In the figure of Prince Myshkin, Dostoevskii has created a mock-Christ, not an *Abbild*, but a *Gegenbild* of Christ. Myshkin is more like an Anti-Christ in the Nietzschean sense. In the German philosopher's work, *The Anti-Christ* (1888), Jesus is characterized as an "idiot": "Aus Jesus einen *Helden* machen! . . . Mit der Strenge des Physiologen gesprochen, wäre hier ein ganz andres Wort am Platz: das Wort Idiot." ("To make Jesus into a *hero*! From a strictly physiological point of view a completely different word would seem more appropriate:

the word idiot.") Moreover, Nietzsche makes an explicit reference to Dostoevskii in this connection: "Man hätte zu bedauern, daß nicht ein Dostojewskij in der Nähe dieses interessantesten *décadent* gelebt hat, ich meine jemand, der gerade den ergreifenden Reiz einer solchen Mischung von Sublimem, Krankem und Kindlichem zu empfinden wußte." ("It is regrettable that there was no Dostoevskii around during the lifetime of this interesting Decadent, by which I mean someone who was capable of feeling the attraction of this particular mixture of the sublime, the sick and the childlike.")

In nineteenth-century radical Christology we see a variant of the phenomenon Sergei Bulgakov has described as "Arian monophysitism," by which he has in mind a doctrine maintaining that there is only one, human nature in Christ. This "immanentism," as he also calls it, is typical of Protestantism and socialism, in which Bulgakov sees its Western, diurnal manifestations, whereas in Russia this immanentism is represented in its nocturnal aspect by the sectarian Castrates and Flagellants.[16] Applied to *The Idiot*, Bulgakov's distinction would correspond to the contrast between Prince Myshkin and his Swiss ideas on the one hand, and on the other Rogozhin with his close affinity with the Castrates.

In this perspective, *The Idiot* may be understood as an experiment in Christology, demonstrating the consequences of a theology in which the risen Christ of the Gospels has been replaced by the all too human Christ of post-Hegelian biblical criticism, as well as by the "christs" the Russian sectarians are known to create among themselves (Bulgakov, *Svet nevechernii*, pp. 5 and 366, n. 12). In this world without Resurrection the dead Christ has become a symbol of the dark, insolent, and senselessly eternal power Ippolit describes in his ekphrasis, a power to which everything in the dual landscape of the novel's central characters is finally subordinated.

The Idiot is not the only novel in which Dostoevskii introduces a central symbol in the form of an ekphrasis. In *A Raw Youth* (1875), we find a similar ekphrastic representation, this time of Claude Lorrain's "Acis and Galatea," one of Dostoevskii's favorite paintings in the Dresden Gallery. The painting had first been used in Stavrogin's "Confession," the so-called "banned" chapter of *The Devils*, and later it made an anonymous reappearance in *The Dream of the Ridiculous Man*, first published in *The Writer's Diary* in 1877.

Yet, what attracted Dostoevskii and his characters in Claude's painting was not his Ovidian subject. In Dostoevskii's interpretation, the symbolic value of the painting is to be found in the idealized beauty of the antique landscape, transfigured by the slanting rays of the setting sun into a representation of man's dream of a Golden Age. "Here, preserved in its memory, is the cradle of European humanity . . . its paradise on earth," according to Versilov's melancholy vision in *A Raw Youth* (III, 7). In Versilov's idea of the painting, however, the sun setting on the first day of European humanity turns into the sun setting on its last day, when people have lost their faith in God and immortality. "All the great surplus of their previous love of Him, He who was immortality, has been turned towards nature, the world, people, every single blade of grass" (III, 7).

But Versilov's dream vision has a third stage, in which just as in Heine's poem "Christ on the Baltic Sea" ("Frieden," from the cycle *Die Nordsee*), Christ appears to the people, reaching out his hands to an orphaned humanity, asking "How could you forget Him?" And the scales fall from everyone's eyes as they join in an "enraptured hymn of the new and final resurrection" (III, 7).

As Malcolm Jones has pointed out, Versilov's vision is the most interesting manifestation of his Romantic idealism, his Schillerism as Jones prefers to call it, using one of Dostoevskii's own terms.[17] But like Heine's verse, Versilov's dithyrambic composition has acquired an additional, post-Romantic dimension. In both works, the figure of Christ has been taken out of its biblical context and brought together with non-Christian elements in a way made possible by the mythological understanding of the Gospel in nineteenth-century liberal theology (Strauss), and of Christianity as a projection of man's deepest desire (Feuerbach).

Versilov's opposite in *A Raw Youth* is Makar Dolgorukii. Versilov is the Russian European, a nostalgic wanderer tormented by a split Faustian mind. Makar Dolgorukii, on the other hand, comes forward as a single-hearted Russian pilgrim in whose words we can already perceive the essence of Father Zosima's teachings about the presence of God's mystery in all.

In Makar's exemplary story about the repentant merchant, life's divine meaning is revealed by the words of Christ from the Gospel, and through the symbolic presence of Christ in the transfiguring ray of light descending over the boy about to drown himself in the painting described by Makar, a painting commissioned by the merchant in memory of the boy he has tormented to death.

In *A Raw Youth*, the symbolic representation of Christ as the light of the world is not confined to Versilov's and Makar's ekphrasis. It is the central symbol of the whole novel. The slanting rays of the setting sun are a recurring motif in the raw youth's account of his own life story. They illuminate the classroom when his mother comes to see him at the boarding school, and later, during his illness, they shine into his "tomb" of a room at the moment when for the first time he hears Makar praying in the neighboring room. It is his mother, however, who gives us the key to the novel's light symbolism, when she tells her son that "Christ is the father . . . Christ will shine even in deepest darkness" (III, 3). Christ is the light of the world. But he is also father. Thus, Sofiia Andreevna, the mother, suggests another main theme in the novel: the raw youth's quest for his father's identity.

A Raw Youth is a fictitious autobiography. Its narrator and central character is the young Arkadii Dolgorukii, Versilov's natural son, whose legitimate father is Makar Dolgorukii, his mother's much older husband. Arkadii's autobiography is the story of his transition from adolescence to manhood. In this process, the contrast between biological and social father is first replaced by an ambiguous constellation in which both father and son, Arkadii and Versilov, relate to Makar as their spiritual father. This is a situation that is only resolved after Makar's death, when Versilov emerges in the role of both husband and father, and the opposition between biological and social father is neutralized. But at this point, Arkadii has freed himself from his father-fixation by internalizing the image of Makar as his Christ-like spiritual father, whose words and ideas he has made his own. "The old life has gone for ever, while the new has only just begun" (III, 10).

From *Crime and Punishment* to *The Brothers Karamazov*, Dostoevskii's novels are experimenting with the possibility of a Christocentric anthropology in the modern world. The church as a social institution, and the relationship between church and state are also reduced to anthropology: a just organization of society depends on the moral rebirth of its individual members.

Dostoevskii's younger contemporary, Nikolai Leskov, saw this differently. Leskov was not primarily a novelist. His favorite genre is the short story, and religion and art are the main themes of some of his most remarkable works, such as "The Sealed Angel" and "The Enchanted Wanderer," both from 1873, and "At the End of the World," published in 1875. But since these works are stories and not novels, they fall outside the scope of our present discussion.

However, one of Leskov's most famous works is a novel, or "Romantic chronicle" as he liked to call it. Published in 1872 under the title *Cathedral Folk* it describes the relationship between church and state in contemporary Russia from the point of view of a provincial archpriest, Savelii Tuberozov, a representative of those members of the Russian clergy who in the last century hoped to bring about a reform of the church from within.

Originally, Tuberozov was modelled after Archpriest Avvakum, the martyred leader of the Old Believers who broke with the official church in the middle of the sixteenth century and whose autobiographical *vita* had created a sensation in Russian literature when it was published for the first time a few years earlier, in 1861. But in the final version, the idea of patterning Tuberozov on Avvakum was rejected and Leskov chose instead to relate the religious zeal of his hero directly to Christ's cleansing of the Temple. Tuberozov sees a parallel between the story in John 2:12–22 and his own castigation of the civil servants. He compares their prayer to the trading in the temple, at the sight of which "not only was our Lord, Jesus Christ, troubled in his divine spirit, but also he took a scourge and drove them out of the temple. Following his divine example, I accuse and condemn this trading with conscience that I see before me in the temple" (III, 21).

On the surface, the story about Jesus driving those that sold oxen and sheep and doves, and the changers of money out of the temple has nothing to do with Tuberozov's situation. But deep down in the landscape of his consciousness, Tuberozov makes a connection between the two, so that the one "slips" into the other, transforming his landscape of action into a variation on the theme developed in the Gospel story. In his act of defiance, his subsequent arrest and imprisonment, Leskov's hero detects the archetypal pattern of Christ's life and suffering. "Our old life" – he says to his wife – "has come to an end; from now on, life will be a *vita*" (III, 23).

At the time when in his *Cathedral Folk* Leskov openly criticized the official church and its clergy, trying in Tuberozov to represent a true follower of Christ, Tolstoi, too, turned to the Gospels for an answer to the religious questions that had begun to occupy him after the completion of *War and Peace* in 1869.

In order to study the New Testament at first hand he decided to take up ancient Greek, and soon he was passionately trying to read the great classical authors in the original. His religious problems temporarily receded into the background. According to his wife's diary, he now wanted to write something pure and elegant, like the works of ancient Greek literature and art. This idea took the form of the novel *Anna Karenina*, begun in 1873 and finished in 1877.

There is, however, in *Anna Karenina*, a reflection of Tolstoi's religious preoccupations in the 1870s. Traveling in Italy together, Anna and Vronskii are taken by Golenishchev, an old friend of Vronskii's, to see the Russian artist Mikhailov and his painting, "Christ before Pilate." According to Golenishchev, Mikhailov is "not without talent, but his tendency is quite a false one. He has that Ivanov–Strauss–Renan attitude towards Christ and religious painting" (part V, chapter 9). The reference is here to Aleksandr

Ivanov's famous painting, "Christ before the People," completed after the artist had come to understand Christ as a historical person in conformity with David Friedrich Strauss's *Life of Jesus*, a book that Ivanov knew almost by heart.[18] To someone like Golenishchev, once known for his "brainy liberal activity," but now complaining that the Russians "do not wish to understand that we are the inheritors of Byzantium" (part V, chapter 7), Mikhailov's representation of Christ as an historical person with pronounced Jewish features is quite unacceptable. Discussing Mikhailov's painting with the artist, Golenishchev again stresses the ideological links between "Christ before Pilate" and Ivanov's art:

> "you have made Him a man-god and not a God-man . . ."
> "I could not paint a Christ whom I haven't got in my soul," Mikhailov said gloomily.
> ". . . Yours is different. The motif itself is different. But still, let us take Ivanov. I consider that if Christ is reduced to the level of an historical person, it would be better to choose another historical theme, fresh, untouched."
> "But if it is the highest theme open to art?"
> "If one looks, there will be others. But the fact is that art won't suffer debate and discussions. Yet in front of Ivanov's picture the question arises to the believer and the unbeliever alike: Is this God or not God? and destroys the unity of impression." (part V, chapter 11)

Golenishchev's reaction to Ivanov's art is reminiscent of Prince Myshkin's response to the Holbein picture in *The Idiot*: "some people may lose their faith by looking at that picture" (II, 4). Although Tolstoi clearly sympathizes with Mikhailov's genuine artistic empathy, he reacted not unlike Golenishchev to the Ivanov–Strauss–Renan attitude towards Christ and religious painting. As Hugh McLean has pointed out, Tolstoi made several statements about Ivanov's art that show that he found it personally unacceptable.[19] One reason for this may be found in his description of the painter Ge's version of "Christ before Pilate," the very subject of Mikhailov's picture in *Anna Karenina*. What Tolstoi finds so praiseworthy in Ge's painting is its unambiguous opposition between Christ and the representatives of this world:

> Christ and his teaching not only in words, but in words and action in conflict with the teaching of the world, i.e. the motif that now as then forms the central meaning of the manifestation of Christ, a meaning that is unquestionable, which has to be accepted by the representatives of the Church, recognising him as God, by the historians, recognising him as an important figure in history, and by the Christians who recognise as the most important in him his practical teaching.[20]

Anna Karenina is Tolstoi's last great work of fiction before his religious conversion. In the 1880s he formulated his own conception of Christianity, based on his Rousseauesque idea of man's natural goodness and on what he now saw as the true teachings of Christ in the Gospel. He accused the official church of perverting the message of the Gospel and rejected everything in Orthodox theology that went beyond his immediate understanding. The church like other social institutions is part of "civilization," and like Rousseau Tolstoi believed that all people were born innocent and that their natural innocence was later ruined by the institutions of civilized society. In order to regain his or her natural goodness and be able to live a true life – not the life of one's animal instincts – every individual must transcend the barriers between self and other and be reborn through love – love not as an emotional impulse, but as a total submission to what Tolstoi in his treatise *On Life* (1887) calls "reasonable consciousness," that enjoins men to renounce their individual welfare. This inborn "reasonable consciousness" or natural ethical law is what according to Tolstoi makes up the quintessence of Christ's teachings. In this sense, Christianity does not occupy a privileged place among the world's religions. Its basic ethical principle, most clearly expressed in the Sermon on the Mount, is common to all the great faiths. They are different expressions of the same "reasonable consciousness" that is part of the natural make-up of every single human being, but which has been obscured and suppressed by modern civilization and can thus only be found in children and simple people.

In Tolstoi's fiction, this natural ethos is already present in the figure of Platon Karataev, the peasant soldier in *War and Peace*, a man without any feeling of an individual selfhood. In him, Pierre Bezukhov sees a possible way out of his own isolation. "To be a soldier" – he thinks as he falls asleep – "To enter with all one's being into that communal life, to be permeated by what makes them what they are. But how to throw off everything superfluous, demonic, the whole burden of the other man?" (3, III, 9).

Pierre's imprisonment by the French, the execution of his fellow prisoners by the enemy, his friendship with Platon Karataev, and his final rescue after Karataev's death, are stages in a process of liminality that eventually leads to Pierre's spiritual regeneration.

Lying next to Karataev in the darkness of the prison shed "he felt that the world that had been shattered was beginning to move again with a new beauty, and on some new unshakeable foundations in his soul" (4, I, 12). And later in life, Platon Karataev "always remained in Pierre's mind the strongest and most precious of all his memories, the personification of everything Russian, good and perfect" (4, I, 13).

In *War and Peace*, Pierre's spiritual death and rebirth is only one of many strains in the novel's thematic texture. In *Resurrection* on the other hand, the theme of spiritual death and rebirth has become the central story line underlying the novel's whole flow of action.

When *Resurrection* was finally published in 1899, Tolstoi had been working at it intermittently for more than ten years. The story begins when as a jury member, Nekhliudov, the novel's central male character, recognizes in Katiusha Mazlova, a prostitute tried for theft, the young girl he has seduced in his youth. Convinced of her innocence and overcome by remorse, he abandons his former way of life and after her conviction decides to follow her to Siberia, where they are both spiritually reborn in a process of conquering their animal instincts and rediscovering their natural, uncorrupted moral selves, which had been obliterated by socialization and acculturation.

This process of change and regeneration in the inner landscape of consciousness in the two protagonists is paralleled in the outer landscape of action by a chain of events that takes them through the life of the Russian gentry, the squalor of the peasants, the courts, the prisons, the deportation of the convicts, and their life in the prison colony. The State and its institutions, the church in particular, are exposed to Tolstoi's ruthless irony and satire, as, for instance, in the chapter describing the prisoners' communion, where we find the following passage:

> the priest lifted the napkin covering the plate, cut the central piece of bread into four parts, dipped it in the wine and then put it into his mouth. He was supposed to be eating a piece of the body of God and drinking a mouthful of his blood. (I, 39).

After distributing "this bread" and "this wine" among the prisoners in front of him,

> he carried the goblet behind the partition where he proceeded to eat up all the little pieces of God's body and drink the remaining blood; then he carefully sucked on his moustache, wiped his mouth, cleaned the cup, and in the best possible mood, the thin soles of his calfskin boots creaking smartly, came out from behind the partition. (I, 39)

In this chapter, which was one of many banned from publication under the old regime, Tolstoi uses his favorite device of "defamiliarization," representing the Eucharist from the point of view of someone uninitiated into its symbolism. The prisoners' mass was the ideal liminal chronotope for such a ludic recombination of the *sacra* of the Orthodox church in order to render them completely meaningless. At the end of the novel, the

Christian message is reinterpreted by Nekhliudov as an extension of his own spiritual resurrection to the whole of human society:

> When he had read the Sermon on the Mount, which never failed to move him, he discovered today for the first time in this sermon not abstract beautiful thoughts . . . but simple, clear and practically realizable laws that if they were implemented (which was perfectly possible), would establish a completely new organization of human society . . . If only people realize this doctrine, the Kingdom of God will be established also on earth. (III, 29)

What we have here is the possibility of a new *communitas*, a resacralization of society according to Tolstoi's own extreme form of rationalistic, ethical evangelism. In the world outside the novel it found a close parallel in Tolstoiism as a particular form of millenarian religious movement.

In his Rousseauesque condemnation of civilization, Tolstoi in *Resurrection* arrived at a radical Christian anarchism that brought him close to the ethical ideals of the radical intelligentsia, described with such sympathy and understanding in the novel. This Christian anarchism was incompatible with the teachings of the Orthodox church. Its leaders were unable to respond adequately to the call for a social renewal expressed in Tolstoi's last novel. After its publication the church denounced its author as a false prophet who "led astray by pride has boldly and insolently dared to oppose God, Christ and his holy heirs." On 22 February 1901 Tolstoi was excommunicated.

Around the turn of the century, Russian intellectual life was charged with millenarian movements and apocalyptic expectations. Sergei Bulgakov spoke of "the apocalypse as the sociology of our time." It was in this atmosphere that Andrei Belyi wrote his apocalyptic novel *Petersburg* (1916) in the years following the revolutionary events of 1905. Belyi brings together characters and plots from nineteenth-century Russian literature – Gogol's Petersburg stories, Pushkin's *The Bronze Horseman*, *The Queen of Spades* and Dostoevskii's *The Devils* – in an apocalyptic struggle between the forces of evil, symbolized by the Bronze Horseman – the incarnation of Peter's city – and his antagonist, the lonely figure of Christ, symbolizing life, love and compassion, on the threshold between good and evil, old and new, death and new life. Nikolai Apollonovich Ableukhov, the novel's main hero, first emerges as a representation of evil, dressed in a red domino and hidden behind the mask of a harlequin, in striking contrast to the figure of Christ in his white domino. But in the course of the action Nikolai undergoes a process of change and regeneration that follows the classical pattern of the Russian novel. In the epilogue, the revolutionary hero has shed his Western rationalism and revolutionary ideas. After a pilgrimage to the Holy Land, he withdraws from the world into the Russian countryside in order to live the life of a hermit, replacing the works of Kant and the neo-Kantians with the writings of the eighteenth-century Greek-Orthodox thinker Grigorii Skovoroda.

Belyi's *Petersburg* was to become the first in series of apocalyptic novels in twentieth-century Russian literature. Other masterpieces of the genre are Mikhail Bulgakov's *The Master and Margarita* and Andrei Platonov's *Chevengur*, both written in the 1920s but only published in the 1960s and 1970s. Now, with the rewriting of the literary canon in post-Soviet Russia, these novels will receive their due attention as the real masterpieces of modern Russian literature.

When the Revolution came, it was hailed as a universal regeneration, and a feeling of *communitas* cut right across the traditional divisions of Russian society. But with the Bolshevik assumption of power and the beginning of the Civil War in 1918, it soon became clear that Victor Turner's general characterization of such situations also holds good for communist Russia: the "movement" becomes itself an institution among other institutions, "more fanatical and militant than the rest, for the reason that it feels itself to be the unique bearer of universal-human truths."[21]

The emergence of the victorious Communists out of the large-scale process of the Civil War is one of the main themes in Boris Pasternak's novel *Doctor Zhivago* (1957). As Russian society is being restructured, the veterans of the Revolution are elevated to a new status: "Numbered amongst the gods at whose feet the Revolution has laid its gift and its burnt offerings, they sat silent and grim as idols; they were men in whom everything alive and human had been driven out by political conceit" (part X, section 7).

In order to understand this description of the new rulers as idols, we have to remember Vedeniapin's opposition between, on the one hand, the "sanguinary mess [*svinstvo*] of cruel, pockmarked Caligulas" of the classical world with its "boastful dead eternity of bronze monuments and marble columns" and, on the other, life after Christ, with whom history as we know it today began. Christ gave us, according to Pasternak's novel, "firstly, the love of one's neighbor," and "secondly, the two main components in the make-up of modern man, without which he is inconceivable, the ideas of a free personality and life regarded as sacrifice" (part I, section 5).

Vedeniapin's conception of human life as a life in history founded by Christ and lived according to his example serves as a generative model for the unfolding of Iurii Zhivago's character in a process that in the end transforms him into a traditional Russian pilgrim, returning to Moscow from Siberia in the spring of 1922, accompanied by a handsome peasant youth:

> Accompanied by his young friend, the tall, gaunt doctor in his unprepossessing clothes looked like a truth-seeker from the people, and his constant companion like an obedient, blindly devoted disciple and acolyte.
>
> (part XV, section 1)

We are reminded here of Father Zosima and the "comely youth, a peasant" in *The Brothers Karamazov* (book VI, chapter 2). In a wider perspective, however, this pair, the old spiritual father and his young disciple, is an archetypal pair in the Orthodox tradition, known from both icon painting (St. John and Prokhor) and hagiography. In Pasternak's novel, the representation of this archetype brings the hero's life-story to its conclusion. It has taken him to the threshold between death and resurrection foreshadowed in his dream before the Siberian exile, where the connection between the sacrificial death of Christ and his own creative work as a poet is already established:

> The poem he is writing is neither about the entombment nor about the resurrection but about the days that pass between them. He is writing the poem "Confusion" . . .
> Glad to be near him were hell, corruption, dissolution, death; yet equally glad to be near him was spring, and Magdalene, and life. – And time to wake up
> . . . Time to wake up and arise. Time for resurrection (part VI, section 15)

In Siberia, Zhivago has experienced the reality of death and dissolution, but he has also been initiated into the mysteries of love, poetic creativity and life, bringing back with him his collection of poems. In these poems the lyrical I discovers his true self by seeing his own life and suffering as a re-enactment of Christ's life and suffering. This accords with Pasternak's own ideas of human history after Christ as expressed in his autobiography *Safe Conduct* (1931). Here he defines the history of our culture as a "chain of symbolic equations" in which the fundamental pattern of the Bible represents the constant element, while the unknown, the new, is the actual moment in the cultural development.[22]

In the Russian novel, the idea of creativity as a repetition with variations on a single underlying pattern took the form of a continuous dialogue with the words of the Gospel about the true meaning of life. In their struggle against the ossified dogma of the Orthodox Church and the atheist theories of Communism, Russian novelists used their artistic imagination to discover new meanings in the already given, opening up the story of Christ in the Gospel to new interpretations and new life.

NOTES

1. Jerome Bruner, "Two Modes of Thought," *Actual Minds, Possible Worlds* (Cambridge, Mass.: Harvard University Press, 1986), pp. 11–43.
2. Michael Carrithers, *Why Humans Have Cultures* (Oxford University Press, 1992), p. 84.
3. Yurii M. Lotman, "Russo i russkaia kul'tura XVIII – nachala XIX veka," in *Izbrannye stat'i v trekh tomakh* (Tallin: Aleksandra, 1992–93), vol. II, pp. 40–99, 79.
4. Yurii M. Lotman, *Roman A. S. Pushkina "Evgenii Onegin"* (Leningrad: Prosveshchenie, 1980).
5. Yurii M. Lotman, "Siuzhetnoe prostranstvo russkogo romana XIX stoletiia," in *Izbrannye stat'i*, vol. III, pp. 91–106 (pp. 99ff.).
6. Yurii V. Mann, *V poiskakh zhivoi dushi: "Mertvye dushi": pisatel' – kritika – chitatel'* (Moscow: Kniga, 1984), pp. 301–23.
7. Victor and Edith Turner, "Religious Celebrations," in V. Turner (ed.), *Celebration, Studies in Festivity and Ritual* (Washington: Smithsonian Institution Press, 1982), pp. 201–19, 202ff.
8. Victor Turner, "Liminal to Liminoid, in Play, Flow, and Ritual: An Essay in Comparative Symbology," in Janet C. Harris and Roberta J. Park (eds.), *Play, Games and Sports in Cultural Contexts* (Champaign, Ill.: Human Kinetics Publications, 1983), pp. 123–64.
9. Aleksandr I. Gertsen, *Sobranie sochinenii v tridtsati tomakh* (Moscow: Izd. Akademii Nauk, 1954–64) 27, 1, p. 217.
10. Douglas R. Hofstadter, *Metamagical Themas: Questing for the Essence of Mind and Pattern* (New York: Basic Books, 1985).
11. Victor Terras, *A Karamazov Companion* (Madison: The University of Wisconsin Press, 1981), p. 52.
12. Christos Yannaras, *Elements of Faith: An Introduction to Orthodox Theology*, trans. Keith Schram (Edinburgh: T&T Clark, 1991), pp. 17ff., 149ff.
13. Richard Peace, *Dostoevsky: An Examination of the Major Novels* (Cambridge University Press, 1971), pp. 262f.
14. Robin Feuer Miller, *Dostoevsky and "The Idiot": Author, Narrator, and Reader* (Cambridge, Mass.: Harvard University Press, 1981), pp. 84, 88.
15. Ernest Renan, *The Life of Jesus* (London: Watts and Co., 1935), pp. 227, 215.
16. Sergei Bulgakov, *Svet nevechernii: Sozertsaniia i umozreniia* (Moscow: Respublika, 1994), p. 5.
17. Malcolm V. Jones, *Dostoevsky: The Novel of Discord* (New York: Barnes & Noble, 1976), pp. 54–64.
18. Mikhail Botkin (ed.), *Aleksandr Andreevich Ivanov: Ego zhizn' i perepiska 1806–1858* (St. Petersburg, 1880), pp. 202ff.
19. Hugh McLean, "Tolstoy and Jesus," in Robert P. Hughes and Irina Paperno (eds.), *Russian Culture in Modern Times*, vol. II of *Christianity and the Eastern Slavs, California Slavic Studies*, 17 (Berkeley: University of California Press, 1994), pp. 103–23.
20. Tolstoi to P. M. Tret'iakov, 30 June 1890, quoted in Hugh McLean, "Tolstoy and Jesus," p. 110.

21. Victor Turner, *The Ritual Process: Structure and Anti-Structure* (New York: Walter de Gruyter, 1995), p. 112.

22. Boris Pasternak, "Okhrannaia gramota," in Pasternak, *Sochineniia*, 3 vols. (Ann Arbor: University of Michigan Press, 1961), vol. II, pp. 203–94, quotation from p. 263.

7

ANDREW WACHTEL

Psychology and society

It is by now a commonplace that the classic Russian novelists – Dostoevskii, Turgenev, Tolstoi – are distinguished by an unparalleled ability to portray the complex inner mental states of their characters. As early as 1856, the Russian critic Chernyshevskii praised Tolstoi for his superlative rendering of the "dialectics of the soul," by which he meant Tolstoi's painstaking dissection of the inner life of his heroes. And in the English-speaking world, Virginia Woolf summed up a review of Tolstoi's *The Cossacks* by remarking: "They do not rival us in the comedy of manners, but after reading Tolstoi we always feel that we could sacrifice our skill in that direction for something of the profound psychology and superb sincerity of the Russian writers."[1]

I have no wish to dispute the near unanimous critical opinion that the Russian novel is particularly attuned to psychological analysis. Instead, in the essay that follows, I would like to ask why Russian novelists have been so concerned with psychology, and, as a corollary question, when this concern has been most in evidence. My central points will be two. First, that Russian novelists, with few exceptions, are concerned with individual psychology because it provides a window onto what might be called social psychology; that is, the individual is crucial not primarily for him or herself, but because he or she is seen to be representative of a larger group. Although this is sometimes the case in the works of non-Russian novelists as well, it seems to me that George Eliot, Thomas Hardy, Henry James, Gustave Flaubert and other masters of European psychological prose are more usually interested in portraying individuals as individuals than are their Russian counterparts. Second, that psychological portraiture is usually associated with disease, or at least, with distress; to paraphrase Tolstoi, all happy individuals have the same psychology, but all unhappy individuals have unique and fascinating psychologies worth exploring. In practice, what this means is that psychological analysis in the classic Russian novel tends to disappear if and when a major character finds happiness and to be

130

foregrounded at those moments when he or she is most diseased. By disease, I do not mean what we in the late twentieth century might recognize as a bona fide mental illness – schizophrenia, manic depression and the like – although some characters suffering such maladies can be identified in Russian literature.[2] Rather, the novels tend to present astute portrayals of general human psychological problems – pride, doubt, lassitude, spite, envy.

Thus, on the whole, Russian psychological prose is concerned with exploring the ramifications of fairly common human failings through careful analysis of the mental states of characters who are meant to be seen as representative of Russians (or types of Russian) in general. The analysis can be carried out in one of two ways; either the character himself is the narrator, in which case he must be sufficiently self-aware to recognize at least dimly his own affliction, or else a third-person narrator able to penetrate, present, and weigh the character's inner thoughts is employed. It will be noticed that the characters treated in this essay are almost exclusively male. This is not accidental; the classic Russian psychological novel generally deals with a weak (read psychologically diseased) male character who is provided with a foil in the person of a healthy woman (who is, therefore, not treated psychologically). The exceptions to this rule, of course, are precisely those Russian novels that transcend this as well as most other models: *The Idiot* and *The Brothers Karamazov* of Dostoevskii and Tolstoi's *Anna Karenina* about which there will be more below.

It is worth pointing out that Russia's earliest great writers of prose fiction, Aleksandr Pushkin and Nikolai Gogol, practically eschewed psychological portraiture altogether, and showed almost no interest in portraying an inner essential self. This was despite the fact that Pushkin at least was well aware of late-eighteenth-century and early-nineteenth-century French fiction with its intense psychological portraiture. Nevertheless, in the brilliant novel in verse *Evgenii Onegin* (1823–31), Pushkin's narrator does not make his reader privy to the characters' inner states. Instead, he provides highly nuanced external description which the reader, who has long been sure that these states must exist within the characters, can use to intuit convincing psychological explanation. The lone exception is in Pushkin's presentation in chapter 4 of a dream by his heroine, Tatiana Larina. Here we are presented with an encoded exposition of her attitude towards the novel's eponymous hero. Through complicated and symbolically laden dream imagery, Pushkin reveals her ambivalence toward Evgenii, her simultaneous desire to be ravished by him and her fears and hopes. It is of course significant that this section is set off as a dream, for here the normal internal laws of Pushkin's novel can be suspended, allowing for a display of complex mental states normally unavailable.

Gogol's famous short stories from the 1830s and early 1840s ("The Nose," "The Overcoat," "Nevskii Prospect") and his epic *Dead Souls* (1842) avoid psychology even more thoroughly than do Pushkin's works. While Gogol does tell us what his heroes are thinking, this disclosure yields no knowledge about a given character's inner life because the thoughts presented are either empty or so metaphorically extravagant that they tell us nothing. The absence of psychological analysis is particularly striking in Gogol's short story "Notes of a Madman." The entire story is composed of the diary of Poprishchin who goes progressively insane. But the narrator has no understanding of what is happening, and, because of his almost complete lack of self-consciousness, the story cannot be said to be psychological prose of the type that will become so characteristic of Russian literature.

By the end of the 1830s, however, the situation slowly began to change, particularly in the work of those writers born after 1815. At first, a burgeoning interest in psychological analysis appeared not in fiction, but rather in the life of the newly appearing intelligentsia. As Lidia Ginzburg has shown in her broad-ranging analysis *On Psychological Prose*, all the narrative techniques that would be used later in the Russian psychological novel, as well as the tendency to link personal and social analysis, can already be found in the letters and diaries of such men as Herzen, Bakunin, Belinskii and Ogarev, well before any psychological novels had appeared.[3]

The first novel in which the incipient interest in the psyche is manifest is *A Hero of Our Time*. Lermontov's novel is composed of five loosely related stories, all revolving around a single individual, Grigorii Pechorin. What sustains our interest in *A Hero of Our Time* as a novel is not the plot (which is fragmentary) but rather Lermontov's gradual unveiling of Pechorin's personality. The novel's main figure appears for the first time triply distanced from the reader – in time, space and narrative frame: we hear about him in the chapter called "Bela" through a story told to the narrator by an old veteran of the Caucasus about events that occurred a number of years previously in another location. The veteran's insistence on and description of Pechorin's remarkable qualities piques our curiosity. The rest of the novel gradually brings this mysterious figure into focus, first through a meeting with him in the present (the story "Maxim Maximych"), and then through three stories supposedly taken from Pechorin's own diary ("Taman," "Princess Mary," and "The Fatalist").

It is in this final trio of stories that Lermontov unveils, for the first time in Russian literature, the complex inner life of a character. Pechorin indeed possesses remarkable abilities, yet he is bored, bilious and a scoundrel. The novel's central concern is to show us why and how such a paradoxical combination has come to pass. What is remarkable about Pechorin (and this will become typical of the type) is the contrast between, on the one hand, his seemingly highly developed self-understanding coupled with his evident talent, and, on the other, his inability to accomplish anything except the production of misery for himself and those around him. The explanation for this lies in the fact that the only psychological categories Pechorin possesses for self-understanding are the polarities of Byronic Romanticism – either/or: an angel or a demon. Through Pechorin's pitiless self-analysis we come to recognize the mechanism of psychological development in which he believes. A person possesses certain internal, clearly defined qualities; depending on how they are received by society, they can either be developed to their full potential or turned into their opposite.

What makes the novel work is not Pechorin's outdated Byronism (which is even parodied by Lermontov through the presence of Pechorin's "double" Grushnitskii in the story "Princess Mary"), but our recognition that the limited poles provided by Romantic psychology are not sufficient to compass him. As the novel progresses, we begin to recognize that although Pechorin seems filled with self-knowledge, something is missing. He is trying too hard to fit his life into the Byronic poles that are all he possesses for self understanding. Byronism is a mask, a disease, which ultimately makes him incapable of self-understanding, despite what seem to be valiant efforts. Interestingly enough, something of the same problem seems to have afflicted Lermontov himself, whose attempts to live the Romantic life climaxed in his own death in a duel at the age of 27.

From the perspective of this essay, however, Pechorin's psychology is less important than Lermontov's characterization of his own novel, which he provided in an authorial introduction added to the second edition (1841). Lermontov begins by complaining about unjust criticisms his book has received, particularly from those who claimed that the main character was nothing but a self-portrait. In response, Lermontov makes the counter claim that Pechorin is best understood not as an individual but as a social portrait: "*A Hero of Our Time* . . . is a portrait composed of all the vices of our generation in the fullness of their development."[4] His novel, Lermontov goes on to say, is not meant to give a cure for the disease he has portrayed, but rather an explication of it. These parallel claims, that psychological analysis serves to portray disease and that what seems to be a nuanced portrait of a unique individual's psychology is best understood as a presentation of the psychology of a group or type, were destined to have a long history in Russian culture. As we shall see, some authors strove consciously to provide psychological snapshots of specific types or even whole generations through the description of individual psychology, others tried to avoid this, but Russian critics and readers always tended to assume that this was occurring.

The character of the "superfluous man," as the Pechorin-type figure came to be dubbed in Russian culture, was treated in a realist rather than a romantic key in Ivan Goncharov's novel *Oblomov* (1859). This outstanding work gives the lie to the belief that the Russian novel is necessarily characterized by grand passions and exciting plots. For what is remarkable about *Oblomov* is that practically nothing whatsoever happens in it; the first 150 pages or so describe neither more nor less than the main character's attempt to get out of bed in the morning. What saves the novel from being as boring as its title character, however, is its subtle focus on Oblomov's inner life. Certainly, Goncharov's ability to explore the hidden recesses of his hero's mind, to ferret out the wellsprings of his action (or inaction as the case may be) and to recognize the possibility of the coexistence in his mind of seemingly incompatible thoughts is light years ahead of Lermontov's. In place of the Romantic dualist view of the mind that dominated Pechorin's, and Lermontov's, vision of self, Goncharov recognizes that the mind is a complex instrument, and that human motivation falls primarily in a prosaic gray area rather than in stark black and white.

The following passage is a fine example of Goncharov's ability to reproduce the complex associative mechanisms of human thought. It appears in the first part of the novel immediately after Oblomov's manservant Zakhar has insulted his master by having the temerity to compare him to others, suggesting that if they can move then so can he:

> He tried to grasp the whole meaning of that comparison and analyse what *the others* were and what he was, and to what an extent a parallel between him and other people was justified, and how gravely Zakhar had insulted him. Finally, he wondered whether Zakhar had insulted him consciously, that is to say, whether he was convinced that he, Oblomov, was the same as "another", or whether the words had escaped him without thinking.[5]

These thoughts about himself and others lead Oblomov to question the very nature of his own being. And in so doing, he must face the fact that he is incapable of doing anything, in short that he is a superfluous man.

> Oh, how dreadful he felt when there arose in his mind a clear and vivid idea of human destiny and the purpose of a man's life, and when he compared this purpose with his own life . . . He felt sad and sorry at the thought of his own lack of education, at the arrested development of his spiritual powers, at the feeling of heaviness which interfered with everything he planned to do; and was overcome by envy of those whose lives were rich and full, while a huge rock seemed to have been thrown across the narrow and pitiful path of his

own existence. Slowly there arose in his mind the painful realization that many sides of his nature had never been awakened, that others were barely touched, that none had developed fully.   (p. 101)

As opposed to Pechorin, who had a convenient theory to explain his superfluity and provide him with a code of action, Oblomov cannot fully explain his inability to realize his own potential. In a sense, the entire novel can be seen as a two-pronged attempt on the part of Oblomov first to answer the question he asks immediately after this moment of insight: "Why am I like this?" and then to escape the deadening weight of his own psychological complexes.

Of these two prongs, the most interesting from our point of view is the former, because Goncharov provides, in the famous section called "Oblomov's Dream," an overtly psychological (as opposed to political or sociological) explanation. The "Dream" (which was, incidentally, the first section of the novel to be published, a full decade before the rest) transports Oblomov back to the idyllic world of his childhood, to the family estate of Oblomovka, an earthly paradise characterized by a cocoon-like softness and safety. And the narrator suggests that precisely the childhood impressions Oblomov drew from this bucolic paradise are what made him what he was as an adult. Because no one around him ever did anything, the boy came to believe that lassitude was the natural order of things. Goncharov suggests that our basic psychological make-up is set in earliest infancy, never to change thereafter no matter what external circumstances might arise.

The rest of the novel, which deals with Oblomov's ultimately unsuccessful attempts to escape from his torpor, either through love or friendship, need not concern us here. What is of cardinal importance, however, is the history of the novel's reception. Immediately after the work's appearance, one of Russia's leading literary critics, Nikolai Dobroliubov, wrote an appreciative essay entitled "What is Oblomovitis?" which forever fixed Russian critical opinion of *Oblomov*. Despite the fact that Oblomov is drawn with a realist's fine brush and seems, at first glance, to be a quite specific character, Dobroliubov saw the novel's hero not as an individual but as a social portrait.

The story of how Oblomov, a lazy Mr Nice Guy, lies around and sleeps and can be roused neither by friendship nor love is not much of a story. But Russian life is reflected in it, we see in it a vivid contemporary Russian type, sculpted with pitiless severity and accuracy. A new word in our social development has been pronounced here clearly and firmly without despair or childish hope, but with the full knowledge of the truth. The word is

Oblomovitis and it serves as a key to the solution of many phenomena of Russian life.[6]

The expectation that a carefully drawn psychological portrait of a literary character is actually meant to be a criticism of Russian society is one that Goncharov may well have shared, for he was on record as having said that the novel can only depict types.[7] Be that as it may, Dobroliubov's article fixed in the mind of the reading public the belief that literary characters were interchangeable with real people, and that the diseased fictional psychologies described by novelists could and should be seen as social psychologies. In the future, few Russian novelists would do anything to overturn this opinion.

Withal, the Russian novelist of the nineteenth century whose works provide the most comprehensive attempt to fix through the portrayal of individual psyches the stages of Russian social development is Ivan Turgenev. Although his characters may lack the shattering power of Dostoevskii's greatest portraits and the astoundingly fine-grained detailing typical of Tolstoi's heroes, Turgenev's central fictional creations provide the best examples of psycho-social types in Russian literature. Such was Turgenev's intention from the beginning of his career; describing *A Sportsman's Sketches* (1852), a collection of short stories of a rather unpsychological bent, Turgenev himself described his method as extracting the essence of his characters. Gradually, in the course of a series of novels starting with *Rudin* (1856) and culminating with *Fathers and Children* (1862), Turgenev perfected his own psychological method, one that was fully in accord with the Russian expectation that individual characters should reflect more general truths about the nation. "Turgenev also indicates that his characters face uncertainties and contradictions within themselves and in their relationships with others that are akin to those the Russian nation as a whole had to confront to establish its own identity and autonomy."[8] That is to say that any problem of personal identity in a Turgenev novel (and in pretty much any other Russian novel for that matter) can be and invariably was read as a problem of national self-definition. It is this fact that lends a certain epic quality to the Russian psychological novel.

Although it is beyond the scope of this essay to delineate exactly the sources of Russia's concern with its national identity, it would not be amiss to note here that the roots of the problem lie in the schism that opened up in Russian society in the wake of the reforms of Peter the Great. Although the process began earlier, Peter was credited (or blamed) with orienting Russia toward Europe and away from Asia and her own national roots. By the end of the eighteenth century, educated Russians were as conversant with European culture as any European of the day, but they had lost touch with the pre-Petrine Russian past. The mass of the peasant population, however, was more or less untouched by Europeanization. The gap between educated Russians and the people, as well as the vague fear of having become nothing but a European cultural colony, dominated Russian thought in the post-Napoleonic period. Its strongest expression was in the "First Philosophical Letter" of Petr Chaadaev (written, characteristically enough, in French in the late 1820s and published in 1836). There Chaadaev lamented the fact that Russians belonged to none of the major families of humankind, and claimed that this outside status precluded Russia from making the progress toward perfection that nineteenth-century thinkers believed to be the birthright of European civilization. Chaadaev's anguished soul-searching found general agreement among educated Russians, who broke into two camps in their attempts to find a solution to this problem: the Slavophiles called for a return to Russia's own roots, while the Westernizers wished for full assimilation with Europe.

Thus, like Chaadaev, Turgenev's main characters (as well as many of Tolstoi and Dostoevskii) are, in attempting to discover their essence, standing in for an entire country that was desperately trying to do the same. Perhaps the best Turgenevan hero to examine in this regard is his most controversial creation, Bazarov, the central character of *Fathers and Children*. Bazarov appears in the novel as an angry young man from a relatively poor background. He believes in nothing except physiology (symbolized in the novel by his constant desire to dissect frogs), convinced that the dualism of the body and mind is specious, and that the way to all understanding is through a thorough knowledge of the workings of the nervous system. In the course of the novel, however, Turgenev gradually, lovingly, and gently, shows us the breakdown of Bazarov's system in the face of human life, which turns out, in essential ways, to be different from the amphibian.

In particular, Bazarov's system crumbles under the onslaught of love, an emotion whose existence he had never acknowledged. Turgenev carefully prepares us to recognize the developments that are occurring in Bazarov's mind by first describing external changes: "Bazarov, whom Anna Sergeevna [Odintsova] obviously favored, although she seldom agreed with him, had begun to show signs of unprecedented perturbation: he was easily irritated, reluctant to talk, he gazed around angrily, and couldn't sit still in one place, as though he were being swept away by some irresistible force."[9] The metaphors Turgenev uses here, of elemental forces and illness, hint that love has softened up Bazarov to such an extent that he has become a candidate to be treated psychologically; that is, he is sufficiently diseased for his formerly impregnable psychic defenses to have been breached.

Bazarov's friend and disciple, Arkadii Kirsanov, notices that something has changed in his formerly rock-solid mentor, and Turgenev's narrator hastens to add:

> The real cause of this "change" was the feeling Mrs. Odintsov inspired in Bazarov, a feeling that tortured and maddened him, one that he would have instantly denied with scornful laughter and cynical derision if anyone had even remotely hinted at the possibility that it existed inside him. Bazarov was a great admirer of women and of female beauty, but love in the ideal or, as he put it, romantic sense he termed lunacy, unpardonable imbecility. He regarded chivalrous sentiments as something on the order of a deformity or disease . . . In his conversations with Anna Sergeevna, he expressed calm contempt for everything romantic more firmly than ever, when he was alone, though, he indignantly perceived the romantic in himself.[10]

The psychology Turgenev describes here is infinitely more complex than that described by Lermontov or Goncharov; whereas their central figures were characterized by either/or, Bazarov suffers from the disease of both/ and. His conscious mind struggles as hard as it can to avoid the conclusions that his subconscious is drawing, and as a result, contradictory world views exist simultaneously within him. Worse yet, when Bazarov finally allows his subconscious feelings to come to the surface in a confession of love, Odintsova rejects him. He realizes, therefore, that he had not only misunderstood himself, but that his analysis of her character (and of the feminine character in general) had been incorrect. His response is to control himself through flight, but it is clear from his actions in the rest of the novel that this temporarily successful effort to master his emotions has so weakened him as to lead to his destruction.

The case of Bazarov is not different from that of most of Turgenev's male heroes. The conscious mind, Turgenev says, functions to protect us from the trauma that unbridled emotion would cause. This view of the mind's workings is part and parcel of Turgenev's overall view of human nature. In the words of one of Turgenev's most sensitive recent readers:

> As Turgenev represents human nature in his works, he contributes to a venerable tradition – going back at least to the stoics in the West and continuing through Freud – that dwells on the susceptibility of human beings to suffering. Within this tradition, the goal of human existence is to minimize pain, not to maximize pleasure . . . Turgenev's psychology [as manifested in his characters], and the ethics derived from it, anticipated Freud in that Turgenev too could be said to have reduced the sources of suffering to three, not so different from Freud's: nature, other people, and the irrational.[11]

This observation leads us to the further conclusion that the novel was, in fact, a substitute for scientific study of the mind in Russia in the nineteenth century. As has been pointed out by the historian David Joravsky, most Russian novelists had nothing but contempt for academic psychology and psychiatry, perhaps because they realized that their own powers of psychological observation and explanation far outstripped anything that contemporary science had achieved.[12]

While in the novels of Turgenev internal psychological analysis is always balanced by external narrative description (as is the case in the passage describing Bazarov falling in love, quoted earlier), in Dostoevskii's novels the psychological takes pride of place. Dostoevskii's primary concern, throughout all his great novels, is to explore the psychology of individuals who are possessed by an idea. Every one of Dostoevskii's major novels has at its center a character whose task is to comprehend the mystery of his own personality. Dostoevskii, like Freud who so admired him, believed that the human mind was an enigma begging to be solved; his central artistic concern was to show, by a process of unparalleled artistic intuition, the ways in which the human mind attempts to hide from itself and then, when this becomes intolerable, discovers its own inner workings. This concern was already apparent in one of his earliest works, the 1846 novella *The Double*. Here Dostoevskii borrows the popular Romantic theme of the *Doppelgänger* but he characteristically shifts the center of interest from the eerie and supernatural to the psychological. The entire narrative interest of the piece comes from our observation of the gradual mental breakdown of the hero, one Mr. Goliadkin, as he tries desperately to escape his self-created double.

What sets *The Double* apart from the novels that Dostoevskii wrote after his return from Siberian exile is that Goliadkin's obsession is primarily personal, while those of Dostoevskii's greatest heroes are social and philosophical. They are, of course, refracted through the very specific characters Dostoevskii creates (which is why his heroes seem far more like individuals than like types). Nevertheless, the idea that the obsessions Dostoevskii portrays are meant to be read as portraits of his age lies at the very foundation of all his ideological novels. In the case of *Notes From Underground* (1864) the link between the diseased individual and the overall state of society (or at least part of it) is made explicit from the beginning. In his short authorial preface, Dostoevskii makes the following startling claim for the inner veracity of his fiction:

Both the author of the *Notes* and the *Notes* themselves are, of course, fictitious. Nonetheless, such persons as the author of such memoirs not only may, but must exist in our society, if we take into consideration the circumstances that led to the formation of our society.[13]

The hundred-odd pages of rambling first-person narrative that follow provide us with a more-than-adequate self-portrait of the Underground Man himself. From the mesmerizing first lines – "I am a sick man. I am a spiteful man. I am an unattractive man. I think my liver is diseased"[14] – we see a person who has literally been devoured by an idea, in this case a hypertrophied belief in determinism which seemed to follow from nineteenth-century materialism. The only impulse as strong as the Underground Man's belief in determinism, it turns out, is his hopeless desire to preserve some kind of freedom of action. All of the degrading, masochistic, and pitiful actions the Underground Man describes are rooted in his paradoxical attempts to find an outlet for his free will. Thus, with supreme mastery, Dostoevskii shows us the psychological dialectic by which the Underground Man, in his hopeless fight against his own belief, has constructed a prison from which there can be no escape.

In *Crime and Punishment* (1866), the first of Dostoevskii's great long novels, the author again focuses on an individual consumed by an idea. Originally, the novel was to have been written in confessional form and it was to be

> the psychological account of a crime . . . A young man, who was expelled from the university, of petit-bourgeois origins and living in utter poverty, through irresponsible thinking, through shaky notions, having fallen under the influence of those strange, "incomplete" ideas which are floating about in the air, has decided to break out of his horrible position in a single stroke. He has decided to kill an old woman.[15]

As Dostoevskii worked on the novel, he abandoned first-person narrative, but the new third-person perspective did not interfere with his ability to depict the inner workings of his confused hero's mind.

In its final version *Crime and Punishment* is a detective story with a twist; from the first pages we know that the murderer was the book's central character, the poor student Rodion Raskolnikov. The mystery is why he murdered and what psychological changes his having done so will effect in him. There is a further twist in that Raskolnikov himself does not fully know why he acted as he did. It is in this sense that the novel is a psychological thriller, for it depicts, with frightening analytic depth, the process by which Raskolnikov discovers his own motivations. Dostoevskii gradually unveils the complex ideas that have taken possession of his hero. The first is the modish utilitarian calculus which tells him that since he would do some wonderful things with the money, and the old pawnbroker he murders does nothing but hoard, then the greatest good for the greatest number will be produced if he kills her and steals the money. This theory is overlapped and partially contradicted by another, the "idea of Napoleon"; that is, the notion that there exists in the world a class of human beings who do not have to follow the moral laws that bind everyone else. Raskolnikov suspects that he belongs to this group, and in part he murders in order to prove it to himself. In the aftermath of the crime, however, confronted by the enormity of his own deeds, Raskolnikov slowly begins to recognize the speciousness of his theories. When he finally chooses to confess to his crimes, he does so primarily because the psychological weight of his guilt becomes heavier than he can bear.

Crime and Punishment also brings up the fascinating issue of when psychology does not appear in the Russian psychological novel. As we have noted before, its primary function is to make clear the illness of individuals who are suffering from ailments which beset an entire generation or class. Thus, it should not be surprising that the psychological approach is abandoned precisely at those moments when Dostoevskii wishes to show that his character is either healthy or no longer representative (or both, since the two often overlap). The most obvious example of this different method of writing comes in the epilogue to *Crime and Punishment*. Raskolnikov confesses his crime, is convicted and exiled to Siberia. Sonia, whose moral purity inspired him to confession in the first place, joins him there. At first, Raskolnikov seems not to have changed much, but after a serious illness, he recognizes the possibility of happiness, of an escape from the psychological demons that have tortured him. Raskolnikov lies in his bunk thinking of Sonia:

> He remembered how continually he had tormented her and wounded her heart. He remembered her pale and thin little face. But these recollections scarcely troubled him now; he knew with what infinite love he would now repay all her sufferings. And what were all, *all* the agonies of the past! Everything, even his crime, his sentence and imprisonment, seemed to him now in the first rush of feeling an external strange fact with which he had no concern. But he could not think for long together of anything that evening, and he could not have analyzed anything consciously; he was simply feeling. Life had stepped into the place of theory and something quite different would work itself out in his mind.[16]

Psychological self-analysis is a sign of illness, and health can only be reached at those moments when it is overcome. This is a paradoxical conclusion when considering the work of the author who is generally conceded to be one of the two great masters of psychological prose; but it is unavoidable. The Underground Man, Raskolnikov, Stavrogin in *The Devils* and Ivan Karamazov are all ill. Of these striking creations, only Raskolnikov is vouchsafed the ultimate happiness of an escape from self-analysis; the Underground Man apparently continues to rave, Stavrogin commits suicide when the secrets of his mind are pierced by Father Tikhon (whom Stavrogin, in one memorable scene, calls a "dammed psychologist"), and Ivan lapses into brain fever at the close of *The Brothers Karamazov*.

When we turn from Dostoevskii to the other master of Russian psychological prose, Lev Tolstoi, we move from a world characterized by tension, extremes of emotion, and psychological obsession to one in which the concerns are much more quotidian. While Tolstoi does provide the occasional character who seems to be a refugee from a Dostoevskii novel (Anna Karenina being the most prominent example), the majority of his characters are portraits of normal human beings with normal human emotions. This does not mean, however, that Tolstoi's analysis is any less subtle or penetrating than Dostoevskii's; they are simply describing different types of worlds. What it does mean, however, is that Tolstoi uses psychology in his novels for different purposes than had his predecessors. Where all the great Russian novelists discussed above based their characters on the concept of type (even if Turgenev's and Dostoevskii's greatest creations rise above it), Tolstoi is fascinated by the uniqueness of each individual. "To say about a person: he is original, good, intelligent, stupid, logical and so forth . . . such words do not give any idea about a person but they pretend to describe him while only throwing you off," wrote Tolstoi in a very early diary entry.[17] The point is that what Tolstoi attempted to do in all his novels was to show how the human personality, which looks like a smooth and finished whole from the outside, is in fact constructed of a mass of frequently self-contradictory elements held in unstable equilibrium by the self.

Tolstoi's interest in and talent for dissecting individual psychological motivations was already apparent in his earliest work, the pseudo-autobiographical novel *Childhood* (1853). The hero of this novel, Nikolai Irtenev, is the first of the line of Tolstoian heroes that includes Olenin of *The Cossacks*, Pierre Bezukhov of *War and Peace* and Konstantin Levin of *Anna Karenina*. Through constant self-analysis, these questing heroes attempt to achieve happiness through self-understanding. In this they function as autobiographical avatars, for Tolstoi's diaries reveal that he himself employed pitiless self-analysis as a tool for improvement and development. As opposed to the heroes of Dostoevskii's novels (who are prevented from reaching self-knowledge because they have been possessed by an external idea), Tolstoi's central characters are held back by far more mundane and realistic enemies: doubt, self-pity, illusion, physical desire.

These enemies, however, are no less dangerous for being prosaic, and, in the Tolstoian universe, the heroes are those who successfully navigate the path to self-knowledge avoiding the diseases of everyday life to which others fall prey. Paradoxically, however, self-knowledge, when achieved, allows the Tolstoian hero to stop thinking. In this respect, Tolstoi may be seen as a precursor to Freud, for he, like his contemporary Dostoevskii, believes that the sign of a complete cure is the overcoming of the need to analyze.

Probably the best illustration of how Tolstoi uses his unparalleled ability to explore the inner life of his characters is *Anna Karenina* (1877). From a psychological point of view, *Anna Karenina* can be read as a contrast between two very different ways of perceiving the world. On the one hand, we have Konstantin Levin, who is introduced at the beginning of the novel as something of a provincial boor, simply unable to grasp the ways and wiles of the city. Tolstoi constantly analyzes Levin's thoughts, but the curious thing about the character is that the more he thinks the less he understands. We are told instead that the only time he truly feels at home is when he is working on his farm, which also happens to be the one place in the novel where he is able, for the most part, not to think. Levin's battle, throughout the novel, will be to learn to trust the instinctual, non-thinking parts of his nature. When he is able to do this, he is happy, although the strength of his mind's desire to understand is such that this happiness is quite unstable. Such famous scenes as the hay-mowing (part III, chapter 4), in which Levin gets so caught up in the physical exertion of the task at hand that he forgets to think, echo the epilogue of *Crime and Punishment* with their shared assertion that thinking too much is a disease which can be cured only by unconscious epiphany.

Anna is introduced at the beginning of the novel as an entirely natural person. She is able to comfort her sister-in-law precisely because of the natural, unthinking, goodness that radiates from her. As she falls in love with Vronskii, however, this naturalness begins to disappear. She has been infected with a particularly virulent form of the disease of self-consciousness. Her marriage, which had given her satisfaction before she began to think about it, turns bitter. However, we are meant to recognize that this change in feeling reflects not the truth about her life, but rather her attempts to justify her affair with Vronskii. As Anna gradually becomes more psychologically aware she becomes a more interesting, even a heroic character (despite the fact that Tolstoi did not wish for this). Self-awareness, however, leads slowly to a kind of solipsism in Anna, and by the end of the novel she lives in an inner world of her own creation; indeed, as is the case with most of the characters I have discussed here, we can say that self-awareness is itself Anna's disease. The last scenes of part VII of the novel depict, in pitiless detail, the results of self-absorption. Anna travels in a railway carriage listening to the innocuous conversations around her. Functioning like a psychological black hole, she swallows and internalizes everything she hears, reinterpreting it to apply to herself and her own perceived condition. For the first time, Tolstoi applied the method that has come to be known as "stream of consciousness" to depict the disjointed patterns of Anna's thought. Unfortunately for Anna, by the end of part VII the disease of self-analysis has advanced to a critical stage. The self-created world of her thoughts comes to an all-encompassing prison, and the only escape is suicide.

Of course, the schema I have described as characteristic of *Anna Karenina* is complicated by the fact that each of the main characters is accompanied by a more or less permanent "unconscious" companion. After a youthful fling with consciousness which she quickly grows out of, Levin's wife Kitty is as naturally and unconsciously good as Anna is at the novel's outset. Vronskii, too, is a primarily unconscious actor, but in his case, lack of self-awareness leads directly to evil. Thus, Tolstoi seems to be saying, the absence of the disease of self-consciousness is not in itself a good. It only becomes one when one has struggled through consciousness and come out the other end. Because they both struggle actively to escape the snares of consciousness Anna and Levin are the central and most similar characters in the novel. That the results of their struggles are diametrically opposite only shows what a dangerous disease self-awareness can be.

The early 1880s brought about a crisis in the Russian novel. With the death of Dostoevskii in 1881, of Turgenev in 1883, and Tolstoi's rejection of literature at about the same time, the giants of the Russian psychological novel had disappeared. It was unclear whether further development of psychology in the framework of the novel would be possible or even whether the genre itself had any life left in it. And indeed, the period from the 1880s through the 1910s proved unpropitious for the Russian novel. Smaller genres dominated at this time. By the 1890s Chekhov had begun to show how the techniques for realistic psychological analysis that had been perfected by Tolstoi could be used in the short story. Even more important, Chekhov expanded a concern with analysis of the mental states of characters into the world of the drama, creating in *The Seagull* (1896), *The Three Sisters* (1899), *Uncle Vania* (1901), and *The Cherry Orchard* (1903) unprecedented masterpieces of psychological drama.

The first Russian novelist to come out of the long shadow of Mssrs Dostoevskii, Turgenev, and Tolstoi and to do something original with the depiction of psychology in the novel was Andrei Belyi (pseudonym for

Boris Bugaev) in *Petersburg* (1916, revised 1922). Belyi's novel flamboyantly avoids the conventions of Realist narrative, foregrounding narrative play, intertextual reference, and symbolic organization. In terms of psychology, it breaks new ground in its attempt to show that all actions (including narrative gestures) proceed from psychological states rather than the other way around. The central psychological concept in the novel is what Belyi calls "cerebral play," which is indulged in by the narrator (in order to create characters), by the characters themselves (in order to create their own internal and external worlds), and by the reader (in order to make sense of and derive pleasure from the narrative). The characters whose minds are depicted for us are Apollon Apollonovich Ableukhov (a high-ranking government official), his son, Nikolai Apollonovich, and Nikolai's erstwhile friend, the revolutionary Dudkin. Each of these characters is remarkable for his ability to create entire worlds via mental processes. Although Apollon Apollonovich is physically unprepossessing, we are told that from his cranium gigantic forces pour forth, both forces that seek to control the growing anarchy and chaos that are enveloping Russian society around the year 1905 and those that create this disorder. "Apollon Apollonovich was like Zeus: out of his head flowed goddesses and genii."

For all his efforts at control, however, Apollon Apollonovich is not even able to keep his own son under control. Nikolai Apollonovich's head becomes identified with revolutionary chaos through its equation with the bomb which he agrees to store for Dudkin. When he absentmindedly winds the bomb up, we know that an explosion will take place in the senator's house within twenty-four hours. In some of the most brilliant passages of the novel, we read in horror as the ticking of the bomb is registered inside Nikolai Apollonovich's head; the mind and the bomb becoming one. In this framework, the narrative itself becomes an arena for psychological discovery. The narrator has enclosed us in cerebral games, which distract us from the awful events about to unfold, but leave our minds, too, in a state of expectation which can only be relieved by an explosion. Instead of viewing the characters objectively (as we are encouraged to do by the conventions of Realism), in Belyi's novel we are meant to think and respond as if we were one of the characters, that is, the reader becomes part of the novel's psychological universe rather than an observer.

The connection of psychology with disease, and the identification of individual characters with psycho-social types is, however, preserved in Belyi's novel, despite all its modernist trappings: Apollon Apollonovich is an incarnation of the bureaucratic state, his mind a microcosm of its collapsing ideology. The hallucinating terrorist Dudkin, who loses his mind by the end of the novel, is, for all his individuality, meant to be representative of the Russian revolutionary class. Finally, Nikolai Apollonovich himself signifies the confused and divided loyalties of the younger generation of the Russian intelligentsia. All three are profoundly ill, as is Russian society as a whole, and Belyi's narrator, with his vaguely out of control cerebral play, is part of the same collapsing universe. Thus, although the narrative techniques for depicting psychology have changed, its function in Belyi's great novel remains analogous to that of its nineteenth-century predecessors.

Although the 1920s saw a renaissance of the novel in Russia, prose fiction in this period was generally more concerned with registering the impact of the revolution and civil war on Russian society than with exploring the inner lives of characters. The man of action became the model figure of Soviet society, and such literary embodiments of this figure as Gleb Shumalov in Fedor Gladkov's celebrated *Cement* (1925) were distinguished primarily by their ability to get the job done rather than by their complex thought processes. There was, however, one major novel of this period, *Envy* (1927) by Iuri Olesha, which employed subtle psychological analysis to thematize the conflict between a cerebral and active approach to the world. *Envy* is narrated by Nikolai Kavalerov, a holdover from pre-Revolutionary Russian culture, a self-pitying failure at everything he puts his hand to and an alcoholic. But Kavalerov's greatest sin is that he thinks too much, and the result is that, like some latter-day Underground Man, he can do nothing but envy the activity of those around him. In particular, his overly cerebral attitude towards the world is contrasted to the transcendent physicality of his sometime benefactor, the materialist sausage-maker of the future, Andrei Babichev. As the novel unfolds, we recognize that the formula "psychology equals disease," which we have come to expect from nineteenth-century Russian literature, is not being used as simplistically as we might have thought. Indeed, Kavalerov is ill, but his envy is accompanied by other traits which we are not so anxious to lose – compassion, aesthetic feeling, emotional responsiveness. Although in theory we should condemn Kavalerov as a hopelessly atavistic representative of the past, we begin to sympathize with him. And despite the fact that Babichev and his adopted son (the soccer player Sergei Makarov) embody the healthy – read unthinking – happiness of the perfect socialist future, we somehow do not like them. Thus, although Olesha's novel seems at first to have endowed his superfluous hero with all the negative and diseased traits of psychologism, by the end of the book, we recognize that the cure may well be worse than the disease. In this respect, Olesha's novel breaks new ground. In the pre-Soviet period, the healthy individual without psychology was often seen as a kind of ideal, a person who had overcome the diseases inherent in Russian culture which he embodied in his diseased state. When the healthy, unpsychological individual became the official societal norm, however, it was possible to see such people from a new angle, and to recognize the dangers as well as the advantages of the state.

Socialist Realism, which dominated Soviet literature between the 1930s and the 1950s had nothing to add to the techniques of psychological analysis that had been perfected by the Realists of the nineteenth century. What is more, those novelists who produced fiction "for the desk drawer" – an expression used to denote work that could not be published under conditions of Soviet censorship – were generally not interested in new or unusual ways of depicting the human psyche. Indeed, such great novels as Mikhail Bulgakov's *The Master and Margarita* or Andrei Platonov's *Chevengur* are almost completely devoid of psychological insight. Some Russian émigré novelists, however, continued to be fascinated by the potential of psychological analysis. In his pseudo-autobiographical novel *The Life of Arsenev* (written mostly during the late 1920s), Ivan Bunin uses masterfully the techniques of nineteenth-century psychological prose to show the interplay of the personal with the literary and historical worlds of his pre-Revolutionary youth and thereby to rescue them from oblivion. Vladimir Nabokov combined the insights of traditional psychological prose with some of the playfulness that characterized Andrei Belyi's *Petersburg* to produce such complex and compelling novels as *The Defense* (1930), *Despair* (1936), and *Invitation to a Beheading* (1938).

In the Soviet Union it was not until the "Thaw" period after 1953 that it became possible for writers with an interest in psychological exploration to turn their attention to an examination of the psyche of Soviet man, a psyche that had been traumatized by the horrors of Revolution, war, collectivization, and The Terror. One such novel is Boris Pasternak's *Doctor Zhivago*, which was originally meant for publication in the USSR but was instead published in Italy in 1957 after having been banned in the author's own country. Pasternak's work follows the life of his hero, Iurii Zhivago, a doctor and poet, from his pre-Revolutionary childhood through the years of Revolution and Civil War until his death in 1929. The novel is, in many respects, a throwback to the Russian nineteenth-century classics, mixing penetrating psychological analysis of the heroes with a broad description of the historical, philosophical issues of the period. But Pasternak does add one significant item to the arsenal of techniques for providing the reader with psychological insight into his main character. As a poet, Pasternak was certainly aware of the limitations that novelistic form imposes on the depiction of a given character's lyrical side, particularly if that character is himself a poet. In *Zhivago*, Pasternak extends the form by providing in an epilogue twenty-five lyric poems "written" by his hero. The poems, which are masterpieces of Russian poetry in their own right, add significantly to our understanding of the mind of the main character, and the coupling of novelistic and lyric extends dramatically the possibilities of the standard psychological novel.[18]

Perhaps the most astute explorer of the post-Stalinist Soviet psyche among authors who could be published in the USSR was the Moscow writer Iurii Trifonov. Of Trifonov's novels, his masterpiece is *The House on the Embankment* (1976). Set in the 1970s, this book describes what we might today call "recovered memory syndrome." In the course of the novel, we watch the main character and central narrator, Glebov, recover and attempt to come to terms with memories of the 30s and 40s, memories he had semi-consciously tried to suppress. In particular, he must relive and confront the cowardice that led to his betrayal of his dissertation advisor and potential future father-in-law. As a parallel to the memories of Glebov, Trifonov introduces a second narrator into the novel, an unnamed man who grew up with Glebov and recalls many of the same scenes. He does so, however, from an entirely different perspective, revealing in the process how distorted Glebov's memories are. The point, it appears, is to show how the conditions of Stalinist Russia encouraged most of a generation to fall into a state of collective amnesia, a state they were unable to escape even when the external reasons for it had disappeared. Thus, insofar as it depicts the psychology of an individual whose psychological diseases mark him as representative of an entire generation, Trifonov's moral psychological novel is a true heir to the nineteenth-century Russian tradition.

NOTES

1. Virginia Woolf, "Tolstoy's 'The Cossacks'," in *The Essays of Virginia Woolf*, ed. Andrew McNeillie, 4 vols. (London: The Hogarth Press, 1987), vol. II, p. 79.
2. It is, of course, extremely dangerous to provide psychiatric diagnoses of literary characters, particularly when one is not a psychiatrist and when the characters themselves were created before the discipline of psychiatry existed. Nevertheless, it seems reasonable to say that such characters as Poprishchin in Gogol's "Diary of a Madman," Goliadkin in Dostoevesky's *The Double*, and the central character of Garshin's story "The Red Flower" are indeed mentally ill in the medical sense of the term.
3. Lidia Ginzburg, *On Psychological Prose*, trans. Judson Rosengrant (Princeton University Press, 1991), see especially pp. 27–101. As Ginzburg puts it in discussing Belinsky: "[He] traced the psychological process in earnest both in its general significance and in its individual specificity, but most importantly in its *details*, details that were still beyond the reach of the novel in the first third of the nineteenth century." (p. 83).
4. Mikhail Lermontov, *Geroi nashego vremeni*, in Lermontov, *Sobranie sochinenii*

v chetyrekh tomakh (Leningrad, 1981), vol. IV, p. 184. English translation from *A Hero of Our Time*, trans. Vladimir and Dmitri Nabokov (Ann Arbor: Ardis, 1988), p. 2.

5. I. Goncharov, *Oblomov*, part I, chapter 8, trans. David Magarshak (London: Penguin, 1954), p. 93.

6. N. A. Dobroliubov, "Chto takoe oblomovshchina," in Dobroliubov, *Literaturnaia kritika*, 2 vols. (Leningrad, 1984), vol. I, p. 344.

7. "It is difficult, . . . and in my opinion simply impossible, to portray a life that has not yet taken form, where its forms have not settled and characters have not been stratified into types." Quoted in Milton Ehre, *Oblomov and His Creator: The Life and Art of Ivan Goncharov* (Princeton University Press, 1973), p. 74.

8. Elizabeth Cheresh Allen, "Introduction. Turgenev Today," in Allen, (ed.), *The Essential Turgenev* (Evanston: Northwestern University Press, 1994), p. xxiv.

9. Turgenev, *Ottsy i deti*, chapter XVII. Translation from Allen (ed.), *The Essential Turgenev*, p. 644.

10. Turgenev, *Ottsy i deti*, chapter XVIII. Translation from Allen (ed.), *The Essential Turgenev*, pp. 646–47.

11. Elizabeth Cheresh Allen, *Beyond Realism, Turgenev's Poetics of Secular Salvation* (Stanford University Press, 1992), pp. 55–56.

12. See David Joravsky, *Russian Psychology, A Critical History* (Oxford: Basil Blackwell, 1989), pp. 118–19.

13. F. M. Dostoevskii, "Zapiski iz podpol'ia," in Dostoevskii, *Polnoe sobranie sochinenii v tridtsati tomakh* (Leningrad: Nauka, 1972–90), vol V, p. 99. Translation in Dostoevsky, "Notes from Underground," trans. Jessie Coulson (London: Penguin, 1972), p. 13.

14. Dostoevskii, "Zapiski iz podpol'ia," p. 99. Translation mine.

15. Quoted in the notes to F. M. Dostoevskii, *Prestuplenie i nakazanie*, in Dostoevskii, *Sobranie sochinenii*, 10 vols. (Moscow: Gosudarstvennoe izdatel'stvo khudozhestvennoi literatury, 1956–58), p. 579. Translation mine.

16. F. M. Dostoevskii, *Prestuplenie i nakazanie*, in Dostoevskii, *Polnoe sobranie sochinenii*, vol 6, p. 422. Translation from *Crime and Punishment*, trans. Constance Garnett (New York: Bantam, 1981), pp. 471–72.

17. L. N. Tolstoi, *Polnoe sobranie sochinenii* (Moscow: Khudozhestvennaia literatura, 1929–64), 91 vols, vol. XLVI, p. 67.

18. This thought was suggested to me by Justin Weir, a graduate student in the Northwestern University, Department of Slavic Languages and Literature.

8

GARY SAUL MORSON

Philosophy in the nineteenth-century novel

When one considers the impact of Russian literature on world literature, one thinks first of all of the novel. Russia excelled in the novel to the extent that the Greeks and the English excelled in tragedy. To the extent – but not in the same way, because Greek and English tragedies offer the defining examples of the form, whereas the Russian masterpieces, while surely the greatest novels, defy, rather than define, their genre.

From the time Russian novels began to be widely read abroad, two features struck Western readers: their inclusion of long philosophical arguments and their violation of the formal expectations of the genre. It was also clear that these features are intimately connected, because it is in part the philosophical passages that turn these novels into "loose, baggy monsters." The essays in *War and Peace*, Levin's internal dialogues on the meaning of life at the end of *Anna Karenina*, Kirillov's mad meditations in *The Devils*, and Ivan Karamazov's "Grand Inquisitor" legend – all these striking sections, which seemed to have few counterparts in Western masterpieces, define the spirit of the Russian novel. Their Russianness, it appeared, lay in their transcendental ungainliness. And while some argued that *War and Peace* would be better without the essays, no one could imagine what Russian novels would be like if all their metaphysical protuberances were lopped off. Their greatness seemed closely connected to their flaws, and this fact offered a challenge to the traditional canon of the novel.

Viewed from a Russian perspective, however, the problem of philosophy in the novel looks rather different. The great nineteenth-century writers were not part of the philosophically obsessed intelligentsia, but rather chose to set themselves apart from it, often expressing unrestrained hostility to it. "In Russia an almost infallible gauge of the strength of an artist's genius is the extent of his hatred for the intelligentsia," observed the critic Mikhail Gershenzon in *Landmarks*.[1] If we allow for Gershenzon's habitual polemical exaggeration, the statement is largely correct. The great Russian novel (and story and drama) was *negatively* philosophical: it was directed *against* the faith in abstract ideas and ideology so common among the intelligentsia in pre-revolutionary Russia and in the rest of the world ever since. Read by Western intellectuals, who were increasingly philosophically inclined themselves, this key fact about Russian novels was lost, and they were sometimes transformed, more or less, into their opposite.

By and large, the great Russian novels are novels of ideas only insofar as they are novels that fight against the primacy of ideas. In their critical evaluation of theory, they are closer to Edmund Burke than to Hegel. Among Western thinkers, some Existentialists and, especially, Wittgenstein were closest in spirit to the Russian novelists they admired.[2]

Russian fiction relentlessly satirized the view, so common to members of the intelligentsia, that life is well lived, well governed, and well understood if approached in terms of the right theory. Thus it developed a set piece, the gathering of the *intelligenty* (members of the intelligentsia), who madly and comically exchange ideological formulae while behaving like children and treating each other with puerile cruelty. The most famous of these scenes is, of course, the chapter "A Meeting" (*"U nashikh"*) in *The Devils*, but there were several others, most notably the visit of Bazarov and Arkady to Kukshina's in *Fathers and Children* and the eponymously smoke-filled gathering at the "great thinker" Gubarev's in Turgenev's *Smoke*. Minor characters in the great novels seem to carry the aura (or smoke) of such ideological meetings with them as they repeat intelligentsial phrases like mantras. In *Crime and Punishment*, Lebeziatnikov (the name means roughly one who "fawns" on ideas), who is described as a participant in one of those "powerful, all-knowing, all-despising, and all-exposing [intelligentsia] circles," intones the formulae of a mind-numbing feminism – progressive husbands should provide their wives with lovers – and a form of socialism in which every aspect of daily life will be regulated. "We've gone further in our convictions," he proclaims, "we negate more."[3] Rakitin in *The Brothers Karamazov*, the Burdovskii crew in *The Idiot*, and Nikolai Levin in *Anna Karenina* mouth similar radical clichés, as do numerous characters in Turgenev and Chekhov. In *Fathers and Children*, Bazarov himself comes to refer to revolutionary truisms as mere "commonplaces in reverse," as shallow as the mindless conservative ones they supposedly supersede.

The whole mad atmosphere of theory-driven *intelligenty* is sometimes evoked in a single telling phrase. The devil who visits Ivan Karamazov mocks him by treating his ideas as if they had been invented by an ordinary *intelligent*. Paraphrasing Ivan's argument that "if there is no God, all is permitted," the devil queries, "That's all very charming; but if you want to swindle why do you want a moral sanction for doing it? But that's our modern Russian [*intelligent*] all over."[4] In *The Cherry Orchard*, Semenov-Pishchik offers an intelligentsial suggestion for saving the estate: "Nietzsche . . . the philosopher . . . the greatest, most renowned . . . a man of gigantic mind . . . Says in his works that one may forge banknotes."[5]

The Russian writers never ceased to satirize the intelligentsial faith that ideas, especially borrowed ones pushed to the extreme, would save the world. As Dostoevskii once remarked, a Russian *intelligent* is someone who can read Darwin and promptly resolve to become a pickpocket for the good of humanity. Such thinkers were millenarians for whom Hegel, Marx and other philosophers took the place of the Bible: for the intelligentsia, Marxism (or Nietzschean philosophy or some other ideology) was Revelation and rival interpretations were heresy. The novelists saw this tendency as at best misguided and at worst extremely dangerous.

If all they had done was point out the absurdity or danger of the intelligentsia's addiction to abstractions, the Russian writers would have deserved a place in literature alongside the other great satirists of ideas, from Aristophanes and Lucian to Swift and Voltaire. But they did something else: they developed a series of *counter-ideas* of their own. In my view, these counter-ideas constitute the most durable contribution of Russian thought. They are what make the Russian philosophical novel an incomparable achievement, both intellectually and aesthetically: for to express these counter-ideas effectively, the Russian writers undertook some radical and brilliant innovations in the form of the novel. Although these innovations made the novels seem formless to many early readers, the novels have come to be regarded as incomparable examples of realism that somehow, inexplicably, rose above their obvious "flaws." I would like to focus on the counter-ideas that seem to me of greatest significance.

No class in Russian history has had a more momentous impact on the destinies of that nation or indeed of the modern world than the intelligentsia.
(Martin Malia)

We get the word "intelligentsia" from Russia, where it came into circulation around 1860. Virtually all commentators have noted that the Russian term did not mean the same thing as its English counterpart (or, for that matter, as the Soviet use of the term). The word is very difficult to define because it was used in various ways, because it changed its meaning somewhat from decade to decade, and, most importantly, because it had honorific overtones: debates on Russia's destiny often took the form of redefining the "true" *intelligent*. Nevertheless, there was a group that almost everyone would have acknowledged as *intelligenty* in the strict sense, and it was this group that most offended the great writers.

One might readily identify three characteristics of the intelligentsia in this sense. First, an *intelligent* was expected to identify above all *as* an *intelligent*. To be an *intelligent* was not like being an Anglophile, a general, or a poet, all of which were compatible with a primary identity as a nobleman. Whereas an English intellectual might be a nobleman or professional who happened to be interested in the arts, a Russian *intelligent* owed his first loyalty, indeed the very sense of who he or she was, to the intelligentsia. A profession was to be pursued simply to make a living, and was to be abandoned whenever the (usually revolutionary) demands of the intelligentsia required. That is the point behind the comment made about Kirillov in *The Devils*: is it wise to hire an engineer who believes in universal destruction?

Second, an *intelligent* was expected to adhere to a particular set of beliefs. From this expectation derived an extreme intellectual conformity and a willingness to slander anyone who disagreed, characteristics that especially offended the major literary figures. Required beliefs differed over time, but they always included a commitment to socialism, atheism, and revolution. Most important of all, they involved a faith that the intelligentsia itself was destined to save society and that others could and might be sacrificed to realize its theories and dreams. "I am beginning to love mankind à la Marat," Belinskii had declared; "to make the least part of it happy I believe I could destroy the rest of it with fire and sword."[6] Nechaev and the terrorists of the 1870s also viewed their contemporaries and people from other groups as so much raw material to be expended in making a revolution, a perspective taken for granted by Lenin and severely criticized in *Landmarks*. Dostoevskii precisely caught the importance of the intelligentsia's belief in itself when he had Raskolnikov divide humanity into a few extraordinary people who have the right to kill and the many ordinary people who serve as mere breeders. Raskolnikov comes to realize that none of his theories for saving humanity really matters to him; what matters is membership of the extraordinary. The intelligentsia's beliefs about economics or the peasant may change, Dostoevskii suggests, but the core idea that will remain is its megalomaniac aspirations for itself.

Finally, an *intelligent* was expected to live a certain sort of properly sordid life. Bad manners like Chernyshevskii's were regarded as essential.[7] The nihilists in *The Idiot*, for instance, treat rudeness itself as a form of good manners according to the radical code – and, as Myshkin wryly observes, they then demand the respect accorded to traditional good manners and take offense at the slightest rudeness directed at themselves, measured against both codes. Eager from radical principle to offend others' dignity, they insist on the most punctilious respect for their own (another form of commonplace in reverse).

For the writers, those beliefs spelled a stifling intellectual conformity. It was clearly impossible to create anything but crude propaganda if one adhered to a code in which anything but certain beliefs was automatically "reactionary." Asked to join a typical intelligentsia "circle," Chekhov replied with a statement of his fundamental values – personal honesty and simple acts of kindness for which "you've got to be . . . just a plain human being. Let us be ordinary people, let us adopt the same attitude *towards all*, then an artificially overwrought solidarity will not be needed."[8] Pressed to break with his conservative friend Suvorin, Chekhov replied by denouncing the intelligentsia's enforcement of conformity. What would such people do if they ever gained real political power? he asked. "Under the banner of science, art, and oppressed free thinking among us in Russia, such toads and crocodiles will rule in ways not known even at the time of the Inquisition in Spain" – a comment which, if anything, was to prove an understatement.[9]

The novel is above all a genre that deals with the particulars of experience, and so it became a tool directed at the abstractions of ideological thinking. One may, in fact, identify a masterplot of an ideological novel: a hero proclaims a set of theory-driven beliefs with great energy and charisma; but in the course of the novel, events take place that reveal to the hero himself that reality is infinitely more complex than theories allow. In *Fathers and Children*, for instance, Bazarov regards love, art, and nature from an entirely "materialist" point of view, and considers romance and beauty to be sheer rot; but, seduced by fragrant spring air, elegance, and a beautiful woman, he finds himself feeling the sort of love that "the minnesingers and troubadours" praised. In *The Brothers Karamazov*, Ivan, who believes that all is permitted, finds himself feeling guilty for a crime he has only desired. In these and many similar cases, the governing trope is what might be called the "irony of outcomes": the lived consequences of a theory, not another theory, refute it. Life ambushes ideology. An "irony of origins" is also often used: we see that what leads a hero or heroine to a set of beliefs is not theoretical cogency, as they seem to think, but some complex psychological factor ideology does not even accommodate but that the novelist traces with supreme subtlety. In *Fathers and Children* we see that Arkady becomes a nihilist so as to seem more grown up, which is, of course, itself a childish thing to do; and so when denouncing all authority he looks to his mentor Bazarov for approval.

There is in such cases a strong metaliterary aspect to this kind of novelistic disproof, because (as in Bazarov's case) the realist, psychological novel is itself a form typically rejected by the ideological hero. Bazarov is quite explicit about that, as are all heroes who bow to the "men of the sixties." The novel responds by making the very rejection of novels and all they presuppose – love, the soul, particularity, and the superiority of experience over theory – itself a central or important secondary theme, as it is in *Fathers and Children* and *The Devils*.

The *intelligenty* typically relied on a strong ethical appeal, and so a central theme of the Russian philosophical novel became a kind of counter-ethics. In one of the dialogues contained in Herzen's quasi-novel *From the Other Shore* – probably his finest work from a literary point of view – one skeptic of ideologically driven hope points to the intense cruelty likely to result from utopian longings. Willing to sacrifice real people for the sake of a theoretical goal, the *intelligent* becomes the cruelest tyrant of all:

> If progress is the end, for whom are we working? . . . Do you truly wish to condemn all human beings alive today to the sad role . . . of wretched galley slaves, up to their knees in mud, dragging a barge with some mysterious treasure and with the humble words "progress in the future" inscribed on its bows? . . . This alone should serve as a warning to people: an end that is infinitely remote is not an end, but, if you like, a trap: an end must be nearer – it ought to be, at the very least, the labourer's wage, or pleasure in the work done.[10]

In *The Brothers Karamazov*, Father Zosima also contends that love and goodness must be directed at particular people in particular situations: love for mere abstractions is always false and turns rapidly into its opposite. He describes a doctor he once knew:

> "I love humanity," he said, "but . . . the more I love humanity in general, the less I love man in particular. In my dreams . . . I have often come to making enthusiastic schemes for the service of humanity, and perhaps I might actually have faced crucifixion if it had been suddenly necessary; and yet I am incapable of living in the same room with anyone for two days together, as I know by experience . . . But it has always happened that the more I detest men individually the more ardent becomes my love for humanity."
>
> (*BK*, p. 64)

This contrast between dreams and theory on the one hand and experience on the other shapes Dostoevskii's plots as well, and so Zosima's comments have real narratological significance. We are told, for instance, that Alesha, though dedicated to God, has the same mentality as the socialists and materialists: he believes in miracles, sudden change, and "immediate action" based on a model, which is why he is so disappointed when the expected miracle fails to occur on Zosima's death: Zosima's corpse unexpectedly stinks and the chance to astonish non-believers is lost. But at Grushenka's he hears the splendid story of "the onion," which suggests to him that a small act of kindness is what God wants, and he performs such an act for Grushenka. When he returns to the monastery, he hears the story of the marriage at Cana read over Zosima's body and he realizes what it is that Zosima has been trying to teach him.

Pause for a moment on the extraordinary choice of this story as the central Christian text of this highly Christian novel. The incident has nothing to do with Jesus' mission – "mine hour is not yet come," Jesus tells his mother when he is reluctant to perform the miracle. Or as Alesha thinks, "was it to make wine abundant at poor weddings that He had come down to earth?" (*BK*, p. 434). In a real sense it was: the Christ of this novel, and the novel about this Christ, teach that goodness comes from small, prosaic, barely noticed acts of kindness. Zosima explains that one does not have to know the consequences of good acts to believe in them, for each small act of good (or evil) shapes another small act in an endlessly complex concatenation of causes and influences beyond human view. Small acts are like seeds bearing fruit with more seeds, an image that provides the epigraph to *The Brothers Karamazov* and is developed at length in *The Idiot*. In *The Idiot*, Ippolit is right for a change when he remarks on one of his rare good deeds: "But how can you tell what seed may have been dropped in his soul? . . . You know it's a matter of a whole lifetime, an infinite multitude of ramifications hidden from us. The most skilful chess-player, the cleverest of them, can look only a few moves ahead . . ."[11] At the end of *The Brothers Karamazov*, Alesha teaches this lesson to the boys. And so the novel turns out to have a double plot, one about the fate of ideologues and passionate men, and the other about unremarkable people who learn small acts of kindness. In *The Devils*, Shatov achieves his brief moment of salvation when his wife is in labor and he realizes that even the right ideology – even the Slavophilism to which Dostoevskii himself was inclined – kills what is real in life, that is, caring for specific people.

A similar contrast underlies many of Chekhov's plays and stories, for Chekhov above all believed in small acts of kindness. Uncle Vania's radical mother neglects him while making notes on the margins of her pamphlet, and the old professor ("I have my knife out for professors," Chekhov wrote)[12] neglects people for dead ideas, while Sonia, the real heroine of the play, is quietly kind to all around her. Even Elena voices the Chekhovian truth when she observes: "You, Ivan Petrovich, are an educated and intelligent man, and I should think you would understand that the world is perishing not from robbers and fires . . . but from all these petty squabbles." Apocalyptic or extremist thinking – "robbers and fires" – distracts us from the small actions that really are life and that shaped Chekhov's distinctive undramatic dramas.

Stated positively, what the great Russian novelists proposed was a revival of casuistry, that is, reasoning by cases.[13] Bakhtin's early treatise, "Toward a Philosophy of the Act," makes this approach, already developed by the novelists, explicit.[14] The tradition he opposes – he calls it "theoretism" – sees ethics as the application of the right rules to particular situations. But in Bakhtin's view real morality must go from the bottom up, not the top down; "oughtness" begins with where I am at a particular unrepeatable moment in a specific situation unlike all others if viewed finely enough. It begins – I begin – with my "singular singularity" (p. 112). "That which can be accomplished by me (right now) cannot be accomplished by anyone else, ever" (p. 112). Consequently, "There are no definite moral norms signifying in themselves, but there is a moral subject . . . on which one must rely" (p. 85).

In an evident allusion to the revolutionaries, Bakhtin cautions that one invites cruelty when one thinks of oneself as a mere representative of some party, historical force, theory, or great idea: in that case, one becomes a mere "pretender" and seeks an impossible "alibi" for one's own ethical choice. But "there is no alibi," Bakhtin repeats. As his later works make explicit, Bakhtin's anti-theoretist view of ethics was indebted to his favorite genre and especially to his favorite Russian writer, Dostoevskii.

War and Peace and *Anna Karenina* are both concerned to demonstrate the superiority of ethically sensitive case reasoning to any conceivable theory. Pierre and Levin reach the Tolstoian truth when they give up their abstract theories and learn to judge by cases. Thus, at the end of both novels Tolstoi describes how his hero judges rightly by giving a list of particular choices – "To Petr, who was paying ten percent a month to a moneylender he must lend money . . . But he could not let off peasants from paying their rent," and so on – a list that goes on for about a page, but he never provides the rule his heroes follow: because they do not follow a rule.[15] They draw instead on the whole experience of their lives and on very close observation of the particular person in front of them. These parallel passages in the two novels illustrate how their plots, for all their differences, resemble each other. In each novel, one hero or heroine believes in an abstraction (Prince Andrei in glory, Anna in romance) that proves as mistaken as it is seductive; whereas the other (Pierre or Levin) comes, after many errors, to see the world casuistically.

When, at the end of part VIII of *Anna Karenina*, Koznyshev asks Levin whether he would kill a Turk about to harm a child before his eyes, Levin answers that he does not know, that he would have to decide on the moment. Though weak theoretically – no rule for how he would make the decision is offered – this is the right answer for Tolstoi. No rule should decide, because the particularities are too unpredictable and the consequences of a wrong judgment, either way, are too terrible. The right thing to do is to develop a good moral sense over a lifetime and then trust one's morally trained eyes over any abstract philosophy. That is why the raising of children is so important a theme in Tolstoi (and Dostoevskii) and why they judge so severely the intelligentsia's tendency to undervalue such prosaic activities. For if one does not develop a significant moral sense in childhood, one can never really make up for it (the story of Vronskii).

Here again we come to the Russian novel's self-awareness. If morality is a matter of sensitive attention to particulars, then novels are the best form for ethical education. More than philosophers' or sociologists' examples, novels provide the richest and "thickest" descriptions of specific moral cases. They educate by example and exemplification, but they do not encourage us to apply theories. The richer, more detailed, and more complex the cases, the better the moral education: which is one reason Tolstoi's novels are so long.

After looking for theories and finding only despair, Levin understands that he was seduced by the "pride" of intellect: "And not merely the pride of intellect, but the stupidity of intellect. And most of all the deceitfulness, yes, the deceitfulness of intellect" (p. 831). But where intellect deceives, an educated attentiveness informs. As Wittgenstein likes to say, "don't think, but look!"[16] Tolstoi's novels – Russian realist novels in general – are conceived as exercises in teaching one to *look*, to see the richness of particular *cases* that theories generalize away.

In fact, it appears that the novel began as a casuistical genre. After casuistry had been discredited philosophically (especially by Pascal in *The Provincial Letters*), it took refuge in more popular publications, and gave birth to something like our advice columns. Daniel Defoe wrote such articles, some at great length and evidently made up. As they lengthened, they grew into his novels. Banished from philosophy, which had come to emphasize the general over the particular, the abstract over the experience, and the timeless over the timely, casuistry thus found a home in the novel. A century and a half later, the Russian novel in effect made this "form-shaping" idea of the genre, an idea that was long forgotten, newly explicit and self-conscious. In so doing, it set itself radically apart from all those who believed in the primacy of theory and rules.

Casuistry was closely related to a set of ideas that I have elsewhere called prosaics.[17] Developed most explicitly by Tolstoi, prosaics became an idea –

better, a sense of life – with which other Russian writers contended. In opposing intelligentsial apocalypticism, for instance, Dostoevskii was torn between a counter-apocalypticism and prosaics. The struggle between these two ideas – between Sonia and Razumikhin, between the apocalyptic and prosaic sides of Prince Myshkin – shapes the peculiar ideological dialogue of his works. Marked as Tolstoian, the prosaic sensibility thereby plays a prominent, though not uncontested role in his all major novels, as well as in *The Diary of a Writer*. It was important to Turgenev as well, and it may fairly be argued that Chekhov became the most orthodox heir of Tolstoian prosaics, loyal to the sensibility of *War and Peace* and *Anna Karenina* even after Tolstoi had rejected those works.

Deeply suspicious of the claims of theory to accommodate the world, prosaics sees the life of individuals and society as fraught with contingency, which operates not just at grand historical junctures but also at every moment of our daily lives. Whereas the impulse of the theoretists is to detect (or invent) some underlying order or law beneath the apparent mess of the world – the dream of a social science – prosaics makes just the opposite assumption. In prosaics, the fundamental state of the social world is mess, and order is always the precarious result of human effort. As Bakhtin was to say, order is a "task," a project posited and never quite completed. Almost unique for his time, Tolstoi relentlessly denies the existence of historical laws, especially the one that seemed the most obvious to his contemporaries, a law of progress.

In *War and Peace*, battle serves as an emblem of concentrated history. The generals who think they can plan battle repeatedly overlook the radical contingency of combat, what Prince Andrei calls "the hundred million diverse chances" that will be decided "on the moment" and that no one can foresee. Tolstoi had a supreme sense of *presentness*, the complexity of each moment leading to outcomes that no knowledge of the past, and no conceivable principles, laws, or strategies would allow one to predict, even in principle. The wise generals, like Kutuzov and Bagration, know this, and are aware that it is line officers, who seize opportunities that arise contingently and unexpectedly, who decide battles. That is why Kutuzov falls asleep at councils of war and recommends, as the best preparation for a battle, not more plans but "a good night's sleep." It is also why the most effective soldier we see is not Prince Andrei, with his dreams of glory and his early faith in military genius, but the utterly untheoretical and un-intellectual Nikolai Rostov, who keeps his wits about him and makes the most of opportunities that arise fortuitously.

Pierre begins the novel as a sort of *intelligent* before the name – the critics condemned Tolstoi for such anachronisms – who believes that either there is a theory to explain life or else there is no such theory, and so all is relative and meaningless. Alternating between utopian hope and metaphysical despair, he consumes theory after theory, each of which parodies some intellectual flaw of the theoretical world view in general. When Pierre adopts Masonic numerology supposedly allowing him to predict when and how Napoleon will be defeated, Tolstoi means us to see all substantive philosophies of history as equally absurd. Of course, Pierre calculates that he himself is destined by history to kill Napoleon, much as the intelligentsia (as a group and often as individuals) imagined itself as the Napoleon destined to defeat Napoleon, or whoever was the enemy at the time. As Porfirii Petrovich insinuates to Raskolnikov, don't we Russian intellectuals all imagine ourselves to be little Napoleons? "Inside every maximalist [*intelligent*]," wrote Sergei Bulgakov in *Landmarks*, "there is a little Napoleon of socialism or anarchism . . . But life is an everyday affair."[18] One reason the "Napoleon idea" plays such a large role in Russian fiction is that it is the opposite of prosaics: it assumes the value of theoretical genius and grand action, rather than small acts of ordinary people in everyday situations.

By the end of the novel, Pierre learns the value of the ordinary, a key tenet of prosaics. "In everything near and comprehensible he had [previously] seen only what was limited, petty, commonplace, and meaningless. He had equipped himself with a mental telescope and gazed into the distance where the petty and commonplace had seemed to him great and infinite only because they were not clearly visible."[19] The telescope he abandons is theory, and he learns to appreciate not the laws supposedly behind experience but experience itself. "Now, however, he had learned to see the great, the eternal, the infinite in everything, and therefore . . . he had naturally discarded the telescope through which he had till then been gazing over the heads of men, and joyfully surveyed the ever-changing, eternally great, unfathomable, and infinite life around him" (p. 1320). He now appreciates in this prosaic sense the words he had learned as a child, "God is here and everywhere." That great reader of Tolstoi, Wittgenstein, was to write: "The aspects of things that are most important for us are hidden because of their simplicity and familiarity. (One is unable to notice something – because it is always before one's eyes.) . . . And this means: we fail to be struck by what, once seen, is most striking and most powerful" (*PI*, section 129, p. 50e).

God must have loved the ordinary events because he made so many of them. For Tolstoi and Chekhov, life is good when it is lived well moment by moment. In one of his late essays, "Why Do Men Stupefy Themselves?," Tolstoi retells a story about the painter Briullov, who corrected a student's sketch. You only touched it a tiny bit, the student remarks, but it is quite a different thing. Briullov replies that art begins where that "tiny bit" begins, and Tolstoi adds that what is true of art is true of life. True life is lived not where noticeable changes occur – where people move about, fight, and slay one another – but where infinitesimally small changes take place.

Tolstoi's description of human psychology depends on his sense of "tiny alterations" of consciousness. When Prince Andrei, listening from the next room, hears the moans of his dying wife in labor, he registers the cry of an infant, and says to himself, "Why have they taken a baby in there?" Of course, a split second later he realizes that his child was born, a conclusion which is so obvious that most of us would never remember the stray thought that passed after an infinitesimal instant. But Tolstoi records the thought, because his technique is to take the smallest mental act that we remember or that other writers record and to show that it can in fact be subdivided much further. This use of "tiny alterations" provides another reason his novels are so long.

Tolstoi further argues that Dostoevskii's Raskolnikov (in *Crime and Punishment*) lived his true life not when he formulated his theories about Napoleon or decided that all is permitted, but when he was just lying on his couch, thinking about the most ordinary events in life. At such moments, so ordinary he rarely remembers them, infinitesimally small changes take place. In Raskolnikov's case, these infinitesimals of mental life lead to the death of the old woman and her sister even though Raskolnikov never quite decided on murder. Tolstoi precisely caught what Dostoevskii was up to here: the murder was the result not of a theory or plan, but of a climate of mind, which is why Raskolnikov can never decide which theory he had in mind and never behaves according to any of his plans.

If history and individual lives are shaped by the sum total of ordinary events, too small to notice, then historical and biographical narratives radically misrepresent the shape of events. They do so for a variety of related reasons. First, as Tolstoi points out, historians typically rely on records, and people generally record only what is unusual or exceptional. Historians are therefore strongly predisposed to underestimate the significance of ordinary events that nobody bothers to record. Something similar happens in novels, which usually rely on dramatic actions to explain a life. Second, both histories and novels rely on a coherent plot, which leaves out loose ends and eliminates contingency: indeed if they do not, critics usually describe the work as flawed. But if life is made by ordinary events, which usually lead nowhere in particular, then this criterion of great art almost compels narratives to lie about *how* events happen.

This line of thinking informs what is perhaps the most famous, and most often misunderstood sentence of Russian literature, the opening of *Anna Karenina*: "All happy families resemble each other; each unhappy family is unhappy in its own way." Happy families resemble each other because their lives are filled with undramatic incidents that do not make a good story, but unhappy lives each have a story: and each story is different. In his notebooks and letters of the period, Tolstoi twice quotes a French saying, "happy people have no history." Plot is an index of error.

If real life is lived outside of plot, then the whole way in which novels are written will have to change. That is basically the reason Tolstoi gives for insisting that *War and Peace* is not a novel nor, for that matter, an example of any received narrative genre. *War and Peace* relies on a form of "negative narration": interest is sustained by dramatic events in the foreground, which, however, are shown to be empty and meaningless, whereas the real story lies where there is no story, on the margins. And so in *Anna Karenina* we have the scenes where Dolly takes pleasure in her children and the joy of the Shcherbatskii parents when Kitty becomes engaged. Chekhov was to make remarkable use of this technique in his undramatic dramas and in many of his stories. When Vania comes out shooting, that is pure theatre in the pejorative sense, but when Sonia or the old nurse quietly care for those around them, we have no drama at all: we have, instead, a sense of what really makes a life valuable and what actually allows it to go on. Chekhov's metatheatre – theatre that shows what is wrong with the whole histrionic view of life contained in the very form of the "well-made play" – transfers to the stage the radical innovations Tolstoi made in the form of the novel.

Tolstoi restores contingency to the world by including a large number of incidents that lead nowhere in particular. When in *Great Expectations* Pip gives a pie to a convict, we know it must lead somewhere or the author would not have included it. But "pies" are given all the time in *War and Peace* and *Anna Karenina*, with no more discernible effect than most of our daily donations. That is why when events do work out novelistically in *War and Peace*, they possess tremendous power, because we know, from the experience of reading, that they very well may have worked out differently. Critics at the time and since have faulted Tolstoi for this mass of contingent details – they are yet another reason Tolstoi's novels are so long – but it is in part their presence that makes the feeling of experience in these works so close to that of life.

In short, a key factor that provoked radical innovations in the form of the novel was a deep concern with the philosophy of time. Whereas the intelligentsia constantly favored models of closed time, in which history had a plot guaranteed to lead to a predetermined utopian ending, several of the great writers favored models of open time allowing for human freedom, contingency, and the unpredictable: in short, for what Bakhtin was to call "surprisingness." "If we concede that human life can be governed by reason, then the possibility of life is destroyed," Tolstoi concludes in *War and Peace* (1354). The existence of laws of psychology or history would reduce people to piano keys or organ stops, complains the Underground Man. There is no libretto to history, declares Herzen in *From the Other Shore*: "In history, all is improvisation, all is will, all is *ex tempore*" (p. 39). "Don't say: *It could not have been otherwise*," wrote Pushkin. "If that were true, then the historian would be an astronomer and events in the life of humanity could be predicted in calendars, like eclipses of the sun. But Providence is not algebra."[20]

The Russian writers also keenly sensed that determinism is already implicitly endorsed by the very plots of traditional novels. This, in fact, was their great insight, leading to dramatic innovations in the form of the novel. They saw, for instance, that foreshadowing already closes down time, because it allows earlier events to be caused by later ones; the characters' sense of freedom becomes an illusion when the reader is given signs of a future already written. Similarly, structure, which by its very nature ensures that all events figure in a pattern, necessarily eliminates contingency and chance. So does closure, which makes all events gravitate forward, to a conclusion that ties up all loose ends. In short, however much a writer might wish to endorse open time, traditional plotting almost forces a model of closed time upon him. How is this problem to be solved?

The Russian novelists came up with at least two remarkable solutions, which I have called "creation by potential" and "sideshadowing."[21] It was the use of these devices, more than anything else, that led to the strange form of the Russian novel. I am suggesting that the incomparable feel of realism of these works – which made Matthew Arnold declare that *Anna Karenina* is not a piece of art but a piece of life,[22] that if life could write itself, it would write like Tolstoi – depends more than anything on a concern with the philosophy of time and its implications for literary plotting.

"Creation by potential" is a form of composition in which the writer literally does not know what is going to happen next, a technique that precludes the very possibility of foreshadowing, structure, and closure. Events are necessarily caused only by prior events and by present chances, and not by a future to which everything is invisibly tending. In his essay "Some Words about the Book *War and Peace*" – note that he called his work a "book," not a novel – and in his drafts for an introduction to the work, Tolstoi promised that he would write so that each part of the work would have "an independent interest . . . which would consist not in the development of events but in development [itself]."[23] *Development itself* – the experience of pure process and autonomous presentness – meant that at each point he would develop potentials he had planted before and would plant new ones for the future; events would simply happen, not tend anywhere; and serial publication would ensure that the author could not go back and correct earlier parts so as to leave out loose ends. Creation by potential ensures that time flows only forward, and it necessarily results in numerous loose ends – that is, it makes the story resemble life as we actually experience it.

This technique was also used to a considerable extent in *Anna Karenina*. Part VIII of the novel devotes considerable attention to the Eastern War, a topic that *could not* have been part of any original plan because when Tolstoi published the first part of the novel that war had not yet begun. For today's readers, history is telescoped, and so we are likely to miss what must have been a striking fact: the author was incorporating events from the real world, chance events outside his control, into the very fabric of his story. *The Idiot* also incorporates reports of real crimes that had not taken place when the first installments of the novel appeared. A still more radical technique results in Dostoevskii's *Diary of a Writer: A Monthly Publication*, in which the work as a whole and many specific narratives in it are deliberately left open to chance events of the real world on which Dostoevskii reported but which he could not control.

In fact, more than one of Dostoevskii's novels was written with the author discovering events as he wrote them. This practice was probably forced on him by financial pressures, but he seems to have made a virtue of necessity. The incomparable thrill we identify as Dostoevskian – something beyond mere suspense – results from the fact that he was as uncertain as his readers and characters of what would happen next, and he managed to convey that uncertainty in the novel itself. Critics often fault *The Idiot* for its "structural flaws" and loose ends, but typically the same critics then remark on the novel's uncanny ability to rise above those flaws. However, there is less paradox here than meets the eye if we recognize that there can be structural flaws only if one insists on reading in terms of structure: *The Idiot*, like *War and Peace*, was created by potential. So, it appears, were other masterpieces of Russian fiction, like *Evgenii Onegin*.

Dostoevskii's novels also may serve to illustrate "sideshadowing." The opposite of foreshadowing, sideshadowing conveys the sense that time is open and that each moment contains real alternatives. For the determinist, and in a plot based on structure and closure, whatever happens had to have happened; the impression of other possibilities is a mere illusion, the product of ignorance recognized as such when the narrative is over. But in the world of sideshadowing, the illusion is inevitability itself. *Something else* was possible at each moment. Instead of casting a foreshadow from the future, it casts a shadow "from the side," that is, from the other possibilities. Along with an event, we see its alternatives; with each present, another possible present. Sideshadows conjure the ghostly presence of might-have-beens and might-bes. Two (or more) alternative presents, the actual and the possible, are made simultaneously visible.

Time therefore appears as a field of possibilities. Each moment has a set of possible events that could take place in it. From this field, a single event emerges – perhaps by chance, perhaps by choice, perhaps by some combination of both with the inertia of the past, but in any case contingently. Dostoevskii's novels typically work by making this field visible. In one scene in *The Devils*, for instance, Liza Nikolaevna and Stavrogin jostle against each other in the doorway after their visit to the mad prophet Semen Iakovlevich:

> I fancied they both stood still for an instant, and looked, as it were, strangely at one another, but I may not have seen rightly in the crowd. It is asserted, on the contrary, and quite seriously, that Liza, glancing at Nikolai Vsevolodovich, quickly raised her hand to the level of his face, and would certainly have struck him if he had not drawn back in time. Perhaps she was displeased with the expression of his face, or the way he smiled, particularly just after such an episode with Mavrikii Nikolaevich. I must admit I saw nothing myself, but all the others declared they had, though they certainly could not all have seen it in such a crush, though perhaps some may have. But I did not believe it at the time. I remember, however, that Nikolai Vsevolodovich was rather pale all the way home.[24]

"Though . . . though . . . however"; "I fancied," "perhaps," "it is asserted quite seriously": with qualification piled on qualification, tentative judgments no sooner made than withdrawn and perhaps ambiguously re-asserted, the narrator claims not to be sure what he himself has seen. Reports of others are probably even more unreliable, and apparently contradictory, though not necessarily groundless. Frivolous people with a taste for scandal seriously say things that differ from what the narrator himself has seen, although of course, he may have missed such a vague event and does not trust his own eyes "in such a crush." He concludes by saying that he did not believe in the reported event – does he accept it now? – and then giving evidence that it might just be true anyway. Moreover, the action in question was checked before it happened – the action that may have taken place was a slap *not* given – and so one has in any case to distinguish between an unrealized possibility and nothing at all.

What we are given here is not one but many possible stories. The real point is that whatever did happen, any of these incidents *could* have happened. What is important is the *field of possibilities*, not the one actualized. By depriving any version of undeniable actuality, Dostoevskii reveals the field itself. The sideshadows crowd out the actual event.

Readers will identify this kind of narration as quintessentially Dostoevskian. His novels proceed by allowing for many possible stories, a sea of rumors, and – as in *The Devils* – the refusal to specify, even for key events, what did actually happen. All this is part of Dostoevskii's war on determinism, his sense that if the tape were replayed, something else might have happened. The most important lesson of sideshadowing is: to understand an event one must know not only what did happen, but also what else might have happened. For Tolstoi, sideshadowing and creation by potential served as ways to illustrate contingency; for Dostoevskii, they demonstrated human freedom.

The sense of open time also implies that we ourselves are not the inevitable product of history, and that, if some other chain of events had taken place, we might see the world quite differently. If that is so, then the hubris characteristic of the intelligentsia's way of judging the past is entirely unearned. Tolstoi, Dostoevskii, Turgenev, and Chekhov were repulsed by that supreme tone of authority with which the intelligentsia judged figures of the past (and their non-intelligentsia contemporaries), sure that, somehow, they were wiser for having been born later (and for having the right intelligentsia theory). In *War and Peace*, Tolstoi mocks what he calls "the stern tribunal" of professors and critics who cast their little stones at Alexander I – in this the tsar was progressive, in that reactionary – as if the critics' view were necessarily beyond question: "All the famous people of that period, from Alexsander and Napoleon to Madame de Staël, Photius, Schelling, Fichte, Chateaubriand, and the rest pass before their stern tribunal and are acquitted or condemned according to whether they promoted *progress* or *reaction*" (pp. 1351–52). Naturally, progress is defined as proximity to the beliefs of the historians themselves.

As there is such a thing as ethnocentrism, the unjust and unjustified privileging of the prejudices of one's own culture, so there is also such a thing as "chronocentrism," which confers unjustified privilege on the prejudices of one's own time. Chronocentrism combines rather easily with a "centrism" of profession. In Tolstoi's phrase, it is "natural and agreeable" for intellectuals to think this way, just as it is agreeable for them to think that the world is best understood in terms of theory and is most likely to be redeemed by the application of the right ideology. For if what we need is not theory, but practical reasoning – in Aristotle's terms, *phronesis* – then how would intellectuals justify their claim to pre-eminence in solving problems? They have never been famed for having much practical wisdom.

The idea that philosophy is about the abstract, the timeless, the general, and the theoretical had dominated European thought since Descartes. The Russian novel gives new life to an older and rival philosophical tradition – extending from Aristotle to Montaigne and revived in our time by Wittgenstein – that places the highest value on the particular, the local, the timely, and on accumulated experience. The insights produced by this way of thinking constitute the great contribution of the Russian philosophical novel and led to the remarkable series of formal innovations that made them aesthetic, as well as philosophical, masterpieces.

NOTES

1. Mikhail Gershenzon, "Creative Self-Consciousness," in Mikhail Gershenzon (ed.), *Vekhi/Landmarks: A Collection of Articles About the Russian Intelligentsia* (originally published in 1909), trans. Marshall Shatz and Judith Zimmerman (Armonk, N.Y.: M. E. Sharpe, 1994), p. 60.
2. On Wittgenstein's debt to Tolstoy, see Allan Janik and Stephen Toulmin, *Wittgenstein's Vienna* (New York: Simon and Schuster, 1973), pp. 177, 200–01, 205, 206, 224, 229.
3. Fyodor Dostoevsky, *Crime and Punishment: A Novel in Six Parts with Epilogue*, trans. Richard Pevear and Larissa Volokhonsky (New York: Knopf, 1992), pp. 261, 266–67. Part V, chapter 1 of the novel is a satirical compendium of radical clichés.
4. Fyodor Dostoevsky, *The Brothers Karamazov*, trans. Constance Garnett (New York: Modern Library, 1963), p. 789. Further references to this are to *BK*.
5. Opening of act III.
6. V. G. Belinsky, *Selected Philosophical Works* (Moscow: Foreign Languages, 1956), p. 168 (Letter to Botkin, 28 June 1841).
7. On such codes of behavior, see Vladimir C. Nahirny, *The Russian Intelligentsia: from Torment to Silence* (New Brunswick: Transaction, 1983), and Irina Paperno, *Chernyshevsky and the Age of Realism: A Study in the Semiotics of Behavior* (Stanford University Press, 1988).
8. Anton Chekhov, letter to I. L. Leontiev-Shcheglov, 3 May 1888, cited in Ernest J. Simmons, *Chekhov: A Biography* (Boston: Little Brown, 1962), p. 165.
9. Anton Chekhov, letter to A. N. Pleshcheev, 27 August 1888, cited in ibid.
10. Alexander Herzen, "From the Other Shore," in Herzen, *"From the Other Shore" and "The Russian People and Socialism,"* ed. Moura Budberg (Oxford University Press, 1979), pp. 36–37.
11. Fyodor Dostoevsky, *The Idiot*, trans. Constance Garnett (New York: Modern Library, 1962), p. 385.
12. Anton Chekhov, letter to Suvorin, 27 November 1889, cited in Simmons, *Chekhov: A Biography*, p. 197.
13. On the tradition of casuistical reasoning, see Albert R. Jonsen and Stephen Toulmin, *The Abuse of Casuistry: A History of Moral Reasoning* (Berkeley:

University of California Press, 1988). On philosophy's turn from the timely to the timeless – from Montaigne to Descartes and after – see Stephen Toulmin, *Cosmopolis: The Hidden Agenda of Modernity* (New York: Free Press, 1990).

14. See M. M. Bakhtin, "K filosofii postupka," in the 1984–85 issue of *Filosofiia i sotsiologiia nauki i tekhniki*, a yearbook (*ezhegodnik*) of the Soviet Academy of Sciences (Moscow: Nauka, 1986), pp. 80–160. For a detailed summary of this essay, see Gary Saul Morson and Caryl Emerson, "Introduction: Reading Bakhtin," in Morson and Emerson (eds.), *Rethinking Bakhtin: Extensions and Challenges* (Evanston: Northwestern University Press, 1989), pp. 5–30.

15. Leo Tolstoy, *Anna Karenina*, the Garnett translation revised and edited by Leonard J. Kent and Nina Berberova (New York: Modern Library, 1965), p. 824.

16. See Ludwig Wittgenstein, *Philosophical Investigations*, trans. G. E. M. Anscombe, 3rd edn (New York: Macmillan, 1958), section 66 (p. 31e). Further references to this are to *PI*.

17. I coined the term "prosaics" in Morson, *Hidden in Plain View: Narrative and Creative Potentials in "War and Peace"* (Stanford University Press, 1987); Morson, "Prosaics: An Approach to the Humanities," *The American Scholar* (Autumn 1988), 515–28; and Morson and Caryl Emerson, *Mikhail Bakhtin: Creation of a Prosaics* (Stanford University Press, 1990).

18. Sergei Bulgakov, "Heroism and Asceticism (Reflections on the Religious Nature of the Russian Intelligentsia)," in Gershenzon (ed.), *Vekhi/Landmarks*, p. 32.

19. Leo Tolstoy, *War and Peace*, trans. Ann Dunnigan (New York: Signet, 1968), p. 1320.

20. Pushkin, "O vtorom tome *Istoriia russkogo naroda* Polevogo" (1830), *Polnoe sobranie sochinenii*, 17 vols. (Moscow–Leningrad: Izdatel'stvo AN SSSR, 1937–59), vol. XI, p. 127.

21. I discuss "creation by potential" in detail in my *Hidden in Plain View*; "sideshadowing" is the key idea of my more recent book, *Narrative and Freedom: The Shadows of Time* (New Haven: Yale University Press, 1994). On "sideshadowing," see also Michael André Bernstein, *Foregone Conclusions: Against Apocalyptic History* (Berkeley: University of California Press, 1994).

22. Matthew Arnold, "Count Leo Tolstoy," in Arnold, *Essays in Criticism: Second Series* (London and New York: Macmillan and Co., 1888), p. 260.

23. L. N. Tolstoi, *Polnoe sobranie sochinenii*, ed. V. G. Chertkov, 91 vols. (Moscow: Khudozhestvennaia literatura, 1929–64), vol. XIII, p. 55.

24. Fyodor Dostoevsky, *The Possessed (The Devils)*, trans. Constance Garnett (New York: Modern Library, 1963), p. 341.

3

THE LITERARY TRADITION

9

SUSANNE FUSSO

The Romantic tradition

All novels are Romantic in the sense that they defy generic categories, combining poetry and philosophy, reportage and fantasy. "Der Roman ist ein romantisches Buch" ("The novel is a Romantic book"), according to Friedrich Schlegel, one of the greatest of Romantic theoreticians.[1] But to speak more strictly, there is such a thing as a Romantic novel, as distinct from other types of novels (realist, science-fiction, etc.). The Romantic novel, mainly cultivated by the German Romantics (Schlegel, Novalis, Eichendorff and, to some extent, Goethe), is a free, lyrical form, often incorporating lyric poetry, concerned less with linear plot than with the exploration of inner spiritual states, of love, the mystical and the super-natural. Another type of novel that may be termed "Romantic" is the tale of exotic adventure in the manner of Chateaubriand and Scott. Both these types of Romantic novel are represented in Russian literature of the early nineteenth century, but only among the works of second-rank writers like Aleksandr Bestuzhev-Marlinskii, Aleksandr Odoevskii, and Nikolai Polevoi. The first two great Russian novels, Aleksandr Pushkin's *Evgenii Onegin* (1823–31, published in full 1831) and Mikhail Lermontov's *A Hero of Our Time* (1840), are already engaged in a struggle with Romanti-cism that in its intensity and explicitness goes well beyond the self-conscious play known as "Romantic irony."[2] From the very beginning the Russian novel, unlike the Russian lyric poem, stands to one side of Romanticism, engaging in dialogue with it but not belonging to it. In this essay I will first provide an overview of the various ways Russian novelists have confronted Romanticism, and then discuss in more detail the reflec-tion of the Romantic legacy, specifically Romantic poetry, in three novels: Fedor Dostoevskii's *The Brothers Karamazov* (1880), Andrei Belyi's *Peters-burg* (1913–14, 1916), and Andrei Bitov's *Pushkin House* (1964–71, published in full in 1978).

It is inevitable that so amorphous and multifarious a concept as Romanticism means different things to different people. Within the Russian context, the general idea of Romanticism has given rise to variants such as "Romantic Realism" (the fantastic, Gothic realism of Dostoevskii and Gogol), and "Revolutionary Romanticism," the literary mode proposed by Soviet writers and critics in the 1920s to capture the heroic and elemental qualities of the Revolution.[3] As might be expected, Russian novelists differ widely in the ways they interpret Romanticism. For Lermontov, Romanticism is primarily the cult of Byron. In many of his lyric poems he explores the Byronic persona: the talented, sensitive, but disillusioned and bitter man whose best hopes and aspirations have been thwarted by the unfeeling world. In Lermontov's lyric this persona is, for the most part, presented with a straight face, but in his great novel it is embodied with savage irony in the compelling but often ludicrous figure of Pechorin, sarcastically dubbed the "hero of our time." Pushkin had, of course, begun the work of demolishing the Byronic hero in *Evgenii Onegin*. Later hypostases include Bazarov, the hero of Ivan Turgenev's *Fathers and Children* (1862), who begins as a hard-headed nihilist rejecting all forms of Romantic idealism but ends by committing what amounts to suicide (dissecting a typhus victim without gloves) in grief over an unrequited love. One of the most complex examples of late-Romantic ironization of the Romantic hero is Karolina Pavlova's *poema*, *Quadrille* (1843–59). A *poema* (narrative poem) in form but a novel in spirit, *Quadrille* offers a feminine perspective on the death of Russian Romanticism, in which the hitherto naive heroine is finally allowed to see through the Byronic hero and to liberate herself from his moral (or immoral) influence.

An essential component of the Byronic myth is the exaltation of Napoleon as a world-historical figure (see, for example, Byron's "Ode to Napoleon Buonaparte" and "Napoleon's Farewell," and Lermontov's "The Last New Home"). The Romantic individualist cult of Napoleon, and his status as a hero capable of influencing the course of human affairs for better or worse, is thoroughly and systematically dismantled by Lev Tolstoi, in his anti-heroic *War and Peace* (1865–69). Tolstoi's theory of history as the study of the laws common to all the equal and inseparably interconnected infinitesimal elements of free will, rather than the study of the movements of "great men," has its narrative counterpart in his presentation of Napoleon as a character in the novel. The "great man" becomes just another supernumerary on Tolstoi's epic stage, and far from the most interesting one.

Nikolai Gogol assimilated German Romantic aesthetic theories early in his career. His collection of stories and essays *Arabesques* (1835) displays at every turn the influence of German thinkers and their Russian popularizers. In his novel *Dead Souls* (1842), this legacy survives in the scene of

Pliushkin's overgrown garden, an aesthetic manifesto that asserts the beauty of imperfection, ruin, entanglement, and fragmentation. Such is the beauty of *Dead Souls*, which combines grotesquely naturalistic descriptions of Russian provincial life with exalted lyrical effusions, which has very little plot and no ending, but which is nevertheless one of the most artistically successful of Russian novels. The novel closest to *Dead Souls* in setting and spirit is Fedor Sologub's *The Petty Demon* (1907), and here again a Romantic aesthetic is provocatively combined with a sharply satirical view of a godforsaken Russian provincial town. The *fin-de-siècle* Symbolist movement to which Sologub belonged, in its preoccupation with the mystical and transcendental, is a neo-Romantic movement. *The Petty Demon* is a compendium of the late-Romantic obsessions catalogued in Mario Praz's classic study *The Romantic Agony*: the demonic, the beauty of the horrid, sado-masochism, androgyny, and synesthesia (the perception of one sense modality in terms of another). This novel's aesthetic manifesto is Charles Baudelaire's 1857 poem "Correspondances," in which "man walks through forests of symbols / That observe him with familiar glances." In a characteristically Russian twist, Baudelaire's lyric persona is parodied in the figure of the paranoid schoolteacher Peredonov, who feels that nature is full of petty human emotions, and that the trees are whispering about him and the sun is spying on him from behind a cloud.

Romanticism remains an important element in the twentieth-century Russian novel. *The Master and Margarita* (1928–40), by Mikhail Bulgakov, includes among its array of intertextual references many allusions to works of Romantic art, particularly works belonging to the year 1830: Stendhal's *Le Rouge et le noir* (*The Red and the Black*), Berlioz's *Symphonie fantastique* (*Fantastic Symphony*), Pushkin's *Skupoi rytsar'* (*The Covetous Knight*).[4] More important, *The Master and Margarita* is one of the most brilliant examples in Russian literature of the use of the supernatural, introduced by Romantic writers at the beginning of the nineteenth century under the influence of E. T. A. Hoffmann, among others. In *The Master and Margarita*, the Gospel account of the Crucifixion is retold in a way that downplays the supernatural, in the Master's realistically textured novel about Pontius Pilate. The charged symbols of Biblical discourse (the fig tree, Christ's garments at the foot of the Cross) are transformed into passing incidental details in a naturalistically observed scene. The Master has turned Holy Writ into a historical document reminiscent of the "historical Jesus" movement in Biblical scholarship. At the same time, the Moscow of the 1930s, in which materialism would seem to have triumphed, is invaded by supernatural forces, as conventional figures of speech ("The Devil take me," "Off with his head") are instantly and magically realized by the Devil's henchmen. The Master's novel invests the narrative of an event long shrouded in legend with the detailed texture and believability of an eyewitness account; the magical and miraculous is transferred to the contemporary scene, forced upon *homo Sovieticus* through the agency of the quintessential Romantic hero, the Devil.

One of the most explicit statements on Romanticism by a twentieth-century writer is to be found in Boris Pasternak's autobiographical work *Safe Conduct* (1931). Pasternak sees in Vladimir Maiakovskii an exponent of the "Romantic manner," which he formulates as the understanding of life as the life of the poet. Pasternak claims that in order to "protect" Maiakovskii from the vulgarity of the similarities between the two of them, he has made a conscious decision to avoid the Romantic manner in his own work. Pasternak sees the Romantic world view as a seductive variant of Orphism and Christianity, in which the poet "posits himself as the measure of life and pays for this with his own life" (Part III, chapter 11).[5] The falsity of the Romantic manner lies in the poet's need for an audience of non-poets, the evil of mediocrity: "Romanticism always needs philistinism, and without the petty bourgeoisie it loses half its content" (part 3, chapter 11).

Although in 1931 Pasternak claimed to have purged his own work of "the Romantic manner," in his novel *Doctor Zhivago* (1957) he offers a poet-hero who, like his real-life counterparts, Maiakovskii and Esenin, partakes of the Orphic–Christian myth. Iurii Zhivago "needs philistinism" in the best Romantic tradition; near the end of the novel, while listening to his friends discussing intellectual topics, he thinks, "The only vivid and bright thing in you is that you have lived at the same time as I have and you have known me" (part XV, chapter 7). This is an echo of Christ's words in the last of the "Poems of Iurii Zhivago," "Garden of Gethsemane": "God has given you the honor / To live during my days." Similarly, the lyric hero of the first poem, "Hamlet," states, "I am alone, everything sinks into Pharisaism." Zhivago clearly "posits himself as the measure of life," the novel is steeped in what Keats called (in relation to Wordsworth) the "egotistical sublime." Nature is constantly echoing the thoughts of Zhivago, sympathizing with him, expressing his essence: "The winter evening breathed an unprecedented sympathy, like a witness who felt it all along with him. It was as if it had never grown dark in this way before, and as if evening were falling for the first time only today, in order to console him, a person orphaned and fallen into loneliness" (part XIV, chapter 13).[6]

The intensity of Zhivago's sense of his own individuality is seconded by the highly Romantic concept of Christianity that is threaded through the novel, presented as the teachings of Zhivago's philosopher uncle. In a brilliant passage comparing the parting of the Red Sea to the Virgin Birth, it emerges that in Christianity's new dispensation, the story of the free human personality has come to replace the epic of nations and leaders: "The individual human life became the story of God, and it filled the expanses of the universe with its content" (part XIII, section 17). Zhivago's Romantic individualism is undoubtedly meant to counter the traces of "Revolutionary Romanticism" that survive in the Socialist Realist novel, in which the Old Testament focus on nations and leaders remains in force.

Beginning with *Evgenii Onegin*, Russian literature has been interested as much in Romantic readers as in the Romantic writer. By Romantic readers I mean readers who identify too strongly with the literature they read, who seek to live their lives according to the books they read, who confuse their own personalities with the personality of the author or characters. In Russian literature the paradigm of the Romantic reader is Tatiana, who falls instantly in love with Onegin because she thinks she already knows him from Richardson's novels. The most famous example in world literature is Flaubert's heroine Emma Bovary, whose prosaic marriage is doomed by comparison with the Romantic visions she has imbibed from her schoolgirl reading. (Romantic reading is often called "bovarism"; in view of Tatiana's historical priority, "larinism" might be more appropriate.) Romantic literature as a whole conduces to the folly of Romantic reading, but the Romantic lyric in particular, with its emphasis on the immediate expression of individual feelings and with the illusion of spontaneity it achieves by eschewing prescribed genres, seems to invite the reader to merge his own "I" with the "I" of the lyric persona. Paradoxically, the most personal of literary expressions is the most transferable to readers removed from the author in time and place, because it seems to have freed the individual of the constraints of society, history, and convention.

As I have said, it is hard to find a distinctly Romantic work among the masterpieces of Russian prose. The greatest works of Russian Romanticism are works of lyric poetry by Pushkin, Lermontov, Evgenii Baratynskii, Fedor Tiutchev, and others. So for the later Russian novel, the quotation of lyric poems is one way of infusing the Romantic spirit into an otherwise realist, modernist, or postmodernist work. When poetry is quoted by characters in a prose narrative, the problem of Romantic reading comes to the fore. I will now consider the role played by the Romantic reading of poetry in three works that brilliantly represent three stages in the post-Romantic development of the Russian novel: psychological realism *The Brothers Karamazov* (1880), modernism *Petersburg* (1913–14, 1916), and Soviet postmodernism *Pushkin House* (1964–71).

Dostoevskii is a good geneticist. When he describes the personalities of a character's parents, one can be sure that the parents' traits will be subtly but distinctly reflected in the character's own personality. Much has been made of Alesha Karamazov's vivid memory of his mother praying to an icon of the Mother of God, a memory that clearly plays a strong role in Alesha's life of spiritual striving under the guidance of Father Zosima.[7] But less attention has been paid to Dmitrii's legacy from *his* mother. Unlike Alesha and Ivan's mother, the daughter of an obscure deacon whose sons gravitate naturally to the clergy and the radical intelligentsia, Dmitrii's mother is a member of the nobility whose son just as naturally becomes a dissolute army officer. She belongs to what the narrator calls the "Romantic generation." Accordingly, her act of virtual suicide in marrying the disgusting Fedor Karamazov is characterized by a phrase from Lermontov, "the irritation of a captive mind" (book 1, chapter 1).[8] Although the phrase is taken from one of Lermontov's most anti-Romantic poems, "Ne ver' sebe" ("Do not trust yourself," 1839), which questions the usefulness and morality of poetry and inspiration, the phrase itself, in Lermontov as in Dostoevskii, is a characterization of the Romantic personality. Thus Dmitrii's Romantic pedigree is established: along with her more obvious traits (passion, boldness, impatience, physical strength) Dmitrii has inherited his mother's link to Romanticism. Indeed the spirit of Russian Romantic lyric poetry plays as vital a role in his fate as devotion to the image of Christ plays in Alesha's.

Dmitrii bears many of the outward signs of the Russian Romantic poet. His early career is markedly similar to that of Lermontov: military service in the Caucasus, duelling, carousing, promotion for exemplary service alternating with disgrace and demotion. Although he possesses great physical strength, his face expresses "something sickly" (book 11, chapter 6), an echo of Lermontov's description of poetic inspiration in "Don't trust yourself": "It is the heavy delirium of your sick soul."[9] His gaze is abstracted, like that of someone listening to an inner voice, a stereotypical feature of the Romantic poet. Most strikingly, in his "confession in verse" to Alesha, Dmitrii explicitly identifies himself with Afansasii Fet's definition of the lyric poet. In an essay on Tiutchev, Fet claims that the poet must combine insane daring with extreme caution. The former quality is expressed in a metaphor that Dostoevskii ridiculed in his 1861 article "Mr. Dobroliubov and the Problem of Art." "Whoever is incapable of throwing himself first out of the seventh floor, in the unshakeable faith that he will soar into the sky, is not a lyric poet."[10] Dmitrii repeatedly promises to accomplish a similar feat: "If I'm going to fly into the abyss, then I'll go straight into it, head first and heels up"; "tomorrow I'll fly from the clouds . . . Have you ever experienced, have you ever dreamed how it feels when you fall off a mountain into a deep pit? Well, I'm flying now, and not in a dream" (book III, chapter 3).

Despite all this, Dmitrii is not a writer of lyric poetry; his complete works consist of three lines of fairly crude verse. He is, however, a reader of lyric poetry. Somehow, somewhere, something inspired this seemingly brutish and debauched army officer to devour and memorize – and take to heart – reams of verse. In chapter 3 of book III, "The Confession of an Ardent Heart. In Verse," Dmitrii speaks to Alesha in a monologue that is a tissue of poetic quotations.[11] Their talk takes place in a typically Romantic setting, a gazebo in an overgrown garden. We are even told that the gazebo was built about fifty years ago, i.e. *circa* 1816, the heyday of Russian Romanticism. The gazebo is decayed and rotten, like Romanticism itself in the 1860s, but Dmitrii's confession demonstrates that the spirit of Romanticism has not decayed.

The main poet Dmitrii quotes in this scene is Friedrich Schiller, who in Germany is not considered a Romantic writer. But Dmitrii does not read Schiller as a German writer; he admits to Alesha that the title "An die Freude" is the only German he knows. He reads Schiller in the translations of Vasilii Zhukovskii and Fedor Tiutchev, translations that are monuments of Russian Romantic poetry in their own right. In the *Diary of a Writer* of June 1876, Dostoevskii claimed that Schiller had been absorbed into the Russian soul through the translations of Zhukovskii and had given his name to a period in the history of Russian cultural development. For Dostoevskii and many other Russians, the period of "Schillerism" is virtually synonymous with "Romanticism."

Dmitrii is a Romantic reader of poetry: he reads the lines as though they had been directed at him personally. For example, he recites a passage from Zhukovskii's translation of Schiller's "Das Eleusische Fest" ("The Eleusinian Festival," 1798), which describes the brutality and degradation of pre-agricultural humanity and ends with the following lines:

> No matter where Ceres looks
> With her sad eyes –
> She sees man everywhere
> In deep degradation! (book III, chapter 3)

It is truly tempting to read this scene of a bereft mother beholding the spectacle of human debasement as having direct reference to the Karamazov story, and Dmitrii does not resist the temptation: "In degradation, my friend, in degradation even now . . . Brother, I think of almost nothing else than that degraded man, if only I'm not lying . . . I think about that man because I myself am such a man" (book III, chapter 3). Dmitrii makes a similar move after quoting (out of order) two stanzas from Tiutchev's translation of Schiller's "An die Freude" ("To Joy," 1785). The final four lines that Dmitrii quotes describe the gifts of Joy:

> She has given us friends in misfortune,
> The juice of fruit, the wreaths of the muses,
> To insects – sensuality. . .
> The angel – is to stand before God!   (book III, chapter 3)

Dmitrii again reads these lines as referring to him personally: "Brother, I am that very insect, and this was said specifically about me" (book III, chapter 3).

In this scene and throughout the novel, Dmitrii's Romantic reading is naive, perhaps, but by no means foolish. Richard Peace has demonstrated that when Dmitrii learns of the cult of Mother Earth from Schiller's ode to Ceres ("Das Eleusische Fest"), he is making contact with a source of spiritual redemption that has its counterpart in Alesha's kissing of the earth after Zosima's death.[12] The theme of wine and drunkenness (marked repeatedly in the various Russian texts Dmitrii quotes by the word *kubok*, "goblet") is of similar importance. Not only is the drinking of wine seen as a sacred, bonding ritual in "The Eleusinian Festival" and "Ode to Joy," but in a poem Dmitrii quotes later, Schiller's "Das Siegesfest" ("The Victory Feast," 1803) in Tiutchev's translation, wine is a healing elixir:

> As soon as blessed wine
> Begins to gleam in the feasting cup,
> Our sorrow will tumble into Lethe
> And go like a key to the bottom.[13]

Dmitrii's resolution, inspired by Schiller, to enter into a holy bond with Mother Earth has its counterpart in Alesha's watering of the earth with his tears. Alesha's epiphany is triggered by his vision of the first Gospel miracle, the marriage at Cana, in which Christ provided wine for a human celebration: "It was not people's sorrow but their joy that Christ shared when he performed a miracle for the first time, he helped human joy . . . One cannot live without joy, Mitia says" (book VII, chapter 4). It is no accident that Alesha thinks of Dmitrii at this moment, for the high significance of wine as messenger and consecrator of human joy is another of the lessons Dmitrii has learned from Schiller–Zhukovskii–Tiutchev. At the moment Alesha is kissing the earth, Dmitrii is bringing wine to a human feast, the party at Mokroe where he and Grushenka acknowledge their love.

Russian Romantic verse continues to sound in Dmitrii's head throughout his ordeal. He is sustained during his interrogation by a line from Tiutchev's "Silentium" (1830?), a line that reminds him that his tormentors cannot have access to his inner world, the world of his soul: "Molchi, skryvaisia i tai / I chuvstva i mechty svoi" ("Be silent, hide yourself and conceal / Your feelings and dreams") (Tiutchev, *Lirika*, vol. I, p. 46). Although Dmitrii remembers the line in a garbled version, "Terpi, smiriaisia i molchi" ("Be patient, be humble, and be silent") (book IV, chapter 4), he correctly applies the poem's moral to his own situation, refusing for as long as possible to allow the interrogators into what he calls his "private life," his inner spiritual world.[14] An even more important moment in which Dmitrii is visited by the spirit of verse comes somewhat earlier: it is his moment of truth in the garden, when he finds himself on the verge of murdering his own father.

When Dmitrii stands in the garden looking into his father's window and sees the old debauchee craning his neck to watch for Grushenka, his greatest fear is realized: he is overcome by physical revulsion for his father, the "personal loathing" that he knows will tempt him to murder. In an earlier novel, *The Insulted and Injured* (1861), Dostoevskii established that it is precisely "Schilleresque natures" who are overcome by murderous impulses when faced with the physical embodiment of moral corruption. In a brilliant scene, the novel's narrator, a Petersburg dreamer, has a long conversation with the depraved Prince Valkovskii, who repeatedly mocks him as a "Schiller." The narrator is overcome by a wave of revulsion as he looks at the Prince: "He produced on me the impression of some kind of slimy creature, some kind of huge spider that I wanted terribly to squash" (part III, chapter 10). Perceptive as all Dostoevskii's villains are, Valkovskii accurately describes the narrator's feelings: "What are you angry at? Just at my external appearance, isn't that right?" (part III, chapter 10).

At this crucial moment in *The Brothers Karamazov*, Dmitrii is for some reason saved from committing the crime that his jealousy and outraged moral feelings are urging him to perpetrate. He offers several interpretations for his decision to turn away from the window without harming his father: God or a guardian angel was watching over him, a bright spirit kissed him, or his mother prayed to God for him (book VIII, chapter 4; book IX, chapter 5). Moments after mentioning his mother to the interrogators, Dmitrii mocks his own story in terms that are highly significant: "Having tragically described how I wanted to kill him and how I had already pulled out the pestle, I suddenly ran away from the window . . . A poem! In verse!" (book IX, chapter 5). It would seem that "a poem in verse" is used here as a synonym for "fairy tale," but combined with Dmitrii's mention of his mother a moment earlier it reminds us that his legacy from his mother is the legacy of Romantic poetry and the high moral teachings

Dmitrii has been able to draw from it. It is no accident that two lines of verse, one by Pushkin and one by himself, float through Dmitrii's head as he stands in the garden: "'I tol'ko shepchet tishina', – mel'knul pochemu-to etot stishok v golove ego" ("'And only the silence whispers,' – this little line of verse flashed through his head for some reason") (book VIII, chapter 4). "'Kalina, iagody, kakie krasnye!' – prosheptal on, ne znaia zachem" ("'The guelder-rose, the berries, how red they are,' – he whispered, not knowing why") (book VIII, chapter 4).[15] Dmitrii does not know why either of these snatches of verse is visiting him at this moment. But the reader does know, if he has read attentively. Dmitrii was a neglected child who never really knew his mother, and learned from his father only about the deep degradation in which humanity abides. Although his mother's Romanticism led her rashly to abandon him, it also sank deep into his soul and made him receptive to another, higher vision of humanity, the vision offered by Schiller, Zhukovskii, and Tiutchev. At the moment of his greatest temptation, it is this vision that prevails.

In *Notes from Underground* (1864), the narrator characterizes the Russian Romantic in terms that are certainly applicable to Dmitrii: "Our Romantic is a broad person and the foremost rogue among all our rogues, I assure you of this . . . We have many 'broad natures,' who even in their final fall never lose their ideal . . . only among us can the most inveterate scoundrel be completely and even loftily honest in his soul, at the same time not ceasing in the least to be a scoundrel" (part II, chapter 1). Dmitrii's view of human nature as a whole is very close to this view of the Russian Romantic: "Even more terrible is the person who already has the ideal of Sodom in his soul but does not deny the ideal of the Madonna either . . . Man is broad, even too broad, I would narrow him." The two lines of verse that Dmitrii himself composes and recites to Alesha and later to the civil servant Petr Perkhotin are an appeal to the nobler part of his own "broad nature": "Glory to the Highest in the world, / Glory to the Highest in me!" (book III, chapter 3; book VIII, chapter 5). These lines have an important counterpart in Russian poetry. They are a naive version of Fet's encomium to Schiller:

> Your voice continually calls
> To that which is human in man
> And that which will not die in the immortal.[16]

Romantic reading can lead to foolish choices, to blindness and self-delusion, as in the cases of Tatiana and Emma Bovary. But in the morally desolate world of the Karamazovs, Dmitrii's naive, enthusiastic reading of

Russian Romantic poetry helps him to "narrow" his own broad nature to give "that which is human in man" precedence over insect lust.

In Andrei Belyi's modernist masterpiece *Petersburg*, Romanticism is mainly associated with the two major female characters, Anna Petrovna Ableukhova and Sofia Petrovna Likhutina. Anna Petrovna, like one of Turgenev's maidens, pours roulades of Chopin out into the Petersburg night in the days before she abandons her husband and son for an Italian singer. The narrator specifies that Anna Petrovna played Chopin, not Schumann. Thus he identifies her with the kind of Romantic piano music that borders on kitsch rather than Schumann's music, which Belyi so aptly called "the Romanticism of realism, tragic to the point of madness."[17] The endearingly silly Sofia Petrovna's Romantic reading is of Pushkin; it is based not on Pushkin's texts but on Pushkin re-Romanticized by Tchaikovsky in his opera *The Queen of Spades* (1890). Sofia Petrovna mentally reproaches Nikolai Apollonovich for failing to be Hermann, the hero of Pushkin's story and Tchaikovsky's opera, and thus depriving her of the opportunity to be the heroine Liza (chapter 3). Nikolai Apollonovich is indeed unlike the dashing, Byronic hero of Tchaikovsky's opera, but in his vulgarity and backfiring ambition he is not very different from the petty bourgeois hero of Pushkin's story.

A less obvious and predictable instance of Romantic reading is associated with Nikolai Apollonovich's father, the cold and mechanical bureaucrat Apollon Apollonovich. Disturbed by the growing unrest among the masses in 1905 Petersburg and by the recent assassination of his colleague Viacheslav Konstantinovich Pleve, Minister of the Interior, Apollon Apollonovich begins to hear in his head a persistent refrain made up of several Pushkin poems, three in particular. To understand how Belyi uses the Pushkin subtexts in this episode it will help to review the poems themselves and their place in Pushkin's career. The earliest is "Chem chashche prazdnuet litsei" ("The more our Lycée celebrates," 1831), written on the occasion of the twentieth anniversary of the opening of the Tsarskoe Selo Lycée that Pushkin attended from 1811 to 1817. The poem is haunted by the recent deaths of several classmates, particularly Anton Delvig, one of Pushkin's closest poetic colleagues. The second poem (in order of composition, not of appearance in *Petersburg*) is a highly personal lyric, "Pora, moi drug, pora! Pokoia serdtse prosit" ("It's time, my dear, it's time! My heart asks for peace," 1834), addressed to Pushkin's wife at a time when he was trying desperately (and unsuccessfully) to obtain permission from the Tsar to retire from government service and devote himself to quiet family life and poetic labor in the country. The last poem is the last Lycée anniversary poem, "Byla pora: nash prazdnik molodoi" ("There was a time: our young festival," 1836). This poem differs from the 1831 anniversary poem in its greater emphasis on Russian history than on personal ties; while still focused on mortality, it speaks of the passing of tsars and emperors rather than intimate friends. The poem is left unfinished; as soon as Pushkin turns from the exploits of Alexander I to those of his nemesis Nicholas I, he breaks off the poem in the middle of a line. According to witnesses at the October Lycée celebration, Pushkin was prevented by emotion from finishing his reading of the poem. He was to die in January of the following year.

Despite the fact that these three poems are so intimately tied to events in Pushkin's life, Apollon Apollonovich, like any good Romantic reader, manages to apply them to his own situation. In chapter 1, after glimpsing a portrait of Pleve, Apollon Apollonovich recalls a line from the 1836 Lycée poem: "And he is no more – and he has left Russia." Apollon Apollonovich immediately asks himself "Who is he?" In Pushkin's poem, "he" is Tsar Alexander I, under whose reign the Lycée was opened in 1811, on the eve of Napoleon's invasion of Russia. But Apollon Apollonovich, after first considering himself to be "he," settles confidently on Pleve (p. 36). The answer to the next question – "And he, Apollon Apollonovich?" – is somewhat more complicated. The question is followed by two lines from the 1831 Lycée poem: "And it seems to me that it's my turn, / My beloved Delvig is calling me." Apollon Apollonovich identifies himself with the lyric persona; in a situation in which terrorist acts and assassinations are multiplying, the phrase "it's my turn" is fraught with ominous significance for him. This idea leads naturally to the final lines of Pushkin's unfinished 1836 poem, "And new storm clouds have gathered over the earth / And their hurricane . . ." The context of these lines is left unclear in Pushkin's fragment, but for Apollon Apollonovich they clearly refer to the unrest of 1905.

Pushkin's lines resurface in chapter 2, in a section entitled "My beloved Delvig is calling me." This scene occurs at the exact moment that Nikolai Apollonovich is receiving the bomb that is meant to assassinate his father Apollon Apollonovich. Accordingly, the forebodings of death already associated with the name Delvig are intensified here. Apollon Apollonovich's train of thought in this scene is subtly described. First the coldness of his offices reminds him of a time fifty years ago when he nearly froze to death while at his country estate:

At that hour of his solitary freezing it was as though someone's cold fingers, heartlessly poking their way into his breast, stiffly stroked his heart: an icy hand led him on; led by the icy hand he climbed up the steps of his career, having ever before his eyes that same, fatal, unbelievable space; there, from there, – beckoned the icy hand; and boundlessness flew: the Russian Empire.

This reminds him of a conversation with Pleve in which Apollon Apollono-vich called Russia an "icy plain"; the memory of Pleve again calls up the lines from Pushkin about Alexander I, followed by a more extensive fragment about Delvig, followed again by the lines about the "hurricane." The use of the name "Delvig" in this section is typical of the virtuosity of Belyi's intertextual play. At first glance it would seem that the figure of Delvig, an indolent, pleasure-loving littérateur and master of Russified classical meters, has little in common with the stiff, soulless bureaucratic world of Pleve and Ableukhov. But in Russian cultural history the name "Delvig" has numerous connections to the semantic fields of "coldness" and "death," the major themes of this section. (1) Delvig was the editor of the almanac *Severnye tsvety* (*Northern Flowers*). (2) Pushkin's 1829 riddle on Delvig's name begins, "Kto na snegakh vozrastil feokritovy nezhnye rozy?" ("Who managed to grow the tender roses of Theocritus in the snows?"). (3) In his *Table-Talk* Pushkin adduced an aphorism by Delvig that has become famous as a characterization of mystical verse: "Chem blizhe k nebu, tem kholodnee" ("The closer to heaven, the colder"). (4) There is a paronomastic connection between the name *Del*vig and Belyi's repeated word "*led*ianaia" ("icy"). (5) Delvig died at 33, and was then remembered fondly and frequently by his numerous literary friends. In the letters and poems of the Pushkin circle, "going to embrace Delvig" becomes a euphemism for "dying."

Of course all of this has less to do with Apollon Apollonovich's consciousness than with the author's designs; it is not by chance that the author has partly taken over the task of quoting Pushkin, by making a line from the 1831 poem the heading of the section. In its approach to characterization *Petersburg* is not in fact a Romantic work, and interest in any individual character's psychology is not maintained for long before being subordinated to the complex symphony of motifs orchestrated by the author figure. By the time the Delvig poem next appears in chapter 7 it is just one more in a series of mechanically repeated refrains, issuing rhythmically from the mindlessly mumbling mouth of the ruined Apollon Apollonovich. The third Pushkin poem, "It's time, my dear, it's time! My heart asks for peace," undergoes a similar process. The first time it appears, in chapter 4, it serves to remind Apollon Apollonovich of a personal problem he has repressed. Pushkin's lyric persona speaks of plans to live with his partner *vdvoem* ("together as a couple"). Apollon Apollonovich is moved to figure out who could possibly be the other half of his own couple:

surely not his scapegrace son, or the common man of the Petersburg streets. This questioning leads him to remember his lost wife:

> Apollon Apollonovich recalled that at one time he intended to live out his life with Anna Petrovna, to move to a little dacha in Finland after ending his government service, but, after all, you know: Anna Petrovna left – yes sir, she left! ... Apollon Apollonovich grasped that fact that he had no life companion (up until this moment he somehow hadn't had time to remember).

Despite this moment of psychological insight, the next time the poem appears it has been appropriated – and rewritten – by the author and used as the epigraph to chapter 7. The word *pora* ("it's time") has been replaced by *ustal* ("I'm tired"), in a metaliterary allusion to the approaching end of the monumental and truly tiring (for author and reader) novel.

Apollon Apollonovich's end combines the motifs of the three poems: the "hurricane" of revolution has sent him into retirement, reunited with his life companion and awaiting death among the snows, where he sees only *teni i teni* ("shades and shades" or "shadows and shadows"), that recall the *tolpa tenei rodnykh* ("crowd of beloved shades"), in the midst of which Delvig dwells. But by this time the implications of Apollon Apollonovich's Romantic reading have been forgotten, submerged in the more grandiose schemes of a novel that is fundamentally uninterested in the individual personality.

In his novel *Pushkin House*, Andrei Bitov takes Romantic reading one step further: his hero is a *literaturoved-romantik* ("literary scholar-Romantic") whose article on Pushkin, Lermontov, and Tiutchev is retold in exhaustive detail by the narrator.[18] Although Leva Odoevtsev is a professional scholar, his article on the "Prophet" poems of Pushkin and Lermontov and *Bezumie* ("Madness") by Tiutchev is really about himself, as the narrator repeatedly reminds us: "It is as fresh as ever because it is not about Pushkin, not about Lermontov, and especially not about Tiutchev, but about him. About Leva" (part I). Indeed the story Leva tells about the three poets – the imperturbable genius Pushkin, the callow adolescent Lermontov, and the treacherous envier Tiutchev – has more to do with Leva's personal life as depicted in the novel than with literary-historical fact. Later Leva realizes that in this article he has been guilty of the same fault of which he accuses Lermontov: an excessive focus on his personal "I" (part III).

But Leva's "I" also implies the "I" of the author figure, who presents Leva's article in his own voice, with ironic asides, corrections, and comments. The epigraph chosen for this section identifies the author with the scavenging narrator of Lermontov's *A Hero of Our Time*: "Recently I learned that Pechorin had died on his way back from Persia. This news made me very glad; it gave me the right to publish these notes, and I took advantage of the opportunity to put my name on someone else's work. God grant that my readers not punish me for this innocent forgery!" (Appendix to part II). As at least one Russian critic has pointed out, Leva's Romantic reading provides the author-figure with a mask to cover his own Romantic reading: "One might say that, making use of his Leva, A. Bitov enters into familiar contact with the great poets."[19] Thus the author of *Pushkin House* joins the long Russian tradition that he himself identifies: the tradition of "one-sided personal relationships with Pushkin" (Appendix to part II). His Romantic reading has to do not with personal experience, as Leva's does, but with his own artistic choices.

Although Bitov would probably reject the label "postmodernist," the intertextuality of *Pushkin House* is rather postmodernist than modernist, as I will explain below. Leva's current scholarly project is a grandiose one: defining the "I" of Pushkin, seen as a muteness, the epicenter of a typhoon, "where there is peace, the point from which the invulnerable genius looks out" (part III). For the postmodern writer, the pure and clear invulnerability of Pushkin's "I" is no longer attainable.[20] Like Leva's imagined Tiutchev, the contemporary writer has fallen into a knowing disingenuousness that is paradoxically more self-betraying than Pushkin's candor:

[Tiutchev] is the first to hide something . . . and as a result he, the one who controls everything so well, does not express himself, but ends up being expressed . . . Only candor is elusive and invisible, it is poetry; lack of candor, even at its most artful, is visible, it is a stamp, craftsmanship's mark of Cain – and, by the way, this kind of craftsmanship is close and contemporary to us in spirit. (Appendix to part II)

The "mark of Cain" in *Pushkin House* is the thicket of quotations, both explicit and implicit, from pre-Revolutionary Russian literature that are used by the author to distance himself from the human dimension of Leva and his story.

Bitov's intertextuality is fundamentally different from Belyi's. Belyi the modernist is still at home in the tradition. He is free and unselfconscious in his quotations of myriad sources, from the most esoteric philosophical texts to popular songs. The postmodernist – especially Soviet – writer is alienated from the history of culture, which has been preserved and petrified by hegemonic forces. Culture is a museum, not a living presence. It is no accident that the climactic scene of *Pushkin House* involves the drunken smashing of the exhibit cases in the eponymous institution, the Soviet Union's most prestigious literary museum. When Belyi quotes, he ranges freely and widely, according to his own erudite whim; Bitov plods predictably through the Soviet school syllabus, as the author openly admits (part II). (In this if in nothing else, Bitov is close to the avowedly postmodernist poet Dmitrii Prigov, whose literary allusions are not dense and obscure like Mandelstam's, but restricted to the range of texts that every Soviet schoolchild should know.)

There is a good excuse for the Soviet writer and reader to lack Belyi's erudition, to be poorly educated, to be unfamiliar with works not on the syllabus. In the Soviet context, reading (and quoting) uncanonized works involves considerable effort and risk. Thus the author-figure in *Pushkin House* is indulgent toward Leva for not knowing Iurii Tynianov's 1929 article "Pushkin and Tiutchev," which Leva in many ways unknowingly repeats (Appendix to part II). Can the reader be similarly indulgent toward Bitov for claiming never to have read Belyi's *Petersburg*?[21] Bitov, a master of irony and self-mockery, is surely alluding to himself as well as to Leva in his notes to Leva's article as published in the journal *Voprosy literatury* (*Problems of Literature*): "The author was also interested in that subtle difference between the 'first' and the 'second,' when the second, for himself, exists with the disinterestedness, the carelessness [literally, 'the lack of looking over his shoulder'] and the passion of the first" ("Tri 'proroka'," p. 166). To put it more bluntly, assuming a pose of willful ignorance can be the only way to free oneself to say one's own word.[22]

Bitov is the author of a Petersburg novel who claims not to have read *Petersburg* but who, like Belyi, places Pushkin's works at the center of his novel and ends it with a man contemplating a sphinx. This brings Bitov dangerously close to the "latest village accounts clerk to discover the integral calculus" whom he mocks in *Voprosy literatury* ("Tri 'proroka'," p. 166). Such feigned ignorance has multiple uses. It can not only empower the author to speak, but can invest his work with added glamor, provided his audience is even more ignorant than he. Bitov displays a sly awareness of this, in the amusing parable he tells about a showing to a supposedly sophisticated Soviet audience of Pasolini's film *The Gospel According to Matthew*. Half the audience reacts judiciously to the film, the other half is stunned and enraptured. It emerges that ignorance has played a major role in this discrepancy:

> The ones who were unconditionally enraptured were the ones who had never read the Gospel, and those who already knew it had a more objective and severe attitude. A simple question-conclusion suggests itself – what produced the impression: the Gospel or the picture itself? The quotation or the film? The honest ones agreed, blushing, that it was the quotation; the dishonest ones agreed without blushing. Thus many of them had been stunned for the

first time by the Gospel, read to them from an interlinear translation by an interpreter sitting in the dark. (part II)

If we take Bitov's self-referential statements seriously, we may conclude that the multitude of obvious, well-worn quotations in *Pushkin House* are meant to hide the unacknowledged, repressed quotations from works not on the syllabus, the ones that lend their aura to *Pushkin House* as the Gospel did to Pasolini's film.

The act of looking back to one's predecessors is fraught with anxiety for any writer, but *Pushkin House* ends with a different anxiety: that of the writer looking forward to a day when his own words will be appropriated and repeated without attribution by a posterity that has forgotten their original source: "Even if the word has been uttered precisely and can survive its own muteness right up to the rebirth of the Phoenix of meaning, does that mean that people will seek it out in the dust of paper, that they will even begin to look for it in its former, let along its true, significance, and won't simply – utter it anew?" (Epilogue). *Pushkin House* ends here, not with the voice of the grandson looking over his shoulder at the great writers who have preceded him, but with the voice of the grandfather prophesying the inevitable corruption, misreading, even oblivion, into which his words must fall in the future. This is the ultimate identification with the "I" of Pushkin.

The evolution of the significance of Romantic reading from Dostoevskii through Belyi to Bitov reflects the evolution of the Russian novel from realism through modernism to postmodernism. Dostoevskii's focus is on the represented world of his characters and on refining his techniques of depicting their inner lives. Accordingly, Dmitrii Karamazov's Romantic reading has profound psychological significance: it fosters a self-knowledge that saves him from committing a soul-destroying crime. Belyi is only secondarily interested in Apollon Apollonovich's flashes of similar insight; the character's Romantic reading plays a subordinate role, as yet another strand in the motley texture of Belyi's modernist apocalypse. For Bitov, the metaliterary impulse has decisively taken precedence over the mimetic. The Romantic reading of the character Leva is of far less moment than that of his author-creator. Bitov uses the Pushkin, Lermontov, and Tiutchev that he and Leva have created for themselves as a means to artistic self-knowledge and self-revelation. As Friedrich Schlegel said at the dawn of Romanticism, "Many artists who only wanted to write yet another novel have by accident depicted themselves."

NOTES

1. There is some debate as to what Schlegel meant by the word "Roman," which now means "novel," but he certainly included under this rubric works of the type that evolved into the modern novel.

2. Monika Greenleaf, *Pushkin and Romantic Fashion: Fragment, Elegy, Orient, Irony* (Stanford, Calif.: Stanford University Press, 1994), has provided an admirably sophisticated and comprehensive account of the role played by Romantic aesthetics and fashions in Pushkin's works. Lermontov awaits a similar study.

3. On Romantic Realism, see Donald Fanger, *Dostoevsky and Romantic Realism: A Study of Dostoevsky in Relation to Balzac, Dickens and Gogol* (University of Chicago Press, 1965). On Revolutionary Romanticism, see Katerina Clark, *The Soviet Novel: History as Ritual* (Chicago and London: University of Chicago Press, 1981); C. Vaughan James, *Soviet Socialist Realism: Origins and Theory* (London: Macmillan, 1973); and Gleb Struve, *Russian Literature under Lenin and Stalin, 1917–1953* (Norman, Okla.: University of Oklahoma Press, 1971).

4. The year 1830 probably points to the year 1930, the year of Maiakovskii's suicide and Bulgakov's telephone call from Stalin. See B. M. Gasparov, "Iz nabliudenii nad motivnoi strukturoi romana M. A. Bulgakova *Master i Margarita*," *Slavica Hierosolymitana*, 3 (1978), 198–251.

5. Where no translator is acknowledged, the translations are my own.

6. Compare Pasternak's early poem, "My sister life": "And the sun, going down, expresses its condolences to me."

7. See, for example, Robin Feuer Miller, *The Brothers Karamazov: Worlds of the Novel* (New York: Twayne, 1992), pp. 19–26. See also Robert Louis Jackson, *Dialogues with Dostoevsky: Deliriums and Nocturnes* (Princeton University Press, 1981).

8. See the detailed discussion of this passage in Susan Amert, "The Reader's Responsibility in *The Brothers Karamazov*: Ophelia, Chermashnia, and the Palpable Obscure," in Elizabeth Cheresh Allen and Gary Saul Morson (eds.), *Freedom and Responsibility in Russian Literature: Essays in Honor of Robert Louis Jackson* (Evanston: Northwestern University Press, 1995).

9. M. Iu. Lermontov, *Polnoe sobranie stikhotvorenii*, ed. E. E. Naidich, 2 vols. (Leningrad: Sovetskii pisatel', 1989), vol. 2, p. 32. In the same passage Dostoevskii includes one more echo of Lermontov: "On i ot prirody byl *razdrazhitelen*" ("And he was *irritable* by nature," emphasis mine).

10. A. A. Fet, *Sochineniia*, ed. A. E. Tarkhov, 2 vols. (Moscow: Khudozhestvennaia literatura, 1982), vol. II, p. 156.

11. The poems Dmitrii quotes were first published in widely accessible journals like *Otechestvennye zapiski* (*Notes of the Fatherland*) and *Biblioteka dlia chteniia* (*Library for Reading*), mainly in the early 1840s. Dostoevskii is careful to establish that Dmitrii quotes only poems that a person like him could reasonably be expected to have access to.

12. Richard Peace, *Dostoevsky: An Examination of the Major Novels* (Cambridge University Press, 1971), pp. 222–23.

13. F. I. Tiutchev, *Lirika*, ed. K. V. Pigarev, 2 vols. (Moscow: Nauka, 1966), vol. II,

p. 131; two earlier lines are quoted by Dmitrii in book VIII, chapter 5 of *The Brothers Karamazov*.

14. In Dmitrii's flawed memory the line from Tiutchev has been contaminated by the words *terpi* ("be patient") and *smiriaisia* ("be humble"), which may come from a Pushkin poem, "Ottsy pustynniki i zheny neporochny" ("Father-hermits and chaste women," 1836). This poem is mentioned during Ivan's conversation with the Devil. There are many connections between Ivan's poetic quotations and Dmitrii's, which there is not room to discuss here. See Frederick T. Griffiths and Stanley J. Rabinowitz, *Novel Epics: Gogol, Dostoevsky, and National Narrative* (Evanston: Northwestern University Press, 1990), pp. 121–22, for a different interpretation of Dmitrii's reading of Schiller.

15. The Pushkin is a garbled quotation from *Ruslan and Liudmila* (1820); the context does not appear to be significant. Dmitrii's utterance is metrically and phonetically shaped like a line (or perhaps two lines) of verse.

16. A. A. Fet, *Stikhotvoreniia i poemy*, ed. B. Ia. Bukhshtab (Leningrad: Sovetskii pisatel', 1986), p. 441.

17. Andrei Belyi, "Vospominaniia o Shteinere" ("Memoirs about Steiner"), manuscript cited in Andrei Belyi, *Petersburg*, ed. L. K. Dolgopolov (Kiev: Dnipro, 1990), p. 535. Page references to *Petersburg* are to this edition.

18. The formulation belongs to V. Turbin, in a survey of literary critics conducted by *Voprosy literatury* (*Problems of Literature*): "Nuzhny li v literaturovedenii gipotezy?," *Voprosy literatury* (1977), no. 2, 82–112; this passage is from p. 108. Unable to publish *Pushkin House* in its entirety in the Soviet Union, Bitov published fragments from it, including his hero's essay on poetry, "Tri 'proroka'" ("Three 'prophets'"; Andrei Bitov, "Tri 'proroka'," *Voprosy literatury*, (1976), no. 7, 145–74.) This strange hybrid of fiction and literary scholarship was published in a scholarly journal (the above-mentioned *Voprosy literatury*) and predictably provoked strong reactions from the critics who were asked to respond to the essay in the journal's pages.

19. S. Bocharov, in "Nuzhny li gipotezy," p. 85. Bocharov, perhaps the most brilliant Russian literary scholar alive today, praises the creative insight of Leva–Bitov's reading of Pushkin and Tiutchev.

20. Compare the impassioned remarks by Leva's grandfather: "Pushkin! How you fooled everyone! After you they all thought it was possible, since you could do it . . . But it was only you who could" (Epilogue).

21. See Ellen Chances, *Andrei Bitov: The Ecology of Inspiration* (Cambridge University Press, 1993), pp. 236, 259; compare Priscilla Meyer, Introduction to Andrei Bitov, *Life in Windy Weather: Short Stories* (Ann Arbor: Ardis, 1986), p. 7.

22. Bitov's narrator and hero of course underestimate the extent to which Pushkin himself "looked over his shoulder"; Pushkin's own richly intertextual works demonstrate that he did not by any means regard himself as "first." Let me note here that the essay "Three 'prophets'" displays a much subtler knowledge of the nineteenth-century literary tradition than the clichéd epigraphs in *Pushkin House* would suggest.

10

VICTOR TERRAS

The Realist tradition

Russian, like Western Realism, is best understood as a reaction against Romanticism, as an attempt, then, to reach out to topical mundane reality (Balzac's *actualité*), renouncing romantic fantasy or escape into an imaginary past and Sentimentalism's abstract discourses on virtue. Realism meant a concern with concrete Russian life, while Romanticism often pursued the exotic and Sentimentalism dealt with humanity in the abstract. In contrast to Romanticism's preoccupation with the extraordinary individual, Realism meant an interest in the concerns of ordinary men and women, in social problems and in the life of the lower classes. Also, Realism meant a faith in literature's calling to be involved in the affairs of real life.

The Russian realist novel, like the realist novel in the West, grew out of existing genres, while often using them as a foil. Gogol's *Dead Souls* (1842) is formally a picaresque novel. Dostoevskii's *Poor Folk* (1846) uses the sentimentalist form of the epistolary novel. His *The Double* (1846) is a "realized" version of a Gothic novel. Lermontov's *A Hero of Our Time* (1840) and Tolstoi's *Cossacks* (1863) "realize" the exotic novel made popular by Aleksandr Bestuzhev-Marlinskii in the 1830s. Tolstoi's *Anna Karenina* (1877) came from the tradition of the family novel. Realism also had roots in satire, in the political pamphlet, and in the physiological sketch. Many of the Russian realists were also active as journalists. The role of the serialized *roman-feuilleton* in the development of the Russian realist novel was significant. Most of the great Russian novels appeared in serialized form, a circumstance that affected not only the novel's composition. The fact that the writing of the novel was still in progress while installments were appearing in print, eliciting critical response, could not fail to have an effect on its content.

The term "realism" (*realizm*) was first used by the critic Pavel Annenkov in an essay published in *The Contemporary* (no. 1, 1849), and was a standard term by the 1860s. But "reality" (*deistvitel'nost'*) was a key term even in the criticism of Nikolai Nadezhdin in the 1830s. His student

Vissarion Belinskii (1811–48) used the term *poeziia deistvitel'nosti* ("poetry of reality") as he championed the realism of the Natural School of the 1830s and 1840s. The notion that literature should deal with real life was taken for granted ever since Belinskii.

The notion of "real life" depends on the beholder. The Christian mystic Dostoevskii no less than the radical materialist Dmitrii Pisarev (1840–68) claimed to be realists. Real life may be perceived as determined mainly by subjective (psychological) or by objective (social) phenomena. As early as 1846 the critic Valerian Maikov remarked that Gogol was a "social," Dostoevskii a "psychological" writer.[1] But beyond the psychological and the social lay more fundamental questions: is reality determined by laws, historical or moral, and does history have a meaning, a *telos*, as was commonly assumed in the nineteenth century? With regard to Russia, Gogol was the first to ask these questions in the famous *troika* passage of *Dead Souls*. It remained an issue throughout the century and after. Questions regarding the direction of Russian history were asked with some urgency by all of the writers discussed here, save perhaps Pushkin.

The rift between traditional demands of form (structure, literary conventions, taboos) and empirical reality was a challenge to the realist. And in addition there was the question of the nature of fiction as such: is it at all possible to make it independent from traditional ballast? Is there any truth in Roland Barthes's contention that realist literature fosters the illusion that we perceive reality without the intervention of language, while the contrary is actually true? In Russia, Dostoevskii, for one, claimed that his more strictly "realist" contemporaries were in fact misrepresenting reality when they mechanically copied the language of ordinary life by "writing from the notebook."

The major Russian Realists, including even those who were politically at the far Left, like Mikhail Saltykov and Maksim Gorkii, were actively opposed to Naturalism, that is, to realist fiction not informed by an idea that explained life and served as a vehicle for changing it. The presence of a revelatory principle in the facts of real life is a central feature of Russian Realism. Hegelians, Slavophiles, Populists and Marxists all believed in such a principle, though they disagreed on its nature. Like many of their Western colleagues, Russian Realists were not content merely to describe the world, but aspired to understand and interpret it. They believed that a realist novelist could penetrate the phenomena of individual and social life and reach out for the essence of the human condition. Moreover, a realist's interpretation of social phenomena was assumed to be in step with history and to have prophetic power. Hence his work laid claim to moral value as it promoted the cause of progress.

Particular novelists and novels were challenged on every single one of these points by critics, who saw the essence of human life differently, who disbelieved in the writer's philosophy of history, and who either doubted that literature had much of a beneficial effect on society or denied that the work in question had any. Pisarev brushed off Dostoevskii's subtle psychological analysis of the murderer Raskolnikov's motive in *Crime and Punishment* (1866), claiming that poverty was the only real motive of the crime. Most critics disagreed with Tolstoi's philosophy of history in *War and Peace* (1865–69). The works of Dostoevskii and Leskov were denounced as reactionary and harmful by radical and liberal critics. Radical critics like Nikolai Chernyshevskii (1828–89) and Dmitrii Pisarev asserted that the social value of literature was negligible and depended entirely on its straightforwardly didactic quality.

Based on a conviction that the relationship between the world of fiction and that of real life is far more complex than realist novelists suspected, some interpretations of Russian realist novels could never have been contemplated by their authors. Freudian interpretations of novels by Tolstoi and Dostoevskii are a case in point.

The modernist Realism of Russian Left Art of the 1920s abandoned the mimetic position of the nineteenth century, as it made art an instrument of social and political change in a predefined direction. Socialist Realism did this in practice, while paying lip service to a Belinskian realist aesthetic.

The great Russian Realists were acutely aware of their novels as works of art. The novel had advanced to the level of art only in the 1830s, when the notion conceived by Schelling and Hegel, according to which the novel was "half art" or "emergent art" (*Kunst im Werden*), a new art form proper to a new age, gained acceptance in Russia. Gogol's *Dead Souls* featured a solemn assertion of the dignity of a realist novel as a "pearl of creation."

Even when the realist novel became the dominant genre of Russian literature, it continued to be, in a way, half art. Novels that were conceived as partisan political statements grew into and were eventually accepted as works of art. Such were *The Devils* (1872) by Dostoevskii, conceived by his own admission as a political pamphlet, and *Anna Karenina* (1877) by Tolstoi, conceived as a work with an explicit anti-nihilist tendency, which was toned down in the course of its progress, though still noticed by leftist critics. The question as to what extent a given novel was a work of art, or what made it one, was rarely asked by contemporaries. It has since become the main concern of sophisticated critics in Russia and abroad.

In its heyday, the *raison d'être* of the Russian realist novel was the discovery and propagation of social, political, or psychological truths. The great Realists perceived their works as pioneering studies of human nature and of Russian society. Indeed, the Russian realist novel is renowned for its penetrating psychological and sociological observations. Critics responded in kind, either approving or rejecting the novelist's conception, but rarely doubting the artist's cognitive powers in principle. The worst a critic could do to a serious work was to reduce it to the status of make-believe entertainment. Some of Gogol's critics did it to *Dead Souls*, much to his distress.

A novel's particular discovery tended to be condensed in characters perceived as typical, though presented as individuals: the superfluous man, the new man (or woman) of the 1860s, the repentant nobleman. These types were understood to stand for tendencies in social life, judged to be positive or negative depending on the critic's ideological position. Goncharov's Oblomov, for example, was a negative type to the radical Nikolai Dobroliubov, a positive type to Apollon Grigorev, a conservative *pochvennik* ("man of the soil"), with both critics accepting his validity as a type.

The realist novel is the most inclusive and most complex form of verbal art. Inside the "box" of a novel various forms of fiction and non-fiction may be packed, more or less integrated with the whole of the text. Russian, like Western novelists, took advantage of the open form of the novel to introduce into their texts digressive essays, diary pages, Platonic dialogues, novellas, legends, anecdotes, idylls, lyric and descriptive passages, and a variety of other material.

The novel's far-reaching freedoms are the cause of an inherent conflict between causal and extra-causal, as well as between paradigmatic and syntagmatic ordering of its elements. Realism *a priori* suggests a certain randomness in the organization of events reported, while the art of the novel asks for "a pattern in the rug." Readers are aware of a contract between themselves and the novelist, though some, and especially the greatest novelists, were inclined to violate this contract in matters of detail, such as psychological motivation, circumstantial verisimilitude, and a discernible plot line.

The realist novelist works under the assumption that his work presents a truthful image of objective reality, granted a certain amount of condensation, simplification, and generalization. But unlike the epic poet who remains impersonal and unidentified, the novelist makes his presence felt in a variety of ways and claims a certain authority over the world he creates. He may set up a narrator who is clearly not the implied author and who may or may not play a role in the narrative. He may speak in his own voice, commenting on his narrative in a more or less committed manner. He may straightforwardly, as Tolstoi in *Childhood* (1852), *Adolescence*

(1854) and *Youth* (1857), or ironically, as Dostoevskii in *The Double*, assume the voice and viewpoint of his hero. He may take a detached position, signalling that he is not a party to the passions played out in his work, as Turgenev does for the most part. He may distance himself from his subject matter intellectually, socially and morally, as Dmitrii Grigorovich (1822–99) and other writers dealing with peasant life usually do. He may let the reader know, in a variety of ways, direct or indirect, that his work, while committed to truth, is still a product of his imagination, a work of literature. Finally the writer may use several of these methods in the same novel, as Lermontov does in *A Hero of Our Time* and Leskov in *Cathedral Folk*.

Even the realist novelist is at times involved in an exercise of Romantic irony, that is, shifting his point of view from objective statement to self-conscious contemplation. Pushkin in *Evgenii Onegin*, Gogol in *Dead Souls*, Dostoevskii in *The Brothers Karamazov* create ironic narrators who, while a part of the world they describe, are also detached from it. Tolstoi the moralist's ironic view of society finds an extreme form in grotesquely estranged visions of social practices. Turgenev ironically juxtaposes what might or ought to have been to what was. There is also the ironic acquiescence of Aleksei Pisemskii (1821–81) in human frailty, as in *An Old Man's Sin* (1861), and the grimly sarcastic acceptance of Mikhail Saltykov (1826–89) of the horrors of Russian life as inevitable necessity, as in *The Golovlev Family* (1875–80).

The tension between the hard facts presented and the manner of their presentation caused some Russian novels to meet with interpretations that were are times diametrically opposed to one another and even to the author's intent. *Oblomov, Fathers and Children* and *The Brothers Karamazov*, to name but the most famous, are cases in point. The dialogic quality of all discourse, postulated by Mikhail Bakhtin, may reveal itself through irony, ambiguity, inner dialogue, introduction of "another voice" in the form of parody, quotations, literary echoes and allusions ("intertext") and various forms of connotation, repetition and emphasis ("subtext"). An intensification of the dialogic quality of the text causes its interpretation to become less certain. If the dialogic quality becomes dominant, as it tends to be in Dostoevskii, multiple interpretations are inevitable.

The dialogic quality of the novel represents only one of several dualities inherent in its structure. A dilemma that beset the realist novelist was the contradiction inherent in a pursuit of objective reality that was yet restrained by the strictures of literary convention. The question of determinacy versus indeterminacy is a key issue for the realist novel. Motivation (psychological, social, ideological) is its fulcrum, yet a certain amount of randomness is asked for to create an illusion of real life. The realist novelist must steer a middle course between structured narrative and the indeterminacy of real life. Choosing the novel's limits in terms of an objective form such as biography facilitates this task. Yet realist novelists often choose an artificial structural scheme, such as a dramatic conflict (Dostoevskii's "novel-tragedies"), a journey (*Dead Souls*), or an hourglass pattern (*Evgenii Onegin*).

Boris Tomashevskii's distinction between *fabula* and *siuzhet,* story and discourse, is particularly important for the realist novel.[2] This is true of many Western novels also, but the Russian realist novel was, for long stretches of time, almost the only forum of social and political dialogue, while in the West other outlets were available for civic thought. The great Russian realist novels are story, argument, allegory, entertainment, and a medium for incidental thought, comment, and observation all at once. The art of it is to allow all these elements to blend into a whole.

The Russian realist novel was very much a part of public life. The appearance of a major novel was a public event. The discussion of a novel invariably turned into a discussion of Russian society and its problems of the day. Novelistic characters like Evgenii Onegin, Chichikov, Oblomov, and Bazarov quickly became part of the Russian educated public's mythology. The realist *roman à thèse* was under the circumstances (censorship, serial publication in journals accessible to a wide readership, a literate and largely partisan audience) well suited to be a medium of public opinion. The nineteenth century believed in causally ordered biography and social history, both of which could be mirrored in a realist novel with a linear plot. When twentieth-century sensibilities moved away from this position, a different type of novel came into existence: Andrei Belyi's *Petersburg* (1913–14, 1916), Fedor Sologub's *The Petty Demon* (1907), Aleksei Remizov's *The Clock* (1908). However, the realist novel made a comeback after the Revolution. Socialist Realism maintained the standards of nineteenth-century Realism by official fiat, but even dissident novels tended to assume the familiar form of a realist novel, Boris Pasternak's *Doctor Zhivago,* for example.

The following descriptions of some of the most important Russian novels do not adhere to a set scheme but merely summarize the most salient traits of each work with regard to the issues raised earlier. While all of these works have a legitimate claim to be realist novels, each has special traits that make a schematic presentation unproductive. Deviations from realist poetics, which vary from novel to novel, are pointed out. There is little doubt that all of the writers discussed here meant to express the truth of Russian life as they saw it. However, in each and every case there were critics who sooner or later stated their disagreement with the author's vision. Some of the novels discussed here, *Oblomov* and *Fathers and Children,* for example, became the object of acrimonious critical debate.

Evgenii Onegin (1823–31, published in full in 1833) is a novel of contemporary manners set in St. Petersburg and Moscow upper-class society, and life in a provincial manor house. It describes a stable society. Its characters are ordinary, presumably typical members of the gentry, ranging from provincial landowners like the Larins to aristocrats of Petersburg high society. Their serfs appear on the fringes of the narrative, without any glossing over of the harsh facts of serfdom. We hear, in passing, that Onegin replaced corvée with rent and that his serfs blessed him for it. Mme. Larin cuffs her servants and "shaves heads," that is, decides who of her serfs will be sent away to serve in the military. Tatiana's heart-to-heart talk with her nurse reveals the gulf between popular and upper-class culture.

Evgenii Onegin is, as Belinskii put it, an encyclopedia of Russian life, if only the gentry's. We hear about a young gentleman's education, his readings, his daily routine in town and in the country. There are vivid descriptions of theater, ballet, balls and family gatherings, with no implied message other than that life in a provincial manor house has a certain vitality that Petersburg high society lacks. The notion that Evgenii Onegin was the first "superfluous man" in Russian literature was read into the text by Belinskii and soon became standard. Pisarev was more accurate when he said in his essay, "Pushkin and Belinskii" (1865), that Pushkin did not go beyond celebrating the life style of his class, though he did bring to literature such *realia* as beaver collars and beer mugs, where chlamyses and chalices had reigned before.

Psychological motivation is given sparingly, but is trenchant, rational and convincing. There are no intimations of hidden depths. Onegin chooses to fight a senseless duel with his friend Lenskii, a mere boy, because it is easier than finding a way to avoid it. Tatiana frankly reveals her – rational and mundane – reasons why she will not have an affair with Onegin, whom she still loves.

The events that make up the plot of *Evgenii Onegin* are indeterminate. Things just happen. The only concession to conventional narrative structure is found in the hourglass pattern of a love letter rebuffed, first from Tatiana to Onegin, then from Onegin to Tatiana. Open-ended as novels go, *Evgenii Onegin* has no real beginning or end. A mock "preface" is inserted late in the novel. *Evgenii Onegin* lacks any obvious message. It has no polemic edge. It does not mind telling the same old story: Mme. Larin's story is repeated in her daughter Tatiana. The dominant mood is one of graceful resignation.

The novel's composition is dominated by sophisticated play with Romantic irony. The author's relation to his text and to his characters is ambiguous and elusive throughout. Onegin is introduced not only as the novel's hero but also as the author's good friend. Tatiana is seen in the company of Prince Viazemskii, Pushkin's intimate friend, yet she is also introduced as Pushkin's muse. Thus, creations of the imagination enter real life – and vice versa, as Pushkin keeps deconstructing his fiction by sober realism. This extends to poetry itself. Lenskii is a bad Romantic poet. Producing the inept lines he wrote the night before his death makes them a realistic detail!

A shifting point of view, such as is found in *Evgenii Onegin*, is not uncommon in Russian realist novels, though it is a Romantic trait. So is the introduction of literary quotations and allusions, literary small-talk, and a pointed shift to the level of literature and away from real life. Like any other realist novels, *Evgenii Onegin* features many digressions: wordly wisdom, idyllic nature scenes, words of wit, lyric apostrophes, vignettes of Russian life, satirical sorties. *Evgenii Onegin* shares with some later novels *(A Hero of Our Time, Oblomov, War and Peace)* the circumstance that it was not composed as an integral whole. Parts of it were printed while the whole was still in progress.

Evgenii Onegin is almost entirely composed of analogously structured fourteen-line strophes, every one of which is a complete poem in itself. Thus the form of the novel is so far separated from its content that it does not conflict with the work's essential realism: the artful is displaced into form. Pushkin's novel in verse has in its content as much objective, unbiased topical as well as universal truth as any Russian novel. It also contains much subjective truth about its author and his art.

Mikhail Lermontov's *A Hero of Our Time* is the first Russian realist *roman à thèse*. The hero's name, Pechorin (from Pechora, a river in northern Russia), suggests that he is meant to be a successor to Onegin (from Onega, another northern river). He is set up as a member of a lost generation, a strong and capable man with no purpose in life – another version of Russian "superfluous man," as Belinskii was quick to point out. Belinskii, who had met Lermontov in person and recognized Pechorin in him, made him a rebel without a cause, for which there is little evidence in the text, though Lermontov, Pechorin's creator, certainly was. It was only Aleksandr Herzen in *Who is to Blame?* who six years later made it explicit that the Russian social order gave an educated nobleman nothing to live or work for.

A Hero of Our Time has a breath of real life mainly due to Lermontov's ability to give Pechorin's diary a personal tone. The reader senses that

VICTOR TERRAS

Pechorin is Lermontov and may suspect that so is the hapless Grushnitskii.
The novel has a faceless though personalized narrator, who hears the first
episode of Pechorin's adventures from one Maksim Maksimych, a character
who became proverbial for well-meaning mediocrity. After a brief encounter with Pechorin, the narrator finds himself in possession of the hero's
diary. The reader thus becomes acquainted with Pechorin step by step.

The novel is open-ended: it has no beginning or end. All we have are a
few disconnected episodes from the hero's life. This is in part due to the
fact that the novel was put together rather than composed: some of the
episodes had appeared in print as separate stories before the whole novel
was published. *A Hero of Our Time* eschews Romantic irony. The pretense
that the narrator, Pechorin, Maksim Maksimych, and its other characters
are real individuals is sustained throughout. Yet the challenge to Pushkin,
announced by the choice of the hero's name, signals literary intertextuality
after all.

The social ambience of Nikolai Gogol's *Dead Souls* (1842) is a step
below that of *Evgenii Onegin*: the same provincial landowners, but no
aristocrats, instead of whom we are introduced to the provincial bureaucracy. Peasants, still at the fringes, do appear as distinct individuals in
vignettes of dead souls, that is serfs, title to whom the rogue Chichikov
acquires from their owners. Gogol makes it explicit that he wishes to deal
with the prose of life. Like Pushkin, he introduces ample prosaic *realia*.
Gogol's characters are ordinary people, who are made into types by
grotesque exaggeration of their main traits, such as the avarice of the old
miser Pliushkin. However, Gogol keeps his characters real by presenting
specific memorable details, such as the bearlike Sobakevich's stepping on
people's toes or the cheat and liar Nozdrev's having his luxuriant sideburns
pulled when caught cheating at cards. Psychological motivation is straight-
forward and uncomplicated. We know that Gogol planned to rehabilitate
Chichikov, but he was unable to provide his rogue hero with any traits that
could make a moral regeneration plausible.

The plot of *Dead Souls* is that of a picaresque novel. Together with a
lengthy flashback in which we hear the story of Chichikov's past, there is
enough factual material for a realist novel of manners. Gogol, like Pushkin,
describes a stable society. But the element of satire is more explicit than in
Evgenii Onegin. The provincial bureaucracy is presented as a corporation
of parasites and extortionists without a useful function of any kind. Unlike
Evgenii Onegin, Dead Souls has a polemic edge. If the reader is willing to
see that Chichikov's fraudulent dealings in dead souls imply that buying
and selling live human beings is perfectly legal, an indictment of serfdom
may be read into the text, hardly Gogol's intent. One can also take a clue

from the title and see *Dead Souls* as an outcry against the terrible lack of spirituality in Russian life. The comic quality of many scenes in *Dead Souls* was perceived by Gogol – and by many of his readers, including Pushkin, who found it a terribly sad work – as an enhancement of the bitter truth about the iniquities of Russian life.

But like *Evgenii Onegin*, Gogol's novel has passages that celebrate day-to-day living and convey an epic sense of gladness. Such are the famous lyric effusions celebrating the Russian language and the boundless expanses of the Russian lands, and, of course, the *troika* passage. Then there are some beautiful vignettes of Russian life, such as the description of a concert of barking dogs at dusk. Finally, there are those Homeric similes, such as when a face that resembles a "Moldavian pumpkin" easily dovetails into an idyllic scene featuring a Moldavian pumpkin made into a balalaika, or when another round and red face calls forth the picture of a hot mead vendor serving his customers from a brass kettle. It is mostly on account of these passages that *Dead Souls* has been called by some the Russian national epic.

The art that illuminates Gogol's world is similar to Pushkin's. The narrator, decidedly personal like Pushkin's, also detaches himself from his story at will and takes off in various directions: a Homeric simile; literary and philosophical musings; lyric effusions; worldly wisdom; apostrophe to the readers drawing them into the author's confidence; an inserted novella, "The Tale of Captain Kopeikin." Like Pushkin, Gogol often displaces the focus of his text from the story to the author's consciousness. He is obviously aware of this and lets the reader know his presence, even if it be from a "splendid far-away."

Gogol's language is often self-serving, becoming foregrounded as the artistic dominant. He delights in the beauties of the Russian language, which he celebrates in a rousing lyric passage. Gogol also uses poetic license in letting his prosaic characters wax poetic far in excess of their personality traits. Thus, Pushkin's verse form finds ample compensation in the poetic quality of Gogol's prose. The subtitle of *Dead Souls*, "A Poem," is justified. *Dead Souls* is a poem, just as *Evgenii Onegin* is a novel. But is *Dead Souls* a realist novel? To contemporaries, and to Belinskii in particular, it certainly was, even though there were voices heard even then that disagreed with this view. When critics of the symbolist period exposed the imaginary nature of Gogol's Russia, it merely confirmed the truism that art and empirical reality are independent of each other.

Ivan Goncharov's *Oblomov* (1859) is a novel which expresses the spirit of its time, a true *Zeitroman*. Its hero is a type that represents the author's understanding of the movements in Russian society which foreshadowed the impending reforms of Alexander II. Oblomov, a well-to-do landowner who lives in Petersburg letting a steward manage his estate, stands for the demise of the old landowning gentry, about to be superseded by a new entrepreneurial class, represented by Oblomov's half-German friend Stolz. Oblomov is sensitive and intelligent, but incapable of any sustained activity and helpless in the affairs of practical life. Stolz is energetic, capable and enterprising, not a bad sort, though a bit of a snob. The novel's plot evolves entirely from the character of its *personae*. Their character, in turn, is determined by their social position. This also goes for some lower middle-class types and servants, described in vivid detail. The petty clerks who extort small bribes from peasant petitioners and Oblomov's devoted but lazy servant are presented as no less a dying breed than Oblomov.

The strength of Goncharov's realism lies in his descriptive detail of things as well as people. His description of life in an old manor house is an unforgettable classic. He is especially strong in creating metonymic details that establish a character in the reader's mind, such as when Oblomov's crooked brother-in-law, a petty government clerk, always points to a signature on a document with his index finger nail-down; when his sister Agafia, who becomes Mrs. Oblomov, is shown time and again with her bare round elbows busy over her kitchen table; or when the obnoxious scoundrel Tarantev's voice is likened to an empty bucket tumbling down stairs.

The structure of *Oblomov* is awkward. It begins with a Sternean hundred-page morning at Oblomov's flat. Several friends show up one after another, resulting in a series of character sketches that have no bearing on what there is of a plot. Oblomov then dozes off and in a dream relives his childhood in Oblomovka, the family estate. He awakens to meet Stolz, who tries to give his friend's life some direction. This leads to Oblomov's falling in love with and courtship of Olga Ilinskaia, a beautiful and well-educated but impecunious young lady. This episode ends quietly when Oblomov cannot bring himself to take the practical steps to make marriage possible. Olga goes on to marry Stolz. The second half of the novel has Oblomov become a boarder at the suburban house of Agafia Pshenitsyna, a widow, barely literate, but a great cook. He eventually marries her and they have a son. Inactive and overfed, Oblomov dies of a stroke at forty and his widow is glad to have their son brought up by the Stolzes, so he will be a gentleman like his father.

Oblomov is rich in symbolic detail. At the very outset, word comes to Oblomov that he has lost his lease, because the wreckers are coming to tear the place down, a transparent hint at the impending emancipation of serfs and subsequent ruin of the parasitic landowner class. The image of flies slowly drowning in the sweet syrup of good old-fashioned Russian *kvass* is symbolic of the fate of Oblomov and the old way of life, as are many other apt and sharply drawn images.

Oblomov has an objective narrator, who occasionally inserts his opinions and comments. In a brief epilogue he quite surprisingly introduces himself as a friend of Stolz – another example of Goncharov's superb skill which shows not only in many instances of sharply observed detail, but also in ingenious legerdemain applied in creating seemingly natural transitions from one episode of the novel to the next.

Ivan Turgenev felt that his novels, all of which are short, were in fact "novellas." They are close to the French *roman à thèse*, a fictionalized discourse on a topical issue. Each of Turgenev's novels illuminates a phenomenon of Russian life and relates to a specific period. The progress from *Rudin* (1856), who here is still a "superfluous man," to the nihilist Bazarov of *Fathers and Children* (1862) and the populists of *Virgin Soil* (1877) covers a full generation. Turgenev's novels were perceived by contemporaries as partisan statements and were discussed accordingly. Even their titles and epigraphs were revealing. *Fathers and Children* was dedicated to the memory of Belinskii, father of the movement that spawned Bazarov. While seeking to take an objective view of things, Turgenev at all times identified himself as a westernizing gradualist liberal. When *Fathers and Children* was attacked by the Left as well as by the Right, he felt obliged to explain his position in an essay, "Regarding *Fathers and Children*."

Turgenev declared that his characters, including Bazarov, were based on personal observation and that his plots evolved from character rather than from any play of the imagination. It seems, though, that current ideas were as instrumental in generating his types as were casual impressions of individuals who crossed his path. Turgenev's novels present ordinary people in ordinary human relations as affected by the times. It is the progress of time and the inevitable changes it brings about that produce new and disquieting traits in ordinary people and ordinary relationships, such as between fathers and sons or between men and women in love. Psychological motivation in Turgenev's novels, while at times subtle, is never provocative. His admirable women act in unexpected ways, considering their background, but not irrationally. When Mme. Odintsova refuses to marry Bazarov, to whom she is erotically attracted, she reasons that marrying this strong man will cost her the freedom she has learned to value above everything.

Turgenev's novels are encumbered by few digressions from the main plot and central theme. Descriptive passages, including Turgenev's superb nature scenes, are designed to create atmosphere. Still, as Apollon Grigorev observed, a Turgenevan novel resembles a canvas with some sections exquisitely finished, some showing well-sketched outlines, and some still blank. In the case of *Fathers and Children* the reader is well informed about the Kirsanovs' past and present, but little is said about Bazarov's past, intellectual maturation and inner life.

Turgenev's impersonal narrator stays in the background, making a pretense of objectivity although he has his sympathies and antipathies. Precisely by virtue of his impersonal quality, Turgenev's invisible narrator sets claim to some authoritative power of judgment and understanding. As for his own ideas and moods, Turgenev projects them on his characters. This also goes for authorial irony. Bazarov, with all of whose ideas save his rejection of art Turgenev said he agreed, fails to live up to any of them and in practice embraces the idealist notions of his antagonist. Pavel Kirsanov, whose personality and biography resemble Turgenev's, suffers the same fate; he who professes an idealist world view, in practice is good only at things material, such as being impeccably dressed and keeping his financial affairs in order. The narrator, though, never makes these ironies explicit.

Nikolai Leskov's *Cathedral Folk* (1872) takes the poetics of the realist novel to the limit in various ways, yet it is still typical of it. Subtitled "A Chronicle," it tells the story of the clergy of a provincial town with a symbolic name: Stargorod ("Oldtown"), concentrating on the 1860s, with flashbacks to pre-reform times. The novel carries an explicit political message, defending old values (the Orthodox faith, the traditional Russian way of life) and putting down liberals, foreigners (Poles, Germans, Jews), and progressive ideas. The novel's characters grow out of its basic tendency. Three clerics of Stargorod stand for the old virtues: Father Savelii Tuberozov, wise, righteous and fiery; Father Zakharia Benefaktov, humble, but firm in his faith; Deacon Akhilla Desnitsyn, a rambunctious giant with the heart and mind of a child. Against them, there stand not only the local liberal intelligentsia and assorted bureaucrats who, it being the time of liberal reforms, make a career of persecuting the conservative churchmen, but even an ecclesiastic hierarchy more intent on serving the bureaucracy than on upholding the Orthodox faith.

Leskov's penchant for personalized and stylized narrative reflects on the novel's structure, as it is put together from heterogeneous elements: the chronicler's narrative; pages from Father Tuberozov's diary; various intermezzi, such as when Nikolai Afanasevich, a dwarf once kept as a pet by an aristocratic lady, tells the story of his life; anecdotes and assorted vignettes, such as a description, extending over several pages, of three human figures gradually taking shape in the mist of morning with the sun rising behind them.

Cathedral Folk, though it has its share of ordinary characters, scores its political points by making its main characters extraordinary. Father Tuberozov is ideally beautiful both physically and morally; toward the end, his life assumes the nature of a martyr's *vita*. His deacon Akhilla is a lusty hero of Rabelaisian proportions. The dwarf overcomes the indignities of servitude to become a kind, sensible and righteous man. The antagonists of the positive characters are grotesquely ugly, physically and morally. Such are Prince Barnovolokov, a government inspector, and his secretary, the scoundrel Termosesov, who denounces Father Tuberozov, causing his suspension from the ministry.

The edifying and moving story of the three churchmen is interlaced with episodes of scurrilous humor, such as the adventures of a skeleton whose possession is a symbol of progress to the liberal schoolmaster of Stargorod, but which to the churchmen is the remains of a human being in need of a Christian burial. Leskov's forte is language. He rivals Gogol in the stylized or sharply individualized speech of his characters, the precision of his descriptions of their physical appearance, the narrator's easy control of the mood of his narrative from warm pathos to amused irony. As in Gogol, the narrator occasionally shows his own face and flaunts his virtuoso command of language. Yet his ample use of concrete realistic detail makes the whole eminently credible.

Lev Tolstoi's *Anna Karenina* (1877) belongs to the tradition of the family novel. It follows the lives of the Levin, Shcherbatskii, Oblonskii and Karenin families, all related by marriage, for several years in the 1870s. In line with the tradition of the family novel, moral concerns are voiced throughout. Some episodes may be read as satires on the depravity and follies of upper-class society. *Anna Karenina* is a *Zeitroman* presenting life in an age of upheaval: the demise of the landed gentry and the ascendancy of capitalism, the crisis in Russian agriculture, confusion in the upper-class family structure, all seen from a vantage point directed backward, rather than forward in time. Embedded in a veritable encyclopedia of Russian life are the tragedy of Anna Karenina and an account of Konstantin Levin's midlife crisis.

All major characters belong to the landed upper middle class (Levin) or to the aristocracy (Vronskii, Anna's lover). Characters from the lower classes appear on the novel's fringes. While ordinary (there are no villains and no paragons of virtue among them), Tolstoi's characters are so strongly individualized they can hardly be perceived as types. The narrative is often conducted on the level of a character's inner life. Psychological motivation is thorough, but leaves open some avenues to the subconscious, particularly as regards the events that lead to Anna's suicide and Levin's suicidal depression.

The structure of the novel is closed only as far as the heroine is concerned. But Anna's tragedy and Levin's searchings blend well into an open panorama of Russian life: a wedding (Levin's), a death (Levin's brother's), a birth (Levin's first child), a ball, a steeplechase, a hunting party, haymaking, and many other masterful vignettes of city and country life.

Tolstoi projects, on the one side, an objective narrator whose consciousness merges with the narrative and its characters, though one senses that many of Levin's experiences, thoughts and feelings are Tolstoi's own. But on the other side, he often detaches himself from his narrative and delivers himself of discourses on a variety of subjects ranging from marriage customs to modern music. In one episode, he takes aim at the literary establishment: Koznyshev, Levin's half-brother, has published an important book, a scholarly work based on years of study; it is ignored or frivolously panned by the critics. An episode involving the painter Mikhailov, who paints Anna's portrait, is devoted to a question that occupied Tolstoi for many years and eventually led to his book *What Is Art?* (1897–98). Tolstoi's position, as it emerges from this episode, is surprising for a realist: he has it that a work of art is conceived wholly as an intuition, technique of execution being secondary.

Also surprisingly, considering Tolstoi's usual adherence to a factual approach to reality, *Anna Karenina* has some traits that are in violation of strict realism. There is a great deal of symbolic foreshadowing and outright symbolism. A blizzard and a fatal accident on the railway that punctuate the inception of Anna's fateful passion, Vronskii's careless move causing the death of his beautiful mare Frou-Frou, and other such details foreshadow a tragic end. Such are also the frighteningly symbolic dreams shared by the lovers. This even goes for some details of plot structure, such as when Kitty realizes she is pregnant immediately after having ministered to the dying Nikolai Levin, symbolic of the eternal cycle of life and death. *Anna Karenina* has a metaphysical subtext, showing men and women searching for a meaning or a direction in their lives. Having shown the futility of them all, Tolstoi lets Levin discover the ideal of a godly life. *Anna Karenina* is a realist novel with some traits that go against the grain of realism. Its moralism also links it with the eighteenth-century novel.

Fedor Dostoevskii's *The Brothers Karamazov* (1879–80), set in the late 1860s, actually describes the 1870s. Post-reform Russia appears in such traits as the emergence of a new breed of entrepreneurs, disintegration of the traditional family, impoverishment and deforestation of the countryside, and a new judiciary featuring trial by jury. The novel introduces a large number of characters from a broad social spectrum: landowners, monks, government officials, intellectuals, lawyers, doctors, townspeople of various backgrounds, servants, paupers, and peasants. There are many descriptions of *realia*: the menu of a dinner party at the local monastery, a shopping spree at the local delicatessen, a doctor's visit to a pauper's cottage, a schoolboy's Sunday morning. A vivid sense of life in a provincial town is provided by the introduction of local gossip, anecdotes and "genre" scenes.

A good part of the narrative is conducted on the level of the principal characters' inner life. Ivan Karamazov's interview with the devil should be viewed as a hallucination. Even characters less central to the action are amply individualized by idiosyncratic speech patterns. The plot combines family saga and local chronicle with high drama and murder mystery, but the entire action is well within the range of the plausible. However, much about the novel's structure is unorthodox for a realist novel: suspense is created by withholding information from the reader; there are flashbacks and some foreshadowing; many inserts of narrative and discourse interrupt the flow of action (Father Zosima's Vita and Wisdom, "The Grand Inquisitor," Grushenka's "Tale of the Onion"). *The Brothers Karamazov* contains ample digressions with no direct bearing on the plot, such as a discourse on elderdom, observations on female hysterics, remarks on a painting by Kramskoi, and so on.

The Brothers Karamazov has a personalized narrator who, in an "Author's Preface," comes forth with an unorthodox program: he believes that the seed of the future is in the extraordinary and will therefore present an extraordinary hero. But then we face, for long stretches, a narrator who sounds like a conservative, worldly-wise provincial gentleman of advanced years. We also hear many other voices: Father Zosima's, Dmitrii's and Ivan Karamazov's, those of the prosecutor and defense counsel at Dmitrii's trial, and many others. All this is well within the realist canon.

The Brothers Karamazov has an anti-nihilist and anti-liberal bias, and proclaims the need for a spiritual regeneration of Russia, represented by Alesha Karamazov. While raising issues of a social and political nature, the novel also advances metaphysical questions such as that of the compatibility of innocent suffering with the existence of God, the dependance of virtue on faith in immortality, the rift between human and divine justice, and the Fatherhood of God. Some features of the novel suggest that it is an allegory of the dilemma of godless modern humanity in search of an Absolute. The realist novel has a metaphysical subtext, provided the reader chooses to see it.

Another subtext is introduced by a host of biblical and literary quotations and allusions. Christ's temptation by the devil is projected into Ivan

Karamazov's tragic failure. His devil is a travesty of and a response to Goethe's Mephistopheles. Throughout the novel there appear thinly veiled putdowns of radical and liberal writers such as Herzen, Turgenev and Saltykov-Shchedrin. Altogether, *The Brothers Karamazov* shows that metaphysical and literary elements may be found embedded in a realist novel without detracting from its objective credibility.

Mikhail Sholokhov's *The Quiet Don* (1928–40) is often read as a twentieth-century version of *War and Peace*, though it is not technically a historical novel, for its action ends only a few years before Sholokhov began to write it. Like *War and Peace* it relates the experience of several families in times of peace and war. The action is advanced largely by historical events. Historical personages make some appearances. A large number of people, some of whom appear only once, are shown engaged in public affairs, in their familial and personal pursuits, and at work. But *The Quiet Don* has some unique traits. It is set almost entirely in a Cossack settlement of the Don region. Its main characters are simple, uneducated people. Members of the upper class and intellectuals appear on the fringes only and are viewed through the eyes of the uneducated. The action is seen from the Cossack's point of view, though the narrator at times affects a somewhat broader perspective.

While the narrator is class-conscious, the character of his *personae* is not exhausted by their social status. The main hero, Grigorii Melekhov, a moderately well-to-do farmer who eventually takes up arms against the Soviets, is an attractive character and a better man than the landless Cossack Misha Koshevoi, who becomes a Communist activist. Love and jealousy, happiness and heartbreak appear independently of political events. The inner life of all characters is uncomplicated. The dialogue, limited to dramatic junctures, is realistic and vigorous. It contains many dialect expressions, as does the narrative. The action features matter-of-fact descriptions of beatings, incest, gang rape, floggings, executions and other shocking scenes. A supporter of the Soviet regime and not himself a Cossack, Sholokhov may have purposely presented life in a Cossack settlement as more cruel and violent than it actually was. There is no moralizing on the part of the narrator, nor does he digress from his narration, except in a large number of masterful nature descriptions. The narrator restrains his own emotions and lets his characters express theirs freely.

While the topic of the novel is clearly defined as the coming of the Soviet order to the land of the Cossacks, it is left to the reader to recognize its political drift. Sholokhov does not present the coming of the Soviet order as historically necessary, but does bring out the reasons why the Bolsheviks prevailed. *The Quiet Don* is one of the purest examples of a truly realist novel among the outstanding novels of Russian literature. It projects an objective view of contemporary life with an emphasis on its social aspect, yet without any preaching or theorizing.

Boris Pasternak, a great modernist poet, followed the example of the nineteenth-century realist novel in *Doctor Zhivago* (1957), his only novel. He made one concession to the lyric bent of his genius, making his hero an amateur poet and adding a cycle of Iurii Zhivago's poems, loosely related to various episodes of the novel.

Doctor Zhivago is one of many novels about the generation that experienced World War I, the Revolution and the coming of the Soviet order. Like Aleksei Tolstoi's *A Tour of Hell*, it has the ordeal of the Russian intelligentsia for its main theme. Iurii Zhivago, a sensitive but passive observer of life, is at the mercy of the cataclysmic events that engulf the country. They deprive him of Tonia, his loving wife, and his children, then of Lara, his second love. He survives until the end of the NEP period sustained by Marina, the third woman in his life, but dies young, a broken man, stifled by the enforced duplicity of Soviet life.

The Revolution is presented as a calamity that befalls the Russian people regardless of their social class, for while it rights the injustices of the old order it brings with it bondage worse than before. The doers fare even worse than the passive sufferer Zhivago. Pasha Antipov, his rival for Lara's love, is a Communist activist who decides that it is nobler to serve the Revolution uncritically than to value one's own opinions. He perishes senselessly. A multitude of other characters appears, whose lives and deaths seem void of meaning, regardless of their political convictions. The entire action of *Doctor Zhivago* is marked by randomness, strange coincidences, and a lack of purpose, not at all due to Pasternak's amateurish composition, as has been suggested by some critics, but rather as a proper reflection of the chaotic condition of Russian life during the period in question. A sustained plot, derived from the character of the novel's *personae*, would have been at odds with the condition of a world profoundly out of joint.

Doctor Zhivago consists of sharply focused scenes scattered over the vast territory of European and Asian Russia, from the first years of the century to an epilogue set toward the end of World War II. A few minor characters stand out precisely because attention is briefly focused on them in a single episode. Meanwhile the main characters, perhaps with the sole exception of Lara, remain remote. We hear Iurii Zhivago's voice frequently and at length, but it lacks immediacy. Having gathered a large volume of impressions and ideas, Pasternak projected them into a panoramic view of life, with a less than perfect effort to mold them into a plot with live characters. In a sense, though, this shortcoming leads to a high degree of subjective realism, once *Doctor Zhivago* is read as the writer's personal and intellectual legacy, an interpretation which is supported by the presence throughout the novel of many memorable discourses embracing topics such as the nature of art, the meaning of history, the destiny of the Russian intelligentsia, Christianity, Jewishness, the meaning of dreams, the Immaculate Conception, and many others.

The third-person narrative of *Doctor Zhivago* has a quality of detachment which has the narrator stay on the outside of the action even as he reports the hideous horrors of war. Pasternak's sense for the concrete detail, metonymic or symbolic, makes certain passages, nature scenes as well as interiors, unforgettable. Such is the rowan tree whose life-sustaining red berries evoke in Zhivago, then a prisoner of a gang of guerillas in the icy wilds of the Urals, the image of a loving women, Lara.

There are several reasons why most of the novels chosen for discussion here date from the nineteenth century. The golden age of the Russian realist novel came to an end around 1880, with the ascendancy of the short story as Russian literature's most representative genre. The very concept of realism came under a two-pronged attack during the first quarter of the twentieth century: to the right, neo-Romantic tendencies took their toll and to the left Marxist ideology branded the objectivity of realism as "pseudo-objectivism." Also, the realist novel was based on a belief that a certain logic was inherent in an individual's biography and a nation's history. Events of the twentieth century caused one to lose faith in this notion, thus depriving the traditional realist novel of its *raison d'être*.

All but two of the novels discussed here offer a broad panoramic view of Russian life: *A Hero of Our Time* and *Fathers and Children* are also the shortest of the ten novels discussed. All but *Evgenii Onegin* and *A Hero of Our Time* show some explicit social concern, while only *Anna Karenina* and *The Brothers Karamazov* may be called psychological novels. All but *Evgenii Onegin* and *A Hero of Our Time* carry a more or less explicit moral or ideological message and in some way all ten pass judgment on the society they describe.

Pushkin, Gogol, Tolstoi, Dostoevskii, and Pasternak combine objective narrative with some subjective contemplation. The same authors also digress frequently from their main plot and introduce some literary discussion into their text. Some elements of Romantic poetics may be found in all ten novels. The great Russian novelists do not offer very pure examples of uncompromising Realism. Some lesser writers, such as the conservative Aleksei Pisemskii, the Populists Fedor Reshetnikov and Nikolai Pomialovskii, the Marxists Maksim Gorkii and Vikentii Veresaev, and even popular middle-of-the-road entertainers like Petr Boborykin and Vasilii Nemirovich-Danchenko are better Realists. However, it does not appear that any of their works contain more truth of any kind than the works discussed here.

NOTES

1. V. N. Maikov, "Nechto o russkoi literature v 1846 g," in Maikov, *Sobranie sochinenii*, 2 vols., 2nd edn (Kiev, 1901), vol. I, pp. 207–10.
2. *Fabula* is the chronological sequence of events, while *siuzhet* is "a sequence of events, artistically arranged." Boris Tomashevskii, *Teoriia literatury*, 4th edn (Moscow and Leningrad: Gosudarstvennoe izdatel'stvo 1928), p. 136.

11

ROBERT RUSSELL

The Modernist tradition

It is common to begin discussions of Modernism with caveats about the difficulty or impossibility of adequate definition. In the introduction to his recent study of Russian literature of the 1920s, Victor Erlich reminds us of Irving Howe's use of the terms "elusive" and "protean" to characterize Modernism.[1] In using these words, Howe may appear to be advocating a free-for-all, permissive attitude to the boundaries of Modernism, and it is, indeed, difficult to see how one can be more prescriptive when faced with the vast range of heterogeneous works of art which are, by common consent, "modernist." Marshall Berman's view of Modernism is more comprehensive than most. For him, it is the artistic expression of an experience of alienation, struggle, and contradiction that has been the normal human condition for an ever increasing number of people for almost five hundred years.[2] Berman's stimulating book contains much that is of value to the student of Russian literature, but I believe that his definition of Modernism, one that includes works by Gogol, Dostoevskii, and even Pushkin, is too capacious. Certainly, given such a definition there can be no opposition between Russian Realism and Russian Modernism; while not coterminous, the two overlap hugely. Such canonical texts of Realism as *Notes from Underground* (1864) and *Crime and Punishment* (1866) are, for Berman, quintessential modernist works because they are concerned with the human condition of struggle, contradiction, and alienation. Fruitful as this idea is for the interpretation of Dostoevskii and Gogol, I prefer to take a narrower and more orthodox view of the chronological limits of Modernism in Russia, from about the 1890s until the imposition of Socialist Realism in the 1930s. The modernist authors of this period were all conscious of the profound break with the past that marked the contemporary age. It was a deepseated, revolutionary change that was realized in many different spheres of human activity: most obviously, perhaps, in social and political life as the Russian Empire crumbled, but also in philosophy and religion, and in scientific thought.

The old certainties had gone, and a mood of anxiety, tension, and restlessness was now the spirit of the age, the essence of modernist sensibility. Formal innovation followed, as artists sought appropriate means of expressing the comprehensive change that had taken place in all aspects of life.

Before turning to the modernist works of the early twentieth century, however, it will be useful to examine more closely Berman's concept of the experience of modernity and its reflection in nineteenth-century Russian literature, since it is one of the peculiarities of the Russian version of Modernism that it developed less markedly in *opposition* to the Realism that preceded it than as a continuation of one important strand of that realistic tradition, the so-called "Gogol–Dostoevskii line." That sense of discontinuity, of a complete break with the past expressed by modernist artists in many countries, was certainly not absent in Russia (one only has to think of the Futurists' pledge to "throw Pushkin, Dostoevskii, Tolstoi . . . overboard from the steamship of modernity"), but in a culture that had already produced Gogol's "The Nose" (1836) and Dostoevskii's *The Double* (1846) it was not necessary to invent completely new images of fragmentation in order to reflect the chaos of the new age. Virginia Woolf may have felt that December 1910 was when human nature changed (see her essay "Mr Bennett and Mrs Brown"), but in Russia the disintegration of the personality and of society that marks the boundary of the modern age had been sensed and expressed earlier. Whereas, throughout much of Europe, the experience of the First World War revealed the extent to which the old stable certainties had gone, in Russia the fundamental shift had come more than fifty years earlier, with the Emancipation of the serfs in 1861. And whereas many artists and thinkers throughout Europe had, from the turn of the century or so, sensed and expressed the impending fragmentation and chaos ahead of its universal recognition, in Russia, once again, that process had taken place significantly earlier in the works of Gogol and Dostoevskii beginning in the 1830s and 1840s. This is not to say that Russian artists of the first two decades of the twentieth century stood apart from the general European modernist trend. Nothing could be further from the truth. But, the Futurists' wish to shock notwithstanding, they had no need to jettison all previous cultural models in order to be able to reflect the age.

For many Russians and visitors to that country, the physical embodiment of modernity, the symbol of a break with the past, was the city of St. Petersburg, founded in 1703. This is not the place to discuss the general significance of St. Petersburg in Russian literature; that has been done elsewhere, including in another essay in this volume. But it is necessary to stress the peculiar hold on the modernist imagination exercised by this "spectral" metropolis, a place which the Underground Man describes as "the most abstract and intentional city in the world" and which Dostoevskii himself referred to as "the most fantastic city" (*Winter Notes on Summer Impressions*, 1863). Certain attributes of St. Petersburg serve to crystallize the sense of fragmentation and alienation that is central to the spirit of Modernism. First there is the contrast between the magnificent public spaces of the city, particularly the palaces and squares lining the Neva, and the overcrowded tenements with their squalid yards and foul staircases that lie just behind; second, there are the extremities of weather and light, particularly the white nights of mid-summer and the frequent dense fogs, both of which can appear to dissolve solid shapes into ghostly outlines ("was it not all an optical illusion, a phantasmagoria?," asked one early nineteenth-century visitor);[3] finally, and perhaps most significantly, there is the fact that this huge city was created in a hostile environment and at the cost of many thousands of lives as an act of will by one man. From Pushkin's *The Bronze Horseman* (written 1833; first published 1841) onwards, St. Petersburg has been presented in literature in terms of the juxtaposition of opposites, struggle, contradiction, lack of certainty, madness: a place where the strangest things can and do occur. To one of the characters in Dostoevskii's *A Raw Youth* (1875), it appears as though the entire city is unreal, a dream, and he wonders whether it might "rise with the mist and disappear like smoke," leaving behind the Finnish bog that had been there before, with, perhaps, just the Bronze Horseman astride his hotly breathing steed in the middle of it (I, 8).

A key figure in the creation of the literary image of St. Petersburg was Nikolai Gogol. The city of his stories "Nevskii Prospect" (1835), "Notes of a Madman" (1835), "The Nose" (1836), and "The Overcoat" (1842) is a protagonist rather than a setting, a place where, as he writes in "Nevskii Prospect," "everything is deception, everything is dream, everything is different from what it seems," one where "the Devil himself lights the lamps." The people who hurry along St. Petersburg's main thoroughfare are reduced by Gogol's narrator to their most striking physical attributes:

> Here you will meet unique sidewhiskers, tucked under the necktie with extra-ordinary and astounding skill, sidewhiskers that are velvety, satiny, black as sable or as coal, but, alas belonging to the Foreign Office alone. Providence has refused to permit civil servants from other departments to sport black side-whiskers; to their very great chagrin, they must wear red ones.

The blurring of the distinction between the part and the whole – Gogol's characteristic grotesque synecdoche – was to strike a chord in several modernist writers, for whom it became a means of conveying intensity of emotion, the disintegration of personality, or essential psychological features. Thus, Maiakovskii's lyrical persona in "A Cloud in Trousers" (1915) cries: "But can you turn yourself inside out as I can, so that you are nothing but lips?"; and the hero of Zamiatin's *We* (written 1920–21, first complete publication in Russian 1952) declares: "imagine a human finger cut off from the whole, from the hand – a separate human finger hunched up, running in a series of hops along the glass pavement. That finger was me" (Entry 18).

In the context of Russian Modernism, the grotesque fantasy of "The Nose" is of particular importance. This story in which a bumptious civil servant, "Major" Kovalev, awakens one day to find that he has lost his nose and later sees it in the guise of a general riding round in a carriage, is astonishingly "modern" for a work written in the first half of the nineteenth century. It is deliberately elusive, with a characteristic dream-like fluidity that extends to every level. Nothing here is stable; character, plot, language, point of view, dimensions, even such a basic category as "animate"/ "inanimate" – all are in constant flux, and there is no fixed point that the reader can hold on to with certainty. One moment the nose is discovered baked in a loaf of bread, the next it is wearing a general's uniform during a service in the Kazan Cathedral and Kovalev approaches it tentatively, since it appears to outrank him. When it is finally recovered, Kovalev tries to stick it back on the smooth place left on his face, but it falls to the table with a dull thud, like something inorganic; later still it reappears in its proper place, once more an integral part of an organism. Some critics have seen in "The Nose" little more than an amusing piece of whimsy, yet the underlying themes of sexual and social anxiety and alienation mark the work as a precursor of Russian Modernism no less clearly than do the stylistic features. A further similarity comes with reader response. The amusement that the reader of "The Nose" is likely to feel will almost certainly be accompanied by an uneasiness that is a characteristic reaction to many of the modernist works of the first two decades of the twentieth century. Gogol's grotesque, unstable fantasy is to find many echoes in the years to come, in works by Belyi, Maiakovskii, Zamiatin, and Olesha, as well as in Kharms's literature of the absurd.

The similarities between Gogol's St. Petersburg tales and the early Dostoevskii have been widely recognized, particularly in the case of *The Double*, which takes thematic and stylistic elements that had been found earlier in "The Nose" and "Notes of a Madman" and relates them to the onset of the hero's schizophrenia. The modernist features of fractured style, anxiety, and social alienation in the city are all to be found in Dostoevskii as in Gogol, but in the younger writer they are more explicitly related to their metaphysical and psychological undercurrents. If Gogol's anticipation of Modernism is instinctive, then Dostoevskii's appears to me to be the result of a profound understanding of the great shift in consciousness that was about to take place and that would be expressed in different spheres of thought by Freud, Nietzsche, Lobachevskii, Einstein, and many others. Dostoevskii both anticipates and, through his enormous influence on twentieth-century art and thought, helps to shape modern consciousness,[4] a process that can be seen nowhere more clearly than in two of the novelist's St. Petersburg works, *Notes from Underground* and *Crime and Punishment*. Here the protagonists' isolation is not only social, but also existential. The question of identity and how it can be determined runs through both works.[5] In their attempts to find out who they are, and in their eschewal of definition by such extraneous factors as class, wealth, nationality, or self-interest, the Underground Man and Raskolnikov are deeply *modern* heroes. Similarly, the uneasy, apocalyptic atmosphere of *The Devils* (1871–72), a sense of being on the edge of catastrophe, anticipates one of the central features of modern consciousness.

The form which Dostoevskii employed for his examination of the existential and psychological condition of modern man was the realistic novel, but it was a new kind of realism, what he himself termed "realism in a higher sense," and in its blend of verisimilitude and fantasy, in its instability and unpredictability, it was exactly suited to the depiction of contemporary life, and was to be a major influence throughout the next century. It is beyond the scope of this essay to examine in any detail the nature of Dostoevskii's realism (a topic that has been extensively discussed by many critics), but one or two examples will indicate the general nature of his innovations. First, there is the depiction of space. The city of St. Petersburg as a whole, its individual streets and buildings, and the rooms inhabited by the heroes of the works are all on the one hand "real," in that their representation is mimetic, and on the other hand they are psychological constructs, spatial analogues of the characters' minds. As has been pointed out by Leonid Grossman, Dostoevskii's depiction of St. Petersburg is the most palpable and accurate in nineteenth-century literature.[6] Yet the city inhabited by the Underground Man is the physical embodiment of his psychological condition, it is "the underground." And Raskolnikov's room seems to change dimensions in accordance with his frame of mind; one moment it is tiny and stuffy, no bigger than a cupboard, the next it swells to accommodate the student himself and several visitors. Likewise, the stifling weather is both the real St. Petersburg summer climate and a metaphor for Raskolnikov's overheated, airless mind. Similar points could be made about the handling of time, which appears to expand and contract as a function of Raskolnikov's consciousness; and about some of the secondary characters, whose inconsistencies become explicable if the characters are seen as in part real (that is portrayed by an objective narrator) and in part projections by Raskolnikov of his own preoccupations.

It is important to stress what Dostoevskii himself stressed: that the world which he depicts in *Crime and Punishment* is no more fantastic than the world of real experience depicted in the newspapers. Modern life in the city *is* intense and chaotic, and if artists are to portray it adequately they must find new forms. It is but a small step from this point to twentieth-century Modernism. That step was taken by Andrei Belyi in *Petersburg* (first version 1913–14, second version 1916, final version 1922). The novel's modernity is evident in the mood of anxiety and alienation that permeates the entire work and that arises out of the awareness of impending catastrophe.[7] That sense of being on the edge of the abyss that is characteristic of the modernist sensibility has, in Belyi's novel, a concrete historical context, since the work is set in the autumn of 1905, when Russia was in the grip of revolutionary turmoil. The plot involves an attempt to assassinate a senior official, Senator Apollon Apollonovich Ableukhov, by planting in his home a bomb hidden in a sardine tin. The first stage of the plan, the placing of the bomb, is carried out by Apollon Apollonovich's son, Nikolai Apollonovich, who is not a revolutionary but who is bound by a promise of help made in a rash moment. Most of the novel is pervaded by an atmosphere of imminent disaster engendered in Nikolai Apollonovich and in the reader by the awareness that the bomb is ticking away and must soon explode.

The absorbing plot and convincing evocation of a particular time and place form the framework on which Belyi hangs his brilliant narrative, which has occasionally been described as the Russian *Ulysses*. The comparison with Joyce's novel is not entirely without foundation; Vladimir Nabokov placed both (along with works by Kafka and Proust) in his list of the four leading masterpieces of the twentieth century. Like Joyce, Belyi writes highly dynamic prose, the normal semantic significance of which is constantly supplemented by rich phonetic patterning and occasionally by experimental typographical layout. In part, the character of the prose is determined by the voice (or voices) of the narrator, who adopts a wide variety of tones from bumbling incomprehension to sweeping lyricism, and who switches between them without warning, thereby contributing to that volatility, that lack of certainty that is a key modernist concept.

The city itself is rendered with minute topographical accuracy necessitating frequent reference to a contemporary street plan, and yet it is simultaneously that spectral, fantastic creation of Peter the Great, mytholo-gized by Pushkin, Gogol, and Dostoevskii, that had become a vital element in the definition of Russia's national identity. Belyi is constantly aware of the works of his predecessors (the Bronze Horseman is a character), as well as the libretto of Tchaikovsky's *Queen of Spades*, and the reader is required to place the events and characters in their cultural environment by picking up the references. St. Petersburg itself, with all its cultural and mythical significance, emerges as the novel's protagonist, every bit as alive as the human characters.

Apart from the work of Belyi, perhaps the outstanding example of the modernist novel in Russia was by Evgenii Zamiatin, in whom modern consciousness can be seen at its purest. For Zamiatin, no true writer could be settled, content with present realities; writers had to be heretics, forever restless, in constant intellectual movement, and provoking a life-affirming and creative anxiety in their readers. As he said in the essay "Tomorrow" (1919–20):

> Today is doomed to die because yesterday died, and because tomorrow will be born. Such is the cruel and wise law. Cruel, because it condemns to eternal dissatisfaction those who already today see the distant peaks of tomorrow; wise, because eternal dissatisfaction is the only guarantee of eternal move-ment forward, eternal creation . . . The world is kept alive only by heretics.[8]

In Zamiatin we can see, perhaps more clearly than anywhere else, the roots of Russian Modernism in the restless spirit of Romanticism. A recurrent image in his work is that of the lone Scythian horseman forever in motion, a figure similar to Lermontov's rebellious lone white sail, and reminiscent of the constant oppositional nature of Pechorin in *A Hero of Our Time* (1840, definitive version 1841): "Where is he galloping? Nowhere. Why? For no reason. He gallops simply because he is a Scythian, because he has become one with his horse, because he is a centaur, and the dearest things to him are freedom, solitude, his horse, the wide open steppe."[9]

For Zamiatin, there can be no immutable truths, for if there were any such fixed philosophical points they would contradict the "cosmic, uni-versal law" of constant revolution, which "is everywhere, in everything."[10] His world view is Einsteinian rather than Euclidean, based on the "speed-ing, curved surfaces" of the new mathematics and the new cosmology rather than the plane surfaces of Euclid and the fixed forces of Newton. Given this view of a universe in constant movement, Zamiatin uses and advocates a correspondingly dynamic literary form. The nineteenth-century Realists' leisurely descriptions of landscape and character are inappropriate in the modern age: "who will even think of looking at landscapes and genre scenes when the world is listing at a forty-five-degree angle . . . ? Today we can look and think only as people do in the face of death."[11] The urgent anxiety of modern life demands brevity, compression, innovative syntax and imagery, and a literary vocabulary enhanced by provincialisms, neologisms, and scientific and technical terms. The syntax of Zamiatin's artistic prose is, in his own words, "elliptic, volatile"; his imagery is "sharp, synthetic, with a single salient feature – the one feature you will glimpse from a speeding car."[12]

Zamiatin was keenly aware of the distinctiveness of modern art. His terms for it were "synthetism" and "neo-realism," and he viewed it as a synthesis of Realism's search for the physical reality of the flesh and Symbolism's obsession with death and retreat from the everyday in quest of the spiritual. On the one hand there was "vivid, simple, strong, crude flesh: Moleschott, Büchner, Rubens, Repin, Zola, Tolstoi, Gorkii, realism, Naturalism"; on the other "Schopenhauer, Botticelli, Rossetti, Vrubel, Churlionis, Verlaine, Blok, idealism, symbolism." The modernist artist returns to the sphere of the first group, to the flesh, but with the full knowledge of the discoveries of the second group. "Thus synthesis: Nietzsche, Whitman, Gauguin, Seurat, Picasso – the new Picasso, still little known – and all of us, great and small, who work in modern art, whatever it may be called – neo-realism, synthetism, or something else."[13] It is clear from this list that for Zamiatin the essence of modern art lies in sensibility rather than chronology. Whitman, for example, was born before Zola, Tolstoi, or Gorkii, yet Zamiatin considers him a Modernist and the others Realists.

Zamiatin's novel *We*, substantially written in 1920 and completed in 1921, exemplifies his views on modern consciousness and its formal expression; indeed, essays such as "On synthetism" and, especially, "On literature, revolution and entropy" can be read as a commentary on and explication of the novel. First, the philosophical position adopted within *We* reflects the view expressed in the essays that revolution must be constant and all-embracing, and that the rejection of all fixed systems of belief, be they religious or political, is a primary requirement for a true artist. In Entry 30 of the fictional diary the following conversation takes place between the rebel I-330 and the mathematician D-503:

"Darling, you're a mathematician. Even more than that, mathematics has made you a philosopher. Well then, name the final number for me."
"Meaning? I . . . I don't understand. What final number?"
"The final one, the highest number, the biggest one."
"But, I, that's absurd. Since the number of numbers is infinite, how can there be a final one?"

"Well then, how can there be a final revolution? There is no final one, revolutions are infinite."

For those brought up in the Single State, taught since early childhood that the revolution which resulted in the foundation of their present society was the last one that would ever take place, such notions of constant revolution are frightening. Surely, argues D-503, those who founded the Single State were right to do so? I-330 wholeheartedly agrees. They *were* right at the time, but, as with all revolutionaries, when they achieved power they tried to prevent anyone else from rebelling against them. Conviction led to dogma and, eventually, the desire to preserve the status quo at all costs. The specific political implications of passages such as this for the fledgling Soviet state are obvious. Although it is undoubtedly the prescience of Zamiatin's novel – its anticipation of twentieth-century totalitarianism – that is its most striking political feature, its satirical reflection of certain aspects of the political, social, and cultural life of Soviet Russia in the Civil War era should not be overlooked, and was sufficient to ensure that it was not published in Russia in the 1920s. Yet to interpret the theme of revolution in the novel primarily on the political plane is to minimize its significance, not least as the philosophical cornerstone of Zamiatin's Modernism.

The concept of revolution advanced in *We* is universal, affecting human behavior, social and political institutions, and natural phenomena alike, and is equated with movement, with energy. The opposite tendency, towards stasis, is also universal, and is referred to by Zamiatin as "entropy," a term which he characteristically borrows from science. Thus, whereas Christ is seen as historically and philosophically revolutionary, the Christian church is portrayed as the true ancestor of the Single State: a deadening body, convinced that it is right in all things, and seeking to stifle opposition to its dogma by rooting out and destroying heretics. Entropy and dogma affect even the apparently objective world of mathematics. The conformist D-503 favors those branches of mathematics concerned with certainty, predictability, integration, and the geometry of plane surfaces and fixed solid objects. His heroes are Euclid, Pythagoras, and the early eighteenth-century English mathematician Brook Taylor, and he appears to have no knowledge of, or no esteem for, those nineteenth- and twentieth-century mathematicians whose work supported philosophical notions of uncertainty and relativity. For Zamiatin himself, as for his heroine I-330, the desire for complete certainty, whether in philosophy, religion, mathematics, or any other area, runs counter to the laws of thermodynamics. As I-330 says: "Surely, as a mathematician, you understand that only differences, differences of temperature, only contrasts in heat, only that makes for life? And if everywhere throughout the universe all bodies are equally warm or equally cool . . . They've got to be smashed into each other – so there'll be fire, explosion, inferno" (Entry 30).

Zamiatin's philosophy provokes unease and anxiety. It permits no comforting notions of eventual peace, no ultimate goal, no heaven, whether on Earth or elsewhere; instead, it promises only "the torment of endless movement" (Entry 28). In this it is modernist thought, strikingly similar in some respects to that of Nietzsche.[14]

A second aspect of the content of *We* that marks it as a modernist text is the prominence of the irrational and the subconscious. There is no evidence that Zamiatin believed in the *primacy* of the irrational, but in the societies which he depicts (not only the Single State but also the middle-class England of "Islanders," 1917) it has been largely suppressed, thereby destroying that balance between reason and the irrational that, he argues, is essential for the wholeness of the personality. Hence his apparent championing of irrationality. Attempting to explain to D-503 who the Mephi are, I-330 says: "Who are they? The half that we have lost. There's H_2 and there's O, but in order to get H_2O – streams, seas, waterfalls, waves, storms – the two halves must unite" (Entry 28). The Single State has split the human personality into its rational and irrational components and has almost succeeded in eradicating the latter. But just as water ceases to be water when either of its two elements is removed, so do people cease to be people when their irrational side is repressed. Under the influence of an overwhelming and uncomprehended wave of sexual desire for I-330, D-503's dormant irrationality is aroused, manifesting itself in dreams, in his synaesthetic perception of the physical world around him, especially his perception of color, and in the increasingly original and creative language of his diary entries.

Among the many influences on Zamiatin, mention should be made of Dostoevskii. Much in *We*, including the role of the irrational in human behavior, and the philosophical issue of the relationship between freedom and happiness, had been encountered earlier in *Notes from Underground*, *The Devils*, and *The Brothers Karamazov* (1880). Like twentieth-century writers the world over, Zamiatin found in the work of Dostoevskii a brilliant artistic investigation of the human condition in the modern age which corresponded in many respects to his own creative concerns.[15] On the philosophical level, however, there is a fundamental difference between the two: Zamiatin rejects all notions of peace and reconciliation in Christ, whereas Dostoevskii and some of his heroes, while finding it impossible to accomplish the "leap of faith," need to preserve the figure of Christ as the only way out of the "underground," the moral and intellectual impasse that is the lot of modern man. Dostoevskii's famous dictum about preferring Christ to the truth if a choice were necessary is diametrically opposed to Zamiatin's relentless refusal to accept any fixed points of belief.

Zamiatin's modernist view of life is expressed in the correspondingly fractured, elliptical prose of *We*. D-503 begins his diary with the intention of explaining to the less fortunate inhabitants of other planets the near-perfect, rational way of life in the Single State. His ideal is total clarity, a transparency of language that would correspond to the transparency of the buildings in the Single State. Almost immediately, however, this ideal is compromised by the intrusion of metaphor, and as the diary proceeds, its style reflects the increasingly chaotic state of D-503's mind. Zamiatin's short, dynamic sentences, punctuated by dashes and frequently tailing off into three dots, are perfectly suited both to his own view of the nature of prose in the post-Einstein age and to D-503's uncomprehending slide into the state of alienation and anxiety, simultaneously exhilarating and terri-fying, that is the modern mode.

The extreme compression of the syntax is complemented by the use of recurrent physical leitmotifs as a kind of shorthand for characterization. The characters are frequently reduced to a single detail that simultaneously suggests physical appearance and personality or function. Thus, I-330 becomes the "X" that is formed in her face by the lines of her eyebrows and the slight furrows from her nostrils to the sides of her mouth and that serves both as a physical identification tag and as an indication of her mysterious inner world. O-90 is constantly described in terms of roundness, a detail expressing her looks, the appropriateness of her name, and the maternalism that is her primary characteristic. The doctor who tells D-503 that he has developed a soul is seen as a pair of scissors, thin, sharp and dangerous. The Guardian S-4711 always appears as a hunched, snake-like figure, the physical embodiment of his ambivalent role as apparent upholder and would-be destroyer of the Single State. His serpent-like shape also acts as a frequent reminder of the mythical level on which the novel operates: the Single State corresponds to the Garden of Eden, the Bene-factor to God, D-503 to Adam, I-330 to Satan, Eve and the serpent. On occasion, when D-503 catches a fleeting glimpse of someone, recognition depends entirely on the leitmotif. This is in line with Zamiatin's view that modern prose must correspond to the pace of modern life, that, as we have seen, the image must consist only of the basic detail that would be spotted from a speeding car, yet it must be capable of suggesting the whole character.

With its rapid, elliptical syntax, its identification of single salient features of physique and character, and its displacement of the "normal" planes of time and space – most evident in stories such as "Mamai" (1920) and "A Story about the Most Important Thing" (1923) – Zamiatin's prose corresponds to his own description of the essence of modern painting. In "On synthetism" he points out that the earthquake in geometric and philosophical thought brought about by Einstein was anticipated by "the seismograph of the new art," which had shattered accepted notions of perspective, the "X, Y and Z axes" of Realism (Zamiatin, "O sintetizme," p. 286). In describing the paintings of his friend Iurii Annenkov, Zamiatin could be describing his own prose: "he has a sense of the exceptional pace and dynamism of our epoch, a sense of time refined to hundredths of a second, the skill (characteristic of synthetism) to provide only the synthetic essence of things" (Zamiatin, "O sintetizme," p. 288).

The painterly qualities of Zamiatin's modernist prose can be seen in his handling of color and light, no less than line. Scholars have sometimes attempted to assign significance to particular colors in *We*. Thus, for example, the light blue of the clear sky above the Single State and the bluish-grey of the numbers' uniforms have been seen as emblematic of that society's predominant rationality; the red of I-330's lips and of the fire that burns inside her as representing the heat of passion and revolution; the yellow of the ancient dress, of the sap that covers everything in spring, and of the eyes of the beast glimpsed through the glass of the Green Wall as suggesting man's struggle for freedom, for escape to the life-giving force of the sun.[16] Yet, useful as these attempts at disclosing the significance of color in *We* have been, they have generally failed to do justice to the complexity of the subject. In a recent article Sona S. Hoisington and Lynn Imbery have, for the first time, shown how subtle and dynamic is Zamiatin's use of color, linking him with modern painters, especially Gauguin, Van Gogh, and Matisse.[17] Hoisington and Imbery demonstrate convincingly that Zamiatin's handling of color is based on *transformation* rather than fixed attributes, and that the opposition between energy and entropy that is the philosophical core of the novel is conveyed through such color transformations. Most of the colors in *We* are, therefore, dynamic and relative rather than absolute in value, which accords with Zamiatin's concept of Modernism.

Like everything else in the Single State, light is perceived by the citizens as uniform and clear, an analogue of their rational lives. D-503 eulogizes the cloudless blue sky and the even light of the "crystalline sun" and is afraid of the fog that occasionally envelops the city, blurring the customary sharp outlines of the glass buildings. On one level, Zamiatin uses different states of light as symbols of the rational and irrational halves of his hero's psyche. I-330 tells D-503 that besides fearing the obscurity of the fog (meaning his irrationality) he also loves it (Entry 13). But, like color, light is also used by Zamiatin in a purely painterly fashion; reflecting and refracting, it can become solid, as in the following examples: "on the mirrored door of the wardrobe – a shard of light – in my eyes"; "a sharp ray of sunlight fractures like lightning on the floor, on the wall of the wardrobe, higher, and then this cruel, flashing blade falls on I-330's thrown-back, naked neck"; "a golden sickle of sunlight on the loudspeaker" (Entries 18 and 19).

The diary form and the increasing unpredictability of the narrator focus the attention of the reader of *We* on the artistic medium itself, as well as on the relativity of perspective. In certain other works of Russian Modernism these issues play an even greater part. The novels of Boris Pilniak, for example, have often been criticized for their dishevelled lack of organization, their repetitiveness (the author habitually incorporated earlier texts within later ones, sometimes with little revision), and their rambling, apparently arbitrary plot development (Donat, the character who, in the early pages of *The Naked Year* [1922], seems most likely to develop into the novel's hero is disconcertingly killed off at the end of the first chapter). Critics from Pilniak's time to the present have voiced the suspicion that his adoption of a modernist stance merely masks an inability or unwillingness to conform to the discipline of consistent plot and character development.[18] Yet to argue thus is implicitly to apply to Pilniak the inappropriate criteria of the realistic novel. *The Naked Year*, which owes much to Belyi and Remizov, is an attempt to convey the elemental chaos of revolution by rendering it in a prose that is itself chaotic to the point of near unintelligibility in places. Pilniak's text is indeterminate; it cannot be tied down to consistency of language, point of view, or moral perspective. It is driven at least as much by phonetics as by plot or characterization, with many paragraphs being structured on particular sound combinations rather than on a core of meaning. And yet, meaning *does* emerge through a deliberate lack of coherence in the literary medium analogous to that in Russian life. Pilniak's prose is an eclectic montage of loosely connected (and sometimes unconnected) episodes narrated in a variety of equally heterogeneous stylistic registers. It is prose that insistently draws attention to the nature of the medium and yet remains representative of Russian reality.

Pilniak's style, with colloquialisms alongside archaisms, and phonetic and rhythmic repetitive patterns, is an example of the manner known as "ornamentalism" practiced by many Russian novelists and short-story writers in the 1920s. Patricia Carden considers ornamentalism to be "simply the name attached to the appearance of Modernism in Russian prose" ("Ornamentalism and Modernism," p. 49). There are advantages in Carden's identification of the two terms, notably the attention which it focuses on the links between Modernism in literature and in the other arts in Russia in the first quarter of the century. In the early work of the painters Goncharova, Larionov and Kandinskii, and the composer Stravinskii, Carden sees "a mood and style reminiscent of ornamental prose," the common features being "a folkloristic primitivism of subject and mood" and "a display of artistic virtuosity" (Carden, "Ornamentalism and Modernism," p. 49). Although this insight into the unifying elements of Modernism in the Russian arts is productive, it serves to narrow the scope of literary Modernism by restricting it to the work of writers who exhibit precisely this combination of folkloric primitivism and formal experimentation. While some of Zamiatin's stories would be covered by this definition, the folkloric elements (though not the primitivism) are absent in *We*. And authors from a slightly later period, such as Olesha, would be considered by most critics to be modernist, although far removed from the ornamentalism of Remizov or Pilniak.

Several significant novels of the 1920s and early 1930s raise the issue of the boundaries of Modernism in Russian literature: can a work be modernist by virtue of experimental form alone, or does Modernism imply a sensibility marked by uncertainty and instability? The question is made more difficult by the chaotic and paradoxical nature of the period – that of the Revolution and Civil War – in which many Russian novels of the 1920s are set. When Pilniak reflects the political, social, and moral uncertainties of the year 1919 in the chaotic canvas of *The Naked Year*, when Konstantin Fedin uses a convoluted chronological structure to suggest the complications of the period between 1914 and 1922 in his *Cities and Years* (1924), or when Isaac Babel depicts the Cossack campaign in Poland in 1920 in a series of interrelated short stories that shock and thrill through the juxtaposition of ethical and aesthetic opposites (*Red Cavalry*, 1926), are the chaos and instability an inherent part of the subject-matter, or are they indications of a modernist sensibility in the authors concerned? There is no comprehensive answer to this question. Many major authors of the 1920s attempted to find formal, aesthetic equivalents of the massive social and moral upheaval of the age, but if Babel's prose, for example, is undoubtedly modernist, Fedin's is essentially traditional, with its roots in the Western nineteenth-century realistic novel and a hero, Andrei Startsov, who is the direct descendent of the superfluous men of an earlier period of Russian Realism. The experimental form of *Cities and Years* derives less from a modernist sensibility than from Fedin's interest in the story-telling possibilities of the Western novelistic tradition which he and other members of the Serapion Brothers felt were absent in the Russian novel, as well as from the structural possibilities suggested by the new art of the cinema. It is one of several prose works of the period given a modernist veneer by the desire to convey some of the excitement and suspense of the adventure novel or of narrative film.

Nowhere can this tendency be seen more clearly than in the early novels of Valentin Kataev, particularly the much underrated *Time, Forward!* (1932). In 1936 Kataev wrote: "The elements of cinematic montage, the very concept of montage became organic for many writers of my generation. . . . *Time, Forward!* is a work constructed literally on cinematic principles."[19] Yet, in contrast to some of Kataev's disturbing late works published between 1965 and his death in 1986, the Modernism of *Time, Forward!* is one of form rather than spirit. Despite its emphasis on movement, the novel promotes stability, combining the formal experimentation of the 1920s with the new political certainties of the Stalinist period.

A more secure place in the Russian modernist canon is occupied by Yurii Olesha's *Envy* (1927), a novel which bears a formal resemblance to *Notes from Underground*. The sense of alienation and existential anxiety experienced by the protagonist, Nikolai Kavalerov, may be linked with the general alienation of the "little man" in Russian literature from Pushkin onward, and, more specifically, with the theme of the "vacillating intellectual" that featured prominently in works of the 1920s. Unable to commit himself to the detested new regime to which he feels superior, and afraid that in its reliance on reason and technology it will shun his essentially emotional and impressionistic apprehension of the world, Kavalerov feels painfully isolated and deprived of a sense of belonging. His ambivalent response to the new world of Soviet society, which he both despises for its supposed lack of humanity and envies because of its vigor and purposefulness, is typical of the heroes of a number of novels in the 1920s, including Andrei Startsov in *Cities and Years*. But unlike other works with a similar hero, *Envy* transcends the topical concerns of post-revolutionary Russia by focusing on the relationship between the observer and the material world, and in this respect it is located in one of the mainstreams of European Modernism. Olesha's concern is frequently with the nature of objects and the defamiliarizing effect of such optical tricks as magnification, miniaturization, reflection, refraction, and observation from unusual angles. Kavalerov's precise and detailed, yet personal, observation of the world around him is reminiscent of the literary Impressionism of Proust and other French writers. When the sharpness of vision is allied to Kavalerov's seemingly endless cascade of unusual and provocative metaphors, the essence of Olesha's modernist prose emerges: fresh, idiosyncratic observation of the surrounding world combined with metaphor that simultaneously renders the physical reality of the object for the reader and illuminates the psychology of the protagonist/observer.

In his 1992 book *Utrachennye al'ternativy* (*Lost Alternatives*), M. M. Golubkov examines the "aesthetic pluralism" of Russian literary theory and practice in the 1920s and shows how, largely as the result of political pressure, Realism, which was simply one aesthetic trend among several, came to be canonized as the only acceptable method for Soviet literature of the 1930s and later decades. The "cultural polycentrism" of the 1920s was replaced by a "monistic" or "monophonic" culture in 1934, and the various modernist trends that had contributed to making the 1920s one of the most interesting periods in the history of Russian literature became nothing more than the "lost alternatives" of Golubkov's title.[20] This analysis of the Russian literary process in the 1920s and early 1930s is hardly original (it has been the standard Western interpretation for many years),[21] but Golubkov's examination of the various branches of modernist prose of the period is of considerable interest. As elsewhere in Europe at this time, the two major divisions of modernist poetics were Impressionism and Expressionism, the former marked by a subjective and hence psychologically significant apprehension of the physical world, and the latter by grotesque deformations, and the absence of individual psychology. The distinctiveness of Russian Modernism, however, lies in the fact that Impressionism and Expressionism are rarely juxtaposed as opposites. Instead, elements of both aesthetic systems are frequently to be found in the same work. Thus, while Expressionism can be most clearly seen in anti-utopian novels such as Zamiatin's *We* and Andrei Platonov's *Chevengur* (completed in 1929) and *The Foundation Pit* (1930), some of its elements can be found in the work of many novelists of the 1920s, such as Gorkii, Kaverin, Tynianov, Bulgakov, and Olesha, who could not adequately be defined as Expressionists. Olesha's debt to Proust might suggest that *Envy* can be categorized as a work of literary Impressionism, yet in some respects such as the presentation of Andrei Babichev and the starkness of the conflict, with the characters drawn up in opposing camps, its expressionistic elements are strong.

Platonov's *The Foundation Pit* is one of the major works of Russian Modernism, a grotesque, expressionist vision of the utopian myths of the first Five-Year Plan period and at the same time an ontological discourse on the relationship between existential essence, flesh, and language. The 1920s saw a widening of the boundaries of literary language in Russia. In itself, *skaz* – the narration of a text in part or in whole through the substandard speech of an uneducated and sometimes morally obtuse narrator – was not new (Leskov in particular had used it to great effect in the nineteenth century), but in the 1920s it became very common. The satirical short stories of Zoshchenko and some of Babel's *Red Cavalry* stories are among the best examples. The incorrect use of "officialese" by semi-literate workers and peasants was also a feature of some works of the 1920s (for example, one of Pilniak's characters uses the memorable phrase *enegrichno fuktsirovat'* – "to fuction enegretically," meaning, presumably, "to function energetically"). But even in a period of linguistic experimentation and eclecticism, the language of Platonov's tales and novels (which Joseph Brodsky described as "untranslatable")[22] is unusually striking. It appears to arise from a confrontation between the colloquial language of the newly and as yet incompletely literate peasants and workers on the one hand and the grandiloquent, slogan-laden "Sovietese" of official *publitsistika* on the other. Disconcertingly, this awkward fusion of linguistic elements is addressed repeatedly to ontological questions. The narrative stance is stubbornly materialistic. Platonov's narrators, their mentality formed by the militant materialism of the 1920s and early 1930s, make no distinction between abstract and concrete, animate and inanimate. Thus, nouns denoting inanimate objects are frequently combined with "inappropriate" adjectives and verbs denoting feelings. In addition, prepositions and cases are used in an unexpected fashion so as to draw attention to particular details. The effect can be strangely disorientating. Here, for example, is a typical extract, taken from the opening pages of *The Foundation Pit*:

> Voshchev grabbed his bag and set off into the night. The questioning sky shone over Voshchev with the agonizing strength of the stars, but in the city the lights had already been extinguished: whoever was able to do so was sleeping, having eaten his fill of supper. Voshchev descended the crumbly earth [*po kroshkam zemli*] into a ravine and lay belly-down, so as to fall asleep and part from self. But for sleep, peace of mind was necessary, its trustfulness in life, forgiveness of experienced grief, and Voshchev lay in the dry intensity of consciousness and did not know whether he was useful in the world or whether everything would manage well without him. From an unknown place a wind began to blow, so that people should not suffocate, and in a weak voice of doubt a suburban dog made known its service.

A strong streak of fantasy, with its roots in Gogol and in Dostoevskii's "realism in a higher sense," is characteristic of many of the most significant modernist novels in Russia, including *Petersburg*, *We*, and *The Foundation Pit*. One of the characters in Platonov's novel is a proletarian "blacksmith-bear" who wages a particularly ferocious class war against kulaks. He is presented as a real bear and at the same time a real blacksmith, and his origins seem to lie simultaneously in folklore and in the realization of a metaphor (native Russian strongman = bear) that is so deeply embedded that it scarcely affects the reader's perception of the bear's animal status. Apart from *We*, however, the most celebrated example of fantasy in the Russian modernist novel is that of Mikhail Bulgakov's *The Master and Margarita* (1928–40), in which farcical comedy coexists with high seriousness, mundane reality with supernatural interventions, twentieth-century Moscow with first-century Jerusalem. Bulgakov's text moves freely in time and space, in the realms of the real and the fantastic, and in matching stylistic registers in a manner that anticipates the "magic realism" of a later era. Some of the principal features of the modernist novel are clearly present here, notably the initially bewildering heterogeneity of the material, the free handling of time and space, and the prominence of the irrational and fantastic. Yet although the novel has a strong apocalyptic element, it lacks the nervous, edgy tenor of much Russian modernist fiction. Its foregrounding of the theme of ultimate justice is reassuring in a way that runs counter to the anxiety and uncertainty of modernity.

Among the many themes of *The Master and Margarita* is one which is particularly relevant to the modernist novel as a whole: the nature of fiction itself and the status of the fictional text. Most major Russian modernist novels are concerned to some extent with the creative process itself. The precise nature of the diary and the full implications of the act of writing in *We*, and the relationship between the Master's novel, the authorial novel, and "real" events in *The Master and Margarita* are but two examples of this concern.

Of course, one must be careful not to imply that metafiction is inherently modernist; fiction about the creation of fiction has existed throughout the ages, and was particularly prominent in the Romantic period. In the age of Modernism and subsequently postmodernism, though, a strikingly high proportion of literary texts are metafictional. In addition to those already mentioned, the novels of Vladimir Nabokov are perhaps the prime example, and it is no coincidence that Nabokov's influence may be detected in the work of several of Russia's postmodernist writers of the present generation, such as Viktor Erofeev and Andrei Bitov. For Erofeev in particular, the aesthetic lessons of the modernist period are very important for the future of Russian literature. In his influential article "Soviet literature: In memoriam," published in 1990, he draws attention to the huge extraliterary weight traditionally attached to creative writing in Russia. It was never enough, he reminds us, for a writer to be simply a writer; under Tsars and Soviets alike he or she had also to fulfil one or more of the roles of mystic, prosecutor, sociologist, and economist, and this extraliterary burden was frequently borne at the expense of the more properly literary aspects of the writer's craft: "while [the writer] was busy being everything else, he was least of all a writer."[23] Attention to the social, political, or philosophical "message" frequently displaced attention to style, to the precise nuances of literary language. Erofeev expresses the hope that Russian writers will shake off their obsession with society and turn inwards to the proper, wholly aesthetic concerns of art, and that literature will become self-sufficient and self-justifying in a way it had rarely done in the past.

Given the chronological boundaries of Modernism adopted earlier (from the 1890s to the 1930s), detailed consideration of the work of Erofeev, Bitov, Sasha Sokolov, and other writers of the late Soviet and post-Soviet period is beyond the scope of this chapter. It is worth noting, though, that the legacy of Modernism is to be seen almost everywhere in serious contemporary Russian fiction. The dazzling artfulness and intertextuality of Bitov's *Pushkin House* (1978); the surrealism of Sokolov; the use of the grotesque by writers such as Liudmila Petrushevskaia, Viktor Pelevin, and Vladimir Sorokin; and the highly volatile, identity-questioning prose of Valeriia Narbikova – these and other aspects of contemporary literature owe much to the tradition of the Russian modernist novel.

NOTES

1. V. Erlich, *Modernism and Revolution: Russian Literature in Transition* (Cambridge, Mass.: Harvard University Press, 1994), p. 1.
2. M. Berman, *All That Is Solid Melts Into Air: The Experience of Modernity* (London: Verso, 1983).
3. The Marquis de Custine quoted in Donald Fanger, *Dostoevsky and Romantic Realism: A Study of Dostoevsky in Relation to Balzac, Dickens and Gogol* (Chicago and London: University of Chicago Press, 1967), p. 105.
4. See Fanger, *Dostoevsky and Romantic Realism*, p. 129.
5. On this point see M. Holquist, *Dostoevsky and the Novel* (Evanston: Northwestern University Press, 1986), p. 36.
6. Grossman is quoted in Fanger, *Dostoevsky and Romantic Realism*, p. 129.
7. On this point see R. Maguire and J. Malmstad, "Translators' introduction," in Andrei Bely, *Petersburg*, trans. and intro. R. Maguire and J. Malmstad (Harmondsworth: Penguin, 1978), p. vii.
8. E. Zamiatin, "Zavtra," in Zamiatin, *Sochineniia*, 4 vols. (Munich: Neimanis, 1970–88), vol. IV, pp. 246–47 (p. 246).
9. E. Zamiatin, "Skify li?" ("Scythians?"), in Zamiatin, *Sochineniia*, vol. IV, pp. 503–13 (p. 503).
10. E. Zamiatin, "O literature, revoliutsii i entropii" ("On literature, revolution and entropy"), in Zamiatin, *Sochineniia*, vol. IV, pp. 291–97 (p. 291).
11. Ibid., p. 293.
12. Ibid, p. 296.

13. E. Zamiatin, "O sintetizme" ("On synthetism") in Zamiatin, *Sochineniia*, vol. IV, pp. 282–90 (pp. 282–83).

14. On Zamiatin and Nietzsche see Peter Doyle, "Zamyatin's philosophy, humanism, and *We*: a critical appraisal," *Renaissance and Modern Studies*, 28 (1984), 1–17.

15. On Zamiatin's artistic indebtedness to Gogol and Dostoevskii, and on the nineteenth-century writers as progenitors of Russian Modernism, see Susan Layton, "Zamyatin and literary modernism," in Gary Kern (ed.), *Zamyatin's "We": A Collection of Critical Essays* (Ann Arbor: Ardis, 1988), pp. 140–48, especially pp. 146–47.

16. See Carl Proffer, "Notes on the imagery in Zamyatin's *We*," in Kern, pp. 95–105; Alex M. Shane, *The Life and Works of Evgenij Zamjatin* (Berkeley: University of California Press, 1968), p. 158; Christopher Collins, *Evgenij Zamjatin: An Interpretive Study* (The Hague: Mouton, 1973), p. 53.

17. Sona S. Hoisington and Lynn Imbery, "Zamjatin's modernist palette: colors and their function in *We*," *Slavic and East European Journal*, 36 (1992), 159–71.

18. For a critical modern appraisal of Pilniak see Patricia Carden, "Ornamentalism and Modernism," in George Gibian and H. W. Tjalsma (eds.), *Russian Modernism: Culture and the Avant-Garde, 1900–1930* (Ithaca and London: Cornell University Press, 1976), pp. 49–64.

19. V. Kataev, "Rovesniki kino," in Kataev, *Sobranie sochinenii*, 9 vols. (Moscow: Khudozhestvennaia literatura, 1968–72), vol. VIII (1971), p. 314.

20. M. M. Golubkov, *Utrachennye al'ternativy* (Moscow: Nasledie, 1992).

21. For a somewhat different view see Boris Groys, *The Total Art of Stalinism*, translated by Charles Rougle (Princeton University Press, 1992).

22. I. Brodskii, "Predislovie," in A. Platonov, *Kotlovan* (Ann Arbor: Ardis, 1979), p. 7.

23. Viktor Erofeev, "Pominki po sovetskoi literature," *Literaturnaia gazeta* (4 July 1990).

4

STRUCTURES AND READINGS

12

ROBERT BELKNAP

Novelistic technique

The power of the Russian nineteenth-century novel depends in part on earlier techniques of novel-writing which most Western novelists had abandoned. This study will concentrate on the particularly Russian relation between plotting and narration, though it must also reckon with the interplay between Russian and the Western novelistic practices in the nineteenth century. In the first Western book on the Russian novel (1881), Melchoir de Vogüé, the eloquent French diplomat, journalist, and gossip, says that for Turgenev the study "of our masters and the friendship and the advice of Mérimée offered precious help; to these literary associations he may have owed the intellectual discipline, the clarity, the precision, virtues which are so rare among the prose writers of his country."[1] This denial that Turgenev is a fully Russian novelist shows that Vogüé recognized something special about Turgenev, but it also led Western Europeans from the 1880s on to recognize that there was something special about most Russian novels. A generation later, Henry James praised the power and richness of the Russian novels, but his letter to Hugh Walpole called them "fluid puddings," and he complained to Mrs. Humphry Ward about Tolstoi's "promiscuous shifting of viewpoint and centre,"[2] perhaps reflecting de Vogüé's description of what he felt on reading Dostoevskii, "the shiver that seizes you on encountering some of his characters makes one wonder whether one is in the presence of genius, but one quickly remembers that genius in letters does not exist without two higher gifts, measure and universality . . . " (de Vogüé, *Le Roman russe*, p. 267). James's prefaces contain the first and most subtle exposition of the novelistic techniques that evolved in the West in the nineteenth century, and his novels may be the least provincial ever written; and yet, somehow, he failed to realize that the rules he presented were not universal aspects of the psychology of art but the conventions of a particular time and place. The Russian inter-dependence between plotting and narration constituted a very different but no less demanding kind of technical mastery, as can be seen in *The Brothers*

Karamazov (1880) by looking at the tight relationship between the spiritual state of the character being discussed and the presence or absence of omniscience in the character discussing him. Many Western critics distinguish novels that tell readers what happens from novels that show them what happens; the Russian novelistic techniques let Tolstoi, Dostoevskii, and others go beyond both these practices and manipulate readers into experiencing for themselves what the characters in the novel are feeling and arguing.

The Russians inherited this literary goal from Rousseau, Sterne and the other sentimental novelists of the eighteenth century. The Russian Formalist literary critics distinguish between two kinds of literary plot, both of which fit the old definition of a plot as the arrangement of the incidents. In the first kind of plot, or the *fabula*, the incidents are arranged in the world where the characters live, so that in the *fabula* a character is always born before dying. In the second kind of plot, or *siuzhet*, the same incidents are arranged in the text, where the death of a character may be presented long before the birth. All novels rely heavily on the interplay between these two kinds of relationship among incidents, but the nineteenth-century Western novel centers on the relation between the *fabula* and character, with characters shaping and responding to the sequence of events. In many eighteenth-century and Russian nineteenth-century novels, the *siuzhet* plays a more important role, and has a closer relation to those crucial figures in all novels through whom we perceive everything else, the narrators. Novels in letters flourished in the eighteenth century partly because collections of real letters and manuals for letter-writing were popular, but also because letters enable authors to trace different careers through the same sequences of incidents and to triangulate a given incident through several sets of responses, so that narration interacts very closely with plot. Russians wrote only half a dozen letter novels in the eighteenth century and only one memorable one in the nineteenth century, Dostoevskii's *Poor Folk* (1846); yet even a markedly Russian novel like *War and Peace* shows Tolstoi's often-mentioned eighteenth-century mentality in the interwoven plotting that uses the lives and consciousnesses of several characters and a chameleon-like narrator to infect readers with Tolstoi's historical, psychological, and moral awarenesses.

Nikolai Karamzin (1766–1826) was the chief early conduit carrying this eighteenth-century tradition from the West into Russian nineteenth-century prose. Karamzin's most famous short story, "Poor Liza" (1792), appealed to the sentiment that expresses itself through tears, but the sentimentalist aesthetic also valorizes the emotions that produce laughter, social action, and many other responses. In Karamzin's "My Confession" (1802), the narrator prides himself on his lack of honor, sanity, and social value, carrying Rousseau's wilful taboo-breaking and gratuitous actions to a level of insulting self-consciousness that bridges the gap between Rousseau's voice in his "Confessions" and that of Dostoevskii's Underground Man.

In his role of follower, competitor, and successor to Karamzin as the central figure on the Russian literary scene, Pushkin seems at first to belong to the Western nineteenth-century novelistic tradition, as Turgenev did in his major novels, and as did many lesser novelists in Pushkin's generation, such as Senkovskii, Polevoi, Marlinskii, Bulgarin, Pogorelskii, Lazhech-nikov, Veltman, or Zagoskin. Certainly Pushkin loved the fashionable and was drenched in Western literature; his *Captain's Daughter* (1836) draws its setting and much of its plot from Sir Walter Scott's *Waverley*. Yet the works of Pushkin that most influenced the later Russian novels were not conventional novels at all. One was *Evgenii Onegin* (1823–31), a novel in verse, and the other was *The Tales of Belkin* (1830), which are usually treated as a group of separate stories. The plotting in *Onegin* follows the standard pattern René Girard ascribes to European novels: desire is imitative and unreciprocated.[3] Onegin rejects Tatiana's love until he sees her loved, and she rejects him when he offers himself to her. But in both of these works, the narrator stands back and reflects upon the incidents in ways that seem sometimes naive and sometimes remarkably sophisticated. The narrator of *Evgenii Onegin* cries out "Alas!" like a sentimental novelist, and digresses like Fielding or Sterne, although he also enters with the reader into conspiratorial judgment of his hero in the manner of Scott or later, Dickens and Thackeray. Pushkin may draw his plots from contemporary Europe, but his narrative technique in *Onegin* retains much of Sterne's or Fielding's or Voltaire's eighteenth-century flexibility and playfulness, with a "preface" at the end of chapter 7 and the *siuzhet* containing much detail about the life and opinions of the narrator which plays no part in the lives of the characters at all.

The Tales of Belkin fall midway through the evolution of the most ambitious Russian prose in the 1820s and 1830s as it recapitulated the long and intricate history of the proto-novel in Europe, moving from collections of individual tales, like Karamzin's, or the *Gesta Romanorum* (c. 1300), to tales linked by a narrative situation, like Marlinskii's *Evenings on the Bivouac* (1823) or Boccaccio's *Decamaron* (1360s), through tales linked by a single narrator like Belkin or Malory's narrator (1485), to tales linked by a single hero, like Lermontov's *A Hero of Our Time* (1841) or *Don Quixote* (1605, 1615). Such evolution never occurs neatly; early techniques often attract late writers more than prescient recent works of isolated geniuses, but the Russians were able to do in decades what took centuries in the West precisely because in addition to the classical sources in epic, romance, Petronius, Apuleius, and others which shaped the Western novel, the Russians had an existing novelistic tradition developed by Emin, Chulkov, and others in the eighteenth century, and, far more important, the rich novelistic tradition of the West to draw on. Belkin breaks Henry James's cardinal rule for a narrator. James's narrators may be wise or foolish, even insane or fanatic, but must be consistently whatever they are, so that "the interest created, and the expression of that interest, are things kept, as to kind, genuine and true to themselves." Moreover, narrators who can see into a character's mind at one moment must not learn what that character is thinking from his countenance at another moment.[4] The introduction to *The Tales of Belkin* states that Belkin died at the age of thirty, while on the first page of "The Station Master," Belkin states that he has been travelling through Russia steadily for twenty years. More important, Belkin begins telling "The Blizzard" with full insight into the mind of the heroine and suddenly switches to the narration of her actions entirely from outside. Pushkin breaks James's rules here not through ignorance or inattention, but simply because other literary needs precluded obedience to such rules. The effectiveness of the *siuzhet* demanded that the reader share Maria's bookish but wholehearted love and also her surprise at the ending of the story. Consistency would have cost him one or the other of these effects, and Pushkin therefore turns to the eighteenth-century tradition of more flexible narrators.

Like *The Captain's Daughter*, Lermontov's first novel, *Vadim* (1834), draws heavily on Walter Scott for its plot and atmosphere, and his *A Hero of Our Time* was the only Russian novel in the first half of the nineteenth century to be judged so accessible to the West that it was repeatedly translated into French. Yet for all its accessibility to Europeans and debts to Scott, Byron, Musset, George Sand, and others, the intricate interplay between its plot and narration sets *A Hero of Our Time* apart from the mainstream Western novels and other narratives of its time. As the arrangement of events in the world the characters inhabit, the *fabula* of *A Hero of Our Time* has an identity whose complexity rivals and intersects that of the narration. Narratively, the voices of Bela, Grushnitskii, or Princess Mary reach the reader through the accounts of Maksim Maksimych or Pechorin, which are filtered through the voice of an "editor" who sometimes selects the materials from "a thick notebook," and always edits at least the names to protect the real people portrayed. And from the 1841 edition on, a preface interposes the outermost voice of an authorial figure who knows that all the others are fictional. Such narrative layering was commonplace in Russia and the West in the 1830s, but these different figures inhabit very different worlds, knowing about different events, and more importantly, seeing totally different mechanisms as organizing these events.

In any novel, the central organizing principle in the *fabula* is usually cause and effect, or its psychological reflex, motivation, but *A Hero of Our Time* also takes the form of a philosophical dialogue on the nature of causality. On the first page of the novel, the "editor" introduces the topic with a question that applies a certain causal system naively, "How is it that four oxen can haul your loaded carriage like a lark, and six of the creatures can scarcely budge my empty one with the help of these Ossetians [inhabitants of the Northern Caucasus]?" This editor's world operates by the laws of physics, or, when he predicts a fine morrow, by appearances. Maksim Maksimych operates in a world of hidden causes, explaining how the Ossetian greed for extra business makes them impede their own oxen, or how the steam rising from a distant mountain presages a blizzard. Though he is the central figure, Pechorin is only a minor narrator in this first story, but he introduces a Byronic system of motivation into a story where Bela, Kazbich, and the other characters have motives out of a Walter Scott novel, "Listen, Maksim Maksimych . . . I have an unhappy character: whether my upbringing made me so, or God made me so, I don't know; I know only that if I am the cause of unhappiness to others, I am no less unhappy."[5] Maksim Maksimych is as naive about such Byronism as the "editor" is about the Caucasus: "'Did the French bring boredom into fashion?' – 'No, the English.' – 'Aha, that's it . . . of course, they always were outrageous drunkards'" (p. 214). Maksim Maksimych introduces not only ethnic, economic, atmospheric, and alcoholic determinism into the causal system; he also uses social class to explain behavior: "What are we uneducated oldsters doing, chasing after you? . . . You're young society folk, proud; as long as you're here under the Cherkassian bullets, you're OK . . . but if you meet us afterwards you're ashamed to offer your hand to one of us" (p. 228).

Maksim Maksimych's causes relate events to one another in the realistic tradition, contrasting not only with the physical causality the editor espouses, but also with the Romantic kinds of causes Pechorin invokes: "These eyes, it seemed, were endowed with some magnetic power' (p. 235); "the bumps on his skull . . . would have astonished a phrenologist with the strange mix of conflicting drives" (p. 248); "We're reading one another in the heart" (p. 249), and so on. For the future of the Russian novel, more important than such phrases are four specially Russian features of causation in Pechorin's accounts: coincidence, including all Pechorin's accidental eavesdropping; the sovereign power of the will, as when Pechorin draws a group of listeners away from other entertaining interlocutors, or makes Grushnitskii miss his shot; the gratuitous actions, motivated not by anything external but by the nature of the character, such as that which makes Pechorin wonder "why did I not want to set out on that path fate had opened to me where quiet joys and heartfelt calm awaited me? . . . No, I should never have adapted to that destiny" (p. 312); and finally, fate, which he discusses throughout, but most especially in the final story.

The complex of Pechorinesque causations never exists alone because his narrative voice never exists alone any more than Onegin's does. At the end of the novel, Maksim Maksimych initially responds to Pechorin's account of an experiment in Russian roulette that appeared to confirm predestination: "Yes sir, It's a rather tricky matter! . . . Still, these Asiatic triggers often misfire, if they're badly oiled . . ." Here, the novel seems to have two *fabula*s, one organizing events according to the rules of practical life and another according to the more exciting rules of Pechorin's world. Lermontov gives Pechorin the last word about fatalism, but it is a curiously indecisive comment on the entire panoply of causal systems that this novel explores in its plot and narration: "[Maksim Maksimych] in general dislikes metaphysical debates."

Lermontov certainly popularized Rousseauesque and Byronic motivational systems that the Russians went on using in close conjunction with their narrative techniques, but the chief explanation for the differences between the Western and the Russian novels of the nineteenth century can be expressed in two words: Nikolai Gogol. Like Karamzin, Gogol has been called the Russian Sterne. It has been argued that the Western Europeans drew a new kind of novel from the tradition of Scott and the "Gothic" novelists because Sterne had carried so many eighteenth-century novelistic techniques to the point of absurdity. The Russians also drew heavily on the sensationalism of Hoffmann and the Gothic novels coupled with the sharp social, moral, and psychological judgment of Scott's novels. Gogol's first novel, *Taras Bulba* (1835), owes much to Scott; yet Gogol also enabled the Russians to go on developing the techniques of the eighteenth-century Western novels they had been reading in translation and in the original for generations. A short story that appeared almost simultaneously with *A Hero of Our Time* gives the clearest illustration of Gogol's departure from the Western European tradition later canonized in Henry James's prefaces.

"The Tale of how Ivan Ivanovich Quarreled with Ivan Nikiforovich" (1835) seems at first to be an almost plotless story of provincial pettiness, anger, and stupidity; two old friends quarrel over an insignificant request and go through their whole lives unreconciled. In the first sentences of the story, the narrator seems to be equally involved in the insignificant: "Ivan

Ivanovich has a glorious jacket! The most excellent! And what lambswool! Whew, go to, what lambswool! I'll wager Lord knows what if you find anybody's like it!" These words give little information about Ivan Ivanovich but a great deal about the narrator. He is still close enough to infancy to love fuzz, to end every phrase with an exclamation point, and to bubble over with enthusiasm at matters that most of us might at most consider nice. Three pages later, this narrator remains enthusiastic and naive, but already has acquired enough control of himself and the world to enter into sociological, statistical, and perhaps biological disputation:

> It has been spread around that Ivan Nikiforovich was born with a tail at his back. But this canard is so absurd and at the same time stupid and indecent that I judge it unnecessary to refute before enlightened readers, who are aware without the slightest doubt, that only witches, and even very few of them have tails at their backs; and they, moreover, belong for the most part to the female sex rather than the male.[6]

Whatever our views on the statistics of caudal preponderance, we all can recognize a much more mature voice than that of the narrator at the beginning of the story. When he appears again twenty pages later, this narrator has developed the voice of a jaded traveler with a clear and ironic sense of the Russian bureaucracy: "The trial then moved with that uncommon speed for which our judiciary is so commonly renowned. They annotated papers, excerpted them, numbered them, bound them, and receipted them all on one and the same day, and placed it all in a cabinet where it lay, lay, lay, a year, another, a third . . ." (vol. II, p. 263). And a few pages later, the narrator has even acquired literary self-consciousness: "No, I cannot! . . . Give me another pen! My pen is faded, deadened, with too thin a stroke for this picture!" (p. 271). Finally, on the last two pages of the story, a conscientious, self-important, tired old man displays no trace of enthusiasm:

> At that time the weather exercised a strong effect on me: I grew bored when it was boring . . . I sighed still more deeply and hurried to make my adieus because I was traveling on a quite important matter, and got into my carriage . . . It's boring on this earth, Gentlemen! (pp. 275–6)

This final exclamation point has nothing in common with those at the beginning of the story. These last words almost coincide with Winston Churchill's to his son-in-law while dying in his tenth decade.[7] Henry James would consider this changing narrator loose and baggy, a danger to the reliability that rests on the integrity of the figure through whom the reader must apprehend everything in the text. And yet Gogol orders these changes tightly. His narrator has rather more of a career than any other character in the story. Readers see the growing decrepitude and pointlessness of the officials, the provincial town and the two Ivans, and without noticing it, they also experience the ageing of the narrator, and his unsuccessful struggle against the pointlessness of his existence. By breaking the narrative rules of the West and giving his narrator a plot of his own, Gogol implicated the reader in the ageing process that is going on all around him.

Gogol's *Dead Souls* (1842) became the most important force in the evolution of the Russian technique of novel-writing well before the novel gained recognition from thousands of bemused readers on the world scene. The *fabula* of the novel derives in large part from that of the typical romance of the road in which a picaro or a more highly placed scamp moves from place to place and extricates himself from scrape after scrape in separate adventures whose organization some critics compare to that of beads on a string. In the manner of Cervantes and Fielding, the *siuzhet* of *Dead Souls* contains digressions, responses to real and imaginary readers, and appeals to the reader's experience which are usually not a part of the world the characters inhabit. In one such digression in the last chapter, the narrator apologizes for the far from exemplary characters who have appeared in part I of the novel: "This is Chichikov's fault; in this he is full master and we must be dragged after him wherever he takes it into his head to go" (Gogol', *Polnoe sobraniie sochinenii*, vol. VI, p. 241). In part, this passage continues the playful mockery of verisimilitude that Gogol learned from Sterne and many others: "Although the time in whose duration they would traverse the hall, the anteroom, and the dining room is a bit on the short side, we will try and see whether we can use it somehow to say something about the master of the house" (vol. VI, p. 23). But blaming his hero for the *fabula* also rejects the idea of a structured plot with a beginning, a middle and an end, confirming the image of beads on a string. Aristotle defined an end as something which needs nothing after it to complete it, but if Sterne and Lermontov had lived longer, *Tristram Shandy* and *A Hero of Our Time* would probably have been longer, and Gogol actually wrote further chapters of *Dead Souls*, which he destroyed; one can always add another bead to a string. With such texts, structural analysis, based on a spatial metaphor in two or three dimensions, may be less useful than algorithmic analysis, based on a metaphor in a single sequence, like time, even though either system of reasoning can be made to work. The diagram on the next page can be described spatially, as a square with helically oriented inflected oblongs and similarly oriented smaller inset oblongs; sufficient measurements would enable a careful reader to reproduce the figure, but it is much easier to use an algorithm or a procedure in time:

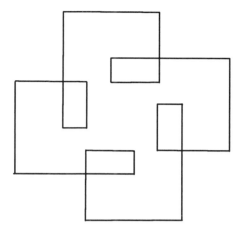

Draw a line one unit long; turn left 90 degrees and draw a line two units long; turn left again and draw a line three units long; turn left again and draw a line four units long; turn left again and draw a line five units long; start over. In this procedure, the action at each step is a reaction to the situation after the last step rather than to a vision of the whole. But because it follows explicit rules, it produces a coherent whole. In fiction, a procedure can produce as elegant and powerful an experience as a structural plan can, but it looks loose and baggy to a nineteenth-century Western sensibility.

In *Dead Souls*, Gogol's rules are accretive and perverse. He adds and adds and adds, and suddenly takes it all away. This pattern repeats itself fractally, at the level of the sentence, of the episode, and of the string of episodes. Chichikov and his two recalcitrant serfs move among landlords with recalcitrant stewards managing recalcitrant serfs, under the aegis of petty officials who cannot control them or be controlled by figures still higher in the fractal hierarchy. Fawning and greed shape the hierarchy at every level, whether the greed be for vodka or a great house, and the protestant virtue, deferral of gratification, exploits the first of these vices for the sake of the second. At each stage of Chichikov's career, in school, as a provincial bureaucrat, as a customs officer, and on his visits to the various town and landed figures, he displays extraordinary discipline until he makes his coup, at which point he loses all control, lets his greed prevail, and has to escape and start over. This pattern of moving from misery into a moment of seeming paradise, and then losing it runs through all of Gogol's best work. Most often, the paradise was never really there in the first place. In Sterne, the anticlimax makes the reader feel foolish or cheated: "Why didn't I see that coming?" or "How could I be expected to know that?" In Gogol, the frustration of expectations grows out of the logic of a situation that always partakes of the weirdness of Russian life. His very sentences have plots, adding, adding, adding, and then suddenly taking away. The last sentence of chapter 6 offers a good example: "Requesting the lightest possible repast, consisting of nothing but pork, he immediately undressed, and curling up under the bedclothes, fell hard asleep, soundly, in wondrous fashion, as only those sleep who are so happy as to know neither hemorrhoids, nor lice, nor overly powerful mental capacities" (Gogol', *Polnoe sobraniie sochinenii*, vol. VI, p. 132). Stupidity is often praised, but Gogol finds a context for the praise that contrasts the experience of Chichikov with that of thousands of insomniacs who do not inhabit the world of the novel. Narration here too has a plot of its own.

Tolstoi and Dostoevskii carried the innovations of their Russian predecessors to their highest fruition. When James called *War and Peace* a "large loose baggy monster" like *The Three Musketeers* (1844), he failed to see it as a novel of ideas that programmed the reader's experience of those ideas with a mastery as disciplined and well-read as his own. Dostoevskii probably was the person who told de Vogüé, "We all emerged from under Gogol's 'Overcoat'." In any case, he often recognized his debt to Pushkin and the two great "demons" in Russian literature, Lermontov and Gogol, as well as to Karamzin and the creators of the nineteenth-century novelistic form in the West, Scott, Hoffmann, Balzac, Dickens, Hugo, and "Gothic" novelists like Ann Radcliffe. Virtually all the important Russian novels in the nineteenth century were written during his lifetime, and his own career paralleled that of the Russian novel in his youth and shaped it in his maturity.

A highly self-conscious experimenter in and borrower of novelistic techniques, Dostoevskii began his career with a novel in letters, a form that had gone out with the eighteenth century. *Poor Folk* is a novel of oppression and compassion and also a variant on the eighteenth-century theme of the libertine who seduces a young girl. The variant comes from Karamzin's "Poor Liza" via Pushkin; Belkin's "The Station Master" had already explored what happens when the seduced girl so enthrals the seducer that he is reduced to marrying her and setting her up in splendor. Dostoevskii shows how the seducer struggles against this comeuppance and finally gives in to Varvara, though he is no great catch for her; she had lovingly nursed his son through a fatal illness and later reciprocated the love of the poor clerk Makar, who longed to starve with her. Dostoevskii's chief literary polemic, however, is with Gogol's "Overcoat," where the poor clerk starves and deprives himself to obtain a coat he needs, and then loses it. Dostoevskii's story is about Makar's paradise lost, but Makar loses a human being and not a piece of cloth.

Dostoevskii's second novel, *The Double* (1846), has a plot that uses many techniques from the tales and novels of Gogol and of E. T. A. Hoffmann. His hero, the disintegrating clerk Goliadkin, has a series of experiences which can be explained as strange coincidences, practical jokes, supernatural events, or the delusions of a perception sinking into madness. Dostoevskii provides strong evidence for each of these plots and no basis for selecting among them, so that the cognitive dissonance drives the reader towards a disintegration very like Goliadkin's. In his major novels, Dostoevskii expands this technique.

In *Crime and Punishment* (1866), when Raskolnikov stands in the room with two bleeding corpses, holding his breath as he listens at the door, inches from his potential discoverers, who may leave or may bring the police, the readers hold their breath, exert their will upon him not to give up and confess, and then suddenly realize that they are accessories after the fact, trying to help this merciless hatchet-murderer to escape. This complicity in the crime alternates with the reader's horror and revulsion at it, just as Raskolnikov alternates between a drive towards murder and escape and a drive towards freedom from the murderous impulse and – after the murder – towards confession. Dostoevskii manipulates his readers into the plot of the novel by never letting them outside the mind of Raskolnikov, or briefly, the two surrogates who share different parts of his situation and react to it very differently, Razumikhin and Svidrigailov. This intensity of narrative concentration on a single figure implicates the readers in his predicament much as readers willed the escape of picaresque scamps in earlier novels. *Crime and Punishment* has a beginning, a middle and an end, but it retains the algorithmic integrity of Gogol and his masters. In *Crime and Punishment*, the shaping rule is not accretive and perverse as in *Dead Souls*, but rather the terrifying alternation between the crime and the punishment, the rational calculation that the destruction of a bloodsucking insect was an action worthy of a great man, and the direct, emotional realization that this was the blood of a helpless fellow human being. Dostoevskii uses his narrative tools to draw the reader inside this vacillation.

Readers have often charged Dostoevskii with undue reliance on coincidence in structuring the plot of the novel, and plainly, Raskolnikov's overhearing a conversation about murdering the old pawnbroker, like his overhearing a conversation indicating that she will be alone the next day, or his finding an axe on his way to commit the murder, all seem to remove his motives from the tight causal system that a proper Western novel would have. In fact, however, these coincidences affect Raskolnikov more by being coincidences than by offering means or information that the plot demands. A central driving force towards Raskolnikov's crime is superstition, and the prevalence of coincidences enhances the power of superstition over him. In the huge complex of concepts, images, and characters that line up on opposite sides of this novel, superstition is associated with science, statistics, social utility, calculation, determinism, control, confinement, murder, escape, and suicide, over against religion, generosity, impulse, freedom, dreams, air, confession, repentance, and resurrection. Svidrigailov, the murderer and suicide, and Luzhin, the calculating controller, compete for Raskolnikov with Sonia's and Porfirii's push toward confession and resurrection. This tension among the characters works with the tension among the associated abstractions to make the reader struggle through the novel with Raskolnikov.

Over a decade later in the history of the Russian novel, *The Brothers Karamazov* has a much more intricate plot than *Crime and Punishment* and a much more elaborate structure working with it. In place of one governing algorithm and one central character, each brother orders his part of the sequence of events according to his own rule. Smerdiakov provokes aggressions that provoke other aggressions that provoke other aggressions until Alesha absorbs aggression in such a way as to end the sequence. Mitia bursts into such trains of action but at the last moment draws away from violence, while Ivan leaves town, or says, "let one reptile eat the other," but finds himself drawn into a destructive role. When a brother's destiny hangs in the balance, Dostoevskii's narrator recounts his thoughts and dreams, but at other times is forced to learn about that character from his countenance. The sequences of events in this novel, distorted according to the signature rules of the different characters, illustrate a central doctrine of the elder Zosima, who compares the world to a causal ocean in which an action at one point may have a good or evil effect at the other end of the earth. A good character may die, but memories and trains of events that person instituted or modified will continue, though they may lie dormant like seeds whose disappearance leads to fruitfulness. Like the plot, with its multiple signature rules for ordering events, the narrative technique leads readers to experience as well as learn when grace is dormant or prevalent in a character and when it is struggling to emerge. In these and many other ways Dostoevskii fashioned a tight and coherent body of plotting and narrative techniques which conveyed his beliefs and doubts to the reader without the use of the spokesmen or unambiguous lessons that earlier novelists had used. Dostoevskii gives the most eloquent apologia he can imagine for a character who rejects God, not to make us agree with the

Grand Inquisitor, but so that our rejection of his position may have been tested by the full glory of its temptingness.

Tolstoi was a subtler novelist than Dostoevskii, but his narrator also breaks the Western rules for the novel in order to exercise our moral faculties. Sometimes, as in the second epilogue to *War and Peace*, or the first sentence of *Anna Karenina*, his narrator enunciates views that transcend the world the characters inhabit, but at other times this narrator treats the fictional characters as if they really existed. These different kinds of pronouncement make Mikhail Bakhtin consider Tolstoi far more didactic than Dostoevskii, in whose works he finds an openness comparable to that of a polyphonic piece of music with no single authoritative voice, so that the reader has to listen to the interplay of many voices to discover the meaning of a Dostoevskii novel. Curiously, however, the debate about Tolstoi's attitudes has raged for over a century. His non-fiction unambiguously propounds a Tolstoianism that rejects sex, alcohol, tobacco, meat, and wealth, partly for the violence or exploitation they entail, but also simply because they make people feel comfortable and deflect them from the real struggle against hunger, war, nationalism, ignorance, bureaucracy, unbelief, and the selfish, vicious or stupid misuse of human possibilities.

The meaning of Tolstoi's fiction remains more debatable and more debated, in large part because readers have not always understood where to look for it. Much of it resides not in the dicta of the narrators but in the understandings built into the plot. Tolstoi carried farther than Dostoevskii a technique that Jan Meijer called "situation rhyme," the use of analogous events time after time in the course of a novel.[8] At the end of *Anna Karenina* (1877), Levin falls subject to suicidal impulses, avoids ropes as possible instruments of self-destruction, and goes about the main business of his life. Taken alone, the passage seems unimportant and unpersuasive, but in the presence of Anna's suicide and Vronskii's botched attempt at suicide, it makes the parallel plots of the novel interact in a way that becomes a moral exercise. In the same way, Kitty's jealousy of Levin for being drawn to Anna's tragic beauty at the end of the novel collides with Dolly's fury at Oblonskii's actual infidelity at the beginning of the novel, and Anna's morbid anger at Vronskii near the end. Kitty's adolescent crush on Anna collides with her devotion to the least Anna-like woman in the novel, Varenka, as her love for Vronskii collides with her love for Levin, and these collisions collide with one another in a combinatorial investigation of overflowing young affection that illuminates Anna's tragic love. The reader's malaise is not psychological, as in Dostoevskii's *Double*, but moral: Tolstoi offers his readers ample proof that Anna is primarily a sinner and ample evidence that she is a victim of a complacent, hypocritical, jealous, and sometimes spiteful society. This conflict matches the goal Tolstoi asserts in *What is Art?* (1897–98). There he sees art as an instrument not for indoctrinating the reader but for infecting the reader with the highest morality and religion of its time. In this sense, like Dostoevskii in his mature novels, Tolstoi is using the action of this novel to force the reader into active judgment. He did not want self-righteousness but the moral strength that comes from difficult encounters. The critics who make *Anna Karenina* a simple morality text for or against behavior like Anna's risk becoming what Tolstoi disliked most: comfortable. The intricacy of the parallels and parallels of parallels infects us with a disputatiousness that emerges in the critical debate and makes this book not moral indoctrination but moral exercise. What Western novelists achieved through the intimacies of narrators, Tolstoi often achieved through plotting that infects us with the moral malaise which Tolstoi considered the highest achievement of his civilization.

Tolstoi and Dostoevskii, more than any others, brought the Russian novel-writing techniques back to the West, where their roots in the Gothic novel and the eighteenth-century novel had fallen into desuetude. From the end of the nineteenth century on, western novelists often use techniques from Russia, from the eighteenth century, and from poetry as modernist departures from the nineteenth-century rules, so that the two strands of novel-writing that had partly separated in the nineteenth century came together in the twentieth. The modernist Russian novelists, like their British and American contemporaries from Joyce to Pynchon, worked to make the reader participate actively in the experience and thoughts of the characters. In Russia, as in the West, modernist authors coexisted with more traditional ones surviving from the nineteenth century, like Tolstoi, Chekhov, and Gorkii, or later authors who revived their techniques, like Sholokov and Solzhenitsyn. But modernist authors like Belyi, Bulgakov, Platonov, and Pasternak inherited the Russian nineteenth-century tradition both directly and in a newly enriched form refracted from the West.

Andrei Belyi's *Petersburg* (1916) draws constant attention to its borrowings from Pushkin, Tolstoi, Gogol, and Dostoevskii, using the depth of literary allusion to make each sentence mean what it says and what its source says at the same time. In this novel about revolution, madness, and the disintegration of a rigid society, Belyi's play upon the borderline between the possible and the supernatural makes his readers vacillate in deepening anxiety not only over an expected bomb explosion but also in that doubt about the nature of the account they are reading, which Freud and others consider the source of the uncanny.[9] Along with the shiver the uncanny gives us, Belyi's cognitive dissonance makes us experience something very like the helplessness at being caught up in a revolution, where all the social, semiotic, and moral structures disintegrate:

> Suddenly like a faceless smile between his back and his skull appeared a greasy neck crease, just as if a monster were emplaced there; and its neck seemed to be a face, as if in the armchair were emplaced a monster with a noseless, eyeless mug, and the neck fold seemed to be a toothlessly disrupted mouth.[10]

Here, as so often in the novel, and in any revolution, what seems to be is not what is, and incidents are connected verbally, or by appearances until a causal or chronological meaning emerges. The nagging insistence of the prose and the repetition of identical as well as parallel events draws readers into the conspiratorial experience.

In the 1930s, Mikhail Bulgakov brought a more playful mind to bear on many of the matters Belyi had approached. Like Belyi, he had a scientific background, had experienced the trauma of revolution, and had experimented with the boundaries of the supernatural in his earlier prose writings. *The Master and Margarita* (still incomplete on his death in 1940) separates the supernatural from the realistic in two parallel plots, one dealing with the death of Jesus in the hauntingly realistic psychological, social, and archaeological detail that Flaubert had perfected in the history of prose forms, and the other dealing with the appearance in Soviet Moscow of a band of wildly supernatural tricksters. The novel draws its readers into the attractiveness of evil and the ambiguity of good, but the supernatural plot produces less of a sense of the uncanny than the circumstantially detailed historical plot set in Jerusalem. Sometimes as in science-fiction, a genre Bulgakov had excelled in, the supernatural is taken for granted and made analogous to the process of literary creation:

> Thus Margarita spoke, going with the master towards their eternal home, and it seemed to the master that Margarita's words flowed just the way the river they had left behind flowed and whispered, and the master's memory, his restless, needled memory started to grow dim. Someone was liberating the master, as he himself had just released the hero he had created.[11]

This world of eternity, where authors and authors of authors, and – by implication – the Author of authors of authors are free to establish any variety of reality they please, is juxtaposed to, but sharply divided from the world where commonsensical mortals react to supernatural events. Horace Walpole had proposed such a division in the preface to his eighteenth-century account of "miracles, visions, necromancy, dreams, and other preternatural events": "Allow the possibility of the facts, and all the actors comport themselves as persons would do in their situation."[12] On the first page of the epilogue, half a page after Bulgakov's extraordinary ending of the account of the Master and Margarita, the narrator of the novel uses a totally different voice: "The writer of these true words himself, while setting out for Theodosia, heard a story on the train about how two thousand people in Moscow had left the theatre literally naked and dispersed to their homes in taxis." These two adjacent points in the text show how Bulgakov juxtaposed different causal systems, not as Lermontov had, to triangulate the same episode, but to establish two different worlds, each with its own narrator, its own causal rules, and its own *fabula*. In each world, the causal rules are plain, and the reader has the option of bringing them together or reading like a Soviet devotee, accustomed to different ways of thinking in different contexts.

In the 1950s, Boris Pasternak was still using a close interplay between plot and narration to shape his reader's experience, and still being charged with novelistic sloppiness for using coincidence to shape his plot. In section 9 of part IX of *Doctor Zhivago*, for example, when Zhivago's health and surroundings become almost unbearable, a sleigh arrives "as if from the clouds" bearing his brother Evgraf, who has more influence than even the local commander:

> "Whence comes he? Whence his might? What is his work? . . . .
> Twice now he has entered my life as a good genius, a liberator, solving all the problems. Maybe, alongside the people encountered in it, the makeup of every biography also demands the participation of a secret unknown power, an almost symbolic figure, coming to help unasked, and in my life the role of this beneficial and hidden spring is played by my brother Evgraf."[13]

Here, as in *Crime and Punishment*, the coincidence exists not to get the author out of the problems he has just created, but because it is a coincidence. It helps to justify Evgraf's status as a secret unknown power, an almost symbolic figure about whom Pasternak is encouraging his readers to reflect and wonder. Evgraf is mysterious, beneficial, and mighty, entering the causal system of the novel much as the creator enters the history of Israel in *Genesis*. In the last chapter of the novel, Evgraf emerges as the figure who has assembled Zhivago's writings, much as an authorial figure had assembled the stories of Belkin or Pechorin.

In fact, Evgraf, as his name implies, is the good writer, a hypostasis of Pasternak, coming to his hero's assistance unasked and inviting the old comparison between literary and divine creators. This comparison between life and a book, God and an author, a reading and history, with all its implications for the relation between the will of the creator and the inertia of the created, underlies the whole plot of *Doctor Zhivago*, culminating in the four last stanzas of the last poem in the novel, where Jesus speaks at Gethsemane:

> The Father, can it be, has not arrayed
> His myriads of legions winging hither?
> So that without a hair of mine disturbed,
> These enemies be scattered altogether.
>
> But no, the book of life has neared a page
> More precious than all shrines of holiness.
> Now what is written has to be fulfilled
> Amen. So be it, let it come to pass.
>
> You see, like parables the ages move,
> And, moving, they can burst into a flame.
> I'll go into the tomb acceding to
> Torture in that book's fearsome grandeur's name.
>
> I'll go, and rise the third day from the tomb
> And, as log rafts float down the stream away,
> Like caravans of barges, centuries
> Will float from darkness toward my judgment day.

This passage gives a vision of a world where history is like a book or parable whose grander meaning precludes certain surface interventions by the creator. Evgraf brings to *Doctor Zhivago* a similar vision, justifying the ways of the author to the character, and by analogy, the ways of God to man. Since the whole novel sets a deeply poetic mind in contact with the most horrendous events in history, its own existence, and most particularly the poems and notes Evgraf has gathered in it, becomes a metaphor and, as a part of history, a metonym for the mystery of how a world or book containing such vast evil can be good.

The evolution of the Russian novel has continued, but Erofeev, Bitov, and many others have entered a tradition which the West has also joined, in part because the Russians had developed an enormously powerful and versatile instrument for working on readers, and in part because it is easier for all of us to assimilate the alien and strange if it is actually our own past.

NOTES

1. E. M. De Vogüé, *Le Roman russe* (Paris: Plon-Nourrit, 1916), p. 197.
2. Henry James, *Letters*, ed. Leon Edel (Cambridge, Mass: Harvard University Press), vol. IV, pp. 619, 112.
3. René Girard, *Deceit, Desire, and the Novel* (Baltimore: Johns Hopkins University Press, 1984).

4. Henry James, *The Art of the Novel*, ed. R. P. Blackmur (New York: Scribner's, 1934). See, for example, pp. 67, 97, 330.
5. M. Iu. Lermontov, *Polnoe sobranie sochinenii v piati tomakh* (Moscow–Leningrad: Akademiia, 1936), vol. V, p. 212.
6. N. V. Gogol', *Polnoe sobraniie sochinenii* (Leningrad: Academy of Sciences, 1951), vol. II, p. 226.
7. Anthony Montague Browne, *Long Sunset, Memoirs of Churchill's Last Private Secretary* (London, Cassell Publishers, 1995), p. 325.
8. Jan M. Meijer, and Jan van der Eng, *The Brothers Karamazov by F. M. Dostoevskij* (The Hague, Mouton, 1971).
9. Sigmund Freud, "The Uncanny," first published in *Imago*, 5 (1919). Cited from Freud, *Collected Papers*, 4 vols. (London: The Hogarth Press, 1924–25), vol. IV, p. 405.
10. Andrei Belyi, *Peterburg* (Moscow: Nauka, 1981), p. 277.
11. Mikhail Bulgakov, *Master i Margarita*, in Bulgakov, *Romany* (Moscow: Khudozhestvennaia literatura, 1973), p. 799.
12. E. F. Bleiler (ed.), *The Castle of Otranto by Horace Walpole, Vathek by William Beckford, The Vampyre by John Polidori, Three Gothic Novels, and a fragment of a novel by Lord Byron* (New York: Dover, 1966), p. 18.
13. Boris Pasternak, *Doktor Zhivago* (Ann Arbor: University of Michigan Press, 1959), p. 297.

13

BARBARA HELDT

Gender

In his preface to *The Brothers Karamazov*, published in 1879–80 and surely the grand finale of the nineteenth-century Russian novel, Dostoevskii as author introduces Alesha as his hero, a hero for the present. The author thereby follows a line of European Romanticism that sees the hero as conveying his time and place, not just literally but also symbolically for others. As Dostoevskii goes further, into the future, he argues that such a hero, though strange, "carries within him sometimes the core of the universal"[1] which his other contemporaries have been torn away from. One could not imagine a woman writer speaking to the universal or prophesying in this unambiguously assertive manner (except in sorrow), much less inventing a heroine to incarnate such prophecy. The heroine of her time in Russia, perhaps because she would have had to be similarly exceptional without any irony on the part of her author, remains unwritten. Women lived within a tradition of total truth, which included their own reality as defined by male writers in the Russian novelistic canon from Pushkin to Solzhenitsyn. A heroine's life terminates abruptly, or ends in marriage, or occasionally survives to a symbolically pregnant widowhood, having no other meaning. There is no Dorothea (the female protagonist of *Middlemarch*), no heroine allowed to make a big mistake and survive into something beyond the maternal. George Eliot wrote in chapter 10 of *Middlemarch* that "among all forms of mistake, prophecy is the most gratuitous." Russian authors of the big novel have believed the opposite, and there was little room for women authors in this tradition which grew up in the 1860s, flourishing too under Stalin and under anti-Stalin (Pasternak, Solzhenitsyn). But there was also a much neglected female tradition of smaller novel writing, beginning earlier, in the 1840s, and continuing today. The issues addressed and the skill with which these narratives proceed make these almost unknown novels seem deserving of more than auxiliary status in the canon, as I hope my reading of three of them will prove. But first some words about gender and the male tradition.

The Brothers Karamazov begins with a veritable flood of female characters who exhibit hysteria, bad choices and a trivial attitude to life in spite of good looks, intelligence and wealth. Dostoevskii seems to take sadistic pleasure in bringing women like Aglaia and Nastasia Filippovna (from *The Idiot*, 1868), women of spirit and whose chief feature is their attractiveness (as opposed to more physically flawed males), to a bad end, and always through their own bad choices. In his last novel none of the woman characters, drawn with a disregard for their own fictive lives, does more than reflect one of the brothers' aspirations. The first woman we hear of is one whose suicide we are told would not have happened had she not found a picturesque setting in which to commit it. The first wife of Fedor Karamazov is said to be similarly influenced by other people's ideas when she leaves her family for an emancipated life in the capital. She dies, offstage. More important, the novel does not enter into dialogue with her inner thoughts at all. Not all secondary characters are similarly mocked and trivialized as are emancipated women.

Woman is the passive body (always attractive; that is its value, a value Tolstoi was to dispute and Dostoevskii felt compelled to reduce to comic proportions, a much-feared value because no other beside bearing children is considered) over which male thinkers conduct learned disputes. Women's hysteria and ill-judgment can be pitied only if the woman is of the peasant class. But all women inspire a healthy fear in men, even in Alesha who fears nothing else. So the appraising eye of the narrator may compare the beauty of Grushenka (a voluptuous businesswoman of twenty-two) with that of Katerina Ivanova (a not so nice lady), but the moment of pleasure is short-lived. Women are part of a contest – against men and against each other. Dostoevskii narratively enjoys pitting one woman against another, and any encounter between females always has a sexual edge for the reader. We look, we fear, and we learn, chiefly through a series of scenes that are highly melodramatic in the sense used by Peter Brooks: "Melodrama is indeed, typically, not only a moralistic drama but the drama of morality: it strives to find, to articulate, to demonstrate, to 'prove' the existence of a moral universe which, though put into question, masked by villainy and perversions of judgment, does exist and can be made to assert its presence and its categorical force among men."[2] Malcolm V. Jones has written of the frightening quality of certain of Dostoevskii's scenes in which "Dionysian elements in life may be harnessed and directed toward positive ends."[3] The gender implications of these statements need elaboration.

To begin with, what do we learn? Can the female reader witnessing male cruelty learn with Alesha or Prince Myshkin to see what is good? There is no female Alesha, although a female anti-Alesha, Lisa Khokhlakova, exists.

Sonia in *Crime and Punishment* differs from Myshkin or Alesha in being an incorporeal prostitute of the imagination, a special and unrealistically portrayed status that the heterosexual author appears unwilling to accord to a character of his own gender (unless Gania Ivolgin can be called a sort of male prostitute). Sonia, unlike Myshkin or Alesha, has no special prophetic gift: her more limited role is reactive.

One important question to keep in mind as we read the Russian novel is: Who is the female reader that the author constructs to do the vast work of identification with a male hero and against persons of her own sex?[4] For Russian novelists, while their particular philosophical dialogue was with men, the immediate audience they preached to and who read their works was in great part female. This would have been true for all the authors who published in the thick journals of the Russian tradition. D. S. Mirsky, Russia's greatest critic, observed almost as a truism in 1920 that "during some five decades of the nineteenth century the vast majority of Russian writers who were generally read were all preachers and teachers."[5] After the thinkers thought and the preachers preached, women were meant to do the work of morality within the family. They are often faulted in the Russian novel for failing to do it or for doing it badly (Sonia and Lisa, like so many other Russian heroines, both have bad mothers), and if, as we have seen, female failure is mocked or trivialized, the reader is given permission not to be morally involved. As we shall see, women writers' own view of the family and their constricted roles within it formed the basis for an alternative Russian novel.

The male-authored Russian novel constructs a woman reader who needs, then, to be converted – away from her "primitive" reactions to her family and educational upbringing, which as in the case of Gogol's Manilova or Druzhinin's Polinka Saks was intended to lead her to a state of matrimony as frivolous as possible. Woman's primitivism, her natural potential as men saw it, should instead be turned toward the cause of the male *intelligent*, who might well have female re-education and emancipation as part of his wider plans for Russia, but hardly as a desirable end in themselves, let alone as his priority.[6] This ethic of forming women through fiction extended easily into the Soviet era: its two-dimensional heroinism at times seems compelling as proto-feminism even to a modern reader. It is only with the most recent novelistic fiction that the teacherly function has atrophied, and that has been seen as a symptom of moral decline even by those otherwise glad to see the end of the Soviet Union (if one reads current debates in such liberal journals as *Znamia*).

That much of Russian fiction is itself autocratic in its attempt to construct an ideal counter-world to the world of Russia and later the Soviet

Union has been seen as strength rather than as an arrogation of power, as ethically positive rather than as reactive to the authoritarian bind from which the novelist cannot free himself. By striking an autocratic tone of his own, the Russian novelist puts his stamp on a world now ruled benignly by authorial beneficence and dispensation. Or is it? The use of women characters in the novels and the absence of non-pastoral peasants would indicate a male ruler at work in his own tsardom. Female characters idealized or demonized, but rarely (the women of the late Tolstoi and Chekhov being notable exceptions) individualized with an inner voice, emerge as the locus of male desire projected onto their bodies (or spirits, if nonsexual body/soul conventions prevail). Women's spirituality becomes in this context the essence and the embodiment of male longing.

The two twentieth-century novels most firmly cemented into the canon make the authority of the male writer the very subject of the text, but also need their love stories, the feminine interest that Gogol and Dostoevskii were able to do without. In Bulgakov's *Master and Margarita* and Pasternak's *Doctor Zhivago*, the heroines, models of those women famously beloved by their living authors, Margarita and Lara, exist in the novels paradoxically almost solely as emanations of the minds of writers/heroes: they indicate their devotion to the writer's "fate," which is of national and prophetic significance, by a recklessness of behavior when confronting the outside world combined with a singleminded servitude within the home – having no children (Margarita's case) or none who might interfere with caring for the writer or to their commitment to household tasks and other proofs of intimacy that enable him to write. Improbability of plot is named the miracle of life in the midst of "historical" events which defy logic. But the very sweep of the narrative, which tolerates nothing less than total submission to the writer's point of view on the part of the reader and female character alike, seems rather clumsy by comparison to the modernist novel that mocks its romantic heritage that was being written elsewhere in Europe. An exact contemporary of *Doctor Zhivago,* Philippe Sollers's *Une Curieuse Solitude*, written in 1957 and published a year later, deals precisely with the role of the woman in the construction of the male narcissism making itself the hero of the text. It is tempting to believe that only in Russia could the same year have produced a novel as unironic as *Zhivago* on the same theme (to almost universal European acclamation: non-Russians seem to value the backward and the primitive in Russia).

If so many of the novels of Turgenev (following on from Pushkin) and Dostoevskii involve the struggle of the hero to reclaim his patrimony (son over father), in the novels by Bulgakov and Pasternak the writer claims his patrimony over the very time he lives in. His virtue made manifest is acknowledged first of all by the woman he has chosen for the job. And, once again, there is no irony involved. Russian male narratives were (and are) embedded in a highly gendered social context, an authoritarian and hierarchical society supported and exemplified by certain masculine ranks and rituals, those of the military, the church and the civil service. Every literate Russian male had a place in one of these rankings at some time in his life. When he became a writer, he was free to establish his own rankings, in a moral hierarchy of his own devising. The rejected allegiances of a former career did not vanish altogether and are often present as a satirized anti-world in nearly every Russian novelist, a rejection of the male career in favor of the higher but no less authoritarian vocation of novelist.

The writer can now spread his wings, answering the question posed by Gogol in chapter 11 of *Dead Souls*: "What does this vast expanse of space prophesy?" The space in which women writers were positioned was considerably less vast. For in topographical terms, certain areas of her own society were closed to the woman writer. She did not visit the gypsies on her own or in groups of her own sex or spend a night on the streets talking to the homeless, as Tolstoi did. Where she faced penalties of social ostracism, the status of the male writer was enhanced by such breadth of experience. Leskov's travels with his commercial uncle, Chekhov's medical visits and Dostoevskii's youthful midnight urban rambles became the stuff of their fiction. Women writers grew up and remained inside houses: domestic interiors or gardens figure as the chief locus of their writing. As Mary Zirin points out: "Throughout the age of Russian Realism, . . . most women writers remained rooted in the provinces, cut off from day-to-day contact with editors and from the stimulation of interaction with other writers. They sent their manuscripts to the two capitals by mail."[7]

Yet unvarnished female reality even within these restricted territories was still too dangerous a proposition to enter fully into female fictional realism. Most women writers – Karolina Pavlova (1807–93) is a prime example[8] – felt compelled to blinker the evidence of their own eyes, putting their experience into a shape narrowly acceptable, that of a more conventional fiction that would be read by young girls who had to be protected from too much knowledge; nevertheless this fiction contained warnings in the form of metaphoric hints of future disappointment and warnings of irony in narrative tone. Domestic violence, childbirth and other painful facets of existence appear more readily in the works of men. Nineteenth-century women writers, aware that protective ignorance of life resulted in the repetition of previous injustice, characteristically ended their narratives, from the early society tale onwards, with plots of escape either mental or physical, sometimes, ironically, escape to a bad marriage and thus re-entrapment.[9] Bitterness and irony, therefore, lamenting the inevitable, take the place of prophetic truth-telling on a grand scale. Nevertheless, this inhibition, which limits female prose-writing in Russia, also constitutes its strength. The constraints of the female citizen of the middle to upper classes became the constraints of the female heroine in the writings of women. Men, paradoxically, often saw their heroines, and their anti-heroines, differently – as freer than themselves in spirit if not in body. They wanted all of Russia to be as pure and as free, a fantasy which forms the basis of many a "realist" male fiction. (We are not speaking of fantastic elements in the realist novel's plot, nor of the writer's creative fantasy, but rather of the creation of women characters to incarnate dreams of a better Russian social world.)

Male writers, trained in rhetoric in the seminar, *gymnasia*, and university, wrote persuasively of their truth, the nation's truth. But, – from Gogol's troika to Blok's vision of Christ leading the revolution – much else is swept aside. It is on the side-paths of writing and not on the major routes that we must begin to look for a realism that a tradition animated by the highest artistic confidence and the noblest of social intentions has ignored, breezed past, or subsumed under its own preoccupations. One of the less major routes is the shorter novel, as written by Turgenev, influenced by George Sand and by women writers popular in their time but until recently all but forgotten (though only the 1860 novella *First Love* is of as high a standard as the best novellas by women).[10] These novels are shorter because they include the family scenes of the male novel but are free of the moral/philosophical/political ballast. Although 1848 was an important year in European politics, two Russian novels written in that year concentrate exclusively on the politics of the family. Avdotiia Panaeva's *The Talnikov Family* and Karolina Pavlova's *A Double Life* both see the family/household unit as the crucial determinant of life in Russia, and in their family units the female side, especially the mother, dominates. The tradition of the female family novel has as its most striking recent achievement the 1992 publication *The Time is Night* by Liudmila Petrushevskaia.

The continuing drama of family life in which women play an active role less often for better and more often for worse is characteristic of many writings by women and of some by men. For the latter motherhood figures more often as a serious component in the formation of the good man, the good writer or, failing these, of the idea of the Russian nation as it could be. Even in Tolstoi the drama of family life forms part of an education novel for men. The tragedy of Aleksei Vronksii and especially of Aleksei Karenin is as poignant as that of Anna Karenina. She learns little of value in the course of the novel; but, because of her, each of the men learns for a time what is valuable in life before losing it again. The two Alekseis share with Anna the same inability to live family life: in their case the reader is clearly shown the male codes by which they live as being the root of this inability. The staid and stoic belief of Karenin in ministerial duty and the ethic of the officer and gentleman adhered to by Vronskii are what each man returns to after Anna kills herself. This return represents meaningless decline for the one and meaningless death for the other. Tolstoi pities them for returning to their empty codes, and thereby makes their fate as tragic as Anna's and better documented in social terms. Anna has been provided, after an early marriage, with no code at all, except for the motherly instincts exemplified by the unhappy Dolly, and these she loses by the time she has her second child. Tolstoi never really shows parenthood in this novel except in the smallest of moments; yet we are encouraged to believe that these smallest of moments, expanded into a code of life, alone could have saved Anna from her fate.

The codes of civic and military honor are fairly clear, embedded as they are in the male character's novelistic behavior and in implied authorial commentary. The code of the male writer in opposition to the national codes exemplified by the nation's rulers has been further reinforced by the majority of critical works on Russian literature. But what of the woman writer, who, both by choice and necessity, takes it as her mission to examine female codes, those relating to family and to motherhood and to self? These codes, not as neatly formulated and ritualized as those of the various male professions, have taken on an aura of sacredness yet remain subsidiary to men's interests. Family life shaped individuals, not citizens (contrary to what most efforts to change it have always claimed); it was not the repository of national virtue but rather of the morality of the closest and most obscure human interactions.

The enormous role played by gender in the formation of the Russian woman, the woman writer and the woman reader, the strategies and forms of legitimation used by them, will hopefully be the subject of as many studies as those devoted to the male canon. These strategies were in themselves arguably of little practical or theoretical concern to male authors, even those who, like Tolstoi, portrayed in devastating fashion the effects of gender roles on men. We need to look for evidence of what women actually thought about their relatively obscure lives wherever such evidence is to be found, even under the guise of fiction, often fiction published under a male or gender-neutral pseudonym. Such pseudonyms for women writing in the nineteenth century include: Nadezhda Durova (1783–1866) who wrote (and lived) as Aleksandr Aleksandrov; Avdotia Panaeva (1819 or 1820–93), who published as N. Stanitskii; Nadezhda

Khvoshchinskaia (1824–89) who wrote as V. Krestovskii; her sister Sofia Khvoshchinskaia (1828–65) as Iv. Vesenev; Mariia Vilinskaia (1833–1907) as Marko Vovchok; Maria Tsebrikova (1835–1917) under various aliases, some like N. R. neutrally gendered; Sofia Soboleva (1840–84) as V. Samoilovich.

The attitude of the woman author to the female life portrayed is at least as complex and ironical as that of Lermontov to Pechorin, with the added awareness of the gender-marked status of the woman writer. Often a lesser or younger heroine than herself is made in the fiction to live a life the writer has escaped from. The heroine is deceived by her family, as the author had been. Having learned that the true betrayer is her own mother, the truth of woman's entrapment becomes evident. Her only hope is to escape from one family into another through marriage, a risky proposition at best. Pavlova and Panaeva let their readers entertain not the slightest hope for their heroines.

Whether she was deprived of formal education, like Panaeva, or tutored at home by the best people available, like Pavlova, a woman's childhood was a prelude to marriage, and her marriage, if it occurred, a relief to the parents whose responsibility toward their sixteen- or seventeen-year-old daughter thereby ended. The unique combination of overprotection and gross neglect that characterized the childhoods described by Panaeva and Pavlova demonstrate that norms for girlhood and young womanhood were a confusion of aims and capabilities by the parents, especially the mother, to whom fell most of the responsibility for seeing her daughter through to the next stage.

The bad mothers in these two novels are incompetents and escapists who negate whatever their daughters may feel and thus betray them. There is no code for raising daughters other than that of hiding them from view and then abruptly putting them on full display. The woman's dimension of the Russian experience seems to consist of two stages: first to suffer oneself (in childhood and in marriage) and then to repeat that suffering through the treatment of one's daughter. What women writers tell us about society is that men opt out of the crucial decisions, that social injustice reduces to family justice, where overburdened and ill-educated women mediate between the need to placate inconsistencies of male authority and male absenteeism and the need to make the daily decisions of a household where custom bears little relation to the actual needs of the inhabitants. In the final novel we will discuss, Petrushevskaia's *The Time is Night*, the themes are essentially the same in 1992, but they are married to the linguistic violence of contemporary speech. These three novelists, as well as other women writers past and present, do not merely add their voices to the male canon: they exist in defiance of the moralizing prophetic narratives that canon writers and their abetting critics and scholars have written as normative and peculiarly Russian in moral sweep. A feminist, gender-aware criticism or one merely cognizant of what has been omitted must necessarily lead to a reconceptualization of the entire tradition of the Russian novel.

Avdotia Panaeva (née Brianskaia) married the writer Ivan Panaev in 1837 and became the common-law wife of the famous poet Nikolai Nekrasov in the mid-1840s. Her *Memoirs*, written at the end of her life, treat not herself but the famous men she knew, the radical circle whose writings and other literary activity formed the blueprint for the socio-political debates to come. It is her only work which has been repeatedly reprinted, reflecting what has been considered important until now.

The Talnikov Family, written under the alias N. Stanitskii, was Panaeva's first work and it occupies a unique place in her writing. Although written as fiction, it is the most autobiographical of her writings, and also the most powerful. Her fiction that followed with titles proclaiming the misery of the married women ("A Woman's Lot," "Domestic Hell"), was published in the leading radical journals. In her writing, marital and family injustice seems somehow reformable, like serfdom. The absolute hopelessness of the family relations of *The Talnikov Family* and its central figure of a mother so negative in character that her children could be happy only when she kept her distance from them hints at human depths unmitigated by any hope of spiritual or political reform. The censor understood the attack on parental authority through the description of an unhappy soul-destroying childhood and did not permit publication. Panaeva never again wrote with such density of specifics. What was called "Critical Realism" in the writing of the day kept its critique on the level of lofty moral indignation; its realism reached for a higher plane. The male censor and the male radical writer thus reached a *modus vivendi*, one which left little real scope for the woman writer who wanted to write about actual conditions of physical and psychological abuse within the family, the place from which so few women ever emerged into public view, and within which they, with so little room to maneuver, were supposed to cast a moral light that would radiate outwards into future generations. *The Talnikov Family* was published only eighty years after it was written, in 1928. It is largely a forgotten work.[11]

It begins brutally with the washing of the corpse of the narrator's six-month-old sister. Neither the father nor the mother weeps; only the nurse weeps, because, as we learn, the baby's early death has deprived her of the material rewards otherwise due to her. Violent death or death from neglect constantly shadows this large household which consists of a mother and father, six children, the mother's two sisters, and the father's sister and mother at the time the narrator begins to "remember herself" at the age of six. The household grows continually: as some leave or die, others are added or born.

The father is described first in all his "savagery" but later mercifully becomes a background figure, absent for most of the day. He starts a game with his three-year-old son: see who can hit hardest. It is a game the adult takes seriously. When the child is hit hard and begins to cry, the father beats him even harder. At this moment the narrator, who has formerly believed that parents have the right not only to punish but also to kill their children, interposes her body between that of her father and brother and receives the blows. The mother finally rescues her bloodied children whose only future defense is simply never to go near their father. But the fairy-tales told them by their nurse have a healing power: when the hero or heroine of the story suffers, the children bribe the nurse with biscuits to give their lives a happy ending. Panaeva has a good grasp of "the uses of enchantment," and also of the uses of bribery in a household where food, not money, was the currency.

The children are excluded from any area of the house their mother occupies; she literally doesn't care whether they live or die. Unable to prevent the birth of her children, she does her best to deny their existence. A series of aunts and governesses inflict punishment on the children in the mother's absence. They are a not disinterested authority: when the children have to go without dessert, the adult's portion is doubled. All the children (eight by then) live in one room, in which the dirty linen for the entire household is also kept. Any food brought in is immediately eaten by the omnipresent cockroaches. This area of the household remains populated only by women and children. Women who did not marry were a lifelong liability, and had the same dependency as children in the household. Of all her children, therefore, the mother liked her daughters least, calling them monsters who would never marry and cruelly describing different parts of their bodies, much as a loving mother would brag of her children's good features, the narrator explains with wistful sarcasm.

The deaths of three sisters and one brother occur in a single sentence. These deaths are clearly the consequence of abuse and neglect, of never being loved. But the narrator makes no such statement directly. Keeping the immediacy of the childhood memory, she lets the adult characters speak for themselves, as they do in family surroundings, but rarely to the outside world. There is probably no other work of Russian literature in which a mother's hatred of her children is depicted so relentlessly. Yet the mother, who has few positive sides to her, is shown at times in a pathetic light, as she changes household rules to oblige a male visitor who is never quite called her lover, or as she keeps household accounts manipulated to her own advantage and to the detriment of her children. The father develops great tenderness for his collection of caged birds, symbolic realism that, again, passes without exclamatory comment in the narrative, merely unfolding as one of the stream of events.

The narrator's only friend from the outside world is the daughter of the laundress. A dialogue between this girl and the more innocent narrator about "kissing" older men in return for presents leads to a warning that, when a girl becomes pregnant from such behavior, her mother throws her out. The author is aware of a worse fate for girls of an unprotected lower class, which the stifling combination of isolation and ignorance inflicted on the relatively higher-class girl seeks to avert. The children of the Talnikov family are cut off from most of life, even from walks in summertime. At one point a kind of grotesque ball is given in their house, ostensibly to acquaint them with society, but really at the request of the mother's lover, who is bored. Hideous rivalries emerge among the unmarried women as they prepare for it. There is a rhythm in the novel of expectation thwarted. Every moment of potential happiness is turned to disappointment or disaster.

The sons eventually leave. They are sent out to various institutions and relatives, one to an uncle who beats him. The other grandmother, who shares that household, is powerless to stop the beatings. The grandmother is loved by the narrator because she confirms the reality of her existence, that her parents do not love her. But the grandmother, powerless before her son and estranged from her husband, increasingly gives way to alcohol, foreshadowing the figure of the grandmother in Gorkii's *Childhood* (1913). That good people have no choice but self-destruction is axiomatic in this novel. Gorkii may point to a way out through social change; but his optimism was ill-founded: the figure of the grandmother who submits to petty male authority within her own family remains a constant in contemporary Russian fiction from Solzhenitsyn's "Matrena's House" (1963) to the novellas of Valentin Rasputin.

Missed opportunities of life, the constant fear of adult power, and especially that of an unreasoning mother, the neglect of all bodily and spiritual needs: these things characterize growing up in the Talnikov household. Rarely has psychological abuse been so skilfully documented, yet no critic has ever put this work with its female narrator on a par with similarly autobiographical fictions of Saltykov-Shchedrin or Gorkii. Panaeva does not prophesy: she makes no overt claim to symbolize Russia in her psychologically detailed girl's point of view of a particular family. *The*

Talnikov Family belongs in our revised canon precisely because of its lack of symbolic pretense and its privileging of the gendered horrors of a Russian childhood.

Our next nominee for canonization is a work of mixed genre which harks back to an ideal of Romanticism, but makes the role of poet accessible to women, as had the women writers of French Romanticism. (The question of which Western novelists influenced Russian women writers and how works were adapted or incorporated into the Russian woman writer's emerging tradition remains to be studied in depth.) Karolina Pavlova (née Jaenisch, 1807–93) considered herself primarily a poet, and thus her only novel, *A Double Life* (1848), has an even more unique place in her writings than does *The Talnikov Family* in Panaeva's. It has gone equally unnoticed, never having been published as a separate book except in English translation. In *A Double Life*, the pain of young womanhood is uncovered not through gradual knowledge but through its opposite, the burial of that knowledge in a receding dream. Pavlova's work is more indirectly autobiographical than that of Panaeva, but the author is present in every line from the very first one, a bit of overheard conversation in a heartbreak salon: "But are they rich?" Her heroine is an ordinary girl who, although she comes from the highest social and economic class, is being steered inexorably towards a life of imprisonment in a marriage with a libertine husband, this time by a well-meaning mother. In this work too, young women enter and leave the rooms of their own house only when their mothers tell them to do so. They are kept totally ignorant of their own lives, present and future. The male characters' chief freedom is that of being able to be elsewhere: they absent themselves while the women maneuver and speed up their plans for the daughters' marriages. The poetry at the end of each chapter of *A Double Life*, preceded by a transitional prose passage of reverie, solitude falling into a dream state, represents a vision of ambiguous sexuality, an inner voice that calls and then is silenced forever. Not poetry written by the heroine herself, it is accessible to her only for a time and in the other life of her dreams. An ordinary woman, she is given no higher calling; there will be no compensation for her real life.

Pavlova rightly realizes that women may write poetry, but they do not become The Poet, the autonomous genius, the prophet. They cannot foresee even their own future. But, by documenting the endless materialism of the female circle, Pavlova demonstrates how innate spiritual qualities are cruelly deceived and destroyed as a girl's expectations of life turn into married adulthood. Predicting the lives of women takes the form of irony and rhetorical lament, reaction after the fact, after the occurrence of the inevitable. Irony and lament, not prophecy, best define the authorial voice of women writers in Russia. It reaches the prestige of national identity only with Anna Akhmatova's "Requiem" (1963), when the worst prophecies were inadequate to daily horror and lament alone could describe them: the lament of the mother for her child, written by a woman, finally became the national symbolism.

The future women writers do foretell seems doomed to be re-enacted *ad infinitum*. Works of Russian fiction today realize all the metaphorical warnings of nineteenth-century women writers. Women are still being left to learn how to live with a vague ethical code of family responsibility unshared by men. Women writers especially, as in the past, write about how lives burdened by ever increasing family cares seem to lead to general misery. In one of the best Russian novels ever written, the scenario is the same, the narrative is female/unreliable, and the time is now.

The Time is Night (*Vrem'ia Noch'*), published in *New World* (*Novyi mir*, 1992, 2: pp. 65–110), documents the night-time of Russia in the fragmentation of the Russian family that has, ironically, deserted its own mother who is, with further irony, also the lamenting voice that speaks for it: a woman's narrative voice violently censors that of her own daughter and of all other family members. Is this a revenge text on the Russian novel itself? Liudmila Petrushevskaia, who began to write from the mid-1960s onward was first published only in 1980. Of late she has written other endgame pieces, but most were sufficiently futuristic or particular to certain circumstances to offer the reader a ladder on which to climb out of the narrative into a saner reality – just barely. "Our Circle" (*Svoi Krug*, 1988), like this work, involves cruelty to a child by a mother for his own good, perhaps. In this earlier novella there is no good and no perhaps. The narrative unravelling of intent, as in Petrushevskaia's other stories in which a wife or mother connives in the holding together of a dubious modern family by eventually compromising its tenuous integrity is clear from the outset, as the narrator indulges in the crude language of power and discipline, layered with age-old female complaint. The vision of Woman sitting like Patience on a monument, and especially of enduring Russian womanhood, is forever laid to rest. The narrative of a female tyrant no longer listened to by her own children becomes the voice of the old Soviet Union at the very moment of its disintegration. But why should it be a female voice?

The Soviet Russian family at the end of its existence will no doubt occupy the minds of future sociohistorians as a horrifying combination of female power and lack of real authority within the context of an almost total deficiency of resources and masculine presence. In some families it would seem that the husbandless mother head-of-household has every interest in evicting a son-in-law once he has fathered a grandchild, since, not being either a mother or child, he lacks any serious voice in the great dialogue between these two. This dialogue is the basis of Petrushevskaia's best plays and stories. Here the voice of the Mother dominates in its hideous self-revelation, its blatant self-justification, narrating all possible aspects of the family in a negative light, cannibalizing and spying upon her own mother, daughter, son and grandchildren while also being the only one strong in her ties to the remnants of the regime that once could support them.

This is the Golovlev family as narrated by Arina Petrovna. This is what Colette called "le mentir-vrai," truth through a verbal fabric of lies and self-deception. We watch the care-giver, this key figure of Russian society, as she goes under, leaving no successor. That she is a hack poet, grotesquely quoting Akhmatova and Pushkin, darkly implies the end of culture also, or at least it suggests the debasement of the very poets of Russia whose resistance to authority is seen by Russians to have built steps to a national future. The subject of all world tragedy is the family at war with itself, its doom threatening the continuation of the nation, though here not quite as nationalism's ideologues foresee. Petrushevskaia's vision is darkly comic, highly parodic. The heroine is grotesquely named Anna Adrianovna, parodying not only Anna Andreeva Akhmatova but also Anna Arkadevna Karenina: "Whether she is struck down by love, by filth or by wheels, it all hurts the same." Save for a few institutions like the madhouse and the penal colonies, the domestic hearth is all that remains of the Nation.

The novella begins with the convention of the found manuscript, a framing device which introduces the author into the text as separate from the narrator. This is an important maneuver, since both are Russian mothers. There is a second reason for the framing epigraph: it imparts a sense of urgency to the reading of the text, which was almost lost altogether. The manuscript has been sent to the busy author by the anonymous daughter of an anonymous mother, their voices shrill against the oncoming night.

The collapse of female domestic virtue in the traditional sense of sympathetic care-giving in a world fraught with uncertainty on the outside is accompanied by a narrative shared by two women, mother and daughter, who in different ways embody that lack of care-giving. This structure reverses the usual course of Russian literature, which upholds female domestic virtue no matter whether the narrator is female (as in the stories of most of Petrushevskaia's immediate predecessors, the published women prose writers of the 1960s) or male, as in the traditional male fiction. The security ensured by compassion and nurture usually provided by the female side has reversed itself in this work into the authority (albeit hollow), instruction and discipline associated with a masculine principle. When this type of overarching passes to the female side, we are encouraged to consider it as a sure sign of any state's collapse.

The conflict no longer situates itself primarily in the struggle for identity of the middle-class heroine, but rather in a struggle for survival of all who surround her. In this connection the ending is ironic. The heroine, having disposed of her family, sits down to write the lines which comprise the title. But this is not the ending of the nineteenth-century heroine epitomized by Nadezhda Khvoshchinskaia's *pansionerka* (boarding-school girl), who must leave her family behind in order to claim her own freedom and selfhood. Petrushevskaia's narrator is the sort of hollow professional subsidized by the very dying social order she now epitomizes in a more horrifically thorough manner than the legislators of Soviet culture ever intended. The very concept of writing as purity of action and the salvation of society is savaged by a woman writer.

The question then arises of whom Petrushevskaia's created writer is writing for, who are her voluntary readers in an age when no one any longer reads because that is the done thing. Can it only be ourselves? All others have departed the scene at the end: the story is over as well as just beginning. All the other characters unto the next two generations have departed into an uncertain future survival without Mother. Only we the readers are listening, her semblables, her sœurs.

This violent wrenching from female dominance that occurs in so many recent works of post-Soviet fiction is peculiar in being as pronounced in the work of women as in that of men.[12] The iron rulers of their domestic establishments and dispensers of the crumbs of wealth that remain in the society bear more than the psychological hatred of their family members: they bear the political hatred of those who grew up in the embrace of the Communist state. The gap between the narrator's stated motive and the results of her verbiage-cum-actions definitely recalls to all former citizens of Communism-land the nurture/discipline gap which permeates their own past. The call to behave came from the women as much as from men; women saw some redemptive virtue in order and discipline. The patriarchal authority of the Soviet state is thus all too easily symbolized as a decadent matriarchy, one in which the matriarch has no real authority to discipline but does so nonetheless.

Russian literature more than any others has been esteemed for its transcendent value, a value placed upon it by Russians and non-Russians, professional academics and ordinary readers alike. This reverent attitude has been copied into the reading of a small body of fiction in particular, one written exclusively by male authors in the case of the novel. Regardless of origins, affinities, verbal materials and devices of narrative, the end product is deemed to possess a high order of cultural significance and extra-linguistic interest. The twin giants of the Russian novel, Tolstoi and Dostoevskii, bring others (Turgenev, Goncharov, Pisemskii) into their orbit whose novels are distinctly less compelling. Goncharov's account of his voyage in *The Frigate Pallada* (1855–57) contains much more intelligent and interesting writing than his novel *Oblomov* (1859), and hardly anyone would read his other novels, much less defend them; the Russian novel commands respect, especially if it contains a prophetic dream, a man who struggles with his life, and a sense of failure at the end. The sense of failure in effect silences the reader: who cannot but respect fictions written in defiance of censorship and repression? Those who have suffered less consider themselves unworthy to demote the ranking martyrs by treating their writing as mere texts. Ideological motivation in Russian authors has been taken for philosophy, social and moral reconstruction, psychological depth, supra-legal ethics and a universally valid view of the meaning of life, decontextualized or rather recontextualized in a Russia of the author's own making and imagining, but often with the readers' own social longings superimposed. The partnership between the Russian novel and its official readers, male master critics, journalists and academics of both sexes, has been a powerful one, worthy of study in its own right.

While Russian poetry rather than the novel has had greater meaning for Russians as historically the first and socially the most recitable texts, it is the Russian novel that has become world property. We might say the property of the West, but the West itself is a peculiar construct of an era of nation-forming and for these purposes it must surely include the educated classes of Asian countries. Russian prophets, most recently Aleksandr Solzhenitsyn in his speeches addressed to Westerners, have extended their past into our future (fortunately, inaccurately). They have produced authority where there is no power, the Russian or Soviet State, simultaneously playing the opposite role in a male power game whose players occasionally occupy both sides of the equation. We may attribute to Russians and their novels a virility and a faith in big answers to big questions we see ourselves in the "West" as lacking. The novelists themselves, however, attribute this same virility and persevering faith to women and to peasants. That this ideal can go badly wrong has been best demonstrated by Richard Wortman in *The Crisis of Russian Populism*, and by Laura Engelstein in *The Keys to Happiness*, her study of the fin-de-siècle. In two recent male novels neither women nor peasants but animals have embodied the ideals of post-Stalinist society. A freed Gulag guard dog in Georgi Vladimov's *Faithful Ruslan* (1975) and a she-wolf with blue eyes in Chingiz Aitmatov's *Scaffold* (*Plakha*, 1987) carry an interior point of view denied to most females of the human species in modern male fiction.

More than any other novelistic tradition, the Russian one relies on prophecy to underline its authority both with regard both to present action and to future retribution. Coming at a time when demands for social justice and the problematic identities of peoples and individuals within an empire were being debated, prophecy was a way of making one's voice heard in journalistic competition. The end of tyranny was proclaimed, or else tyranny was accommodated and a better world prophesied, as a parallel entity. At the same time that women, as objects of the debate, their bodies scrutinized by the male gaze, had their own voices muted, ignored, buried in family papers filed under male family names, parodied as too strident, edited by male publishers and criticized, if they did appear in print, by the lords of criticism, masters with their own male disciples, who had different agenda. The last of these master critics, Bakhtin, described the novel as a non-canonical genre, one welcoming many voices; but a gendered voice was not among his considerations. The great debate of Russian writers and critics seems to carry on in the same vein.

Our present understanding of the Russian novel needs to be revised from the current notion of grudging inclusiveness of a few women authors as adjuncts. Male writing is (also) gendered; it is partial (both partial to itself and describing only a part of the world it occupies). Women's writing is an authoritative voice in disguise, lacking the sort of tradition of counter-authority in Russia until Anna Akhmatova literally embodied both Russia and the voice of Russia, brilliantly combining the iconographic image of Russia as suffering lamenting woman (Yaroslavna's lament in the medieval masterpiece *The Igor Tale*) with the normally male voice of the prophetic speaker for Russia. Akhmatova cleverly drew to her the major formalist critics and wrote poetry that they could tackle as both of and new to the canon.

We must carefully consider the question of whether our past study of Russian literature and particularly the Russian novel according to its value as a substitute for liberal institutions in a nation that has otherwise lacked them has not led us to repeat the novelist's belief that the novel in Russia is not just literature, but a repository of truth, morality and even superior craft, when what we should be doing is studying "new" novels, ones not admitted on the basis of lacking a philosophy, an ideology that gives it "scope." We should at the same time re-examine our love of the canon, and do so even on the basis of old-fashioned aesthetics. Much writing on Dostoevskii in particular has flown in the face of common sense about his difficulties in narrating and reconciling implausibilities, to redefine his very problems as solutions. We might look upon Dostoevskii, the author we began with, as a skilled writer of melodrama, but because he is obsessively Russian, melodrama with a value-enhancing national megaphone attached. The Russian novel as we know it from the male canon is a national genre, despite its European roots. Russian novelists read the latest European novels and often entered into the dialogue with women writers like George Sand or George Eliot. The debate with the European novel was, in part, a gendered one. It may have been one reason for the ascent of a narrative voice that must assert, by omniscience or trickery, a point of view that is anything but multi-voiced or bi-gendered in its quest for absolutes. Chekhov, who could not conceive of a character who propagated the Truth as doing otherwise than curtailing the freedom and selfhood of others, never wrote a novel: though some of his stories (for example, "The House with an Attic") in which lives are ruined by Truth-dominance, seem certainly to be commentaries on the novelistic tradition which continued into his own writing lifetime.

The family dramas women writers describe may be written as realism, neo-Romanticism, or postmodernism, like the three we have examined. Satisfied to remain on the level of everyday horror and loss within a family, they do not blare out the message of wider national significance that Lermontov, Gogol, Dostoevskii, Bulgakov, Pasternak, or Solzhenitsyn so obviously weave into the fabric of their narrative. The reader of the Russian novel is conditioned to be repaid with a construct of Russia, one fed by devices of suspense and articulations of terminal states of mind, in return for the effort of reading hundreds of pages, whether over a few days or, like the contemporary reader, in serialized form over months. If women's novels present families as microcosms of the State, their fathers are more often absent than despotic. Absence can result in even greater despotism, as women are left to "rule." But it is striking that the loving father-daughter plot, so crucial to the Verdi opera of the same time, is not foregrounded in the Russian novel. It surfaces at the beginning of the twentieth century in fiction for girls, in the works of Lidiia Charskaia (1875–1937), where a girl must demonstrate bravery to win her father. In novels for adults, however, Daddy in the form of father or husband has problems of his own and the female characters generally take them on, to the exclusion of all else. (Examples are the old Count and Princess Mariia in *War and Peace* or Sonia and her father in *Crime and Punishment*.)

To return to a problem we raised earlier: how can the woman reader constructed by these texts which show women to be so unlike ourselves, either weak or superior in the extreme, distinguish herself from or relate herself to these women characters? She is not voluptuous, arbitrary in her judgments, prone to act and speak without reflection. She is, judging from the constructed reader of women's journals, the mother of daughters, thereby multiplying her importance several times into the next generation. She is not as unimportant to the life plot as she is to the central plot of the novels. The reading communities of women in nineteenth-century Russia have yet to be studied. I would like to infer for the moment that the popularity of novels about women on the fringes of respectability, or who led lives of danger and were punished, had the effect of the sensation-novel on readers who were forced to lead more closeted lives. They enjoyed reading about women they could never meet, let alone become, and flirted with scenarios of danger without a happy ending.

But when these readers read women writers (in spite of the compromises they had to make even to be published), all the irony employed and all the protective artistic distancing of author from heroine still led them back into their own world, a world quite different from that of the canonical male text, in words they may have felt powerless otherwise to articulate. As today's readers begin to recover Russian literature in all its variety, we can also begin to think about its first readers who were women. These first female readers of the Russian novel are the ones Karolina Pavlova dedicated her work to, the "mute sisters of my soul."

NOTES

1. F. M. Dostoevskii, *The Brothers Karamazov*, books I–X.
2. Peter Brooks, *The Melodramatic Imagination: Balzac, Henry James, Melo-drama and the Mode of Excess* (New Haven and London: Yale University Press, 1976), p. 20.
3. Malcolm V. Jones, *Dostoevsky and the Novel of Discord* (London: Elek, 1976), p. 22.
4. My thinking about the demands that particular texts made upon their women readers has been focused by a recent work of English criticism: Kate Flint, *The Woman Reader 1837–1914* (Oxford: Clarendon Press, 1993).
5. D. S. Mirsky, *Uncollected Writings on Russian Literature*, ed. by G. S. Smith (Berkeley: Berkeley Slavic Specialties, 1989), p. 46.
6. See my *Terrible Perfection: Women and Russian Literature* (Bloomington and Indianapolis: Indiana University Press, 1987).
7. Mary F. Zirin, "Women's Prose Fiction in the Age of Realism," *Women Writers in Russian Literature*, eds. Toby W. Clyman and Diana Greene (Westport, Conn. and London: Greenwood Press, 1994), p. 78.
8. See my introduction to Karolina Pavlova, *A Double Life*, 3rd edn (Oakland, Calif.: Barbary Coast Books, 1990), pp. i–xxii.
9. For outlines of such plots, the reader is referred to Catriona Kelly, *A History of Women's Writing 1820–1992* (Oxford: Clarendon Press, 1994).
10. Overwhelming evidence of the great numbers of acclaimed women authors can be found in Marina Ledkovsky, Charlotte Rosenthal, and Mary Zirin (eds.), *A*

Dictionary of Women Writers (Westport, Conn. and London: Greenwood Press, 1994). How subsequent generations of critics and publishers allowed them to be "lost," and why, will be the subject of future research.

11. The text I am using was published in B. S. Meilakh (ed.), *Russkie povesti XIX veka*, 2 vols. (Moscow: Goz. izd. khudozhestvennoi literatury, 1952), vol. 2, pp. 263–357.

12. The following paragraph summarizes part of an argument made elsewhere by me in "Gynoglasnost': Writing the Feminine" in Mary Buckley (ed.), *Perestroika and Soviet Women* (Cambridge University Press, 1992), pp. 160–75.

14

CARYL EMERSON

Theory

In the nineteenth century, after decades of imitations, translations, and a tradition of bawdy native prose, Russia began to challenge the West as the home of the greatest novels ever written. Are Russian "theories of the novel" comparably rich? The current fame of Mikhail Bakhtin might suggest that this is indeed the case. But Bakhtin was a pioneer: he began work on the novel during the 1920s, with what he considered to be only scattered and unsatisfying critical precedent at his disposal. He repeatedly declared that the protean nature of this genre, its unsystematicity and generosity of form, had made the very question of an adequate theory of the novel awkward for any literary tradition. Since the novel outgrows every definition imposed upon it and can incorporate its own parody without ceasing to be itself, its formal study does not reward that drawing of boundaries upon which respectable theory rests.

For this reason, many discussions claiming to provide a "theory" or "morphology" of the novel in effect provide a *history* of novels. The literary historian devises a chronology of select novel-types (picaresque, sentimental, utopian, psychological), attaches it to larger literary periods, and then appends to this structure valuable information about authors, origins, plot invariants, or the literary market. But such chronologies fall short of a unified concept of the genre, as the great comparativist Aleksandr Veselovskii acknowledged in his 1886 essay "History or Theory of the Novel?"[1] Veselovskii viewed the novel as the endpoint of a lengthy process of narrative individualization. A fixed, shared "we" was gradually replaced – by way of tragic drama, the chivalric romance, and the Italian novella – with an uncertain, self-orienting "I," a process that represented in miniature the victory of "unity of content" (the ego of the storyteller) over the ancient unity of performance. Veselovskii concluded that this sequence was sufficiently operative in all cultures to justify an immanent theory of the novel. All the same, he adds, the theorist would do well to "eavesdrop as often as possible on the lessons of history. The history of any literary genre is the best verification of its theory."

Soviet academic work on the novel has followed suit. E. M. Meletinskii's *Introduction to the Historical Poetics of the Epic and the Novel* (1986) is deeply indebted to Veselovskii in its historicism and comparativist scope, and G. N. Pospelov's theory of "implicit forms" rests upon four historically evolved types of relationship between individual and community.[2] By far the best known Marxist variant of the genetic-historical approach within the Russian orbit is the work of the émigré communist Georg Lukacs. In his idealist, pre-Marxist study *Die Theorie des Romans* (1920), Lukacs viewed the epic as the product of an integrated world and the novel as the genre of a "transcendental homelessness." In his later Soviet-Marxist writings, he combined formidable erudition, poetic imagination, and a traditional plot-and-themes methodology with positivist Hegelian principles and class determinism to reaffirm, in an oldfashioned way, humanity's eventual victory over despair through the medium of art. Lukacs's work remains one of the few enduring analyses of the classic European novel to come out of the Soviet 1930s.[3]

Among Soviet critics dissatisfied with the genetic-historical approach was Boris Griftsov, whose brief monograph *The Theory of the Novel* was published in 1927, just as Bakhtin was turning his attention to the genre.[4] Celebrating the novel as the "sole verbal artwork of modern times," a "half-art" that can absorb any other form "with no theoretical prejudices" (p. 10), Griftsov admits that such tolerance has made the genre inaccessible to theorists (his own methodology is conventional, a historical survey of novel-types as they unfold within a single tradition, the French). He finds fault with most of his predecessors. The novel did indeed emerge from rhetoric (such was Gustav Shpet's explanatory thesis), but it was only when rhetoric had ceased to serve strictly ethical goals and had already decayed into casuistry that the novel came into its own as a vibrant fictional form. No genre so rich in singular examples can be covered "historically" or paradigmatically. Its evolution is difficult to demonstrate since one cannot distinguish between imitation and convergence. And, although Formalist studies were then the fashion, novels are not well served by them since little attention was paid to the boundaries *between* prose genres (prose genres were assumed simply to "grow in" to one another). Lukács's *Die Theorie des Romans* was not a theory of the novel at all but "metaphysical speculation on one of its principles" (p. 6). Not surprisingly, Griftsov's "several methodological conclusions" are almost all negative warnings (pp. 140–48). Do not tie the evolution of the novel to literary schools. Do not attempt an exhaustive typology, for there are never enough categories to cover all variants and no list of distinctive features will ever be sufficient. And as regards immanent principles, he comes up with only one: "the novel lives by controversy: by quarreling, by struggle, by a contradictoriness of interests, by contrasts between what is desired and what actually exists" (p. 147).

As theory, this conclusion is thin. Bakhtin will pick up where Griftsov ends. In a Formalist spirit, Bakhtin will specify a "dominant for the novel," the primary feature defining its "literariness": this very motif of contradiction and struggle. But Bakhtin will distance this struggle from any crude identification with real-life battlefields or social class. He will relocate it within the novel's own professional medium: the contradictory, multi-voiced utterance. And language, thus understood, becomes a carrier not of plot, economic pressures, or formal literary devices, but of consciousness itself, a consciousness intended to benefit first and foremost the densely populated, *created* world of the novel and not primarily the creators and consumers of that world (authors, readers, analysts). Only then, from this theoretically grounded position, will Bakhtin reintegrate literary history into his prosaics and reopen the question of genesis.

Before turning to Bakhtin, however, we must consider briefly the heritage and alternatives. For what we recognize today as "theory" – the quest for laws, invariants, initial conditions – does not have its strict equivalent in the critical thought of most students of the novel. In Russia, a rich body of commentary did accumulate around the genre. But it was most often linked with individual prototypes rather than with organizing principles. Several discrete Russian attitudes toward the mission and function of the novel might be distinguished.

The first might be called, broadly, the "realist." In an essay on Lukacs and Bakhtin, the French Slavist Michel Aucouturier properly notes that "the theory of the novel in Russia suffered precisely from what made its practice so successful there: the crushing domination of a realist aesthetic."[5] According to this aesthetic, the intent of novelistic prose (in contrast to epos, lyric, or drama) is representational and mimetic: it is perceived as non-autonomous *vis-à-vis* the real world that contains it, and – as is so often the case with cultural artefacts in the Russian context – expected to serve society, progress, civilization. In such a scheme, the novel's origins are frequently traced to epic narration, with its broad scope, open form, public quests and "choral" embodiment of conscience.

If a single figure exemplifies this mimetic-realist approach to the novel it is Vissarion Belinskii, the "founder of Russian literary criticism" in the 1830s and 1840s. Conceding to the low reputation of the genre in Russia,

Belinskii made little attempt to defend the novel as art. (Bestselling eighteenth-century journalist-novelists such as Mikhail Chulkov or Fedor Emin had been ignored or rebuked by the Enlighteners; Sumarokov, speaking for an official high culture dominated by neoclassical poetics, remarked that novels were rubbish written by ignoramuses and, since they lacked all moral instruction, could not be ranked with works of pure imagination.) Aesthetic criteria were assumed to be secondary. As Belinskii saw it, the purpose of novels was two-fold: either historical-patriotic – to "portray the life of our ancestors" – or moral, to expose social and political ills. As he wrote in 1834, any European poet of talent might have written Pushkin's "Fountain of Bakhchisarai" or "The Gypsies" – but in their setting and diction, Mr. Bulgarin's wretchedly written novels were unmistakably Russian and their very crudeness enabled them to "render a service not to literature but to society."[6] As Russian Realism matured, the aggressively long, thematically untidy Tolstoian novel would become its trademark. Since the realistic Russian novel was "more real than life itself," theory was presumed by many to be as irrelevant to the one as to the other.

At the far extreme from the realistic-mimetic is a concept of the novel as carrier for utopian scenarios and social fantasy – which, in the Russian context, often came with a polemical, exceptionalist charge. The canonical prototype here is Nikolai Chernyshevskii's *What is to be Done?* (1863), arguably the most influential of all Russian novels, with its vision of cooperative societies, unproblematic personalities and futuristic dream sequences. A half-century later, Chernyshevskii's classic text inspired the doctrine of Socialist Realism, proclaimed by Maksim Gorkii in 1934, which privileged the novel over all other genres.[7] Socialist Realist production was theory by fiat. In the name of the Soviet State and its victorious proletariat, Gorkii made explicit what had been only implicit earlier: that the Russian novel's most distinctive traits are (and I draw here on Donald Fanger's categories for the "Russianness of the Russian Novel") its formal anomalies, its insistence on an alliance and communion with readers rather than a stance of alienation, and its contrariness – that is, its adversary stance toward whatever critics in the West thought the genre to be.[8] If novels in the West European tradition were about romantic love, then Soviet novels would be about industrial production.[9] If doubt, despair, individual psychology and tragic endings had entertained the bourgeoisie, then mass psychology, the vigor of folklore and myth, and uniformly cheerful closure would inspire the Soviet readers of Soviet novels. The "West within" – the nineteenth-century superfluous man – would be replaced by the positive hero, who was a variant on the Orthodox Christian ascetic saint.

Andrei Siniavskii, writing as Abram Tertz in the 1950s, provided the best theoretical statement on this sort of novel from within its own Soviet system, in his essay "On Socialist Realism?"[10] According to Tertz, the Socialist Realist novel was a text with a Purpose, a closed future, answers in advance and heroes devoid of doubt. As such, it was the culmination of "social" and didactic thinking about the novel – but, Tertz intimates, it was ultimately a failure. Pretending to reflect reality in its "revolutionary development," such texts were in fact sentimental, utopian, phantasmagoric, and thus closer in many respects to classicism than to Critical Realism. In secular times, he argues, it is not possible to construct a persuasive narrative solely out of cults of personal courage, public self-confidence, and material productivity (however praiseworthy those virtues), if there is no respect for the individuating, ironizing imagination.

A third approach to the novel, the "ethical-religious," overlaps with the other two but is justified on different grounds. If both "mimetic" and "utopian-fantasy" novels tend to spread out horizontally in their plots and seek resolution in a socially-defined purpose, then religious narratives devolve upon a single spiritualized point and can work with tiny casts, even within a single consciousness. Here belong Romantic and neo-Romantic concepts of the novel; here also the confessional or repentant novel-memoirs of error and resurrection, written by such widely different practitioners as Karamzin, Dostoevskii, Tolstoi, Andrei Belyi and Solzhenitsyn. Such prose can celebrate the fantastic, mystical, meta-worldly, and even – as in some Symbolist and postmodernist works – can welcome the altogether inexpressible. Science in the strictly rational or utilitarian sense is abjured, and "literary science" becomes a sort of blasphemy.

What links these writers, first and foremost, is the conviction that the beautiful and the good must coincide, and that the task of literary art is to guide the reader toward an innerly beautiful truth. This truth is *real* – as real as bread, boots or social justice – and can be pursued within the quotidian times and places of the conventional realist novel. But this truth is also transcendent. It must therefore preserve some autonomy from its immediate environment, for its testing-ground remains the individual soul. When, on the eve of the Great Reforms, Turgenev divided character-types in Russian literature between "Hamlets" and "Don Quixotes," he slightly favored the latter – because the mad knight's willingness to posit an ideal, however ridiculous, at the very least paid homage to a value outside himself, above himself, and was not cravenly dependent upon the material proofs of the world. Likewise, arguing in the early 1860s against the radical social critics, Dostoevskii insisted that a striving for moral beauty and transfiguration is the most "useful" of all possible utilitarianisms, the most precious contribution that art can make to life.[11] Such justifications for moral narrative run like a bright thread through Russian literary history. The most powerful twentieth-century proponent of this view – one that individualizes human beings as it unifies them, calling upon each of us to repent – is Aleksandr Solzhenitsyn. As the novelist argued in his 1970 Nobel Prize Speech, only one reliable means exists for creating a common bond between all the widely different values, experiences and sufferings that govern and divide the world, and that is literature.

We arrive now at our final category, "aesthetic" approaches to the novel, designed to uncover structural principles and draw attention to the novel's own artfulness. Such an approach is perhaps the only home for "theory proper." It was late in coming, for nineteenth-century Russia – so under the sway of mimesis when it came to prose – rarely subjected the novel to theoretical speculation as a formal artistic object. And when this mimetic aesthetic was challenged, first by the Symbolists and then (from another direction) by the Russian Formalists, it was in a spirit quite hostile to everyday "content." In the novels most favored by Formalist analysts, content (what we would recognize as "plot events" and personalities changing over time) was subverted, diluted by digressions, made problematic, and kept emotionally at bay. For it was, after all, that ancient fascination with character and storyline that had always made novels so popular, so able to pull us in, and that provided an easy escape from the challenges issued both by life and by the constructs of art.

In order to break down the allure of novels, early Formalists who worked on prose simply refused to acknowledge the presence of whole, emotionally integrated novelistic worlds. They either insisted, as did Boris Eikhenbaum in his early work on Tolstoi, that prose art was not modeled on real-life experience at all but rather the reverse, that life was a deliberate "rehearsal" of new literary strategies; or, as Viktor Shklovskii argued, that long prose narratives were constructed (and thus should be read) solely as "parts" – built, as it were, from the bottom up. In this matter of genesis and structure, Formalists were guided in their thinking about novels by what they valued in artistic production generally: "literariness" (*literaturnost'*), "defamiliarization" (*ostranenie*), parody, and similar devices applied either as irritants or as stimulants to inert verbal material. They drew on Dickens, Cervantes, Sterne, Sir Arthur Conan Doyle – and also on Pushkin, Gogol, Lermontov, Lev Tolstoi, Dostoevskii, Rozanov and Belyi. Of the Formalists whose work is most central to novel theory (Shklovskii, Boris Eikhenbaum, and Iurii Tynianov), Shklovskii was the most consistently inventive and reductionist. It is significant that Shklovskii's pronouncements came closest to constituting an autonomous "theory" of the novel, but were the least adequate to their subject. The research of his two colleagues, who resorted (or retreated) to more traditional approaches, was more satisfying and has proved more durable.

Beginning in the early 1920s, in a series of provocative essays ("The Structure of Fiction," "The Making of *Don Quixote*," "Dickens and the Mystery Novel," "The Novel as Parody: Sterne's *Tristram Shandy*"), Shklovskii devised a "grammar" for novels – or rather, for what he considered the "typical," that is, the ideal, novel.[12] His schema reduce even the most complex psychological narrative to a mechanical stringing-together of parts into wholes: puns become motifs, motifs are expanded into episodes, episodes into plots, and plots (often via "stepped" or "staircase" construction) into novels. Shklovskii treats these accretive components as elements to be valued by the novelist largely because they are so easily manipulated from the outside: framed, obstructed, braked, and laid bare. Such processes are their own reward. Plot with any larger purpose is an embarrassment or an accident; even in so powerful a figure as Don Quixote, character is assumed to be born out of the novel's structure and not the other way around.

But as Jurij Striedter, one of the Formalists' most sagacious critics, has noted, Shklovskii's reductionism is a rather complex affair.[13] The device of *ostranenie* ("defamiliarization") could be applied either ethically – linking it with social and moral criticism – or purely aesthetically. An example of ethical defamiliarization would be Shklovskii's references in his 1917 essay "Art as Device" to Tolstoi's "Kholstomer: The Story of a Horse," or, more famously, to Natasha at the Opera from *War and Peace:* in such situations, social or artistic convention is indeed "laid bare" but not on behalf of any neutral, disinterested perception of reality. Tolstoi frees up a scene through parody only to reattach it immediately to his own moral code. Theoretically, Shklovskii feels more at home with the second, purer, ethically neutral type of *ostranenie*, that which loosens art from life for its own sake. Its sole purpose is to revitalize our curiosity about life, which, paradoxically, entails reassuring us over and over that art is *not* life, and especially not the tedious, shabby everyday life that in Russian has its own derogatory term, *byt*. Shklovskii sees defamiliarization at work everywhere. In novels as different as *Evgenii Onegin, Tristram Shandy, Don Quixote, Little Dorrit,* and Belyi's *Kotik Letaev,* Shklovskii assumes that the novelist's primary aim (and that which justifies the great length and complexity of novels) is to mislead and surprise the reader by constructing – and then violating – an expectancy.

To be sure, this method serves some novels better than others. It is hampered by an exceedingly static notion of "surprise," in which reader, work, and outside context are so unchangingly homogenous over time that the identical devices continue to shock and delight, and also by an unrealistic faith in the power of parody to remain surprising (or even mildly interesting) over long stretches of text. Most unsettling, perhaps, in its implications for the novel is the Formalist passion for "newness at any price," predicated on the dismal thought that the material of the world, unless consciously deformed in some way, can offer no more than the same familiar old content. Familiarity is likened to aesthetic death. Now, stable content is indeed what many readers love in their favorite novels. But in principle, Shklovskii resists any appreciation of novels as "contemporary epics of the everyday," lovingly devoted to accumulation and conservation of detail. He insists that in novels as elsewhere, "a poet removes all signs from their places; an artist always incites resurrections among things."[14] Pushkin and Sterne, with their self-conscious poeticity, heightened sense of symmetry and masterful play with convention, lent themselves readily to this type of analysis. But the indifference of Formalist theory to any sustained quest undertaken by a complex, earnest personality – indeed, to any emotional reaction other than surprise – severely limits its scope. Neither the creating author, the created characters nor the receiving reader are credited with any *cumulative development over time*; and thus a model that is adequate to folktales, fables, short stories and detective fiction fails to register the one thing that novels have in such abundance: space and duration.

As Jurij Striedter remarks, therefore, Shklovskii's theory of the novel works wholly well only at the extremes of the genre (p. 36). It can be applied to tightly plotted, formulaic prose (mysteries or detective stories), or to novels with no plot at all or with trivial or parodied plots. But it excludes values that a common reader might seek in novels: psychological motivation, inner crises that are real but not the reader's own, a narrator willing to invest emotionally in the telling of a story, a world view that invites us to risk something by entering it. Little wonder that Shklovskii devoted one of his most insightful essays to Vasilii Rozanov's late, quasi-fictional collections of aphorisms and scattered domestic observations, *Solitaria* and *Fallen Leaves*.[15] But few readers of novels, I believe, would agree with Shklovskii that Rozanov's "bushels" of dead leaves, designed as a tribute to the pre-Gutenberg era and intended to herald the end of literature, are a powerful new literary device and a brave new genre: "novels without motivations."

In his major Formalist works on Russian prose from his early period (1918–24), Boris Eikhenbaum was as much of an innovator as Shklovskii – but less willing to provoke controversy at any price.[16] Sensitive to biography, to the problems of psychology and to individualized literary style (notably the stylized oral folk discourse known as *skaz*), Eikhenbaum considered *ostranenie* a rather crude device, overly dependent on the reader's personal emotional, or even physiological, response and thus a threat to a work-centered poetics.[17] Indeed, his special contribution to a theory of prose, quite Aristotelian in its inspiration, was to exile from the realm of art the raw spontaneous reaction – what he called *dushevnye* emotions – and demonstrate an author's commitment to designing impersonal, technical, so-called *dukhovnye* (that is, spiritual-aesthetic) emotions.

To this end, scandalously, Eikhenbaum took on the most canonized "civic" and "realist" writers of the Russian tradition, Gogol and Tolstoi. What mattered for both, he argued, was not the outside world and its ethical dilemmas but the creation of a literary work as a dynamic system. In his analysis of "The Overcoat," for example, he tried to show how Gogol constructed two competing narrative lines – one pathetic and the other comic – whose conflict is stage-managed solely by verbal mimicry, not by any concern for the poor hero's psychology or fate. In the first installment of his huge Tolstoi project (*Molodoi Tolstoi* [*The Young Tolstoi*], 1918–22: the only volume that can be called Formalist), Eikhenbaum put forth the startling thesis that Tolstoi's early diaries were not a *cri de cœur* but something akin to emotional "stylization," an exaggerated literary plan projected onto life. In its extreme demands and inevitable fallings-short, this stylized diary then served Tolstoi as a practice ground for the great repentent novelistic character-studies to come: Olenin, Bezukhov, Levin, Nekhliudov. Continuing to whittle down the myth of the autobiographical or confessional novel, Eikhenbaum's essay "On Tolstoi's Crises" argues that throughout his life – not only in 1881 – Tolstoi was in a state of crisis and revolt, largely against the two clichés that governed the nineteenth-century novel: heroism and romantic love.[18] When Tolstoi later shifted to a "deliberate primitivism" and displayed more enthusiasm for proverbs than for realistic narrative plots, this was less a moral turn on his part than it was a reaction against the preoccupation with detail that was the hallmark of the realistic novel.

In his early work on Tolstoi, then, Eikhenbaum marshalled Tolstoi's horror at imitativeness to bolster the Formalist claim that literary creativity is motivated largely by parody of earlier forms – even in the work of the century's most driven literary moralist. However, in the final chapter of his study on Lermontov (which deals with Lermontov's prose in the context of the Russian novel of the 1830s), Eikhenbaum reveals his good sense and scholarly fastidiousness in the face of counter-intuitive Formalist dogma. He implicitly parts company with Shklovskii on the genesis of novels, and questions as well Shklovskii's thesis that the quest for newness, self-conscious narration and a laying-bare of formal devices (along the lines of Sterne) is the primary drive-belt of literary development. Surveying the Russian novel-writing community of the 1830s, Eikhenbaum notes that its most active practitioners – writers of widely varying talent, such as Marlinskii, Dal, Veltman, Bulgarin, Odoevskii, the now-forgotten Voskresenskii – mastered with marvelous ease not only the framing and beading techniques for building long narratives out of short stories but also all the trademarks of Sternean narration: quarrels with one's readers, prefaces occurring in the middle of the book, bumbling lyrical digressions, unmotivated play with the plot. Anyone, it seemed, could get good at these banal devices – and rather than prick readers on to a greater awareness of life and art, such conventions had begun to anaesthetize them. The best novelists were already parodying themselves at it. As a genre, the Russian novel was standing still.

It was Lermontov's achievement, then, in his *A Hero of Our Time,* to do the genuinely new thing. He invested old-fashioned psychological unity in a single hero, found satisfactory natural motivation for descriptions and events by means of interlocking narrators, and thereby brought the "tiresome play with form" to an end. The road was open for the great realistic novel masterpieces. Here Eikhenbaum, while remaining a Formalist, shows himself willing to serve the individual artwork with the theory, and not – as so often is the case with the more pugnacious, aphoristic Shklovskii – illustrate a bold theoretical premise with snatches of fictional text.

As a theorist of literature, our third exemplary Formalist critic, Iurii Tynianov, never turned his attention to the novel *per se*. For a mind so partial to functions and systems, it would have been an unruly genre of choice. But Tynianov was the sole Formalist scholar actually to practice novel-writing on a wide and successful scale (his fine "novelizations" of the lives of Kyukhelbeker, Griboedov, and Pushkin); for all his abstract schematics in the realm of theory, he had a keen practitioner's sense of the organic growth of novelistic worlds from within. One area where Tynianov applied his ideas on stylization and parody to two Russian prosewriters of genius is especially relevant, for it provides a model (surely of great importance to Bakhtin) for the emergence of Dostoevskii's psychological novel out of Gogol's grotesque masks and types. In so doing, it altered the way literary influence itself was understood.

In "Dostoevskii and Gogol: Toward a Theory of Parody" (1921), Tynianov tackles the problem of creative parody – but not merely as a means for making something strange.[19] Working within the orthodox Formalist assumption that "the essence of parody lies in the mechanization [the deadening or bowdlerization] of a device," Tynianov shows how Dostoevskii struggled with and transcended Gogol, first through the homage of imitation and stylization and then, by degrees, through exaggeration and parody. In the process, Dostoevskii distorted and recombined Gogolian phrases; he reanimated Gogol's heroes and introduced them into his own characters' world view, forcing his own heroes to read them and be appalled at them. Gradually, the vacuous Gogolian mask and literary "type" – verbal patter sounding over empty space – were either exposed as such or else became the very different Dostoevskian mask, under whose stunning, static, but ultimately demonic exterior (Svidrigailov, Stavrogin) a genuine personality or character was always ripening. Tynianov intimates that such a complex, multifaceted portrayal of character, the hallmark and pride of the realistic novel, could not have resulted from any mere imitation of real, lived life. Real life has other tasks – and neither the time nor the controlled skill required to work out the necessary forms. Novelistic technique like this could only be the fruit of an intensely competitive *intra*-literary evolution. And thus "creative parody" presents itself as a central subject for Formalist research.

Tynianov's second major contribution to a theory of the novel – his writings on literary tradition, evolution, and "literary fact" – was less tied to issues of individual influence.[20] In fact it worked in the opposite direction. Tynianov insisted that the literary historian must deal not solely with masterpieces, which always defy systematic categorization, but with the many small, routine, popular examples of a genre, whose very ordinariness permits us to see clearly their generic functions and formal elements. Here the novel was superb material, for from the 1830s onward, in Russia as in the West, it stood unrivalled in accessibility, popularity, and number of mediocre bestsellers. By encouraging work on the mainstream novel, Eikhenbaum and Tynianov, by the mid-1920s, had inspired a school of prose studies that added greatly to our knowledge of individual Russian novelists (especially Bestuzhev-Marlinskii and Veltman) and of vital pre-novelistic genres (most importantly, the sentimental tale and literature of travel).[21] Among the students of that school was Lidia Ginzburg.

Lidia Ginzburg's work on narrative, and especially her 1971 monograph *On Psychological Prose*, is arguably the most comprehensive synthesis of Russian thinking about the novel (in its mimetic, utopian, religious-moral and aesthetic phases) outside the Bakhtinian framework. Tynianov's most talented pupil, Ginzburg was also an enthusiastic promoter of Belinskii and a close student of human psychology – which received its most subtle literary reflection, she felt, in the prose of Lev Tolstoi. Hers is an impure, revisionist Formalism with a human face, one that had learned from Lev

Vygotskii, Carl Jung and William James. "I've never been too bothered by whether or not literary scholarship is a science," she confessed in an interview in 1978.[22] She was certain, in any case, that it was not a progressive science; and although some theorizing was essential for precision, any strict structuralist approach "becomes benignly amorphous as it gets more theoretical." Only formulaic genres such as folklore and mythology can be elucidated in that way, she remarked; in complex works, "formalized precision can often lead in practice to utterly arbitrary interpretations."

Ginzburg's contribution to a theory of the novel in *On Psychological Prose* might be summed up in three basic theses.[23] First there is the "human document" and its role in the molding of fictional character. Art is never separated from life, she insists; we continually aestheticize real-life events and genres, and our behavioral models, personal letters, memoirs, and fantasy-variations on the outside world move back and forth across the art–life border. When depicted in art, human personality is not a structure in the sense of a strict pattern or a straitjacket (the way Belinskian "type" is often erroneously understood); but it *is* a structure in the dynamic sense that it integrates impressions over time in a recognizable way and gives shape to values or potentials projected into the future. Drawing on Saint-Simon's *Mémoires*, Rousseau's *Confessions,* Montaigne's *Essais*, and in the Russian context on Bakunin, Belinskii, and Herzen, Ginzburg discusses various stages in the "capturing" of personality (Classical, Sentimental, Romantic). Only with the novelists of the early Realist period, she claims, is a binary concept of character – the juxtaposition of fixed, opposed, ideal attributes (duty versus love, head versus heart) – replaced by a fundamentally different and genuinely developmental model.

Ginzburg identifies this new model of explanatory psychologism in the novel with "*obuslovlennost'*," the "conditionedness" of our cumulative, albeit transitory, existence.[24] She attributes the technical breakthrough to Lev Tolstoi, and a careful analysis of his theories of the psyche constitutes Ginzburg's second thesis. Tolstoi devised an artistic method for displaying the dynamics of the mind in all its variety, hesitation, and inarticulateness. He could depict personality as completely fluid and yet – here was his wizardry – as fully, even instantly identifiable. Expose us to one of these bumblingly fluid Tolstoian heroes and immediately we know "who he is," even though individuation in Tolstoi's texts is neither essentialist nor coded in psychoanalytic categories. The characters are open to "life in general," to the unstable stimulations of conversation as a social act. But no matter how they flounder and beg for direction, no omniscient narrator can help them out: because from one minute to the next the heroes themselves do not know what they wish to say, how they will manage to say it, or how they wish to appear.

In brief, Ginzburg as critic does for Tolstoi the novelist what Bakhtin does for Dostoevskii. She makes him the pinnacle of that long search in literature for a means to reflect the multiplicity and openness of consciousness. Bakhtin, it might be recalled, dismissed Tolstoi as a "monolithically monologic" writer who insisted on owning every idea in his fiction and practiced "absolute language" in his novels;[25] Ginzburg has no patience with that verdict. In her opinion, Dostoevskian heroes – if compared with their Tolstoian counterparts – are selfish, socially useless, rhetorically unpersuasive and rather artificial constructs; for "the protagonist of a novel of ideas cannot by its very nature be the projection of an empirical personality" (p. 245).

Ginzburg's third thesis, on ethical evaluation, reconnects her with the social and moral categories of Russian novel criticism. Literature is indeed bound up with ethics, she writes, but in Eikhenbaum's spirit she insists that our ethical reactions to art are not naive: these reactions are *designed* by authors in accordance with ordered aesthetic norms. By assuming static natures and "typological masks," rationalist and classicist poetics could control readerly reaction rather easily – "a man lied; therefore he was a liar" (p. 334). The age of the realist novel, however, coincided with the challenge of atheism and moral relativism. Norms were in dispute, God did not exist, nature was seen as in flux, and novelists – Herzen, Tolstoi, Gorkii – were expected to work out systems of *non*-religious ethics. In principle such systems could not hold. The psychological novel, built on introspection ("its material was the self-aware and self-observant individual" [p. 335]), could not trust its own transitory voices. Thus surrogates for ethical systems were found, in determinism, in the unmasking of convention, in a substitution of honest *striving* for actual achievement. The psychological stereotype in literature had moved from static opposed qualities, through stable (yet dynamic and productive) features, to the purposeful, but only partially free, impulse (p. 344). Here Tolstoi, fascinated as always by the ways in which we are not free, provides a valuable "typology of impulses" (p. 363). It classifies the outer limits of free initiative recognizable in an era where both human nature and ethical choice were seen as conditioned and severely constrained.

In addition to Ginzburg, the other force in literary theory inspired by Russian Formalist thinking is, of course, the structural semiotics of the Tartu School. But with the exception of the work on *Evgenii Onegin* by Iurii Lotman, one of the world's great Pushkinists, the Tartu semioticians did not produce theories of the novel as a genre. Interesting local commentary – say, Lotman on the role of "home" in Bulgakov's *The Master and Margarita*[26] – does draw on novels, but the fact that Structuralism deals more inventively with categories of space than of time has tended, perhaps, to distance the supremely temporal novel from its theoretical purview. For unmatched insights into the potential of novelistic time, we must turn to the final and greatest Russian theorist of the genre.

Mikhail Bakhtin came slowly to the novel. By the time of his seminal essays of the 1930s – "Toward a Prehistory of the Novelistic Word," "The Word in the Novel," "Epic and Novel," and his lengthy study of the chronotope[27] – he had been writing and lecturing as a moral philosopher and phenomenologist for over a decade. The novel eventually became the literary receptacle for those values that Bakhtin most prized: individual responsibility and irreplaceability; "participative autonomy" (committing to the risk of interaction, but "without an alibi," that is, in an unrepeatable time and place); the ability to be guided in life by a series of "provisional consummations"; and lastly, a willingness to see difference rather than sameness as the ground both for human compatibility and for literary science. Thinking as a philosopher, Bakhtin had discovered the potential of the *dialogic utterance* to transmit and preserve individual experience in a maximally accurate, flexible manner. And in place of the quest for a static essence that had fueled Hegelian aesthetics (and many other nostalgic sociologies of the novel), he recommended that we begin closer to home, by engaging language "novelistically" to express relatedness in process.

Bakhtin arrived at a theory of the novel, then, only after he had worked out an approach to language as a whole, and after he had exposed what, for him, were the flaws in a "materialist aesthetics" (as exemplified by early Formalism). He challenged the Formalists' indifference to content, their exile of the linguistic and experiential products of everyday life from the realm of art, their "physiological hedonism" in devices like defamiliarization, and, centrally, their assumption that to "specify" something meant to *isolate* and then to manipulate it.[28] For in fact, Bakhtin maintained, specification occurs only when discrete, vulnerable entities are brought into contact, when a boundary is drawn between two selves and when each self then risks to be changed by interaction across that boundary.[29] This dynamic, so alien to a Formalist understanding of literary professionalism, lies at the base of Bakhtin's non-referential – that is, *responsive* – theory of language, arrived at long before he began to theorize about novels.

Bakhtin's approach to specificity, and to the whole vexed problem of "totality" once the specific has been achieved, is one convenient point of entry into his theory of the novel. In brief, his argument is this. An aesthetic reaction (unlike our scattered everyday acts of attention) is a reaction to the *whole* of something: to an integral field, or to the whole of another consciousness. As a reaction, it can be grasped only from the outside; but it must also intuitively sense the other's internal reality, a task realizable only by a mind that is permeated with love. (For this reason, Bakhtin would not acknowledge a "hermeneutics of suspicion," so central to postmodernist investigations of literature.) The artistic whole is a recognizable unity or "unit", and here Bakhtin prefers the word "uniqueness" (*edinstvennost'*) to "unity" (*edinstvo*), since an artistic "unit" is neither homogenous nor closed. It includes an awareness of what is beyond it and what is *not yet*, of what can be brought into being only by future interactions – and even then only partially. Thus the whole is never a matter of merely "filling in": clarifying the plot, or carrying out routine acts of catharsis or closure. Totality can only be the result of past history *plus* present and (unknown) future potentials. And whereas all artistic genres provide some opportunities for such totality, none, Bakhtin came to believe, could accommodate it as generously as the novel.

This understanding of wholeness enabled Bakhtin to move beyond several dead-ended molds into which the novel as a genre had been cast. It freed him, first, from rhetorical explanations, which defined the novel as non-art or as half-art. Such definitions had impeded the quest for an aesthetics of the genre, since, viewed as a branch of rhetoric, the novel could be judged "integral" and "whole" merely by its degree of mimesis, by its success at reflecting the outside world "as it supposedly was." It also improved upon early Formalist attempts (largely by Shklovskii) to account for the rise of the novel, all of which faltered when it came to a vision of the novelistic whole (the Formalists, more comfortable with tidier units like puns and folktales, ultimately could not conceptualize the novel except as an accretion of smaller atomized parts). And Bakhtin's special feel for novelistic wholeness freed him, finally, from the Hegelian anxieties suffered by literary theorists like Lukács, for whom, in the spirit of Romantic anticapitalism, the novel remained a "degraded epic in search of a lost totality."[30] This search might be bracing and even beneficial, as Lukacs felt it was ("The novel," he wrote in chapter 4 of *Theory of the Novel*, "is the art-form of virile maturity, in contrast to the normative childlikeness of the epic"); but for the Hegelian, the genre was always problematic. And it was doomed.

For Bakhtin, the novel was not a problem. It was a philosophy for living. While examining its dynamics there was no need to seek, nor to pose as an ideal, any all-encompassing totality. Since wholeness is achieved not at some timelessly abstract level but only in tiny personal acts of reaction and "consummation" (*zavershenie*), and since such acts routinely entail communion with another consciousness whose reciprocal duty it is to reward us with temporary finalization in turn, the more *different* parts or relationships that an entity (a human being or a novel) could assemble and sustain, the healthier and more whole that organism would become. Over his long life, Bakhtin proposed four different rubrics to grasp this proliferating, diversifying spirit of the novel, each of which realized a different sort of wholeness or totality. With a survey of these four approaches, each nourished by previous Russian speculations about the genre but reducible to none of them, my own essay will conclude.[31]

Bakhtin's first focal point for the novel was *polyphony,* a term he coined in his book on Dostoevskii (first edition 1929, revised 1963). It describes a process by which the author supplies his protagonists with a guiding idea, places them within a minimally defined plot, and lets himself be guided by the dialogues that emerge. The idea for polyphony grew out of Bakhtin's early meditations on authors and their created heroes, inspired, some have suggested, by Christian scenarios of humility and renunciation. In an almost kenotic gesture, the polyphonic novelist voluntarily relinquishes some of his authorial rights – *not,* as is often mistakenly supposed, his rights to authorship, but only his right to express a truth directly, from an unreachable authoritative position. The prerogative of "direct truth" is distributed to the novel's heroes, whereupon plot events become weakened and unforeseen (just as events appear in ongoing life to their participants – hence "realistic"), and characters' thoughts and words *about* these events become more prominent. Their dialogues engage eternal questions, for which compositional resolution is always insufficient; thus readers from all times and locales are drawn in and encouraged to "author" as well. The entire polyphonic novel, then, becomes the locus for "creative eventness" (*sobytiinost'*), where all participants (author, characters, successive generations of readers) are larger than the external plot that happens to contain them. And for that reason, all parties to the novel are equally uninterested in coinciding with any predetermined or prejudged concept of a whole. Indeed, Bakhtin admits as much: such an approach to novels is not designed to yield a traditional "whole." But integrative value is not absent. Under polyphonic conditions, an ideal whole is dependent upon a sense of balance, fair play, full access, equal relations across a boundary. To be sure, this ideal of verbal receptivity and reciprocity led Bakhtin to overstate some phenomena he saw at work in Dostoevskii's prose and to ignore others. He is a poor reader of violence, of silent scenes and well-crafted endings. He greatly underestimates the grip of Apocalypse and revelation. And what is at stake with Satan's three temptations in the wilderness, "mystery, miracle, authority," cannot really be addressed within a polyphonic structure.

Bakhtin did not consider polyphony an attribute of all novels. But in every novel, he felt, some trace of the dialogic principle was always a factor. To measure this trace, he devised a typology of single- and double-voiced words (inspired by Dostoevskii and indebted to Tynianov's work on stylization and parody). Double-voicedness in a text could be mapped precisely; it had all the rigor of a Formalist "device". But now, consciousness had become the dominant.

Bakhtin's second approach to the novel was to consider it that prose genre maximally marked by *heteroglossia* (*raznorechie,* "vari-speechedness"). He thereby expanded the dialogic principle from individual words in local contexts to the larger arena of stylistics, and placed the novel (in opposition to the epic) squarely in a zone of tangible, "present-tense contact." Heteroglossia is also a fact of everyday life; according to Bakhtin, the tendency of all language is to fragment, multiply, individuate, and rebel. The novel, however, is not just chaotically multi-voiced; it is art, and its special artistic province is *dialogized* heteroglossia: different points of view embodied in "voice zones" and intentional hybridizations that test one another and question each other's boundaries and authority.

In this happy and open multiplicity, where is a sense of the whole? Here Bakhtin re-enters the field of literary history with his own thesis about the rise of the novel – but it is history of a highly eccentric sort, quite different from either liberal or Marxist–Lukacsian theories on the rise of the novel as a bourgeois epic (in matters of art, Bakhtin was never overly impressed by economic or dialectical determinants). According to his dialogic model, the vernacular novel arose in those areas and epochs – Rome, the Middle Ages – that had become mighty crossroads and "marketplaces." Hitherto self-sufficient cultural worlds exposed one another's language or world view as inadequate to any singular truth. What was once considered a whole suddenly began to be perceived as no more than a part. So the heteroglot novel, while in itself never constituting a finished whole, furthers the cause of wholeness by embracing its role as a *supplement,* as that which fills out and thus makes more true any singular vision of the world.

Bakhtin's third framework for studying the novel is the *chronotope* (literally, "time-space" marker). In certain ways it is his most traditional and accessible concept. The events of our lives, Bakhtin argues, register on us in terms of the time and space that contain them, which in turn condition the types of personality that can take shape within those parameters. Literary genres reflect these differences. In our mental fantasies as well as in our libraries, the primitive mechanical chronotopes of Greek romances and comic strips coexist with more sophisticated matrices. But Bakhtin came to believe, with a Hegelian positivism unusual for him, that all chronotopes were *not* equal. The novel had a task, almost a teleology; its fate was to march forward toward ever more subtle individuations of personality. Early novels are based on chronotopes of random chance, reversible time, metamorphosis, and magic. Their unageing heroes perish or survive against an unchanging or miraculously malleable backdrop. In contrast, the most advanced novels (the prose of Goethe, Dostoevskii, and the great nineteenth-century tradition in general) value a maturing human being acting within an evolving, recognizably realistic world. In such novels, integrity and wholeness is the lot of individuals who feel themselves to be effective agents and genuine creators. Crucial to advanced chronotopes, then, is that set of virtues central to Bakhtin's early "architectonics": irreversible time, differentiated space, and answerable consciousness. For Bakhtin, the most important of these dimensions is the temporal. In complex chronotopes, personality always looks toward what it has *not yet become.* Its heroes do not ask: "Who am I?"; they ask, rather: "How much time do I have to become something else?"

Bakhtin's final approach to the novel is the route of the *carnivalesque.* It differs markedly from the other three, which are grounded in mortal time and in cumulative, personalized dialogic processes. Carnival, in contrast, is a utopian moment: reversible, timeless, faceless, and defiant of death. Originally investigated by Bakhtin in his doctoral dissertation on Rabelais as part of an anonymous "folk culture of laughter," the carnival spirit is also manifest in pre-novelistic authored genres (menippean satire and Socratic dialogues), and in certain character-functions crucial to the novel's ability to resist centripetal "pull" toward a single center, usually by mocking social convention: the roles of the rogue, the fool, the clown. Previous Russian scholars had also linked folk carnival and laughter to the rise of the novel (for example, Veselovskii and later Leonid Pinskii). But Bakhtin capped the deed by combining their traditional literary history with the more daring, early Formalist idea that parody and travesty were the essential energy fueling the "typical novel" and its special self-consciousness.

Beginning with the idea of laughter as deliverance from terror and thus as release of new potentials, Bakhtin developed this – his fourth – marker for the novel around the *body* rather than the word. His earlier categorizations of the novel had been dependent upon talk, upon "how things sound"; carnival was above all an image. The distrust Bakhtin had always felt for disembodied systems now unfolded into a hymn of praise – at times trivial, at times inspiring – to the "*double-bodied image*" (*dvutelyi obraz*), a grotesque body that was as open to a Rabelaisian world of things as the "double-voiced word" (*dvugolosoe slovo*) is open to the world of dialogic exchange. The wholeness or integrity to be sought in novels of this sort is nothing less than cosmic. The carnival body, and the texts that contain this body, do not know death (dying and giving birth are simultaneous); its parts are collective and interchangeable; it can ingest anything. In fact, its primary role is not to communicate personal ideas or attributes at all but merely to *mediate*.

And herein lies the difficulty of the carnivalesque as a theory of the novel. Above all, novels have at their disposal *voices, consciousness*, and *time*. They are sustained and speaking expanses of narrative text, encumbered with memory. Yet the productive and affirmative aspects of carnival are all contained in an allegorical timeless instant, in what Bakhtin calls the "ephemeral truth" that is inherent in "the victory of laughter over fear." This victory is the realization that things can be different, that death need not be terrifying, that even a Great Terror – at least from within one's own consciousness – can be laughed down.[32] The fact that these moments pass, are embedded in violence, or are brought on by hallucination or drunken ecstasy does not distress Bakhtin. Carnival time and space works in utopian novels, not in mimetic ones; it is not responsible enough, nor enough attached to real personalities, to be embodied over a sustained period in realistic novels with advanced chronotopes. Bakhtin can create his dazzling reading of Rabelais only by paring off its Renaissance humanism.

Bakhtin's vision of the carnivalesque novel has become the most contested aspect of his legacy. For all its popularity in the sheltered academies of the West, in real-life post-Soviet Russia the carnivalesque has been seen more often as a Stalinist idea, an embodiment of the Big Grinning Lie that only a wholly deluded or drunken populace could tolerate. Indifferent to real death, to individual privacy, to sane modes of productivity, the carnival vision has seemed to many of Bakhtin's compatriots as one more example of those sorry Russian extremes, utopia and anarchy. When the dust finally settles on carnival, its most durable identity might well prove to be not its materialist, monist, or grotesque veneer but rather its association with such doctrinally central aspects of Eastern Orthodox Christian thought as the anti-Platonic elevation of matter, the miracle of Incarnation, and a commitment to salvation in and through the body.[33]

What can be said, in summary, about Bakhtin's contribution to Russian theories of the novel? His corpus of thought is *not* a synthesis of Russian thought on the subject, and for two reasons. The first has to do with the nature of Bakhtinian "struggle." From Hegel's *Aesthetics* to the present, the novel has been defined in terms of the human beings who sorrow or triumph within it: the novel is either "a conflict between the poetry of the heart and the prose of everyday life that opposes it" (the sentiment is Hegel's), or it is the subjective inner struggle of isolated personalities against a rational, hostile, objective world. Bakhtin embraces struggle, but at the level of words, not personal fates. For him, the novel is above all the home of many wonderful, unwinnable, unlosable *wars with words*. It does not need any special pathos of loss, and can always be read as inspiration by anyone who is still alive and able to talk back.

And second: on balance, this most energetic and inspired theorist of the novel was not particularly in quest of a *theory*. For theories ultimately require a grouping together of attributes, a search for similarities, a setting-up of patterns whereby like attracts like and the unlike is subordinated in an explicit hierarchy. And for all his strengths as a taxonomer, this Bakhtin is reluctant to do. Differences, endlessly proliferating, attract him far more. He values the novelistic genre as the best ground for fostering a climate of differentiated communication: thus novels grow effortlessly out of hetero-glossia, all languages have potentially equal rights, and the novelist ideally becomes the benign organizer of a symposium. But is this in fact why most novels are written? The deeper one looks into Bakhtin's concept of the novel, the more it becomes a mixing chamber of virtues, tolerance, philosophy, spiritual consolation. Like so much of what is richest in Russian philosophy, Bakhtin on the novel is exceptionalist, shapeless, inspirational – and attempts too much. His conclusions, examined closely, often do not answer to the specific realities of the text, nor of literary history. And the closer, therefore, his remarkable body of thought resembles both the practice and the criticism of Russian novels themselves, a verdict that Bakhtin would welcome with a smile.

NOTES

1. Aleksandr Veselovskii, "Istoriia ili teoriia romana?," in A. N. Veselovskii, *Izbrannye stat'i*, ed. M. P. Alekseev *et al.* (Leningrad: Khudozhestvennaya literatura, 1939), pp. 3–22, especially p. 22.
2. E. M. Meletinskii, *Vvedenie v istoricheskuiu poetiku eposa i romana* (Moscow: Nauka, 1986); G. N. Pospelov, entry on "Roman," in V. M. Friche and A. V. Lunacharskii (eds.), Literaturnaia entsiklopediia, 11 vols. (Moscow, 1929–39), vol. IX, pp. 773-95. See also Arpad Kovacs, "On the Methodology of the Theory of the Novel: Bachtin, Lukacs, Pospelov," in *Studia Slavica Hungarica*, 26 3/4 (1980), 378–93.
3. See Georg Lukacs, *The Theory of the Novel*, trans. Anna Bostock (Cambridge, Mass.: The MIT Press, 1971); Georg Lukacs, *Studies in European Realism* (New York: Universal Library, 1964); and, for the best secondary study of Lukacs's literary criticism in any language, J. M. Bernstein, *The Philosophy of*

the Novel: Lukacs, Marxism and the Dialectics of Form (Minneapolis: University of Minnesota Press, 1984).

4. B. A. Griftsov, *Teoriia romana* (Moscow: Gosudarstvennaia akademiia khudozhestvennykh nauk, 1927). Further page references given in text.

5. Michel Aucouturier, "The Theory of the Novel in Russia in the 1930s: Lukacs and Bakhtin," in John Garrard (ed.), *The Russian Novel from Pushkin to Pasternak* (New Haven: Yale University Press, 1983), pp. 227–40, especially 227–28.

6. V. G. Belinskii, "Literary Reveries (An Elegy in Prose)," trans. anon., in Christine Rydel (ed.), *The Ardis Anthology of Russian Romanticism* (Ann Arbor: Ardis, 1984), pp. 450–70, especially p. 466.

7. See "Address Delivered to the First All-Union Congress of Soviet Writers" (August 17, 1934), trans. Julius Katzer, in Maxim Gorkii, *On Literature* (Seattle: University of Washington Press, 1973), pp. 228–68.

8. Donald Fanger, "The Russianness of the Russian Nineteenth-Century Novel," in Theofanis George Stavrou (ed.), *Art and Culture in Nineteenth-Century Russia* (Bloomington: Indiana University Press, 1983), pp. 40–56.

9. For two classic theoretical treatments, see Katerina Clark, *The Soviet Novel: History as Ritual* (Chicago and London: University of Chicago Press, 1981), and Gary Saul Morson, "Socialist Realism and Literary Theory," *The Journal of Aesthetics and Art Criticism,* 38/2 (Winter 1979), 121–33.

10. Abram Tertz (Andrei Siniavskii), *"The Trial Begins" and "On Socialist Realism"* (1959), trans. George Dennis (Berkeley: University of California Press, 1960), pp. 147–219. In practice, Tertz argues, Socialist Realism is much closer to the eighteenth century (the impulse to exalt and memorialize, "religious self-conceit") than to the corrosive nineteenth century, so governed by parody and irony. "Socialist realism starts from an ideal image to which it adapts the living reality," Tertz concludes: this is either classicism or "revolutionary romanticism," but it is *not* a form of Realism.

11. The best discussions of this aspect of Dostoevskii's aesthetics in English remain: Robert Louis Jackson, *Dostoevsky's Quest for Form: A Study of his Philosophy of Art* (Pittsburgh: Physsardt, 1978), especially chapter 5, "Two Kinds of Beauty"; and Joseph Frank, *Dostoevsky: The Stir of Liberation, 1860–1865* (Princeton University Press, 1986), especially chapter 7, "An Aesthetics of Transcendence."

12. See Viktor Shklovskii, *Theory of Prose* (1925), trans. Benjamin Sher (Elmwood Park, Ill.: Dalkey Archive Press, 1990), chapters 3–7.

13. Jurij Striedter, *Literary Structure, Evolution, and Value: Russian Formalism and Czech Structuralism Reconsidered* (Cambridge, Mass.: Harvard University Press, 1989), part I, "The Formalist Theory of Prose and Literary Evolution," especially pp. 25–26. Further page references in text.

14. From "The Structure of Fiction," chapter 3 of Shklovskii, *Theory of Prose,* p. 62.

15. Viktor Shklovskii, "Literature without a Plot: Rozanov," chapter 9 in Shklovskii, *Theory of Prose,* 189–205; quote occurs on p. 201.

16. Eikhenbaum's writings on prose most relevant to a theory of the novel are: "How Gogol's *Overcoat* is Made" (1918), trans. Robert A. Maguire, in Maguire (ed.), *Gogol from the Twentieth Century* (Princeton University Press,

1974), pp. 267–91; "On Tolstoi's Crises" (1920) (see note 18); *Molodoi Tolstoi* (Petersburg: Z. I. Grzhebin, 1922), trans. as *The Young Tolstoy* by Gary Kern (Ann Arbor: Ardis, 1972); *Lermontov: A Study in Literary-Historical Evaluation* (1924), trans. Ray Parrott and Harry Weber (Ann Arbor: Ardis, 1981).

17. For a fine discussion, see Carol Any, *Boris Eikhenbaum: Voices of a Russian Formalist* (Stanford University Press, 1994), especially chapters 2 and 3.

18. Boris Eikhenbaum, "O krisizakh Tolstogo" (1920), published in *Skvoz' literaturu: sbornik statei* (Leningrad: Academiia, 1924), trans. as "On Tolstoi's Crises" in Victor Erlich (ed.), *Twentieth-Century Russian Literary Criticism* (New Haven: Yale University Press, 1975), pp. 97-101.

19. Tynianov, "Dostoevskii i Gogol': k teorii parodii" (Petrograd: OPOIAZ, 1921); translation of part I as "Dostoevskii and Gogol: Towards a Theory of Parody, Part One: Stylization and Parody," in Priscilla Meyer and Stephen Rudy (trans. and eds.), *Dostoevskii & Gogol: Texts and Criticism* (Ann Arbor: Ardis, 1979), pp. 101–17; translation of part II by Victor Erlich as Jurij Tynjanov, "Dostoevskii and Gogol," in Erlich (ed.), *Twentieth-Century Russian Literary Criticism*, pp. 102–16.

20. See especially Jurij Tynjanov, "On Literary Evolution" (1927), in Ladislav Matejka and Krystyna Pomorska (eds.), *Readings in Russian Poetics: Formalist and Structuralist Views* (Ann Arbor: University of Michigan Slavic Publications, 1978), pp. 66–78.

21. See, for example, their *Russkaia proza* (1926), translated into English as: B. Eikhenbaum and Yu. Tynjanov, *Russian Prose*, trans. and ed. Ray Parrott (Ann Arbor: Ardis, 1985).

22. Lidiia Ginzburg, "Razgovor o literaturovedenii," in *O starom i novom: stat'i i ocherki* (Leningrad: Sovetskii pisatel', 1982), pp. 43–58, especially pp. 46–47.

23. Lydia Ginzburg, *On Psychological Prose*, trans. and ed. Judson Rosengrant (Princeton University Press, 1991). Page numbers included in the text.

24. In an otherwise excellent translation, Judson Rosengrant renders this key word as "causal conditionality," which obscures the participial, "acted-upon" quality so central to the term.

25. For an expansion of this idea, see Gary Saul Morson, *Hidden in Plain View: Narrative and Creative Potentials in "War and Peace"* (Stanford University Press, 1987), especially chapter 1, "Tolstoy's Absolute Language," pp. 9–36.

26. See Yuri M. Lotman, "Symbolic Spaces," in Lotman, *Universe of the Mind: A Semiotic Theory of Culture*, trans. Ann Shukman (London: I. B. Tauris & Co., 1990), pp. 171–201, especially 185–91.

27. These essays are translated as *The Dialogic Imagination: Four Essays by M. M. Bakhtin*, trans. Caryl Emerson and Michael Holquist (Austin: University of Texas Press, 1981).

28. This task is accomplished in Bakhtin, "The Problem of Content, Material, and Form in Verbal Art" (1924), trans. Kenneth Brostrom and included as a Supplement in Bakhtin, *Art and Answerability: Early Philosophical Essays by M. M. Bakhtin*, ed. Michael Holquist and Vadim Liapunov (Austin: University of Texas Press, 1990), pp. 257–325. For a summary and simplification, see Gary Saul Morson and Caryl Emerson, *Mikhail Bakhtin: Creation of a Prosaics* (Stanford University Press, 1990), pp. 78–83.

29. In Bakhtin's opinion, we can never be passive analysts, because an object

acquires specificity only once we have assumed a relationship toward it. "It is this relationship that determines an object and its structure, and not the reverse; only when a relationship becomes capricious or arbitrary from our side does the world begin to disintegrate, do we risk to succumb to the power of the random, and do we begin to lose ourselves *as well as* the stable determinateness of the world" (my translation). See Bakhtin, "Author and Hero in Aesthetic Activity," in Bakhtin, *Art and Answerability*, p. 5.

30. For a reasoned discussion of this difference, see Prabhakara Jha, "Lukacs, Bakhtin and the Sociology of the Novel," *Diogenes*, 129 (Spring 1985), 63–90, especially 73.

31. These four approaches are covered in more detail and from a different angle in Morson and Emerson, *Mikhail Bakhtin: Creation of a Prosaics,* chapter 6 (for polyphony); pp. 139–42 and 309–17 (for heteroglossia); chapter 9 (for the chronotope); and chapter 10 (for the carnivalesque).

32. Mikhail Bakhtin, *Rabelais and his World*, trans. Hélène Iswolsky (Bloomington: Indiana University Press, 1984), pp. 90–91: "It was the victory of laughter over fear that most impressed medieval man . . . Through this victory laughter clarified man's consciousness and gave him a new outlook on life. This truth was ephemeral; it was followed by the fears and oppressions of everyday life, but from these brief moments another unofficial truth emerged . . ."

33. For discussions of carnival and its implications for prose from this perspective, see Charles Lock, "Carnival and Incarnation: Bakhtin and Orthodox Theology," *Journal of Literature and Theology*, 5, 1 (March 1991), 68-82; and Alexandar Mihailovic's *Corporeal Words: Mikhail Bakhtin's Theology of Discourse* (Evanston: Northwestern University Press, 1997), chapters 5 and 6.

GUIDE TO FURTHER READING

For reasons of space, this list is restricted to books, mostly published in English within the last two decades. They have been selected by the editors from lists of further reading provided by the contributors. Many of them contain further extensive bibliographies of their own.

Allen, Elizabeth Cheresh and Morson, Gary Saul (eds.), *Freedom and Responsibility in Russian Literature* (Evanston: Northwestern University Press, 1995).

Antsiferov, N.P., *Dusha Peterburga* (St. Petersburg: Brokgauz-Efron, 1922, repr. Paris: YMCA Press, 1978).

Bakhtin, M.M., *The Dialogic Imagination*, trans. Caryl Emerson and Michael Holquist (Austin: University of Texas Press, 1981).

  Problems of Dostoevsky's Poetics, trans. Caryl Emerson (Ann Arbor: Ardis, 1981).

Belaia, Galina, *Zakonomernosti stilevogo razvitiia sovetskoi prozy* (Moscow: Nauka, 1977).

Belknap, Robert (ed.), *Russianness: Studies of a Nation's Identity* (Ann Arbor: Ardis, 1990).

Berlin, Isaiah, *Russian Thinkers* (London: Hogarth Press, 1978).

Berman, Marshall, *All that is Solid Melts into Air: The Experience of Modernity* (London: Verso, 1983).

Bernstein, J.M., *The Philosophy of the Novel: Lukacs, Marxism and the Dialectics of Form* (Minneapolis: University of Minnesota Press, 1984).

Bethea, David, *The Shape of Apocalypse in Modern Russian Fiction* (Princeton: Princeton University Press, 1989).

Billington, James H., *The Icon and the Axe: An Interpretive History of Russian Culture* (London: Weidenfeld and Nicolson, 1966).

Bradbury, Malcolm, and McFarlane, James (eds.), *Modernism 1890–1930* (Harmondsworth: Penguin, 1976).

Brown, Deming, *Soviet Russian Literature since Stalin* (Cambridge University Press, 1978).

  The Last Years of Soviet Russian Literature: Prose Fiction, 1975–1991 (Cambridge University Press, 1993).

Brown, Edward J., *Russian Literature since the Revolution*, rev. edn (Cambridge Mass.: Harvard University Press, 1982).

Brown, Edward J. (ed.), *Major Soviet Writers: Essays in Criticism* (New York: Oxford University Press, 1973).

Bushmin, A.S. *et al.* (eds.), *Istoriia russkogo romana*, 2 vols. (Moscow: AN SSSR, 1962–64).

Chances, Ellen, *Conformity's Children: An Approach to the Superfluous Man in Russian Literature* (Columbus: Slavica, 1978).

Clark, Katerina, *The Soviet Novel: History as Ritual*, 2nd edn, repr. with a new afterword (University of Chicago Press, 1985).

Petersburg: Crucible of Cultural Revolution (Cambridge University Press, 1995).

Clyman, T.W. and Green, D. (eds.), *Women Writers in Russian Literature* (Westport, Conn.: Greenwood Press, 1994).

Dolgopolov, L., *Na rubezhe vekov: O russkoi literature kontsa XIX – nachala XX veka* (Leningrad: Sovetskii pisatel', 1977).

Eikhenbaum, B. and Tynianov, Yuriy, *Russian Prose*, trans. and ed. Ray Parrot (Ann Arbor: Ardis, 1985).

Erlich, Victor, *Modernism and Revolution: Russian Literature in Transition* (Cambridge, Mass.: Harvard University Press, 1994).

Fanger, Donald, *Dostoevsky and Romantic Realism: A Study of Dostoevsky in Relation to Balzac, Dickens and Gogol* (University of Chicago Press, 1965).

Fennell, J.L.I., *The Emergence of Moscow 1304–1359* (London: Secker and Warburg, 1968).

Freeborn, Richard, *The Rise of the Russian Novel: Studies in the Russian Novel from "Eugene Onegin" to "War and Peace"* (Cambridge University Press, 1973).

The Russian Revolutionary Novel: Turgenev to Pasternak (Cambridge University Press, 1982).

Garrard, John (ed.), *The Russian Novel from Pushkin to Pasternak* (New Haven: Yale University Press, 1983).

Gibian, George, *Interval of Freedom: Soviet Literature During the Thaw 1954–1957* (Minneapolis: Minnesota University Press, 1960).

Gibian, George, and Tjalsma, H.W. (eds.), *Russian Modernism: Culture and the Avant-Garde, 1900–1930* (Ithaca: Cornell University Press, 1976).

Gifford, Henry, *The Novel in Russia: From Pushkin to Pasternak* (London: Hutchinson, 1964).

Gillespie, David, *The Twentieth Century Russian Novel* (Oxford: Berg, 1996).

Ginzburg, Lydia M., *On Psychological Prose*, trans. and ed. Judson Rosengrant (Princeton University Press, 1991).

Golubkov, M.M., *Utrachennye al'ternativy: formirovanie monisticheskoi kontseptsii sovetskoi literatury: 20–30-e gody* (Moscow: Nasledie, 1992).

Grivtsov, Boris, *Teoriia romana* (Moscow: Gosudarstvennaia akademiia khudozhestvennykh nauk, 1927).

Hamm, Michael F. (ed.), *The City in Russian History* (Lexington: The University Press of Kentucky, 1976).

Hayward, Max, *Writers in Russia* (London: Harvill, 1983).

Hayward, Max, and Labedz, Leopold (eds.), *Literature and Revolution in Soviet Russia 1917–62* (London: Oxford University Press, 1963).

Heldt, Barbara, *Terrible Perfection: Women and Russian Literature* (Bloomington and Indianapolis: Indiana University Press, 1987).

Hosking, Geoffrey A., *Beyond Socialist Realism: Soviet Fiction since Ivan Denisovich* (New York: Holmes and Meier, 1979).

Kasack, Wolfgang, *Dictionary of Russian Literature since 1917* (New York: Columbia University Press, 1988).

Kelly, Catriona, *An Anthology of Russian Women's Writing, 1777–1992* (Oxford University Press, 1994).

A *History of Russian Women's Writing 1820–1992* (Oxford University Press, 1994).

Kemp-Welch, A., *Stalin and the Literary Intelligentsia 1928–39* (London: Macmillan, 1991).

Layton, Susan, *Russian Literature and Empire, Conquest of the Caucasus from Pushkin to Tolstoy* (Cambridge University Press, 1994).

Ledkovsky, M., Rosenthal, C., and Zirin, M. (eds.), *A Dictionary of Russian Women Writers* (Westpost, Conn: Greenwood Press, 1994).

Leighton, Lauren, *Russian Romanticism: Two Essays* (The Hague: Mouton, 1975).

Lotman, Iu. I., (ed.), *Semiotika goroda i gorodskoi kul'tury: Peterburg* (Tartu: Uchennye zapiski Tartuskogo Gosudarstvennogo Universiteta, 664, Trudy po znakovym sistemam, 18, 1984).

Maguire, Robert. *"Red Virgin Soil" Soviet Literature in the 1920s* (Princeton University Press, 1968).

Mathewson Jr., Rufus, *The Positive Hero in Russian Literature* (New York: Columbia University Press, 1958)

Meletinskii, E.M., *Vvedenie v istoricheskuiu poetiku eposa i romana* (Moscow: Nauka, 1986).

Mersereau Jr., John, *Russian Romantic Fiction* (Ann Arbor: Ardis, 1983).

Moser, Charles A., *Antinihilism in the Russian Novel of the 1860s* (The Hague: Mouton, 1964).

Moser, Charles A. (ed.), *The Cambridge History of Russian Literature*, rev. edn (Cambridge University Press, revised edition, 1992).

Morson, Gary Saul, *Narrative and Freedom: The Shadows of Time* (New Haven: Yale University Press, 1994).

Muchnic, Helen, *From Gorky to Pasternak: Six Modern Russian Writers* (London: Methuen, 1963).

Nabokov, Vladimir, *Lectures on Russian Literature*, ed. Fredson Bowers (London: Weidenfeld and Nicolson, 1982).

Paperno, Irina, and Delaney, Joan, *Creating Life: The Aesthetic Utopia of Russian Modernism* (Stanford: Stanford University Press, 1994).

Parthé, Kathleen F., *Russian Village Prose: The Radiant Past* (Princeton University Press, 1992).

Praz, Mario, *The Romantic Agony*, trans. Angus Davidson, 2nd edn (Oxford University Press, 1970).

Reeve, Franklin, *The Russian Novel* (New York: McGraw Hill, 1966)

Ryan-Hayes, Karen, *Contemporary Russian Satire: A Genre Study* (Cambridge University Press, 1995).

Sakharov, Vsevolod, *Stranitsy russkogo romantizma* (Moscow: Sovetsakaia Rossiia, 1988).

Seeley, Frank F., *From the Heyday of the Superfluous Man to Chekhov* (Nottingham: Astra Press, 1994).

Shatalov, S.E., *et al.* (eds.), *Istoriia romantizma v russkoi literature. Romantizm v russkoi literature 20–30-x godov XIXv. (1825–40)* (Moscow: Nauka, 1979).

Shepherd, David, *Beyond Metafiction: Self-consciousness in Soviet Literature* (Oxford: Clarendon Press, 1992).

Shklovskii, Viktor, *Theory of Prose* (1925), trans. Benjamin Sher (Elmwood Park, Ill.: Dalkey Archive Press, 1990).

Simmons, Ernest J., *Russian Fiction and Soviet Ideology: Introduction to Fedin, Leonov and Sholokhov* (Stanford University Press, 1990).

Slonim, Marc, *Modern Russian Literature from Chekhov to the Present* (New York: Oxford University Press, 1953).

Soviet Russian Literature: Writers and Problems, 1917–1977, 2nd edn (New York: Oxford University Press, 1977).

Striedter, Jurij, *Der Schelmenroman in Russland: ein Beitrag zur Geschichte des russischen Romans vor Gogol'* (Berlin: Harrassowitz, 1961).

Struve, Gleb, *Russian Literature under Lenin and Stalin* (New York: Routledge and Kegan Paul, 1971).

Terras, Victor, *A History of Russian Literature* (New Haven: Yale University Press, 1991).

Terras, Victor (ed.), *Handbook of Russian Literature* (New Haven: Yale University Press, 1985).

Tertz, Abram (Andrei Siniavskii), *On Socialist Realism* (New York: Pantheon, 1961).

Todd III, William Mills, *The Familiar Letter as a Literary Genre in the Age of Pushkin* (Princeton University Press, 1976).

Fiction and Society in the Age of Pushkin: Ideology, Institutions, and Narrative (Cambridge, Mass.: Harvard University Press, 1986).

Todd III, William Mills (ed.), *Literature and Society in Imperial Russia, 1800–1914* (Stanford University Press, 1978).

Vogüé, Eugène Marie Melchior de, *Le roman russe* (Paris: Plon-Nourrit, 1886).

Wachtel, Andrew Baruch, *The Battle for Childhood: Creation of a Russian Myth* (Stanford University Press, 1990).

An Obsession with History: Russian Writers Confront the Past (Stanford University Press, 1994).

Wellek, René , *A History of Modern Criticism 1750–1950*, 7 vols. (New Haven: Yale University Press, 1970–91), vol. vii, *Criticism on the Continent of Europe 1900–1950*.

Zelinsky, Bodo (ed.), *Der russische Roman* (Düsseldorf: August Bagel Verlag, 1979).

INDEX

Note: Index covers pages 1–290. Works are listed under author's name but are indexed in detail under individual titles (italics for complete books, roman in quotation marks for short stories).